MÁS QUE UN INDIO

MORE THAN AN INDIAN

School of American Research
Resident Scholar series

James F. Brooks
General Editor

Figures

Acknowledgments

This book has been a long time in the making. It was first conceived in a preliminary family visit to Guatemala, two months after our daughter Amalia was born, and the English version will finally be out of my hands just after her twelfth birthday. It has occupied a major place among my intellectual and political commitments and, equally important, in our collective life as a family, during much of that time. This makes it impossible to neatly separate professional debts of gratitude from the many sources of support for me personally, and for our family, which I also want to acknowledge.

A number of families and individuals helped us make Chimaltenango and Guatemala our second home. We are especially grateful to the Echeverría-Curruchiche, Ramírez-Moreira, Armira-Camey, and the Chirix-Tiney families, and to a number of others, including: Nora England, Marcie Mersky, Bob Rice, Elisa Miller, Rick and Betty Adams, Tani Adams, and Irma Otzoy. Doña Luisa and later Doña Aura cared for the girls, generously sharing their warmth and kindness, as well contributing hard work to help keep the household together while Melissa and I were at work. Although much of this research was carried out alone, I do want to acknowledge the crucial support of three research assistants: Silvia Barreno, Salvador Castellanos, and Edgar Meléndez.

Guatemalan scholars and institutions guided, facilitated, and enriched the research in innumerable ways. I am especially grateful to Clara Arenas, executive director of the Association for the Advancement of Social Science in Guatemala (AVANCSO), whom I sought out soon after reaching Guatemala. My multifaceted involvements with AVANCSO from that time on, culminating with that organization's commitment to publish this book in Spanish, contributed immensely to my sense of connection with the best of Guatemalan social science, and to the specific goals of my project as well. Clara also read and commented extensively on an early draft of the manuscript. My subsequent involvements with the Center for Mesoamerican Research (CIRMA) also enriched the research and expanded its scope. Through these two institutions, and other parallel activities, I had the opportunity to engage with and learn from a great many intellectuals in Guatemala. Among these, I have a special debt of gratitude to Marcie Mersky. We worked together closely in the research and thinking for chapter 4 and, more generally, Marcie offered an invaluable font of knowledge and critique on the matters central to this book. In addition, I would like to thank: Rick Adams, Santiago Bastos, Arnaldo Batz, Luisa Cabrera, Francisco Calí, Marta Elena Casaús Arzú, Demetrio Cojtí, Edgar Esquit, Christa Little-Siebold, Rolando López, Morna MacCloud, Irma Otzoy, Gustavo Palma, Demetrio Rodriguez, Guillermo Rodriguez, Pakal Rodriguez, Enrique Sam Colop, Claudia Samayoa, Arturo Taracena, and Gabriel Zelada.

This project began when I still worked at the University of California, Davis, and followed me to Texas in 1996. Two dear friends and colleagues at Davis were especially important in the initial conceptual phase: Stefano Varese and Carol Smith. Carol's engagement continued for the entire process; I deeply appreciate her role as sharp critic and sounding board, including her thorough reading of the manuscript. At the University of Texas, I have benefited much from dialogue and exchange with a number of colleagues and graduate students, including: Mark Anderson, James Brow, Nora England, Karen Engle, Richard Flores, Jennifer Goett, Ramon Gonzalez, Juliet Hooker, Brandt Peterson, Bryan Roberts, Shannon Speed, Katie Stewart, Angela Stuesse, Mauricio Tenorio, João Vargas, Irma Alicia Velásquez Nimatuj, and Kamala Visweswaran.

I am especially grateful for the opportunity to participate in a series of activities sponsored by the Center for African and African American Studies, which helped to galvanize my commitment to the critical race perspective that this book puts forth. Edmund T. Gordon, the center's director, my friend and comrade in nearly twenty-five years of shared political and intellectual endeavors, contributed immensely to the content and contours of this project. Critical readings of drafts, co-taught seminars, discussions of key analytical problems, and collective work on these very problems in other parts of Central America add up to more *compañerismo* than one can reasonably hope for in a lifetime (and we still have another twenty-five years ahead).

I had the opportunity to present nearly every piece of this book in one forum or another outside Guatemala and Texas, which improved the work considerably. In the context of these visits, colleagues also read drafts and provided critical feedback. For this help, thanks to: Ana Alonso, Charles Briggs, Pamela Calla, Kanchan Chandra,

MÁS QUE UN INDIO
MORE THAN AN INDIAN

Racial Ambivalence and Neoliberal
Multiculturalism in Guatemala

Charles R. Hale

School of American Research

Resident Scholar Book

School of American Research Press
Post Office Box 2188
Santa Fe, New Mexico 87504-2188
www.press.sarweb.org

Co-Director and Editor: Catherine Cocks
Manuscript Editor: Rosemary Carstens
Design and Production: Cynthia Dyer
Proofreader: Sarah Soliz
Indexer: Vivian Newdick
Printer: Edwards Brothers, Inc.

Library of Congress Cataloging-in-Publication Data:

Hale, Charles R., 1957-
   Más que un Indio = More than an Indian : racial ambivalence and
neoliberal multiculturalism in Guatemala / Charles R. Hale.
      p. cm.
   title: More than an Indian.
   "A School of American Research Resident Scholar book."
   Includes bibliographical references and index.
   ISBN 1-930618-60-3 (pa : alk. paper)
   1. Mayas–Ethnic identity. 2. Mayas–Politics and government. 3. Mayas–Social conditions.
4. Ladino (Latin American people)–Ethnic identity. 5. Ladino (Latin American people)–Cultural
assimilation. 6. Ladino (Latin American people)–Attitudes. 7. Guatemala–Race relations.
8. Guatemala–Economic conditions. 9. Guatemala–Social conditions. I. Title: More than an Indian.
II. Title.

F1435.3.E72H35 2005   972.81–dc22

                             2005031419

Cover illustration: Día de Guadalupe celebration, Chimaltenango, December 12, 1997. Ladino children dressed as Indians march in procession through the town to the church, where they have their photographs taken. © Charles R. Hale

Contents

For Sofia, born when this study began,
and for Martin, whose inspiration lives on

Marisol de la Cadena, Dario Euraque, Jeffrey Gould, Linda Green, Brett Gustafson, Maria Lagos, Claudio Lomnitz, Florencia Mallon, Beatriz Manz, Rosamel Millamán, Don Moore, Diane Nelson, Nancy Postero, Karin Rosenblatt, Orin Starn, and Kay Warren.

In the summer of 2003 I was a resident scholar at the School of American Research, which gave me a much-needed respite from other responsibilities, and the opportunity to craft the book in its final form. I could not imagine a more conducive environment for this task, with stimulation from other fellows, especially Nancy Scheper-Hughes and Gelya Frank, and the SAR staff, in particular James Brooks and Catherine Cocks, and lots of glorious solitude. Mt. Atalaya also provided quiet daily encouragement. As editor of the SAR Press, James invited me to publish with them; both James and Catherine provided invaluable support and advice throughout. I am deeply grateful to them for having seen promise in this project, and for moving it forward so expeditiously. At a crucial point in the manuscript preparation, I also received an enormous boost of aid from Vivian Newdick. Vivian's meticulous editorial scrutiny helped the manuscript take shape, and her acute substantive comments stayed with me as a priority "to do" list, through to the final revisions. I could not imagine having a more dedicated, thorough, caring, and patient copy editor than Rosemary Carstens; perhaps because she is an author herself, she works with an acute understanding of how hard it is to let go. Marta Maria Bianchi did an excellent translation of the first draft, which allowed me to receive feedback from Chimaltenango friends.

Material support for this research came from a number of sources, which I also gratefully acknowledge. A collaborative research grant from the National Endowment for the Humanities provided core support for our longest stint in Chimaltenango, supplemented by generous research leaves from both UC Davis and UT Austin and with summer research funds from the Teresa Lozano Long Institute of Latin American Studies. In a later phase the project received additional monies from the Ford Foundation (Mexico Office) and institutional support from CIRMA. Special thanks goes to Jeff Gould, Carol Smith, Dario Euraque, Anabella Acevedo, and Tani Adams, for participating in this collaborative adventure. Thanks also to AVANCSO, especially Clara Arenas, and Dan Church Aid, for help in making the Spanish language version possible.

Not only was this project a family affair in the logistics of life and research in Guatemala but, also, it stayed with us through the seemingly interminable phases of writing and revision that followed. The burdens of bringing such a project to fruition take their toll. Amalia and Sofia have grown up with this book, and in the process have developed a mild hostility toward my computer, which makes voracious demands on time that might otherwise be theirs. It doesn't seem quite right to thank them for their forbearance, since they didn't get much choice in the matter. I hope that their own connections with Guatemala and Guatemalans will serve as partial compensation. My parents have been a mainstay throughout our Guatemala years; their visits to Chimaltenango added a dimension to the research experience that I cherish. My father's readings of this work over the years have been an especially reliable and valued source of critical support. His own disciplined, original, and thoroughly engaged approach to scholarship will always be an inspiration to me, with an influence that is deepened because we approach our work in such different ways. Words fall far short in thanking Melissa, for being all that she is, and for all that she has contributed to this book over the past decade. I'm not sure how I could have been so fortunate that the love of my life would also be such a superb critic, a sage source of council, an inspiring health worker, and a wonderful companion in all facets of research and writing.

To carry out field research of the sort that yielded this book required the consent of dozens of people who granted formal interviews, and the help of many more with whom I engaged in informal conversations and participant observation. Given my general decision to keep these research subjects anonymous, I cannot thank them by name. My enormous debt to them all is best expressed in the text itself, which represents a selection of their words and practice. I hope they feel accurately rendered in these pages, and that they take my interpretations as a respectful, if provocative, invitation to further reflection and dialogue.

CRH
Austin, Texas
July 2005

The School of American Research gratefully acknowledges the support
of the Ethel-Jane Westfeldt Bunting Foundation
for the writing of this book.

Preface

El ladino suele discriminar al ladino que no discrimina al indio; y mas lo
discrimina si se pone de parte del indio. He gozado esta discriminación.

(Ladinos regularly discriminate against ladinos who do not discriminate
against Indians. Even more so if the ladino takes the side of the Indian.
I am proud to have suffered from this discrimination.)

—*Luis Cardoza y Aragón*

As the Pan-American Highway makes the steep climb westward, leaving behind the
congested, contaminated tangle of Guatemala City's Calzada Roosevelt (Roosevelt
Boulevard), the human geography turns indigenous. Hand cultivated patches of *milpa*
(traditional corn and bean cultivated plots) begin to appear on the hillsides, roadside
signs announce Maya-sounding place names like Santa María Cauqué and Santo
Domingo Xenacoj, and women wearing indigenous *traje* (clothing) go from being a
distinctly marked minority to the norm. As the road reaches a crest just past
Sumpango, the valley of Chimaltenango comes into full view, a verdant plain, lined on
the southeast by a ridge of hills, punctuated by two prominent volcanoes. Kaqchikel
Maya who lived in this valley before the arrival of Europeans called their principal set-
tlement *Bok'ob*, which means "shielded city," a reference to the surrounding hills.
Although Spanish colonizers established a presence early in the sixteenth century, and
rechristened the place in the tongue of their Mexican indigenous guides, Kaqchikel
Maya always remained the vast majority in Chimaltenango and in the region that
would later become a department of the same name. To this day, the census reports the
Chimaltenango department to be some 80 percent indigenous, a proportion that has
remained roughly the same for the last century. The gateway to the vast indigenous
highlands, Chimaltenango marks the beginning of, to adapt a phrase from Guillermo
Bonfíl Batalla (1987), Guatemala *profunda* (deep Guatemala).

1

A second look along the same highway from the capital city to Chimaltenango troubles this image of gradual transition to Guatemala profunda. The road is lined with enormous warehouses that serve as maquila production sites, which hire hundreds of workers from the area, mainly young indigenous women. Interspersed with the milpa are crops of a very different sort—luxury vegetables, berries, and flowers—sold fresh through intermediaries on the international market. During peak hours buses to and from the capital city are jammed with passengers traveling daily the 55 kilometers for work or studies, turning Chimaltenango and surrounding towns into bedroom communities. Chimaltenango city itself, after being leveled by the devastating earthquake of 1976, was rebuilt with rebar, cinderblock, and corrugated metal roofing, giving the urban landscape a generic, third-world feel, with very little that appears distinctively indigenous. The section of the highway directly adjacent to the city is lined with an array of hardscrabble storefronts, their walls covered with highway filth: a *"pinchazo"* (tire repair shop), the Manantial de Vida Eterna (Spring of Eternal Life) evangelical church, a mortuary, a hardware store, and a string of twelve brothels with alluring names like *Buen Gusto, Descanso Feliz,* and *Fogata* (Good Taste, Happy Resting Place, and Campfire). This second look recasts Chimaltenango as the epi-center of an intense process of cultural and economic change, with an ambiguous relationship to things indigenous: a space that left Guatemala profunda far behind, for what Nestor García Canclini (1989) has termed *culturas híbridas* (hybrid cultures).

Anthropology, whether carried out by national scholars or foreigners, has a well-established preference for Guatemala profunda. Hundreds of monographs have been written on indigenous peoples, covering nearly every highland *municipio* (township), while there are at most a handful of works on the other half of the population, people who identify as ladino, mestizo, or criollo Guatemalans. Even given the widespread postmodern skepticism of bounded identities and claims to authenticity, many anthropologists have a residual aversion to the hybrid spaces that thrive in Chimaltenango: brothels with Salvadoran sex workers whose clientele include the mainly indigenous conscripts from the nearby army base; a vibrant twice weekly market where generic commercialism has subsumed indigenous particularity; poor neighborhoods where youth wear baggy clothing and listen to hip hop, and cinderblock walls feature graffiti that mark gang territories (see figure 1). While the *Ruta Maya* travel guide may be too blunt for academic sensibilities, anthropology has in effect heeded its recommendation: "[Chimaltenango city is]...mostly just a place to change buses, with little to detain you."[1]

Curiously enough, my motives for making Chimaltenango the central place of this study were not all that divergent from those that would have led most to avoid it. The spaces of cultural hybridity did come to fascinate me, and I soon took a certain pleasure announcing that I lived in Chimaltenango and then watching eyebrows raise. My principal interest, however, was to carry out a study in alignment with the Maya rights movement that had been on the rise since the late 1980s. From the early days of this movement, Chimaltenango has been a central place for Maya organizations to locate;

Figure 1. Cholo gang graffitti. The Cholos were one of the most popular gangs in Chimaltenango during my principal year of fieldwork. The 18 refers to one of the two principal gang moieties, apparently taken from the streets that divide gang territory in Los Angeles, CA. The other moiety number is 12. This photograph was taken on a street in a neighboring department. Photo credit: Christa Little-Siebold.

by the early 1990s it was home to dozens of Maya NGOs, with specializations covering the spectrum from community development to language rights, some with local areas of influence, others regional and national. The processes of economic and cultural change underway make Chimaltenango an odd choice for the central place of Maya cultural rights activism. The Maya organizations located there do not have an especially strong connection with the urban population that surrounds them. Their rationale, rather, is more logistical than political. Solidly within the indigenous highlands, yet only an hour from the capital city, Chimaltenango allows Maya organizations to move easily between the two worlds, taking advantage of minimal urban amenities, while operating within a majority indigenous milieu. This strong, visible presence of Maya organizations, in turn, also made Chimaltenango an ideal location for what became the main focus of my study: ladino responses to Maya ascendancy.

Ladinos in Chimaltenango, as in the rest of the highlands, are heterogeneous but generally dominant in relation to the indigenous majority. Self-identified ladinos occupy a wide range of social and economic positions, from manual laborers to elite politicians and landowners. Moreover, to state that the city's population is 20 percent ladino leaves out a large and growing sector of *chimaltecos*—like the gang members from poor neighborhoods—who refuse both sides of the ladino-Indian binary that guides official efforts to determine who is who. Amid this heterogeneity, however, people who identify as ladino generally have absorbed an ideology of racial superiority in relation to Indians: viewing themselves as closer to an ideal of progress, decency, and all things modern, in contrast to Indians, who are regrettably and almost irredeemably backward. Until recently, this ideology had a resounding echo in the local and regional racial hierarchy: from middle-class positions upward, ladinos predominated and Indians did not belong. Organizations associated with the Maya movement have confronted these conditions with a wide variety of strategies, which advance Maya rights and challenge ladino racism. Their success on both fronts, however partial, has been impressive. One measure of this success, in turn, is that ladino political sensibilities have changed: they have ceded some ground, assumed a self-critical stance toward the overt racism of the elder generation, and repositioned themselves as cautious advocates of multicultural equality.

This study documents and probes these ladino positions, both in Chimaltenango city and in the surrounding municipios. My topic took shape initially as a product of the most elemental methodological principle of activist anthropology: talk over research ideas with the people with whom you are primarily aligned, in hopes of producing knowledge that might be useful to them. The original idea I brought to these discussions with Maya friends and colleagues focused on coalitions: under what conditions could Mayas and ladinos work together on relatively equal footing? Without overtly discouraging this topic, they pushed me in a different direction, saying "we really need you to study them [ladinos]." Gradually, the idea of studying ladinos took hold. As the study's scope and purpose evolved beginning in the mid-1990s, I had ample opportunity to discuss the research design and the preliminary results with Maya colleagues. But the requirements of the research itself placed limits on this interaction. I carried out only a handful of interviews with Mayas, and never made Mayas the subjects of ethnographic scrutiny, except when the purpose was to observe Maya-ladino interactions. I spent the vast majority of my research time in exclusively ladino settings, which in turn reflects the still largely segregated character of social spaces in the region. Especially when asked to share their hopes and fears in relation to the rising power of their Maya counterparts, most ladinos would only give candid answers when there were no Mayas listening in.

In addition to the advantages that Chimaltenango offered as a field site for my study, family considerations played a central role in my decision. My wife, Melissa, is a family physician, with a longstanding interest in public health and popular education. After a survey of organizations doing this kind of work, she settled on the Asociación de Sevicios Comunitarios de Salud (Association for Community-Based Health Services or ASECSA), an organization based in Chimaltenango that trains health promoters to work in rural communities across the country. We also sought a place with quick access to high quality medical care for Amalia, who would arrive in Guatemala at age two months, and for her sister, Sofia, who would join us two years later. After an initial stint in the cramped quarters of an apartment in the middle of town we settled in to a rented home in the middle-class neighborhood of Las Quintas, with a walled-in garden where the children could play, and a beautiful view of the Acatenango volcano. In good anthropological fashion, we lived in roughly the same conditions, and with many of the same daily routines, as my principal research subjects.

During the first years that we lived intermittently in Chimaltenango, 1993 through 1996, the country was still in the early stage of a profound transition. Although the return to democratic rule had formally begun in 1985, the militarized state remained on a war footing. Details of the army rampage against civilians in the early 1980s were beginning to circulate more widely, both a sign that times were changing, and a vivid reminder of the brutality of the same state actors and institutions that continued to rule. People talked in hushed voices, if at all, about the guerrilla; they still assumed, based on past experience and current analysis, that opposition to the government could result in disappearance, torture, or death. When we first took Amalia to a pediatrician who cares for Guatemala City's elite, he asked casually about my work, and followed up, just as casually, on my reply: "Anthropology...isn't that what Myrna Mack was doing when they killed her?" An elite and decidedly right-wing chimalteco, who offered us his house to rent, had the same reaction, and put it in the form of friendly advice: "Stay away from politics in your investigations, Carlos. You know what happened to Myrna Mack."[2] All relationships had multiple layers, revealed or not depending on degrees of *confianza* (trust); most people still could not fathom the idea of processing their traumatic memories of the period of armed conflict because, in their minds, that period had not yet come to an end. In one of my first exploratory trips to Chimaltenango I contacted a left-leaning ladino intellectual and political actor, on the recommendation of a mutual friend. He agreed to pick me up on the corner of Chimaltenango's central plaza at 10:00 a.m., but never showed up. The long wait, watching one anonymous driver after another pass, gave me plenty of time to worry about how I would ever gain enough confianza with people to carry out this study. His evasive apology later only deepened these concerns: why would ladinos, left, right, or center, agree to open up with me?

Yet the great enigma of Guatemalan society at that time was the entangled presence of two disparate political conditions: pervasive continuing effects of state terror amid a democratic transition whose protagonists portrayed that political violence as a thing of the past. The atmosphere of democratic transition, however partial and confusing, was indispensable to the viability of my research plan. The bizarre attempted self-coup of President Jorge Serrano Elías in June 1993 had provoked widespread indignation, sending the clear message that powerful forces in the country, from the military to the business elite, had no stomach for a return to military rule. Spurred on by the dramatic achievement of Santiago Atitlán in 1990, indigenous communities throughout the highlands were organizing to eliminate army presence and put an end to the civil patrols. Maya organizations, at first low profile and cautious, had begun to find their collective voices, and were rapidly becoming major actors in the national political arena. Rigoberta Menchú, who maintained a semi-clandestine status as late as 1991, was now established as a Nobel laureate, directing a well-endowed foundation devoted to Maya rights and social justice. Even in Chimaltenango, where changes often followed in a faint echo of national-level trends, we felt the political thaw. Although the enormous army base would remain on the former grounds of the Pedro Molina teachers' school for another decade, the concerns of the military turned from defeating the insurgency to governing a postwar society. In general, the victors' arrogance was almost certainly a more important impetus for the political opening than a commitment to democratic values. Ladino political elites would never have been receptive to my study had they not felt so secure about their victory. Early on, I gained an appointment with Don Miguel Angel Rayo Ovalle, a man of impeccable upper-class ladino pedigree who served as Chimaltenango's governor.[3] I presented him with a letter describing my proposed research on economic development and ethnic relations in Chimaltenango. With an enthusiasm that mystified me, and little time for details, which came as a great relief as well, he gave me his blessings—*"este estudio me cae como anillo al dedo"* (this comes like a ring on my finger)—and issued me a letter of support.

From the start my research was a family affair, which created its share of anxieties and difficulties, but also helped immensely to make it possible. Having children in tow accentuated our worries about health, highway safety, kidnapping, and the shocking rise of violent crime. Early on, while running a workshop with community-based midwives, Melissa handed one-year-old Amalia to one of the participants so she could focus on the tasks at hand. Suddenly, the woman and Amalia were both nowhere to be found, and no one knew what had happened. For an hour or more, Melissa searched frantically and switched into emergency mode, sure that someone had snatched the child for ransom. The woman eventually returned, cheerfully announcing that she had decided to take Amalia for a long walk to the market, to allow her mother to work unperturbed. Anxious moments like that one, however, were more than outweighed by the rewards of being in Chimaltenango together, and by the research doors that my family helped to open. Having a family transformed perceptions of me, from a suspicious outsider to someone with an identity at least in part like everyone else. My first experiences with ladinos beyond formal interactions and interviews, sharing the intimate spaces of conversations around the kitchen table, invariably occurred not as a research initiative but, rather, because Melissa, Amalia, Sofia (and I) were invited over to eat.

We became especially close to two ladino families, one whose members have no presence in this book, and the other who occupies a central place. I cannot explain this contrast here, beyond a general reference to the inevitable tension between one's relationship to people as research subjects and as friends. For whatever reason, Yolanda Valencia and her family seemed to thrive on that tension. I first sought out Yolanda on a hunch in 1994; she worked in an office dedicated to adult literacy, and I associated literacy work with a social and political outlook that would make it likely that she and I were of like minds. We began to talk regularly; eventually she invited our family to dinner with hers; little by little we got to know the entire extended family network. In November 1997 Yolanda's daughter Elena got married to Héctor, and they asked Melissa and me to be their *padrinos de matrimonio* (marriage godparents). By the time that week of activities had ended—from Elena's "farewell" party, to the wedding itself, to the long discussions afterward revisiting the emotion and complexity of it all—Chimaltenango felt like a second home. Yet it was a peculiar sort of home, for me at least, since these people with whom we were growing close were also my research subjects. Yolanda affirmed and enjoyed this dual role: she is intellectually curious, confident, and self-reflective, oriented toward research of sorts in her own work. Her comfort with the dual role, in turn, helped to put me at ease. When I finally thought I had finished the research and began to conceive this book, I presented Yolanda with the proposal that her family provide the narrative anchor. She agreed, and this initiated a new research phase of filling in gaps, going together to interview additional family members, and finally, an intense work session in Austin, when she presented her feedback on the Spanish translation of the first draft.

The Valencia family in some respects follows the pattern of what they would call—with a hint of self-mockery—"typical ladinos," and in other ways they are utterly anomalous. Yolanda's father Luis would have beamed with pride at the designation, proceeding to regale us with details of his family line of solid European stock, deeply invested in the boundary between ladinos and their Indian inferiors. Don Luis and Doña Concha would surely have concluded that Yolanda married well, since Alejandro came from a family of Chimaltenango's ladino elite, a clear step upward from the rural township where the Valencia family had its roots. Luis and Concha would also have nodded with approval when, in 1971, Yolanda decided to abandon her university studies in law to raise a family. For the next decade Yolanda and her family lived in a typical middle-class ladino milieu, not especially wealthy but comfortable, with private school for the kids, regular participation in ladino elite sociability, and with extra money for occasional vacations outside the country. During this phase of her life Yolanda was completely immersed in ladino society, and took on the manner and attributes of someone who occupies a higher rung in the racial hierarchy. Perhaps the only visible sign of the transformation to come was that Yolanda had grown restless with her homebound existence and decided to resume her studies, this time in Pedagogy.

The next two decades brought a process of change that set Yolanda radically apart from most of her Chimaltenango peers. Alejandro was killed in 1984, under circumstances that would never be clarified; after a brief exile in the United States, Yolanda returned, and dedicated the next fifteen years to her career and to raising her children, with support from a tight-knit and loving extended family. She became a professor in the Chimaltenango campus of the San Carlos University, and later combined this with a position as director of the literacy program DIGEA and an increasingly active role in local politics. When I met Yolanda she already was reflecting critically on these multiple strands of work, eager to analyze all aspects of the changing relations between ladinos and Mayas, both her own, and those of ladinos chimaltecos in general. In part, Yolanda's receptivity to discussions about race matters was a direct product of the

Maya efflorescence. Especially given that all three facets of her work life—literacy, university teaching, and local politics—put her in daily contact with indigenous people, she experienced Maya contestation directly and needed to figure out how to respond. In part it was a critical transformation of her own making. Many ladinos took Maya contestation as an affront and responded with defensive bitterness; they most surely would have shied away from the vulnerabilities of a dual role as informant and friend, which Yolanda, in contrast, clearly relished. Yolanda fully "came out" as a ladina dissident in 1998, when she and Genaro became *compañeros* (partners in a committed relationship), and decided to live together.

With the addition of Genaro, the Valencia family came to encompass the entire political spectrum of Guatemalan ladinos, from the right-wing and racist old guard, to the revolutionary, adamantly antiracist Left. Genaro was born in Escuintla, and grew up mainly in the capital city, but his family on his father's side was from Chimaltenango. He made periodic visits back to Chimaltenango as a teenager to visit his grandparents, who held significant amounts of land on the outskirts of the city. During these visits, he became good friends with Alejandro, and met Yolanda in passing. Genaro went to medical school at the San Carlos University during the tumultuous mid-1970s, became a physician, and went to work in the public hospital of Escuintla, which had become a hotbed of political activism. Through his work with radicalized health and religious workers, he developed ties with the rising tide of revolutionary opposition to the military regime; in 1980, he found himself on a list of ten people targeted by the right-wing death squads. He went into hiding and within two days six of the ten had been killed. Soon thereafter, Genaro was spirited out of the country and began work with a hospital in the Nicaraguan town of Somoto, on the front lines of the contra war. At the end of 1982, Genaro returned to Guatemala, now as a member of the Guerrilla Army of the Poor or EGP, and spent the next ten years in the lowland jungles of Quiché department, dispensing medical care to guerrilla combatants and their civilian allies. He left the guerrilla in 1994, fed up with what he viewed as the leaders' abandonment of their revolutionary ideals; he worked in Mexico and Spain before returning to Guatemala in 1997. Genaro continues to affirm the ideals that led him to become politically active twenty-five years earlier, and speaks of his first few years in the jungle as a deeply transformative experience, a chance to work together with indigenous people according to egalitarian principles, to catch a glimpse of a new society in the making. By the end of the 1980s, the allure of this social transformation had begun to fade; he continued for a number of years out of commitment to his comrades, but with deepening cynicism about the possibilities for change and great indignation toward the hypocrisy and opportunism of the revolutionary leadership. To this day, Genaro displays the qualities that made him, by all accounts, a much loved compañero-doctor: a high and demanding political idealism combined with a keen sense of the absurdity of the human condition, a fervent and principled critic of injustice with an unusually generous endowment of *humor chapín* (a uniquely Guatemalan sense of humor).

For a long time Genaro responded to the invitation to be included in my study with affable refusal. I met him first in 1997, before he had reconnected with Yolanda. A mutual friend, who knew of my study, insisted that an interview with Genaro would challenge all my conclusions about ladinos, and she arranged for us to meet. The conversation was cordial but distant; he said he'd call me when he had some free time to talk further, but never did. Long after Genaro and Yolanda were living together, and their Chimaltenango house had become our base for return visits every summer, Genaro still made it clear, in contrast to everyone else in the family, that he did not want to appear in my book. Meanwhile, Genaro's established presence in the family deepened the process of change underway, from moderate dissent to outright rebellion against the trappings of ladino respectability. Yolanda retained a solid foothold in that ladino world, through work and social networks, but in the inner circles of home and family, in thought and practice, they moved steadily toward the margins. Instead of tea on a Saturday afternoon, their compound would be host to Maya ex-guerrilla and their families, Genaro's friends from revolutionary days, who live in nearby settlements created after the 1996 peace accords. Instead of well-kept gardens, the grounds in back of the house have the overgrown feel of Macondo, surrounded by cement walls with irreverent and incendiary graffiti (for my favorite, see figure 2). Only in my final session with Yolanda, when she came to Austin to comment on the draft, did I finally learn the reason for Genaro's refusal. He worried that any study of ladinos could only end up being an apology for ladino dominance and wanted no part of such an endeavor. After reading the draft, Genaro changed his mind and sent word with Yolanda that he would like to be interviewed after all. Just before concluding this manuscript, Genaro and I had a daylong conversation about his life, an interview I drew from in final revisions and in writing the epilogue.

Although at times I was tempted to make this book into a narrative focused primarily on the Valencia family, this would have prevented me from achieving my principal objectives. The Valencia family, and especially Yolanda, play a crucial role in this study in two respects. They helped me immensely, to figure out who was who, to set up interviews, interpret the results, and generally to navigate the layered complexities of ladino society in Chimaltenango. They also served as research subjects, representing one pole on a wide continuum of ladino stances toward their own identity, racial privilege, and responses to the Maya challenge. Although I do not spare them critical scrutiny, and Yolanda herself insists on an ample dose of self-critique, the Valencia family in general represents an encouraging transformation toward a category of what might be called ladino race progressives. Indeed, as I write these lines, in January 2005, a debate rages in the Valencia household: Yolanda insists on remaining "ladina" while Genaro and her son Camilo argue that a crucial step toward antiracist practice is to renounce the ladino heritage altogether in favor of a newly construed identity as mestizo. This debate—inconceivable in most middle-class ladino households in Chimaltenango—is symptomatic of the broader point: it would have been profoundly misleading to draw general conclusions about ladino responses to Maya ascendancy

Figure 2. "If priests gave birth, abortion would be a sacrament!" Valencia home wall painting. Photo credit: Charles R. Hale.

from the Valencia family. Since I wanted to provide Maya activists and intellectuals with a complete and candid view of the dominant group who are their adversaries, it was crucial to register the whole range of standpoints, and to analyze the center of gravity of ladino political sensibilities. While Yolanda and Genaro continue to be of this ladino world, they are so deeply critical of it that I sometimes worry that their position is too contradictory to sustain.

The central conclusions of this study, then, derive from field research with more than one hundred ladinos and ladinas, who occupy a wide range of social positions, over a period of about twenty-four months beginning in 1994 and ending in the year 2000. I carried out most of this research myself, at times with the help of research assistants, rarely with any significant involvement of my family. It involved travel to fifteen of Chimaltenango's sixteen municipios (excluding the distant and inaccessible Pochuta), pursuing structured interviews and specific categories of quantitative data collection. The most valuable flashes of insight in this study, however, came not from this planned and systematic data collection but from the chance encounters, informal conversations, and serendipitous openings that participant observation makes possible. One Sunday, for example, I shared a relaxed afternoon with Don Caralampio and Don Rigoberto, two elderly ladino men who previously had been key players in local politics. Now, they both lamented (while sipping rum and munching on chorizos wrapped in hot tortillas), Indians have taken over the municipio, leaving ladinos on the sidelines. Don Caralampio recounted how he had resigned in disgust from the city council when indigenous *concejales* (city councilors), encouraged by the mayor, had taken to switching into Kaqchikel, the indigenous language, excluding him from the proceedings. Mention of the current mayor reminded them of the last time they had an indigenous mayor, twenty years earlier, and how different that experience had been. They chuckled as they remembered how Don Edelberto ended his term in close alignment with town ladinos, and with an angry indigenous constituency who felt betrayed. The chuckle turned to hearty laughter as Don Caralampio recounted what Edelberto, primed with a few drinks, would blurt out to his fellow carousers: *"No quiero ser un indio más, sino más que un indio"* (I don't want to be just one Indian more, I want to be more than an Indian).

Más que un indio—a phrase that two decades ago expressed an Indian's self-denigrating desire for upward mobility in a racist society, ironically enough, captures the predicament of ladinos like Don Caralampio and Don Rigoberto today. At times begrudgingly, at times with the fervor of recent converts, most ladinos in Chimaltenango now accept the idea that indigenous Guatemalans merit better treatment than they received in the past. They now affirm respect for indigenous culture, agree that racism should be eliminated, that the principle of equality should reign, echoing the Guatemalan state's endorsement of "multiculturalism." Yet these same ladinos also harbor deep anxieties about the prospect of Maya ascendancy, anxieties that condition their resolve, and undermine the very egalitarian principles that, in another register, they heartily endorse. We can best understand these sensibilities, I contend, as racial ambivalence, which embodies desires for two incompatible social outcomes: they want to shake free of their racist past, to live according to a more egalitarian ideal; yet they also believe, and continue to benefit from the structured belief, that ladinos are "más que un indio." What follows is an ethnography of this "más que un indio" predicament, and of the partially successful efforts of some ladinos to combat its effects.

Yolanda, her family, and to a lesser extent Genaro, appear in every chapter of this ethnography, but play an especially prominent role in the last two, where I reflect on the possibilities for Guatemala, and ladinos in particular, to move beyond their racist past. My argument revolves around a central paradox that race progressives like Yolanda acknowledge but also inevitably embody. The deep, pervasive ladino desire for intercultural relations with Mayas, and the closely related commitment to cultural equality, stand both as unquestionable evidence that old regime racism is fading, and as the first salvos in a new mode of governance that is just beginning to take hold. To espouse intercultural equality, many ladinos have come to intuitively understand, requires them to give up very little of their inherited racial privilege, and produces only minimal changes in their position in the racial hierarchy. Moreover, these principles can provide a highly effective defense against Maya demands that advance more radical goals. This paradox, expressed in raw and at times homely ways in Chimaltenango, has a more elaborated parallel in the global shift to neoliberal multiculturalism.

At this broader level as well, recognition of cultural rights and equality signals both dramatic shift away from the assimilationist policies of times past, and a more effective way for states to govern culturally diverse societies, while toeing the line of neoliberal political and economic reform. The paradox of neoliberal multiculturalism, like ladino racial ambivalence, is that a progressive response to past societal ills has a menacing potential to perpetuate the problem in a new guise.

Yet the very thrust of this critique also points to a more encouraging alternative scenario. The problem, of course, is not the newfound principles of cultural respect and equality in themselves, but rather, the slippage between these principles as future goal versus description of conditions already achieved, which diverts attention from persisting inequity and injustice. For the most part, ladinos continue to think about their immediate political environs, and about Guatemalan society in general, as if they were the majority and the Indian population were a minority to be managed through the application of high principles and tough love. Once this standpoint is abandoned, the equality ideal can take on a very different political valence, a mandate to actively dismantle the racial hierarchy, an invitation to consider the possibility of indigenous (majority) rule. The point is not that the Maya of Guatemala naturally think alike and could easily be represented as a bloc; nor is it that Maya are somehow inherently more democratic than ladinos. It is, rather, that they have been systematically and structurally subordinated *as indigenous people,* and that a full application of the equality principle would assign special priority to rectify this basic problem.

When confronted with even fairly moderate versions of this more expansive notion of equality, most ladinos in Chimaltenango cry foul. When the occasional ladino dissident supports this notion, expressed as active solidarity with Maya efforts to take their rightful position in Guatemalan society, their peers view their motives as suspect, traitorous, or perhaps a little bit crazy. Yolanda told me recently, for example, that her colleagues at the university have taken to ridiculing her because she gives so much extra time and attention to her Maya students. Genaro's militancy would provoke even stronger reactions, except that he's already so completely *fuera de la canasta* (outside the norm), by virtue of having been a *guerrillero* (guerrilla combatant). This resentment toward the "race traitor" is an old pattern that Luis Cardoza y Aragón observed in Guatemala many years ago, and that surely can be found the world over where stubborn racial hierarchies persist. Arguing in part by analogy with my own experience in the United States, and in part from a decade of study and reflection in Guatemala, I am convinced that an active, visible political alignment of this sort is an essential first step for people who occupy a dominant position in the racial hierarchy and who want to practice the equality principle without allowing it to become a menace. It is a first step only, with no guarantees, fraught with ambiguity and contradiction. If this book, as it circulates in Guatemala, contributes to critical awareness of the need to take this first step and to candid discussion of the difficulties that follow, while also lending hearty support to those ladinos (or mestizos) courageous enough to try, its principal objective will have been achieved.

The Maya Movement in Guatemala through Ladino Eyes

> Moya does like to imagine a Guatemala so evolved from its present darkness
> that one day a future president, a cultured and worldly man, addressing the
> United Nations, might *choose* to do so in Tzutuhil Maya, his first, his native
> village tongue. And if Moya himself should ever gain such ultimate power,
> claro, what a sweeping land reform he would enact, returning, ipso facto,
> much ancestral land. Perhaps the most just Guatemala, or at least one expres-
> sive of the interests of the majority, would be one that Moya, no lover of farm
> life or of any form of ethnic nationalism, would feel compelled to flee, if only
> out of boredom—to Paris, with a clean conscience at last, vos!
>
> —*Francisco Goldman,* The Long Night of the White Chickens *(1992)*

For many years to come, historians will be at work crafting a full explanation for the
remarkable social transformation that has occurred in Guatemala over the past two
decades. Beginning in the early 1960s, armed opposition movements fought the
Guatemalan state, first as isolated guerrilla *focos* (small, isolated groups), then, in the
late 1970s, as part of massive popular mobilizations that engulfed much of the majority indigenous highlands region. They promised radical social change in language and
imagery familiar to the Left throughout Latin America: social equality, material well-
being, and political voice for all. The Guatemalan counterinsurgency state rose to the
challenge and, with aid from the United States and its allies, defeated the guerrilla
militarily—by as early as mid-1982—and went on to punish would-be civilian supporters of the guerrilla with unspeakable brutality. Indigenous communities bore the
brunt of this army rampage, and the draconian measures of social control that followed. Yet long before anyone could imagine a definitive end to the internal armed
conflict, the efflorescence had begun.[1] Quietly at first in the mid-1980s, but with
steadily increasing strength and numbers, indigenous Guatemalans organized,

13

demanded rights, contested racism, affirmed their culture and identity as Mayas, and raised their collective voices in national politics.

The transformation is profound and irreversible. In the early years—through the 1980s—Maya efflorescence expressed an incongruous mix of sensibilities: part exuberant movement for civil rights, part defensive (even semi-clandestine) struggle for survival in the shadow of a repressive state. By the late 1990s, Mayas had established themselves as subjects of collective rights—however limited and contested—and as political actors that no aspiring politician could afford to ignore. Ladinos encompass a wide range of social positions, far too diverse to engender a single response to these changes. But it is safe to observe that ladinos' generally privileged position in Chimaltenango's racial hierarchy has begun to break down. Two images from my field notes serve as bookends for this period of change. *Before*: A priest from a rural *municipio* (township) explains the organization of space during the mass. Benches in the front, each with a plaque with the name of a prominent ladino family; Indians sitting on the floor in the back. *Now:* A politician from that same municipio muttering that ladinos cannot even think of running for mayor because Indians, the strong majority, always vote for their own. I do not want to overstate the novelty. Indigenous political assertion has deep historical roots, and the transformations leave an enormous unfinished agenda. Even with such provisos, gains in indigenous empowerment stand beyond question. One telling index of this empowerment is the anxiety of many ladinos, who fear their longstanding dominance may be slipping away.

I caught my first glimpse of this Maya efflorescence in June of 1989. Carol Smith and Nora England, two North American anthropologists who worked closely with Maya organizations, called a meeting with about ten key Maya activist-intellectuals, to consider their proposal for collaborative research and writing on the Maya movement. They invited me to offer a comparative perspective, based on my work in Nicaragua. These Maya leaders exuded the vibrant, edgy, fresh energy of a social movement just beginning to flower. They spoke of reclaiming Maya culture and identity, and then, gradually, of applying this radically different cultural logic to every facet of social existence, from language and education to development and politics. One of the first Maya movement books, *Cultura Maya y políticas de desarrollo* (1989), had just been published by COCADI (Cakchikel Coordinator for Development), and the introductory chapter conveyed this energy; that COCADI had opted to publish the chapter anonymously dramatized how dangerous they still considered these ideas to be.[2] While agitated and a little impatient with all the work that lay ahead, these leaders' strategy—whether out of necessity or careful design—had a moderate, evolutionary feel.[3] They had opted for what Antonio Gramsci called a "war of position": creating the trench work of organization and consciousness, deferring frontal battles until later.[4]

Upon leaving Guatemala, I stopped in Mexico and confronted a sharply contrasting view of this Maya efflorescence. A ladino friend who directed an NGO with close ties to exiled guerrilla and leftist organizations called a gathering of people from this network—all ladinos—to hear my report from Guatemala on the Maya movement. Faced with dismal prospects for anything even remotely approaching victory, the group found images of Maya efflorescence both encouraging (more proof of what they might have referred to as the indomitable spirit of struggle of the Guatemalan people) and deeply troubling: Who was really leading this struggle? Toward what ends? Against whom? That evening, my friend received an unannounced visitation from a high-ranking member of the URNG (National Revolutionary Unity of Guatemala) and, somewhat nervously, I gave my report to him as well. Analytically sharp, authoritative, and slightly intimidating, this URNG official had three reactions. He studied the COCADI book at length, and attached great significance to a footnote in the essay by Demetrio Cojtí (a leading Maya intellectual), which states that former dictator Efraín Ríos Montt had been correct in referring to the distinct indigenous language groups as "nations."[5] He expressed alarm at the number of North American anthropologists working in alignment with the Maya, including one in particular: it is no coincidence, he asserted, that Richard Adams is back in Guatemala. Adams, he continued, is an architect of *"el nuevo plantamiento indígena"* (the new Indian position).[6] Then, in a final reflective moment, he said ladinos have to overcome their "anguished" response to Maya ascendancy, perhaps by acknowledging their own Indian cultural roots. "We need a serious study of the ladino," he concluded. These leftists had responded to the Maya "war of position" not with outright rejection but with ambivalence, a sensibility I would later find to be common across the political spectrum.

This book tracks ladino responses to the Maya efflorescence, with primary ethnographic grounding in the highland department of Chimaltenango. True to our calling to side with the downtrodden, most anthropologists have attempted to tell this story from a Maya perspective, assigning central importance to indigenous voices, experiences, and practices.[7] While drawing on this rich and extensive existing literature, my analysis departs sharply from it by focusing primarily on ladinos. Yet by situating the fieldwork in a predominantly Maya highland department, this study also departs from recent anthropological work that has taken national-level political actors and institutions as ethnographic subjects.[8] While I do put forth an analysis of state and transnational arenas, my principal point of entry into this local-national-global web of relations is local interactions: the ladinos whom Mayas encounter in their daily routines of school, church, commerce, work, local politics, and increasingly, in various forms of sociability. While it is common for ethnographies that focus on the Maya to flatten, homogenize, or simply ignore ladinos, the rationale for reversing the ethnographic gaze is not simply (as traditional anthropology would have it) to "fill in" the ethnographic record. The stakes are much higher: by tracing the thoughts and practice of provincial ladino power holders since the mid-1980s, I contend, we can help explain how the Maya efflorescence came about, and why, in recent years, continued efforts toward Maya empowerment have begun to founder.

While sustained study of ladinos as actors in this unfolding political drama has been scant, Maya efflorescence has sparked much scrutiny of and self-reflection on

Figure 1.1. In Search of Ladino Identity. "Amid so much ethnic discussion, what really is a ladino?" The Sunday magazine section of the Siglo XXI, one of Guatemala's principal newspapers, 6 October 1996.

ladino identity, which highlights important questions, but ultimately frames them in ways that are apt to yield incomplete and unsatisfying answers (figure 1.1). What does it mean to identify, or be identified, as ladino? Do ladinos share a common set of cultural characteristics? How are these commonalities, and the identities themselves, changing? The problem arises when scrutiny of the dominant identity fails to encompass analysis of the material and ideological underpinnings of racial dominance, and when identity formation is conceived in isolation from daily interactions with others, isolated from the flow of sociopolitical process. While training a bright light on ladino identity does work to undermine the still widespread universalizing equation of "ladino" with "Guatemalan," it runs the risk of shoring up a new form of inequality, exercised through a new idiom: multiculturalism. According to this mindset, ladinos condemn the racism of times past, claim that these problems have for the most part been resolved, and call for relations of tolerance and mutual respect among all identity groups (often summarized in Spanish as *interculturalidad*). Paradoxically, such calls for intercultural equality are clear signs of progress, and yet they also tend to frustrate and derail ongoing efforts by Mayas to contest ladino dominance.[9]

This critique of "identity talk" leaves me positioned in respectful disagreement with two major currents of work on the topics. My insistence on situating ladinos within a power-laden racial formation stands in tension with the theoretical inclination to deconstruct race and identity, to displace generalized notions of structural and ideological power with the cultural analysis of fluidity, heterogeneity, difference.[10] My emphasis on ethnography and, more specifically, the ethnography of social interaction and political process, however, stands in tension with those who, in their salutary focus on racialized power, end up neglecting how people negotiate, contest, and maneuver within these spaces of structured inequality.[11] The attentive reader will note how these two principal theoretical emphases—structural-ideological power and fine-grained political process—themselves also stand in tension, especially for analysis of dominant actors. How to situate ladinos within Guatemala's racial hierarchy, without reducing them to scripted actors in a play whose ending is known in advance? How to register the variation and multiplicity of ladino lives, without losing sight of the pervasive backdrop of their relations of dominance with Indians? Suffice it to say here that I respond to this dilemma not by seeking a neat resolution or synthesis, but rather, by keeping the tension in place, allowing one mode of analysis constantly to disrupt and trouble the other. In the concluding chapter, I revisit this problem, reviewing the analytical insight and political contributions—as well as the quandaries and new research questions—that a study using this approach yields.

Although ladino angst around questions of their own identity is on the rise, it is not entirely new. At least since 1971, when Carlos Guzmán Böckler and Jean-Loup Herbert provoked their (mainly ladino) readership by dubbing the ladino a "*ser ficticio*" (ficticious being), ladinos have regularly been taken to task for their ambiguous intermediary status: denied entry to the elite category of the Euro-Guatemalans who they fruitlessly emulate, yet deeply invested in being everything modern and civilized that indigenous people are not. My own field notes from the late 1990s are filled with expressions of angst along these lines from ladinos themselves: "We have no identity," one informant insisted. "The very term," he went on, "means liar, thief, imposter; ladino identity needs to be decolonized or abandoned altogether." Yet this identity angst alone does not necessarily challenge ladino dominance, and in some respects may even help to obscure it. In Guatemala, as in many parts of the world, identities have become politicized, and cultural difference has become a key idiom through which political struggles unfold. To think of identity itself as the end of these struggles, however, is to take identity politics as a given, rather than to probe critically its effects. With or without identity angst, ladinos continue to occupy the upper rungs of the racial hierarchy out of proportion with their numbers. Moreover, many are inclined to act, individually and collectively, to defend that privilege, which makes them powerful arbiters of Maya cultural-political assertion. Although this racial hierarchy certainly is changing, it shows little signs of going away.

This ladino entwinement with Maya politics has become more evident in recent years, as an impasse has come clearly into view. The first phase of national-level Maya assertion provoked great alarm in the ladino establishment, best epitomized by the opposition to the candidacy of Rigoberta Menchú for the Nobel Peace Prize, and the anxious political commentary in the aftermath of her award. The cover of *Crónica*, Guatemala's *Newsweek*, encapsulates this anxiety is an especially dramatic fashion (figure 1.2). Certain Maya political proposals emitted at that time, such as the idea of political autonomy for indigenous peoples, generated such hostile responses from national-level power holders that prudence dictated abandoning the topic.[12] Other more moderate initiatives failed for different reasons. For example, most Maya organizations strongly supported a May 1999 referendum to reform the Constitution in favor of indigenous rights, but failed to mobilize indigenous voters to counter opposition and fend off defeat.[13] A year later, scandals over misuse of abundant international funding generated by the 1996 Peace Accords wracked many Maya organizations, deepening the sense of internal fragmentation and self-questioning.[14] The organizations that seem to have weathered this storm most successfully are ones that have been considered peripheral to the Maya movement.[15] Yet more important than these setbacks—arguably momentary and easily overcome—a certain kind of success has made the impasse more serious and intractable. Power holders at all levels of Guatemala's political-economic system have endorsed their own versions of "multiculturalism," selectively including Maya demands and, in some cases, inviting Maya leaders to hold positions of power. Demetrio Cojtí explained it this way, as he pondered one such invitation: before, they simply told us "no," now, their response is "*sí pero* (yes but)." My research attempts to explain this impasse, to ask what lies behind the "sí pero."

The responses of ladinos in Chimaltenango, as they confront and come to terms with Maya efflorescence, both illustrate and help to constitute this impasse. Among innumerable informal conversations, and roughly 150 formal interviews, I rarely found ladinos who defended the previously well-established doctrine of indigenous people's racial inferiority. Apart from these exceptional few—generally members of the elder generation—they all firmly, often fervently, endorsed the principle of equality between Mayas and ladinos. Although frequently troubled by some facets of the Maya efflorescence, they had no appetite for return to the past when, by their own account, an odious racism prevailed. At the same time, their anxieties often came embedded in a substratum of race-inflected premises: Indians are treacherous, conniving, vengeful, and clannish; they are prone to practicing "reverse racism" against ladinos; they have cultural attributes that leave them ill-prepared for the rigors of modernity. These premises do not add up to an assertion of overt racial inferiority; moreover, ladinos of

Figure 1.2. Anxieties about Maya efflorescence. "Indigenous Power. What are their objectives? Integration or division? Revenge or Justice? Peace or Conflict?" Crónica, 16-22 October 1992.

this generation and social position rarely affirm an explicit racial identity of their own. Instead, they unload the entire discussion onto the realm of culture: seeking an identity for themselves that befits their own newfound egalitarian ethic; encouraging spaces of intercultural dialogue with Mayas; affirming indigenous people's right to their own culture and identity. Yet paradoxically, these egalitarian sensibilities do not require ladinos fully to acknowledge ongoing relations of racial dominance, much less to dismantle them. This paradox is the crux of what I call racial ambivalence.

I devote considerable effort to understanding racial ambivalence, not as individual predicament, but as collective political sensibility and structured social condition. The phrase refers, most simply, to an incongruity between the way people think about race and the position they occupy in a racialized social hierarchy. Ladinos manifest racial ambivalence when they repudiate racism, express support for the ideals of cultural equality, and view themselves as practicing these ideals, and yet, maintain a strong psychic investment in their dominance and privilege in relation to Indians.[16] In many cases, documented amply throughout this book, this psychic investment betrays continuities from the previous era: discourse about Indians that, while straining to avoid classic racist premises, comes to the same conclusion through the sanitized idiom of culture.[17] Yet as the emergent form of racial hierarchy comes to predominate, we can expect even these more subtle continuities to recede, displaced by a generally ascendant ethos of multicultural tolerance and equality. In this emergent mode, people then tend to defend the persisting racial hierarchy not with universalizing premises about Indian inferiority, but rather, carefully drawn distinctions between worthy and unworthy Indians, authorized and prohibited ways of being Indian. Racial ambivalence, in these conditions, rests on the premise that most Indians remain at the bottom of the social hierarchy because they, for one reason or another, belong there.[18]

First and foremost, I want this book to convey how racial ambivalence feels. How do ladinos think about their own racial dominance, especially as they face the prospect of losing it? How do they mediate among the range of responses to this challenge: fear, anxiety, strategic repositioning, solidarity, guilt, anger? How do we connect these responses—often individual and contradictory—to the social transformations that Maya efflorescence has ushered in? My response to this last question brings the book's central argument into focus. Ladino responses to the Maya efflorescence in today's Guatemala come as an entangled, contradictory, and at times consciously troubled combination of two basic sensibilities: a desire for equality, and an equally deep reluctance to cede racial privilege. This ambivalence, in turn, runs parallel to a broader process of change in Guatemala, and beyond: a shift to neoliberalism as the predominant mode of governance. Although at first many portrayed the neoliberal reforms that swept the region in the past two decades as primarily economic policy mandates, gradually we have begun to see neoliberalism also as processes of subject formation: processes that shape and transform individual subjects and collectivities, as well as economies. Like ladino racial ambivalence, the ideology of neoliberalism affirms cultural rights, and endorses the principle of equality, while remaking societies with ever more embedded and resilient forms of racial hierarchy. This parallel, I argue, signals a great menace to indigenous movements, and to their potential allies—a rough equivalent to the twentieth-century ideologies of mestizaje, assimilation, and unitary citizenship for the new millennium.

Positioning amid the "Opposition"

I placed political considerations at the forefront of my selection of a specific research topic. I wanted my work to contribute to the process of indigenous empowerment underway in Guatemala, and I sought to formulate the specific topic through dialogue with the protagonists. In my first trips to the country, I had the good fortune to engage a number of leading Maya activist-intellectuals in conversation, to ask them about their research priorities. One response came through with striking frequency: "Don't study Mayas, study the ladinos. Find out what *they* are thinking about us." In one of those trips, I picked up Demetrio Cojtí from the San Carlos University, and we stopped for a quick dinner at a nearby Wendy's. In that incongruous setting of scrubbed clean, brightly lit, tacky global commercialism, he said the same thing in a more sophisticated form: "What we need, Carlos, is a department for the study of the opposition."

At first jarring and counterintuitive, the idea of studying ladinos grew on me. I enjoyed the reactions that Mayas had to this topic as a conversation opener: bemusement, followed by a joking comment to effect that "now it's their turn," and (I fancied) an increased measure of trust. It also seemed to me that anthropology had yet to muster an adequate response to Laura Nader's call, of some three decades past, to "study up" as an act of solidarity with those underneath.[19] Moreover, this focus also resonated with my incipient sense—engendered in part by residual sympathies with the Left, in part by pragmatic political analysis—that Mayas would not be able to go it alone, that it would be important to know under what conditions some ladinos might become their allies. My encounters with those exiled ladino leftists in Mexico, and especially, the chance conversation with a high-ranking official of the URNG, seemed to point in this same direction: a moment of openness, a desire for collective reflection on questions of race, identity, and cultural difference. I began with a series of straightforward questions: What do ladinos think Mayas are up to? How do ladinos respond to Maya ascendancy? With what effects?

However neatly this topic came together in theory, when I actually began the research, the central problem seemed both ubiquitous and elusive. On the first day of our arrival in Guatemala as a family, the front page of the leading newspaper trumpeted my key research question—with the help, perhaps, of a mischievous layout person (figure 1.3): under what conditions could these two women, the petite fair-skinned beauty queen and the angry indigenous activist with fist clenched in the air, actually occupy the same national space on reasonably equal terms? Informal and chance encounters, from early on, evoked my topic in other ways. An elderly prospective landlord in Chimaltenango had what I took to be a classically indigenous phenotype, but evinced a frightful racism toward Indians. At a social event to mark the publication of a book by OKMA, a Maya linguistics collective, I gravitated toward a group of ladinos standing in the corner. Upon hearing that I was an anthropologist a man in the group put the question to me out of the blue: "I want to know why Indians always cry at fiestas. I have noted that pure Indians start to drink at times like this, and they always begin to cry." Taken aback, I turned to the courtyard, full of people, mostly Mayas, socializing and dancing to the marimba, not one drunk or crying. Fortunately another man in the group saved me from my dumbstruck state: "There is a wonderful short story by Miguel Angel Asturias," he noted with authority, "read it and you'll find the answer." Yet for all this ubiquity—filling pages of field notes from those initial months—to begin systematic research on this topic proved difficult. Many ladinos turned reticent when it became clear I wanted to study *them*; most were trying hard to carry on cordial relations with Mayas, and did not take kindly to my inclination to scratch beneath the surface; they were more comfortable giving me advice on how to study Indians as, in their understanding, anthropologists properly do.

To meet this challenge I drew on a disparate combination of approaches, from

Figure 1.3. Two Guatemalas. "Hostess. María Fernanda Morales Pellecer, Miss Guatemala, beautiful contestant for the throne of Miss Latin America, is the hostess of 22 candidates, representing the same number of countries. Protest. Right, more than 600 representatives of the Communities of People in Resistance (CPR) protested yesterday to demand that the Government recognize them as civilian non-combatants, and demanded that the Minister of Defense order that they stop the bombardments [by the Guatemalan military]." Prensa Libre, 11 September, 1993.

activist research methods (explained more fully later on), to the most conventional trick of the trade: entering the community by living there, and turning to a "key informant" as guide. We lived in Chimaltenango, the capital city in the department of the same name, as a family, for roughly twenty-eight months, spread over five years. During all of that time, my wife Melissa worked with NGOs in clinical and public health, occupying the immediately comprehensible, and generally welcomed, category of "internationalist." Our older child, Amalia, attended preschool; together, Amalia and Sofia served as our emissaries to the family-centered world of Chimaltenango. We developed a circle of dear friends, both ladino and Maya, although we often socialized separately with each. While I talked openly with all of them about my research, and familiarity helped generally to ease suspicions, those in one family, and one person in particular, really understood what I wanted to do. That person liked the idea and, gradually, nearly adopted the project as her own. As I go back over my notes from those months, I am struck by how many leads Yolanda dreamed up, interviews she arranged, how much insight she provided. We became close friends, later *compadres* (fictive kin), and to some extent confidants in our respective endeavors; yet throughout, Yolanda continued to be a key informant as well.

Yolanda seemed to relish her contradictory role. She readily pointed out and sharply criticized ladino racism, and helped arrange interviews with people who espoused ideas that she deplored. "Don Federico is a proponent of the extermination thesis," she would say, "you really need to talk with him."[20] As director of the Chimaltenango office of quasi-governmental DIGEA, Yolanda worked out a scheme for me to visit each of Chimaltenango's sixteen municipios accompanied by a DIGEA staff person, who helped me collect data and open doors. I often accompanied Yolanda on her own trips to outlying municipios, for ceremonial activities (inauguration of public works, civic holidays, patron saint festivals, and so on) that are the stuff of local politics. A well-connected and generally well-liked figure at the departmental level, Yolanda would inevitably find her way to the head table, or to some inner sanctum, where notables (all or mostly ladinos, all or mostly men) drank rum and talked politics; and she would always pull me along with her.[21] In 1996, Yolanda became a city council member (*concejal*) in the Chimaltenango municipal government, and through this position, offered a constant flow of insight into the inner workings of local power relations. She also held a faculty position in the Department of Pedagogy of the San Carlos University, and taught classes at its Chimaltenango branch. She regularly pressed me into service as guest lecturer in her classes, and I took the opportunity to subject her students to my research questions. Yet while Yolanda worked, as we often joked, as an informal (and unpaid) research assistant, she, her family, friends, and associates were also research subjects. To the extent that my analysis focused on racial ambivalence and the like, these conclusions applied in varying degrees to them as well. I now marvel at her self-confidence, her capacity for serious self-reflection, her ironic self-effacement, and her faintly perverse sense of humor, which somehow all worked together to make this role possible. Or, as her compañero Gerardo might have said, in one of our many boisterous evening discussions of such matters around the kitchen table: "No, don't give her so much credit. That's just typical ladino hypocrisy." We had one of those sessions each time I returned to Guatemala, and after reviewing recent political events, nearly always dismal in their details, Yolanda would summarize the discussion with the same refrain: "*Guatemala no se compone*" (Guatemala will never fix itself). That refrain could be applied to ladino racial dominance as well. It is a fine line, to be sure, between critique of ladino racism as an impetus for change, and as a means to distance oneself from the problem. Like most progressive ladinos in Guatemala (and like most progressive whites in the United States), Yolanda did some of both.[22]

Yolanda and her family will appear in every chapter: to raise a key point of analysis, to provide an epitomizing example, to contextualize, probe, and complicate a conclusion. In part, this will help break with standard anthropological practice: the key informant, after being duly introduced at the outset, often fades into the crowd, to enhance the authentic and representative feel of the ethnography that follows. More commonly still, the facilitating conditions of fieldwork, the means of access to the research subjects, often involve details a little too compromised to reveal fully. While at times I exercise this authorial prerogative of reserve and discernment as well, these details in general form an essential part of the story that I want to tell: the daily workings of the ladino world in Chimaltenango, and the everyday practice of ladino dominance. In part also, the Valencia family plays a prominent role in this ethnography because its collective story is so remarkable, and so evocative of the central topics of this book. Their living members animate a tumultuous seventy-five years of Guatemalan history, and occupy a wide range of positions in this drama: both visceral opponents and sympathizers of the 1944–1954 October Revolution; a career army officer and a veteran guerrilla doctor; victims of state repression and a new recruit to the army; unapologetic racists and biting critics of ladino racism. Without going further afield, they provide a definitive antidote to facile statements about "the ladinos," which fail to take this great heterogeneity into account. Yet I have no desire to portray them as typical. Yolanda, especially, has a truly unusual pair of traits: a deep immersion in ladino society, and a capacity to take a distanced, sharply analytical view of every facet of that world. With all the complexity such a position entails, this made her a superb key informant.

During those kitchen-table sessions, although conversation often settled on topics of race—in addition to sex and politics—it was always a challenge to figure out what to take seriously. It would have been the height of gullibility to draw conclusions from some of what was said, a new page in the book of those Anglo ethnographers of "Mexican culture," who Américo Paredes lampooned so deliciously decades ago.[23] The Valencia family variant of the *chingadera* (banter laden with humor, irony, and mutual ribbing), similar to its Mexican counterpart, involved off-color jokes, constant roasting of one another, an ability to find perverse humor in the most deadly serious matters, and (perhaps a more uniquely chapín contribution to the genre) explanations of political events through recourse to outrageously convoluted and cynical conspiracy theories. (One of my favorites: Chimaltenango's mayor, facing a social movement intent on ousting him, announced one day that he had been subject to an attack the night before. Kitchen-table conversation favored the theory that he had secretly ordered his own house riddled with machine-gun fire, in an attempt to bolster his image as a courageous public servant, under siege from unruly thugs.)

Amid all this chingadera, the conversation at times turned serious, as family members would describe how they and others thought about one topic or another. One such moment came about as I elicited their help in answering a tricky question I had been grappling with: did ladinos think of themselves as different from Indians in cultural terms, or as a matter of racial biology? Yolanda began by invoking the views of her parents' generation: "True ladinos are a separate race, with no admixture with Indians except at a time too remote to be relevant, and the cultures of the two groups have very little in common. For that reason, we are ladinos, *not* mestizos." She then rehearsed the critique of this position, which everyone around the table knew well:

ladinos are thoroughly mixed, an assertion of absolute biological difference between ladinos and Indians is paramount to racism. As the conversation went on, however, they began to reflect on their own premises, describing in detail the differences between ladino and Indian—the nose, hips, thighs, skin color—and indicating their own deep emotional preference for the ladino. As the conversation proceeded I felt my discomfort level rising, a sensation that they were constructing—ambivalently, reluctantly—a portrait of Indians as inferior other. Perhaps sensing the danger, Yolanda suddenly interjected, "Even the farts." What? *Yo, cuando monto a una camioneta, puedo distinguir entre los pedos de los dos*" (When I get on a bus I can distinguish between the farts of the two). I protested the absurdity of her statement, everyone laughed at my earnest tone, and the conversation reverted back to chingadera. Yet that moment of serious reflection stayed with me.

The subtle continuity between progressive ladinos and their racist forebearers is not lost on Mayas, who comment frequently about what they perceive as disdain, just beneath the surface of a more civil and courteous demeanor. My notes record an informal dinner conversation with two Maya friends, husband and wife, talking about a ladina co-worker, whom they consider to be racist. The idealist of the two, he muses: "These are new times, maybe gradually she'll come around." His wife vehemently disagrees, "That's the way she is; just accept it; she'll never change." He turns pensive, and we stay quiet for a long time before he speaks again, "Then when will Guatemala change?" When indeed?

The Race-Culture Conundrum

Don Caralampio, a ladino man of about sixty years, lived in the municipio of San Andrés Itzapa, just down the road from Chimaltenango. He had retired recently from a mid-level office job in Chimaltenango's town hall. Don Lampo collected data for me, and when I arrived to receive his report he often would take me next door to his sister's house, where he could give the conversation a little more *ánimo* (spirit), with an eighth of rum, and delicious Itzapa sausages cooked on the open fire. Don Lampo's sister, Erendira, had been an elementary school teacher in Itzapa for some twenty years; she lived with a second sister, Miriam, who had two children in the states. They lead a comfortable rural middle-class existence, advantaged in relation to the majority Indian population, but not especially wealthy or powerful.

One afternoon, as we settled in at the table in Erendira's kitchen, she and Miriam sat down with us. Toño, a teacher friend of Erendira, soon showed up and joined the conversation. Toño was from nearby Zaragoza, an anomalous municipio because it is majority ladino; Zaragoza ladinos are known to be overtly hostile toward Indians. When Toño left, Erendira went to great lengths to criticize Zaragoza and to draw a sharp contrast between herself and Toño: "I have learned, as part of my vocation as teacher, to treat everyone equally. Toño is still a discriminator." Don Lampo joked with Erendira about the difficult task of "taming" Toño, and continued drawing a general contrast between Indians and Zaragoza ladinos: the zaragozeños do have "the advantage of physical appearance; there are some beautiful young girls there. But they lack motivation and they're too self-centered. The Indian *"tiene deseo de superarse"* (has the drive to better himself).[24]

Miriam, who had remained silent up to that point, suddenly exploded with a torrent that directly contradicted the case for equality that Erendira and Don Lampo had just laboriously built: "I don't like Indians," she said, wrinkling her nose, scrunching her body, shaking her head in what seemed almost a physical aversion. "They are thickheaded, bothersome, and dirty. Who knows where that thick headedness comes from, you even see it in the children. *Traen algo en la raza*" (They carry something in the race). Taken aback, I returned the conversation to the contrast with Zaragoza: did discrimination against Indians still exist in Itzapa? Erendira said no, we are much more "unified" now; Don Lampo agreed, but added that some remnants remain. As if to confirm Don Lampo's correction, Miriam started in again. I asked her how she would feel if her daughter married an Indian. *"Dios guarde"* (God save us) is all that she could muster, before returning the question to me, "Imagine taking off the *corte* (indigenous skirt), all that filth underneath, weeks without bathing." Erendira intervened weakly, suggesting that poverty had something to do with it. The conversation continued, until Don Lampo tried to close it on an analytical note: "The indígenas' major goal is to get back the land taken from them at the time of the Conquest. If they didn't spend so much money on marriages and other ceremonies, they would have achieved that goal by now." This allusion hit a cord with Erendira, who began to vent her own frustration with "the Mayas":

> They do not have the right, historically, culturally, they do not have the right
> to call themselves Mayas. By the time of the Conquest, the Maya Empire had
> disappeared; when the Spanish arrived, there was already a mixed people here.
> There were Toltecs who came from Mexico, and by that time the Maya had
> completely disappeared. Afterwards, the Spanish came, and found a mixed
> culture… Legally the indigenous people claim they are Mayas and this is a
> lie…. There are no pure Mayas left.

Erendira then returned to her teacher's calling: help them "superarse." Even when they better themselves, she reflected in conclusion, "some indigenous characteristics just don't go away." Don Lampo followed up:

> They are mistrustful. It is as if they are angry that you [ladinos] have more
> than they do (*Como que les da coraje que uno tiene las cosas*). I see this when they
> work for me on my farm. Instead of taking care of things, they are destructive.
> A few Indians are good, but only a very few.

Thanks to a growing body of critical historical work, we now know a lot about nineteenth-century racism toward Indians in Guatemala, which persisted largely intact until 1944.[25] Within a highly differentiated socioeconomic structure, Indians occupied the bottom rung, often in spaces set apart as "Indians only." Economic exploitation and political exclusion went hand in hand. Even the tiny indigenous sector that did accumulate capital could not translate wealth into status recognized by society's power holders.[26] A harsh ideology of racial inferiority accompanied and justified this stark social inequality. Even during the period of social democratic reform (1944–1954), among progressive ladino politicians who dismantled the statutory institutional pillars of this racism (for example, forced labor laws), these premises ran deep. Although Left and Right disagreed vehemently about the reforms, they both applied the civilized-barbarian dichotomy to distinguish ladinos from Indians, and used animal analogies to describe the Indians' deplorably backward state. Embedded in the common sense of the time, these premises not only failed to offend the sensibilities of the progressive legislators, they seem to have gone largely unnoticed.[27]

Strong vestiges of this classic racism persist to this day, and still shape the experiences of indigenous people, but they are subject to increasing challenge. Early in my fieldwork, I met Irma Otzoy, then a Maya PhD candidate in anthropology, for lunch in Zone 1 at the Café Swiza. The waitress took my order, and to my astonishment, abruptly turned around and headed toward the kitchen without even making eye contact with Irma. I later heard many other such stories from other professional Maya women: how ladinos assume they are domestic workers, and proceed either to ignore them, or (more insultingly still), offer them a job cleaning their homes! In 2002, a capital city restaurant closed its doors to Irma Alicia Velásquez Nimatuj, a PhD candidate at the University of Texas at Austin, reportedly stating: "Women with *traje típico* (Indian clothing) cannot enter here." Along the same lines, a 1995 opinion column in *La Prensa Libre* inveighed against indigenous people who gather at the Plaza on Sundays:

> I condemn the Indian hordes that arrive on Sundays to spread their filth in the central park, the Plaza of the Constitution. It's not just that these people don't bathe—and as a result, expel fetid odors—but also, that their presence frightens civilized people. This once clean and decent space now looks more like a zoo. There, on Sundays, the unfortunate state of Guatemala is in full view: alienated Indians exhibiting cultural underdevelopment in the extreme. These dimwitted slovenly creatures! If I were President I would have them fumigated.[28]

Hundreds of such insults surely occur on a daily basis in Guatemala, under conditions of anonymity that make them difficult to record, much less contest. Yet, in great contrast to the legislative debates a half-century earlier, when racism is brought to public awareness today, "enlightened" ladino power holders react with critical indignation. The *Prensa Libre* editorial provoked condemnation from well-positioned ladinos across the political spectrum; the corporate owner of the restaurant in the Velásquez incident issued a public apology, and the outcry gave rise to a legislative initiative that would "typify" racial discrimination.[29] While these responses may have a disingenuous feel, addressing symptoms rather than root causes, repudiation still sends a strong message. Ladino power holders find this overtly exclusionary racism unacceptable, and incompatible with the new social order in the making.

As classic racism has receded under the pressure of Maya activism, ladino self-critique, and various pressures from above, racial ambivalence has emerged to take its place. The sensibilities that constitute racial ambivalence might be arranged in a continuum, with Miriam at one extreme, through Don Lampo and Erendira, and with "race progressives" like Yolanda and her family at the other pole. Lampo and Erendira represent the most common position among my ladino informants in Chimaltenango. Their general thinking about Indian-ladino relations has three main features. First, they are explicitly and, at times, vehemently critical of classic racism, which they readily acknowledge once prevailed, still persists, but is rapidly fading into insignificance. As a result, the logic goes, racism itself has diminished as well. Second, they make every effort to talk about differences between Indians and ladinos in cultural terms. This includes both affirming observations about positive features (for example, Don Lampo's comments about how Indians are unified and industrious), and critical attention to negative characteristics, which place Indians at a disadvantage. Third, they deny or downplay ladino racial privilege, and view indigenous mobilization as a threat to social peace and justice: "The most militant Mayas," ladinos will often add with a shudder, "have become racist toward us." Together these three engender a dramatic reversal: seizing the high ground of antiracism, yet defending ladino racial privilege, and portraying Indians as responsible for their own persisting subordination, all in a socially acceptable idiom.

Viewed in historical perspective, these emergent racial sensibilities embody a curious delayed effect: classic racism has only become a subject of systematic critique in the moment of its decline and near-certain demise. Through the 1970s public critique of classic racism was rare and muted. Foreign academics tended not to "see" race in Guatemala, because prevailing racial meanings did not fit with the folk models of race in other places (especially the United States).[30] They depicted and analyzed social inequality principally in terms of cultural difference, and by the mid-1960s, stopped using race completely as a conceptual category, substituting the more flexible, porous, and culture-focused concept of ethnicity. Some Guatemalan scholars followed suit, while others sharply criticized this approach as "*culturalista*," insisting instead that the "Indian question" be viewed through the lens of class analysis. From both the *culturalista* and *clasista* perspectives, race did not appear analytically salient. Far from unified, ladino scholarship on Indians in the 1960s and 1970s covered a range of positions deeply at odds with one another; even among intellectuals of the Left, debates raged. One line of inquiry, guided by a fusion of French anthropology and anticolonial thought in the tradition of Franz Fanon, did introduce a highly influential critique of ladino racism into teaching, scholarship, and political work.[31] Yet this reflection, however important in intellectual terms, remained muted politically until the mid-1980s, when the rise of Maya collective agency imbued it with a more powerful and urgent content.[32] Soon thereafter, the second part of the delayed effect came into play. When the critique of classic racism grew prominent, and growing numbers of ladino power holders rose to endorse its message, the main object of this critique already had begun to fade. Today most ladinos chimaltecos view people like Miriam as outliers, anomalies, sources of embarrassment.

Given this shift, to insist on using the terms "race" and "racism" to analyze changing relations between Mayas and ladinos runs the risk of making everyone a little uncomfortable. It could be misunderstood as a reintroduction of race as biology, especially ill-advised, given that most people have successfully moved to the higher ground of cultural difference. It could also appear as a conceptual step backward, away from the capacious flexibility of ethnicity theory, back toward the rigidities of the race concept. It could even be seen as a violation of anthropological first principles, imposing a framework, a way of looking at the world that the actors themselves do not share or endorse. Increasingly, ladinos portray themselves as belonging to a pluralist identity category, encompassing a range of phenotypes, with identity boundaries drawn along the lines of cultural commonality and difference. Why do I insist on the term "racial hierarchy" for something that my ladino informants are straining to rethink as "cultural difference"? Could I be fanning the embers of racial antipathy, just as they are beginning to turn cold?

My approach here, and throughout this book, is not to downplay this divergence between my own understandings of the race-culture conundrum, and those of my ladino interlocutors, but rather, to highlight the problem, and then subject it to critical analysis. As historian George Stocking (1993) and others have shown, in the early twentieth century neither intellectuals nor the general public in the United States made a rigorous distinction between the two. Then came a series of social forces which, over a half-century or so, yielded the repudiation of scientific racism, yanked race and culture apart, made culture the operable concept of social analysis, and relegated race to the realm of biology.[33] US-based academics then made two additional complicating moves: we determined that race as a biological concept has no scientific value; and we continued to use the notion of race as social construction—to analyze how people (in the United States, Guatemala, and most other places) continue to assign deep social meanings to race, and to reproduce racial hierarchies. These later conceptual refinements have given rise to widespread slippage between general understandings of race as biology, and academic analysis of race as social construction.

In Chimaltenango this slippage is just as serious, but with different coordinates. Since the repudiation of classic racism is more recent and still far from complete, use of the term race (*raza*) generally conjures up, in the minds of both ladinos and Mayas, assertions of Indian people's inherent (biological) inferiority. Moreover, since Maya activists do not explicitly claim a racial identity as part of their discourse of rights and redress, there is little impetus for giving the race concept a positive value in relation to their political struggle. Consequently, rather than endorse the idea of race as social construction both ladinos and Mayas, when they hear the word "race," are apt to think "biology" and when they hear "racism," they think of people like Miriam. They are inclined to agree that race should be expunged from the lexicon in any effort to depict the identity of ladinos and Mayas and the relations between them, except when referring to remnants of the classic racism, which both groups generally agree needs to be left behind. My contrasting inclination to highlight race finds its rationale in two empirical observations. Racial hierarchy persists, despite the term's banishment. Most ladinos allow race-as-biology reasoning to seep back into their otherwise adamantly cultural discourse (as occurred in the kitchen-table discussion with Yolanda and her family). Taking these observations as point of departure, I have opted to use race as social construction in reference to how social hierarchies and identities are constituted and to the meanings ladinos assign to the world around them. This might be framed as a respectful invitation to dialogue with those who have made different choices, focused on two questions, presumably of common concern: How can we most rigorously characterize and explain the persisting inequities between Indian and ladino in Guatemala? What modes of analysis best inform effective strategies for eliminating these inequities?

Scholars have noted widely the divergence—between race and culture, between academic and popular understandings—and have taken three positions on how to proceed. Historian George Fredrickson (2002) acknowledges the slippages but still attempts to hold the line, focusing primary attention on what he calls "overtly racist regimes," which meet a rigorous five conditions that boil down to domination through an ideology of inherent biological inferiority. Cultural studies theorist Stuart Hall (2000) insists that race and culture are so intertwined and mutually implicated that it is folly to distinguish between forms of racism that highlight one or the other. Instead, Hall traces how racial and cultural reasoning come together to form an overarching ideology, in specific empirical contexts. A third position, applied to the United States by Eduardo Bonilla-Silva (2003), and to Europe by Etienne Balibar (1991) and Pierre-André Taguieff (2001), uses the notion of "neo" or "cultural" racism, to direct attention to how culture has become the articulating principle of racist thought and practice.[34] I defend this third position for Guatemala today, because it offers a substantive basis for engagement with my ladino informants' emphatic insistence that they have changed. We need a means to analyze the remaking of racial hierarchy, while fully hearing ladinos' adamant claims to have abandoned biological reasoning, and their use of cultural difference as a means to explain persisting indigenous disadvantage.

The notion of "cultural racism" opens the way for this analysis, marking both continuity and change. Ladino power holders inherited a social formation that systematically favored ladinos over Indians. Ladinos are, for the most part, deeply invested in defending this inherited privilege, especially as it comes under increasing challenge from Mayas. At the same time, Maya political assertion, combined with other forces, has led most ladinos to view classic racism as unseemly, wrong, and ill-advised. Instead, they have embraced a new series of premises, which express both their newfound commitment to racial equality and their deep fears of Indian ascendancy.

Among these premises, the commitment to equality is crucial: it places them in line with the modern multicultural ethos, on the side of justice rather than oppression. Yet these same egalitarian principles also engender fear and anxiety because they open the way for collective Maya empowerment. Especially since Maya are the majority, "equality" could become the driving force behind a radically transformative social and political movement. This ambiguity in the political valence of cultural equality, in turn, is played out in the struggle over indigenous culture. The more Mayas organize to achieve collective empowerment, the more ladinos perceive their negative cultural traits coming to the fore: they are treacherous, untrustworthy, and ultimately dangerous. We respect indigenous culture, they regularly proclaim, but we must draw a distinction between healthy, forward-looking cultural difference, and its destructive or dysfunctional counterpart. Otherwise, the idealistic dream of Maya empowerment could turn into a nightmare. Suddenly, the move to empowerment and equality has become highly conditional: as if to say, "We respect cultural difference, but within limits."

The shift to cultural racism forms part of a broader transformation in Guatemalan society, whose full trajectory has not yet been revealed. In one scenario, these forces of change transform society toward gradual elimination of racism and the achievement of intercultural equality. Had I written this book in the mid-1990s, my analysis might have unfolded with this more uplifting scenario in mind. However, accumulating evidence since the 1996 Peace Accords suggests otherwise: the Maya movement stands at an impasse; ladino responses have turned preemptive; powerful institutions well beyond Guatemala are finding ways to contain cultural rights activism through appropriation rather than suppression. From this standpoint, rather than a waystation in an uplifting course of egalitarian social change, ladino racial ambivalence takes on different attributes: a political project to remake racial dominance in a gentler, less offensive, and more sustainable guise.

Neoliberal Multiculturalism

This remaking of racial hierarchy in Guatemala forms part of a broader process of political restructuring, which has yielded new forms of governance and contestation. Within Latin America, the Central American revolutions of the 1980s represented the apogee—and as it turned out, the death wail—of confrontation in the previous cultural-political register. Central American societies had all the characteristics—at times exaggerated to the point of cruel parody—of corrupt, predatory capitalism, with obscene levels of inequality and social exclusion, held together by brute force. Even if realities were considerably more complex and varied, such images provoked deep political revulsion and widespread social mobilization, with hopes of seizing state power and remaking society along radically egalitarian lines. At crucial moments in the late 1970s and early 1980s, this prodigious collective energy outstripped actually constituted guerrilla movements, and swept up thousands of civilians, who felt aggrieved and sensed change in the air.

In Guatemala, like Nicaragua and El Salvador, initial bursts of social mobilization met with state repression, which provoked popular outrage, multitudinous marches, and funeral processions, followed by greater repression, and so on, until political contention took on a grim military logic. During the initial phase, faculty and students of the San Carlos University (USAC) often found themselves on the front lines, and suffered accordingly. On 8 June 1977, the regime killed Mario López Larrave, a much-admired lawyer and activist who defended the economic and political rights of workers.[35] A large crowd of angry capital city inhabitants followed Larrave's coffin to the cemetery. Ten years later, on the eve of the democratic "opening" the USAC workers syndicate created a mural to commemorate this "illustrious lawyer and defender of the working class," which depicts a crowd of workers in militant pose. The last stanza of the eulogy reads, in classic revolutionary prose:

y miles de puños   and thousands of clenched fists
calientes por luchar   primed for struggle
en las calles milenarias   in the millenarian streets
de la patria   of the motherland
hasta la victoria final.   until victory is won.

On closer examination the mural provides an apt portrayal not only of the rousing energy of collective struggle, but also of what that conception of struggle sorely lacked. Although the country has an overwhelmingly Indian population, especially among the "millenarian" masses, the mural sends a different message. Using standard Guatemalan criteria of phenotypic and cultural markers, an observer of the mural would assume that the people in militant pose are not Indian (figure 1.4). Unlike, for example, the political imaginary depicted in classic murals of the Mexican revolution (compare figure 1.5), racial heterogeneity and indigenous culture played little role in these Guatemalan artists' imaginings of the struggle, and presumably, of the "*victoria final*" (final victory). Research on the revolutionary period, as it has gradually moved beyond the polarized narrative frames that the conflict itself produced, reinforces this conclusion. Indigenous peoples mobilized and fought the regime with whatever means available, but rarely as architects of the struggle; they generally lacked the power to shape the direction of political change in their own image.[36] Some persisted in a contradictory struggle from within, others bit their tongues, but especially after the military tables turned, the vast majority of indigenous foot soldiers simply abandoned the Left. Revolutionary intellectuals and leaders were not completely deaf to these concerns. They condemned classic racism and affirmed the principle that all participants would reap the fruits of universal equality. In worlds of such brute inequality and exclusion, this promise of universal equality had deep resonance; if the ideal had been realized, benefits may well have outweighed limitations. As it happened, disparities between egalitarian rhetoric and authoritarian practice, combined with adamant denial of Maya cultural rights as a principle of revolutionary politics, proved toxic. The

Figure 1.4. Homage to López Lavarre. Mural located on the main campus of the San Carlos University, Guatemala City. Photo credit: Irma Alicia Velásquez Nimatuj.

Figure 1.5. Diego Rivera, El Reparto de Tierras, 1924. Fresco. Universidad Autónoma de Chapingo, Edificio de Administración. http://www.diegorivera.com/murals/reparto.html

prospect of definitive military defeat amplified the problem. By the mid-1980s, critique of the uncomprehending and racist character of the ladino Left had become a standard refrain among Maya activist intellectuals.

This critique achieved remarkably widespread endorsement in Guatemala, and throughout Latin America, in the years that followed. In the face of the global crisis of leftist thought and the plummeting legitimacy of "socialist" alternatives, the

Guatemalan Left learned quickly. By the early 1990s, most ladino-led organizations aligned with the revolutionary movement had embraced some version of Maya cultural rights, provoking cries of "opportunism" and "hypocrisy" from the ladino establishment and Maya activists alike.[37] Soon enough, important members of this same ladino establishment would follow suit. Although ladino elites had no trouble endorsing any critique of the Left, to countenance Maya cultural rights required a greater mental leap; most had been raised to believe in the strict binary between ladinos as beacons of modern Guatemalan nationhood, and Indians as backward and destined to be governed. The displacement of this binary epitomizes a much broader shift underway. Latin American states are moving to condemn racism, affirm rights to cultural difference, and represent their societies as "multicultural." In the modernizing wing of Guatemala's political-economic elite, and especially among those closely associated with the international donor community, Maya rights activists found new allies, as powerful as they were unlikely.[38]

In the wake of this unlikely alliance the debate begins, revolving around the contention that a new mode of governance has emerged. The shift away from national ideologies that promoted assimilation, toward endorsement of cultural rights and intercultural equality, has occurred with striking uniformity across the region, beginning in the mid-1980s. This shift has coincided with the ascendancy of economic policies and political practices grouped together by the omnibus term "neoliberalism."[39] According to advocates' self-justifying narrative, the previous model failed in its own terms, clearing the way for a return to the sound economic principles of open markets, free capital flows, and structural adjustment of local economies according to global economic principles, unhindered by local political considerations.[40] Critical theorists of the neoliberal turn contest this assertion of "natural failure," and by extension, portray the conflict over economic principles as part of a broader ideological struggle over basic notions of rights and the distribution of societal resources. This makes for distinct readings of the prefix "neo": a reapplication of classic liberal economic principles versus a new political project, which deploys liberal doctrine in novel and unexpected ways.[41]

Even among those who think in terms of a "neoliberal political project," there is much debate over the specifics. Some argue that these two dimensions of neoliberal politics—aggressive market-oriented economics and state-sanctioned multiculturalism—stand in stark divergence and tension with one another. An explanation emerges from this position that emphasizes institutional change: "democratization"—another correlate of the neoliberal turn—combined with unintended consequences of the dismantling of the corporate state, opens new spaces for mobilization from below. Market-oriented reforms place an especially heavy burden on indigenous and other impoverished sectors, which provides further impetus for mobilization. The aggregate pressure of these indigenous movements, in turn, gives rise to multicultural reforms in otherwise strictly market-oriented social policies.[42] I find this account to be generally valid, persuasive in its attempt to highlight the interaction of institutional change and "from below" indigenous politics, but lacking in two key respects. It neglects both the great capacity of neoliberal regimes to shape individual and collective political sensibilities and the key areas of compatibility between neoliberal ideology and certain versions of indigenous rights.

Proponents of neoliberal governance reshape the terrain of political struggle to their advantage, not by denying indigenous rights, but by the selective recognition of them. These two closely intertwined assertions—focused on the ideological thrust of neoliberal regimes and the work neoliberalism does—combine to yield a framing argument of this book. While neoliberal reforms may have begun in archetype form as individualist, market-oriented policies strictly in the realm of economics, they did not stay that way for long. To become dominant as economic policy, they had to encompass a political project, with aspirations to reshape relations between state and society, forging a new basis for legitimacy and governance. While the standard references to trimming social service budgets and decentralization begin to describe this transformation, we need to go further, to encompass ideological dimensions: newly formulated notions of the ideal citizen, rights and responsibilities of citizenship, emergent ideals for relations among people now understood as culturally different. Far from being exempt from these processes of "subject formation," indigenous peoples (and other protagonists of cultural rights) are their principal targets. While indigenous people engage in widespread and at times intense resistance to the neoliberal establishment, this flow of political activity does not stand outside or immune to processes of neoliberal subject formation. Those who make such a claim fall prey to assumptions about indigenous authenticity that, ironically enough, have become a standard component of the neoliberal ideology itself. In important respects, indigenous cultural rights activism and neoliberal economics are neatly compatible. In classic liberal political theory, declarations of "universal equality" always emerged in implicit contrast to a silenced "other," to unworthy souls against whom fully deserving subjects of rights could be defined.[43] Neoliberal ideology inverts these "strategies of exclusion," insisting on the inclusion of cultural difference (and by extension collective rights) as subjects of rights.[44] The recognition of cultural difference gives states and, equally important, civil society and transnational organizations, greater prerogative to shape the terms of political contestation, to distinguish between authentic and ersatz expressions of identity, between acceptable and disruptive cultural demands. Neoliberal multiculturalism thrives on the recognition of cultural difference, and by extension, on high-stakes distinctions between those cultural rights that deserve recognition and those that do not.[45]

A project, not a conspiracy, neoliberal multiculturalism in Guatemala has its share of rough edges, unevenness, and internal strife. In part, this follows from a variant of the same ambivalence referred to earlier, located at higher, more powerful levels of the global system. The World Bank, along with its Latin American counterpart, the Inter-American Development Bank (IDB), has championed the notion of "development with identity," and devoted significant resources to indigenous organization, participation, and cultural rights. Two wings of World Bank policy have emerged—orthodox economists and multiculturalist "sociologists"; they regularly clash in high-stakes intra-institutional battles, which divert attention from the areas of compatibility between the two.[46] Similarly, neither the Guatemalan state, nor the national-level economic power holders, has effected a clean transition between the "old" liberal principles and the "new." Attempts to reform the Constitution in keeping with the multicultural principles of the 1996 Peace Accords ended in failure in May 1999, when some 60 percent voted "no" in the nationwide referendum.[47] Whether this opposition reflects the persistence of classic racism, as documented in the ethnography/exposé of Marta Elena Casaús Arzú (1991), or submerged fears of indigenous militancy combined with liberal inclinations for tolerance, is difficult to know. I suspect the latter. In any case, voices of overt support for classic racism, powerful and pervasive as they may be, no longer form a stable, viable political bloc. In the international arena, multiculturalism has come to be associated with modernity itself; a growing bloc of the "modernizing" Guatemalan elite has followed this cue.[48] A multicultural ethic, however contested, has been woven into the social fabric—in ideas about development, electoral politics, and educational policy—to an extent that makes the prospect of turning the clock back very difficult to imagine. Neoliberal multiculturalism in Guatemala, like elsewhere in Latin America, comes with expansive rhetoric that calls forth visions of sweeping change. It also contains a powerful encoded message, which ladino power holders are coming to decipher and embrace: you can support multicultural reforms, pursue "development with identity" and other cultural rights agendas, without placing ladino racial dominance in jeopardy.

Provincial, middle-class ladinos in Chimaltenango provide a window on this transformation, both the fear, anxiety, and uncertainty it provokes, and the general inclination to embrace, rather than resist, the course of change. Ladinos chimaltecos are not powerful actors in Guatemalan national politics, not to mention in global arenas of neoliberal multiculturalism. Nonetheless, following the lead of those who have criticized the "impact model" of globalization analysis, I do not frame this study as an inquiry into the impact of global processes on local race relations.[49] Rather, I contend, we should be able to break into "the global" at any particular locale, and read broader processes from there. In their responses to Maya efflorescence, ladinos chimaltecos have become pioneers of their own local variant of neoliberal multiculturalism, embracing the new ethic of cultural equality with great urgency, because daily relations with upwardly mobile indigenous neighbors and co-workers stand in the balance. They have tried to set limits on indigenous ascendancy with similar urgency, because they feel the threat of displacement so directly. This challenge to racial dominance has palpable effects: indigenous domestic workers have lost the requisite subservience; ladinos can no longer win local elections; ladinos can no longer apply to certain jobs; international aid programs often pass them by. The incentive for adopting a modern stance toward indigenous peoples, combined with liabilities such as these, engenders ambivalence: endorsement with pause, enthusiasm mixed with resentment. From a strictly local perspective, this ambivalence appears anomalous or transitory; viewed more globally, it reappears as a key feature of neoliberal multiculturalism itself. Although more transparently fearful and awkward, ladino racial ambivalence has striking parallels, for example, to the mixed messages of multilateral development institutions such as the World Bank, which support indigenous rights and promote economic policies that deepen indigenous structural poverty and economic misery. Because ladino responses are so raw and near the surface, they may be especially helpful in our effort to understand the political project of neoliberalism, and the predicament it creates for indigenous activism across Latin America.

The critical analysis of neoliberalism put forth in this book also presents the study of "identity politics" with a challenge. Although less than two decades have passed since Maya activists raised their voices in protest against Right and Left alike for the neglect of cultural rights, many of the basic conditions that provoked these protests no longer prevail. While ladinos still dominate in power relations of nearly every sort, they now respond to the same call for recognition and inclusion in strikingly different ways: "We agree in principle; here is how we already encourage indigenous participation," or, in response to especially effective and persistent protest, "Can I offer you a job?" As proponents of neoliberal multiculturalism become ever more deeply invested in shaping cultural rights rather than denying them, this shift helps explain the impasse that many indigenous rights movements now confront. The moment when Maya identity politics represented a frontal challenge to the state has passed, giving way to a phase of much greater involvement of powerful actors in the formulation of identity-based demands, intense negotiations from within powerful institutions, and inevitably, greater internal dissention within the movements themselves.[50] If the quintessential indigenous demand in the formative phase of Maya identity politics was to achieve state recognition, the greatest challenge now is to prevail in negotiations over what that recognition actually means in practice. Even the demand for autonomy, the culmination of indigenous empowerment in the previous era, faces this dilemma. The neoliberal state no longer opposes indigenous autonomy in all its forms; its preferred response, rather, is to concede limited autonomy, in the form of decentralization, participatory budgeting, and various other types of limited local control, and to draw the line there. This, in turn, shifts the grounds of struggle, away from strict binaries (individual versus collective rights) toward a more fine-grained discernment: at what point do state concessions stop being a move to neutralize the opposition, and begin to have real potential for political transformation?

A parallel version of the same skepticism toward identity politics must apply to provincial ladinos, as they confront their identity crisis and reconfiguration. Ladinos' anxious ruminations about their own identity direct attention to the central problem. Constituted historically in relations of racial dominance, ladino identity must be "decolonized," as some have argued, or simply abandoned, according to others. Granted this response is found mainly among the most progressive, reflective, and self-critical, and granted it does produce a healthy humility and openness in daily relations with Mayas. Yet it also runs the risk of reframing the political task precisely according to the logic of neoliberal multiculturalism. Everyone has an identity; each identity deserves recognition and respect; we all must embrace the goal of making our identity "right," living it to the fullest, and so on. This framing acknowledges neither the deep fissures within a given identity category, nor the inequities to be overcome before true intercultural dialogue could begin. Neoliberal multiculturalism holds out the promise of both equality and cultural recognition, but grants only the latter, and then promotes intercultural exchange anyway. Under these conditions, multiculturalism produces mutual incomprehension and strife, evidence that many ladinos take to confirm their suspicions that indigenous people were not ready or completely deserving in the first place. Although identity-based demands still offer a powerful basis to contest racism and to challenge the blind universalism of the national-popular, these goals alone easily fall prey to the very governance regimes that these movements set out to oppose. Transformative politics awaits a rekindling of the collective militancy of that USAC mural, reconstituted to encompass the full range of structural inequities, and to contest the emergent mode of governance, which recognizes cultural rights whose limits already have been set in advance.

Activist and Conventional Research Methods

To draw a distinction between "transformative" and "neoliberal" multiculturalism immediately invokes broader questions about the politics of research. To some extent in my study, I defend the distinction with data collected through conventional means. I demonstrate, for example, how ladinos may question their own identities, affirm the principle of cultural equality, and yet sustain relations with Mayas that keep structural inequities clearly in place. Further, I demonstrate that intercultural dialogue under these conditions subtly undermines the very goal of equality that ostensibly has motivated the dialogue in the first place. The term "transformative," however, causes problems, because it promises an answer to the implicit question—"toward what?" However amorphous and malleable the utopias of the previous revolutionary era, they did invoke reasonably clear answers to that question. Under the weight of critical analysis, bitter experience, and ideological embattlement, those utopias have lost their resonance. Most of the protagonists of this ethnography—ladino and Maya alike—have little appetite for these utopias' return, yet offer no alternative in their place. As a result, the point of reference for the term "transformative" turns from imagined outcome to an imagined political process: mutual recognition, roughly equal material conditions, and—a condition to which this study speaks most directly—an inclination on the part of ladinos for an actively antiracist stance in shaping relations with their Maya counterparts.

This provisional resting place allowed me to implement an activist research methodology, without presuming to have a more coherent answer to the "toward what" question than my informants did. The argument is straightforward. Rather than suppress our political principles and alignments in preparation for research, we encourage them, and allow them a major role in shaping the formulation of the research topic. We then refine and develop the topic in dialogue with those with whom our political alignments are strongest. The research unfolds in constant dialogue with these allies and interlocutors, who take a deep interest in the results because they have played an active role in conceiving the project to begin with. On pragmatic grounds, obvious advantages accrue: these interlocutors become enthusiastic key informants and facilitators of the project's success. On epistemological grounds, this approach has the potential to yield better research outcomes because it involves the researcher integrally in the very processes that he or she seeks to understand. Activist research is justified not by the "good" it does (a matter best left to a separate political judgment), but by the data and understanding that result when research subjects themselves perceive the research as aiming to produce "good" or "useful" results, in a project at least partly of their own conception.

In some respects, the research carried out for this book followed and implemented this activist research design. From the outset, based on general knowledge and political principles, I had a strong alignment with the Maya movement and wanted Maya activist-intellectuals to be the privileged interlocutors in my formulation of a research topic. Discussions with Maya intellectuals at the outset served a dual purpose: to broach the question "What do you think it would be important to study?" and to begin an ongoing effort to map the terrain of Maya cultural politics. My mild skepticism of assertions made in the name of a unified Maya movement came from previous political analysis and experience: ties to and residual sympathies with the Central American Left; a taste for class analysis focused both on hierarchy within Maya organizations and their relations with non-Mayas; a general stance toward indigenous politics, which combined solidarity with an eye for contradiction. Following these inclinations, I sought out parallel conversations with ladinos of progressive or leftist affinities.[51] Growing interest among Maya activists in the study of ladinos converged with progressive ladinos' desires to engage in dialogue and relations of cooperation with the Mayas. Despite the different framings of the two sets of processes—a portent of the chasm that my research would document—this convergence seemed to have produced an ideal activist research topic.

Once I confirmed this topic and began to implement an activist research design, however, I confronted difficulties at every turn. Chimaltenango had the makings of a highly conducive site for this research: a logistical center for Maya organization; a substantial ladino population—20 percent department wide, higher in the departmental capital—that had been obliged, increasingly, to make space for upwardly mobile Mayas; and a history of intense social mobilization. Yet the problem of finding privileged interlocutors who would readily endorse the topic proved challenging. I looked first for settings where Mayas and ladinos worked together, on reasonably equal footing, toward goals that encompassed an ethic of antiracism and intercultural cooperation. I found none. The numerous Maya organizations, on the whole, included only

Mayas; equally numerous ladino-led NGOs (mainly oriented toward "development") worked with indigenous communities, often with indigenous staff, but in a generally hierarchical manner, which Maya activists criticized bitterly. These ladinos would have welcomed a North American anthropologist, assuming the subjects of research were Indians, but they did not relish becoming primary research subjects themselves. When focused on the relatively powerful, activist research faces a dilemma from the outset: people are rarely inclined to participate in research aimed to reveal their own power and privilege. Yet without their participation, the method loses its innovative activist edge.

I confronted this dilemma through a dual course of action: beginning to collect data on ladinos chimaltecos using conventional methods, while continuing to seek out activist research settings for my work, and hoping that eventually the two would meet. During about eight months in 1994 and 1995, I worked two days a week with the Asociación para el Avance de las Ciencias Sociales (AVANCSO), the only major social science research organization in Guatemala that practices activist research as a matter of policy. I joined a research team, including two Mayas and three ladinos, recently formed to study relations of gender and ethnic inequality. Partly at my initiative, the team expanded their research methods to include a second component (dubbed "*Producto 2*" or second product): a series of exercises to scrutinize relations among members of the research team, as a means to reflect more deeply on Maya-ladino relations. Despite strong support from the team and AVANCSO director Clara Arenas, this methodological innovation did not prosper. Producto 2 exercises generated candid and challenging discussions, which gradually grew more intense; although the team had a wonderful ability to mediate tensions with good humor (Producto 2 was shortened to P2, and then pedos ["farts," but also, "problems"], as in, "please, no more of Charlie's pedos today"), the intensity took a toll on morale, and on the team's ability to meet pressing research deadlines. This Producto 2 effort, although interesting in theory and fascinating in some of its results, did not persist. For this and other reasons, I eventually took leave from active participation with the team.

An ongoing commitment to activist research led AVANCSO to another effort of intercultural dialogue, which Arenas asked me to facilitate in June 1996. With the signing of a definitive peace accord imminent, and the Maya efflorescence in full swing, progressive ladinos had "intercultural relations" and the "new project of the nation" urgently in mind. A group of leading ladino intellectuals had recently been formed, motivated by deep concerns that the Maya intellectual-activists spoke too little with "*ladinos solidarios*," (ladinos who practice solidarity toward Indians) and that public ladino voices in response to Maya efflorescence had turned increasingly to incomprehension and backlash. This group proposed to create a "Franja de Diálogo Intercultural" (Space for Intercultural Dialogue), which would open and strengthen channels of communication between progressive ladinos and Mayas. After discussion with trusted Maya, ladino, and foreigner friends, I agreed to facilitate the effort, on the condition that the first rounds of dialogue take place exclusively among ladinos. We selected sixteen leading ladino intellectuals and, to prepare for our first meeting, I carried out an extensive interview with each of them, probing their own identities, their perceptions of Mayas, their fears and hopes for post–Peace Accords Guatemala. One of the first findings of these interviews was a central divergence on the question of identity: roughly half the group insisted that, as a matter of political principle, they were not ladinos, but rather mestizos; the others just as adamantly defended the ladino identity category on political and cultural grounds. Discussions on this, and a whole range of crucial issues, were candid, engaged, and productive.

Work with the Franja fit the key criterion of activist research design—direct participation together with the research subjects in a process that combines efforts to engage the problem at hand—and this work as facilitator turned out to be the most exciting, intense, and illuminating research activity during my entire twenty-eight months of fieldwork in Guatemala. Yet the project did not prosper. After the third "internal" meeting, some participants (mainly the male group members) grew impatient with the intense introspection; more generally, we lacked a clear sense of how to achieve the Franja's principal goals of preparing the ground for constructive, challenging dialogue with Mayas. Although the specific contents of this process must remain confidential by prior agreement with the participants, the process deeply influenced my thinking nonetheless, as I explain in chapter 5. Yet as a dynamic, ongoing activist research program, which might have oriented my work among ladinos in Chimaltenango, the effort failed.

During the year between July 1997 and July 1998, my longest single stretch living in Chimaltenango, I worked with various organizations and efforts, each of which at best only partially fulfilled the activist research mandate. I played a substantive role in the Centro de Investigaciones Regionales de Mesoamerica (CIRMA), as board member and participant in the conception of a major research initiative on interethnic relations. An essay prepared for the project forms the basis for the analysis of regional history presented in chapter 2. I carried out a research project on identity and politics in marginal neighborhoods of Chimaltenango, in support of an organization called "Solidarity with Children and Youth" (SNJ), which works with marginalized youth. This research opened my eyes to the rising salience of the mestizo identity category among poor barrio dwellers, a transformation that I examine more closely in chapters 2 and 6. I collaborated with the Chimaltenango team of the United Nations Commission on Historical Clarification, in particular with its coordinator Marcie Mersky, working out an analysis of the initial period of mobilization in Chimaltenango, which directly informs the argument presented in chapter 3. None of these initiatives, however, developed into a full-fledged activist research endeavor. It proved especially hard to forge sustained connections between my research activities and an ongoing political process of dialogue and cooperation between Maya and ladino, to which I hoped my work ultimately would contribute.

Even with the failure of more ambitious activist research goals, the rationale for employing such methods remains strong. As others have noted, fieldwork "failures" often generate key insights into precisely the problem that one has set out to study.[52] This is especially true with activist research, when part of the analytical focus is a failed political initiative—a crucial source of data and reflection in its own right. More substantively, the experience of working with these organizations—even if an activist research endeavor did not prosper—provided invaluable insight into the topic that, working as a lone researcher, I would surely have missed. Finally, the "failures" also bring us to rethink the practice of activist research among the relatively privileged and dominant. In the absence of a site where Maya and ladino worked together, under roughly equal conditions, toward common political ends, I opted to continue research in Chimaltenango using conventional means. With most of my research subjects (all ladinos), I carried out interviews, put in much time as participant observer, and collected data using methods indistinguishable from those recommended in any conventional methods textbook. Still, by formulating the original research questions in consultation with Mayas, by successive efforts to situate the research in processes of Maya-ladino dialogue, and by periodically presenting Maya allies with the results, I kept the activist character of the research intact.[53]

My findings will no doubt challenge and provoke my ladino interlocutors. I encountered considerable rank racism, and widespread expressions of more subtle and nuanced disdain toward Indians, on which I report fully here. Some, no doubt, will be appalled or feel betrayed by my candor. I also found widespread condemnation of racism, and expressions of desire for equality, which I take seriously as markers of profound change in racial sensibilities, especially in contrast to previous generations. This provided a point of engagement for the critical and open-minded, to explore with them why fruits of this change have been so slow in coming. With distance and antiseptic clarity, ladino racial ambivalence might be portrayed as a form of contradictory consciousness, an odd combination of sharply critical insight into the inequities of the social formation, and a blind eye to the very ideas and practices that help keep these inequities in place.[54] Yet immersion fieldwork in this milieu, with its shared daily routines and special occasions, blurring of boundaries between friend and research subject, is bound to take the edge off these contradictions, to make them appear more tolerable, as they bring the "informant" to life as a friend, a *comadre* (fictive kinswoman), an individual with good qualities and foibles, just like everyone else. In other words, "successful" immersion among a relatively powerful and dominant social group brings forth a measure of contradictory consciousness in the researcher as well.

One antidote to this problem is the apt reminder that this analysis is not only about individuals, but also, about social structures and processes more powerful than any particular individual's intentions, qualities, or desires. I do make recourse to this line of argument here, in my attempt to frame the study with concepts like racial ambivalence and neoliberal multiculturalism. Yet to depend solely on this antidote tends to reduce individual actors to abstract expressions of the structures they occupy and, in so doing, undermines the very purpose of doing ethnography in the first place.[55] In contrast, I keep my portrayal of ladinos, especially ladinos solidarios, as multifaceted and contradictory as I came to know them, and I confront the danger of my own contradictory consciousness through a different means: racial border crossing. The sharpest corrective to my occasional tendency to let the empathy of ethnographic immersion overshadow my broader political objective came from ongoing involvements with Maya friends and colleagues (who were not research subjects). They would scrutinize my research findings, nod in all-too-familiar recognition at my data on persisting racism, and receive my reports about a new ethic of equality with deep skepticism. These reactions, often in the course of long conversations, almost always without ladinos present, repeatedly brought the study back to its more structural groundings, not via social theory, but rather, through vivid, painful reminders of the profoundly racialized world that Mayas continue to experience. This study consistently probes the contrast between that world—in which ladino racial dominance persists, remade but not eliminated—and the ideal world of intercultural equality that most ladinos desire, strain to portray, and see themselves as helping to create.

This conception of research topic and method, along with various other factors, has yielded a decade-long involvement with Guatemala curiously at odds with that of most foreign Guatemala scholars. On the one hand, I have maintained close ties with Maya-centric intellectual-activists, and foreign scholars of this ilk, and learned a lot about Maya cultural politics without making the Maya subjects of my research. One evening, over dinner with two Maya friends, we laughed until our stomachs hurt. After one story—about a leading (married) Maya intellectual who, in an interview with a Scandinavian journalist, explained with great sincerity that "in Maya culture there is no adultery," at the very time that he was known to be taking up with his secretary—one of them stopped abruptly and said, "We're not supposed to be telling you this," at which we laughed again and they continued, confident in the knowledge that my research focused on ladinos. That confidence will not be broken. On the other hand, this study drew me closer to various ladino worlds than is common among foreign scholars of Guatemala interested in indigenous politics. The effort to take ladinos seriously as actors in the unfolding drama of their relations with Mayas, and to do activist research with them, situated me squarely within the (progressive) ladino intellectual milieu. I became close with ladino (or mestizo) intellectuals who grappled with their own identities, their relations with Mayas, their visions for a new Guatemala. I learned also of these ladinos' profound resentment of many white North American scholars who, in their view, arrive with romantic desires to contribute to Maya people's emancipation, and in the process erase ladinos as anything more than alienated epiphenomena of an oppressive racial formation. I endorse that critique, while also recognizing its potential to be a defensive backlash against ladinos' loss of their privileged role as intermediaries between the Maya and the "modern" outside. Each border crossing—between Mayas, progressive ladinos, and various groups of foreign intellectuals—helped me to critically interrogate the standpoint that would have developed if I had "stayed put," aligned primarily with one group. After sizing up this research strategy and practice, a Maya friend and colleague offered a less charitable interpretation:

"You just want to stay good with everyone." She noted how my own privileged position creates the illusion of being above the rough and tumble of racial conflict in Guatemala, of being able to size up everyone with the requisite distance, rationality, and rigor. This critique gently points to my own complicity in the racialized social relations I have set out to study. My response is to subject that very complicity to analysis. The making of ladino racial dominance, I argue in the final chapter, forms an integral part of the remaking of racial dominance on a global scale; racial ambivalence has striking parallels among whites, even progressive whites, in the United States. To conclude in this way, at least draws attention to the disparity—all too common in anthropology—between great passion for the travails of faraway peoples, and studied disengagement with similar problems and struggles much closer to home.

The Politics of Racial Difference

This book argues against the image of gradual progress in Guatemala away from a highly undesirable form of racial hierarchy, toward intercultural equality. Significant change along these lines has occurred, and to highlight these advances would make for a more upbeat account and perhaps help to encourage such change further in the future. Such an interpretation also would resonate deeply with the view that many of my ladino informants hold and, very likely, would want the reader to endorse as well: their repudiation of classic racism; their unreserved embrace of the principle of equality; and their increasing knowledge of the Maya, which has replaced a lamentable lack of knowledge with greater respect and recognition. This portrayal invites skepticism on a number of grounds, not as completely false or misleading, but as profoundly incomplete. Its partiality becomes especially evident in the face of such critical questions as: How does racial hierarchy persist now that classic racism has been repudiated? Does this celebrated deepening of knowledge of the "other" also allow the exercise of new forms of power?[56] Newfound intercultural sensibilities among ladinos in Chimaltenango have given rise to a racial ambivalence, a divergence between their self-perceptions and their position in Guatemala's racial hierarchy. This racial ambivalence, in turn, fits within the global emergence of neoliberal multiculturalism, which promotes the cultural rights of indigenous peoples while perpetuating their economic and political marginalization. Rather than an expression of incremental progress, both neoliberal multiculturalism and its Guatemala-specific variant have the makings of a menacing political project, informed by deepened knowledge of the Maya. Recognition of certain key Maya demands, often adopting the very "language of contention" that Maya activists themselves deploy, generates a powerful capacity to punish those demands perceived as militant, unyielding, or dangerous.[57]

In advancing this contention, I do not claim to be able to discern the ideal formula for achieving Maya collective rights or, more generally, for the daunting problems of social justice in culturally pluralist and highly unequal societies such as Guatemala. My argument is much more modest. It focuses on observable effects of the changes that have occurred, and maps their trajectory to date. Most importantly I argue that, however positive the change, the conditions now in place are not conducive to the kind of transformative process that the discourse of intercultural equality promises to set in motion. Ladinos have become complacent with the high ground of their newfound commitment to cultural equality, inclined to burden Mayas with the responsibility for their own ongoing subordination, quick to see "reverse racism" in Maya acts of cultural-political contestation. These sensibilities reproduce the divergence between ladinos' political sensibilities and their place in the racial hierarchy, making equal dialogue with Mayas a constantly expressed desire, which stands in constant tension with the unequal social relations between the two. Broadly speaking, Mayas have two choices in the face of neoliberal multiculturalism: to occupy the category of "*indio permitido*" (authorized Indian) or to refuse the invitation completely.[58] Both open possibilities for a Maya "war of position," especially when they go on to challenge the very premise of a sharp dichotomy between the two. But the potential for fragmentation, cooptation, and sheer perplexity is enormous, and in the absence of a clear strategy, both choices are apt to reinforce the impasse.

This analysis brings up a final dilemma, which the practice of activist research should have helped me to resolve. In political terms, this book makes a wager that direct dialogue between Mayas and (at least some) ladinos, starting with hard issues like cultural racism, is the best way to achieve some form of "racial healing."[59] This racial healing, in turn, would lay the groundwork for the strongest possible organized confrontation of persisting racial hierarchy. Yet my efforts to connect this research with interracial political work along these lines, on the whole, did not prosper. I did work with a number of initiatives that meet this description; they produced exciting but ephemeral results. In Chimaltenango, they simply did not exist. Throughout Guatemala, the predominant means to confront the problem of ongoing racial hierarchy follow two different strategies. One is Maya-centric cultural and political organization, which I support, but fear is ill-equipped to achieve its own stated goals. The second course is the one many of my ladino informants would favor: to contest classic racism; maintain an air of civility; open space for the indio permitido; expect slow progress as this civility begins to seep in and mistrust dissipates; confine further critiques and doubts to conversation around the kitchen table. Disturbingly, at times I've sensed that some Mayas prefer this second course as well. Why reveal the kitchen-table talk of ladinos who are trying to be civil? We have to keep living with them, after all.

In my defense, I can point in a qualified way to ladinos solidarios like Yolanda's family. They struggle with the issues that I raise here, at times provoked by painful confrontations with Mayas who question their commitment and sincerity. Yolanda has the uncanny ability to embrace her ladino identity, and the privilege it entails, while at the same time being fiercely critical of it. This stance has an element of precisely the racial ambivalence my analysis intends to reveal. Yet Yolanda remains open to criticism, constantly reflecting on and willing to change her practice, always ready to savor the irony of her own predicament. I fancy myself a more coherent and principled antiracist than she, but then again, I have not been subjected to such a bright light of anthropological scrutiny. Without denying a certain ambivalence of my own, I present Yolanda's racial sensibilities as the contradictory but strangely resilient foundation on which the political wager of this book has come to rest.

two

Provincial Ladinos, the Guatemalan State, and the Crooked Path to Neoliberal Multiculturalism

Excuse the comparison: plantation owners domesticate their cattle by giving them salt in canoes, and at times even feeding them with their hands; in this way, they coax them into the corral. We would do the same: giving the illiterate Indian the opportunity to come in from the hinterland, to have contact with city people.

—*Progressive congressman, arguing in support of reforms favoring Indians*
in 1953 congressional debate. Quoted in Palma Murga (1991)

We already have issued invitations to women from Nebaj, who will attend the Presidential House, attend visiting dignitaries, to demonstrate how proud we are of our cultural diversity and our indigenous heritage.

—*Oscar Berger (later president of Guatemala)*
during the presidential campaign of 2004, 12 October 2003.

On 26 April 1998, two assailants entered the San Sebastián parish residence in Zone 1 of Guatemala City and brutally murdered Monseñor Juan José Gerardi.[1] The previous Friday evening, in the main cathedral a few blocks away, the Catholic Church project for the "recuperation of historical memory" (REMHI), over which Gerardi had pre-sided, presented its four-volume report. An overflow crowd, including a large number from rural communities who had been victims of the violence, listened with rapt attention as REMHI spokespeople, including Gerardi himself, summarized the

47

findings, and assured us all that "*la paz se construye con la verdad*" (peace is forged with the truth). My notes, written the next morning, recorded "a strange sensation," knowing that we live today under the authority of the same state that has just been assigned responsibility for unspeakable brutality against its citizens a little more than a decade ago. Yet while the assassination of Gerardi and the impunity that followed dramatize this continuity, stepping back from the gruesome particulars of this case, changes in the mode of state governance appear more striking still. Massive state violence has subsided; social conflict and political turmoil, still ubiquitous, occur along multiple, crosscutting fault lines, extremely difficult to follow using familiar political maps. While indigenous people, the primary victims of state violence in the previous era, still engage in resistance, increasing numbers also participate in these new webs of governance. In the midst of a candlelight vigil on the Tuesday after Gerardi's killing, I marched with Anselmo, who quickly relieved me of my illusions that this vile act might serve as a catalyst for a mass movement against impunity: he lamented the anemic political response in great contrast to funeral marches in the late 1970s that went on for miles, venting raw, spontaneous outrage against the "*ejército asesino*" (army of assassins).

This chapter places Guatemala's current regime of governance in historical perspective, with a focus on ladino power holders and the evolution of ladino-indigenous relations in Chimaltenango. My story begins with brief consideration of the reformist decade (1944–1954), and then pays special attention to the golden era of ladino dominance from 1954 to the mid-1970s, when the Chimaltenango social formation returned, in many ways, to the status quo ante. Those whom I came to know as the "older generation" (ages 60–80) were in their prime during this era, still largely unperturbed by the social earthquake of revolutionary conflict and Maya efflorescence on the horizon. While in no sense static or conflict-free, ladino society of that period did embody a collective mindset and ideology of racial dominance, grounded in the central premise that Indians were to be kept separate and unequal.[2] When viewed as two distinct racial ideologies—one positing inferiorized difference, and the other universalized equality—a curious inversion comes to light. While in many ways Guatemalan society returned to the status quo ante in the post-1954 period, the state never completely abandoned the assimilationist ideology developed during the preceding reformist decade. To the contrary, the state embraced what I call disciplinary assimilation, conveyed and justified in various guises, from integrationism to developmentalism, to the counterinsurgency fervor of the early 1980s.[3] During this same period, most ladino power holders in Chimaltenango continued to defend the separate and unequal doctrine. The post-1985 process of democratization gave rise to a reversal of these two positions. The state made halting moves toward recognition of Maya cultural difference and endorsement of multicultural rights, while most ladinos chimaltecos abandoned the separate and unequal ideology in favor of disciplinary assimilation.

To examine this inversion is to focus attention on key differences between provincial elites and national-level state ideologies, which in turn help to explain the evolving social and political conditions that indigenous chimaltecos confronted. The commonplace assumption that national and provincial elites think and act in lockstep is directly called into question. At the same time, I point to a basic commonality that transcends this difference: both provincial elites and national-level actors have responded to the challenge of Maya ascendancy with ambivalence. Disciplinary assimilation expresses outward support for the principle of racial equality, while in practice granting rights only to those Indians who submit to a ladino-dominant mold. State-endorsed multiculturalism acknowledges indigenous cultural difference, but reserves the prerogative to decide which rights are legitimate and which go too far in threatening the integrity of society and nation. Provincial ladino power holders express this ambivalence in an especially visceral and transparent way: distancing themselves from the racism of elder generations and, in the same breath, using their newfound commitment to equality as rationale for keeping Maya empowerment at bay. I conclude proposing that this racial ambivalence is a key to the workings of the two modes of governance. Both assimilation and multiculturalism offer considerable enticements to the racially marginalized, and both place sharp limits on the terms of inclusion, limits held in place by the threat of coercion. Nowhere is this contradictory fusion more evident than in the Guatemalan army itself. Much analysis of the army in politics has emphasized the repressive apparatus, with ample justification, yet this has led to neglect of the army's egalitarian and populist message, which makes the omnipresent threat of coercion all the more effective.

Yolanda, true to form, provided the ethnographic entrée for some special insight into the army's profound ongoing role in daily affairs of Chimaltenango. I often called her first thing in the morning to ask about important upcoming events related to my research, and to plan the day's activities. That morning, 29 April 1998, she said she had an especially good invitation, but sounded tentative and would only reveal the details in person. I went to her office immediately and discovered the reason for her hesitancy: an invitation to a ceremonial lunch at the city hall, to celebrate the fifteenth anniversary of Chimaltenango's military base 302, scheduled for the very afternoon of Monseñor Gerardi's funeral! We deliberated briefly, thinking that we could jump in the car and make the hour drive to the capital in time for the funeral, and then decided, at my impetus I'm sure, that the event—disgusting though it might be— was too important to miss. A few hours later, we were headed for the *salón municipal* (town hall), listening to a radio broadcast of the funeral on the way. With Yolanda's invitation in hand, we sat at a table toward the back. At the head table sat a half-dozen army officers, all former *comandantes* (political-military commanders) of the base, along with other military and civilian authorities.

From a long series of speeches, mostly by ex-commanders of the base, we learned that the event had come about at the initiative of the *asociación de locatarios* (small-scale vendors association), and especially from association president Leticia Flores, an indigenous woman of hardscrabble background. Flores spoke first and gave a disconcerting speech that mixed a rousing call to defend the interests of her association with eulogies to the army "that has shed blood for our security," and especially "to our ex-command-ers of the base, who did so much for Chimaltenango." Flores made one ambiguous ref-erence to Gerardi, in the course of a call for peace that starts "with the heart"—a phrase that more than one of the ex-comandantes echoed in their own speeches. Although no one uttered Gerardi's name again in the public ceremony, he had to be on everyone's mind when one ex-comandante, now a general, intoned: "We want peace with the heart, not of a document. If this is a peace of revenge, vengeance, and finger-pointing, there will be consequences even worse than those of the tragic period that we just con-cluded." Another speaker portrayed that "tragic period" on a more upbeat note: "This base penned many brilliant pages in the book of our national history. *Se jugó el destino de Guatemala en Chimaltenango* (In Chimaltenango, the fate of all Guatemala was deter-mined)." Each speech ended with the obligatory, "*Que Dios a todos les bendiga*" (May God bless us all). The final presenter, an army spokesperson, read a letter from Flores to the Ministry of Defense requesting increased funds to support the army's invaluable efforts against common crime (*delincuencia*) in Chimaltenango. After the applause, as waiters scurried to supply the tables with plastic plates of lunch and bottles of rum, I felt vaguely nauseated by my own chosen approach to "ethnography."

Suddenly, as I was beginning to contemplate my exit, a man from the head table approached ours, took Yolanda's hand, and motioned for her to join them there. She gave me a querying look, I hesitated, and nodded; she then grabbed my arm and the three of us made our way to the front of the salon. I took a seat at the table next to Colonel Cifuentes, a man in his early fifties from Momostenango, an ex-commander of the base who had passed the heat of the war in the embattled Quiché department and currently was director of the Adolfo Hall Military School in Santa Cruz del Quiché. The waiters supplied our table with imported Johnny Walker whiskey rather than domestic rum; with plenty to drink, and a relaxed, celebratory atmosphere, the colonel spoke at length, and with candor, about any topic I chose to raise. Intensely analyti-cal, he relished grappling with difficult issues. He spoke with the confidence of the victor, determined to instruct and convince me, but without recourse to the superflu-ous rhetoric of the speeches we had just heard. Two hours later Yolanda and most everyone else had left, and I made a wobbly trek home to my computer to reconstruct the conversation. I quote it at length here to convey a full sense of his mindset, illus-trative of army ideology in transition from counterinsurgency death machine to insti-tutional ballast for the neoliberal state.

> It is inevitable: little by little the country is going to become integrated. But
> if it does it too fast, people's customs are violated. The parents are still *sencillo*
> (humble); it's the kids who want Rolex watches and all that. It is going to be a
> kind of modernization. Little by little people are going to integrate, and those
> customs are going to be left behind. But the process can't be forced. If people's
> expectations are raised beyond what society can provide, it creates
> conflict.
>
> [Our society] is getting more and more mixed. In my town,

Momostenango, before there were thirteen [ladina] families. All kinds of racism and segregation were practiced.... Now, those people no longer exist. They're either gone or mixed. It's a different reality now, of mixing, no differences. *Tratamos con el alcalde, por ejemplo, sin ninguna distinción* (We treat the [Indian] mayor, for example, as if he were one of us).... (Indians) have customs that just don't change very rapidly. It has to be little by little, without raising big expectations.

The army is a great motor of integration. We teach [indigenous people] many things, and with that they return to their communities changed. Brush your teeth, shave, dress well, eat at the table and not on the floor—these are all the values that they learn. Ninety percent return to play productive roles in their communities. The army is the great executor of interculturalidad (intercultural relations). We have a very sacred saying that goes, "*al poner el uniforme, todos somos iguales*" (the uniform makes us equal). This is our practice. There is no difference between cultures. The concept of cultural difference doesn't exist in the army.

Lo maya (the notion of things Maya) has been created by a series of private interests. If you go to the community level, you won't hear them talking about lo Maya. It's the NGOs [with] lots of foreign money that want to raise the Maya question. [They have] good intentions, but they can do a lot of damage. Lo maya... is a combination of the Christian cross and outside symbols. There's nothing old there. With the advance of modernization and change, all that's going to disappear. Little by little, differences are going to disappear. Of course class divisions remain. That can't be so easily erased. That's everywhere.... But *lo étnico* (ethnicity) tends to disappear. It happens in the history of all peoples.

Cifuentes defends a classic ideology of modernizing assimilation, with a gesture toward recognition of cultural difference, a strong assertion of equality between ladinos and Indians, and an implicit assumption that everyone, sooner or later, will conform to the dominant cultural mold. He invokes the notion of mestizaje in support of this ideology, and presents the army as the quintessential motor of egalitarian cultural integration. He also clearly identifies the major threat to this vision of gradual progress: no longer leftist revolutionaries ("we did away with them"), but radicalized Maya cultural activists. Echoing an earlier statement by General Otzoy, vice-minister of Defense in the previous government, Cifuentes assured me, "The next conflict in Guatemala will be ethnic."[4]

This overtly coercive and egalitarian ideology of assimilation, I will argue, played a crucial role as bridge between the doctrine of separate and unequal that prevailed through the mid-1970s, and the emergent neoliberal multiculturalism of the 1990s. An ideology of assimilation, which included the full array of effective sociopolitical practices, came late to Guatemala relative to most of the rest of Latin America. As Arturo Taracena and his collaborators have argued in a recently published revisionist history, although the state professed universal citizenship and equality for all in abstract statements of principle (what they call "primary discourse"), in daily practice an ethos of segregation and "differentiated citizenship" prevailed.[5] Striking exceptions—like the famous act of liberal dictator Justo Rufino Barrios that turned residents of San Pedro Sacatepéquez into ladinos by decree—end up proving the general rule: in the daily, on-the-ground workings of governance in such areas as education, labor laws, land distribution, local government, and effective citizenship rights, ladino power holders did everything possible to relegate Indians to separate social spheres. Not until after 1944, when the reformist agenda of the October Revolution began to take hold, did the idea of generalized assimilation become a concrete possibility. It may appear counterintuitive to observe that the Armed Forces, the same institution that put an end to the October Revolution in 1954, would later reintroduce an assimilationist ideology similar to that of the deposed regime. The enigma fades, at least in part, if we note the progressive roots of one sector of the Armed Forces, producing dissidents like Luis Turcios Lima and Marco Antonio Yon Sosa who would become guerrilla leaders, and organic intellectuals—perhaps including my lunch mate Colonel Cifuentes—who neatly fuse populist, egalitarian impulses with the brute authoritarianism of military power.[6] The political logic of this fusion has played a greater role in the success of the military's devastating stranglehold on Guatemalan society than many analysts have wanted to acknowledge: without a residual populist, egalitarian allure, the military could never have achieved its own goals with such efficacy.

Between the "Liberation" and the Earthquake, 1954–1976

On the eve of the 1944 October Revolution that brought Juan José Arévalo to power, ladinos in Chimaltenango awoke to horrifying news. In the municipio of Patzicía, some 30 kilometers west of the departmental capital of Chimaltenango, indigenous people rose up against the town's ladino residents, killing thirteen adults and one child. The uprising had eminently local causes, articulated in complex ways with national political turmoil.[7] General Jorge Ubico, dictator between 1931 and 1944, had fled, leaving a short-lived caretaker government in the hands of General Federico Ponce Vaides. A growing opposition movement led mainly by urban, middle-class progressive ladinos sought to oust both Ubico and Ponce who, in turn, attempted to mobilize the support of indigenous people to fend off the threat. Whatever the specific local detonators of the Patzicía conflict, these national-level articulations clearly played an important role as well, given that indigenous people in neighboring municipios, such as San Andrés Itzapa, had planned similar actions for precisely the same night. Ladinos must have felt great relief, and a burst of confidence in the new government, upon hearing two days later that the army, deployed urgently to Patzicía, had meted out appropriate punishment: some 300 indigenous inhabitants of Patzicía were summarily killed, and dozens more were brought back to jail in Chimaltenango. Fifty years later, when I asked Don Lalo, a retired Chimaltenango teacher, about these traumatic events, he remembered clearly and added with a chuckle, "The army brought them here in trucks, tied up like pigs." Like Don Lalo, most ladinos chimaltecos whom I interviewed—even those born well after 1944—could recount this Indian uprising and killing of ladinos in great detail; these same interviews reveal that, until very recently, the gross disproportion of Indians killed in the incident had no place whatsoever in the story line.

Although ladinos chimaltecos formed part of the core supporters of the reformist government that began in 1944—spurred on, no doubt, by a perception that Indians had been manipulated into supporting the old regime—this unity did not last. Yolanda's family, who still lived mainly in Comalapa at this time, illustrates the extent of the intra-ladino conflict that prevailed. Her father, Don Luis, and various aunts and uncles of his generation, remember the last years of the revolution with a shudder: the *"camaradas"* (comrades) called them *"cangrejos"* (literally, crabs, or backward looking reactionaries), and persecuted them so relentlessly that they had to sleep in the *barrancos* (wooded valleys) for weeks on end to avoid arrest. Although the camaradas clearly had closer ties to the indigenous population, they were mostly ladinos with a reasonable standing in the community, usually associated with one of the leftist political parties. Many of these progressive ladinos would no doubt have been almost as deeply concerned as their cangrejo adversaries at the thought of indigenous empowerment.

Yet whatever the intentions of the universalist reforms, they had the effect of opening space for indigenous mobilization, which in turn quickened and radicalized the pace of change underway.[8] Deepening indigenous mobilization and militancy, especially around agrarian issues, put Chimaltenango ladinos' support for the Arbenz regime to the test. Don Victor Duarte, a ladino who (in retrospect at least) remained loyal to the October Revolution, remembers that the conflict culminating in 1954 split his family down the middle. He summarizes the state of affairs in Itzapa with frank simplicity: *"Si la liberación no hubiera entrando, hubiera generado un conflicto racial"* (If it had not been for the liberation, there would have been a racial conflict).[9] Jim Handy, a leading historian of the revolutionary decade, draws the same conclusion in a more generalized form:

> Fear of ethnic conflict, of violent Indian uprising inspired by the relaxation of centuries of vigilance, helps explain ladino reaction to the relatively moderate reforms of the revolution. It was this fear, as much as any other element, that helped prompt the overthrow of the revolution in 1954. (1989:204)

Although the so-called Liberation in many ways turned the clock back to status quo ante, certain gains toward universal citizenship made in the previous era could not be reversed. The single most potent symbol of the pre-1944 regime—vagrancy laws that produced obligatory labor for the plantations—had been derogated and would never be revived. Yet this victory meant relatively little, since even during the revolutionary decade plantation owners soon learned that laws were unnecessary: an ample flow of labor continued, induced by brute necessity. The elimination of literacy requirements that barred most indigenous people from the right to vote and the declaration of principle in favor of universal education also remained in place after 1954. Schools that had been founded to implement this principle—like the "federated" elementary school of Chimaltenango—continued to accept both indigenous and ladino students. Yet these and other continuities from the revolutionary decade did little to prevent ladino power holders from reconsolidating their near monopoly control over Chimaltenango's political economy. These prerogatives of dominance, in turn, came with a newly reiterated "separate and unequal" principle of social organization.

Ladinos interviewed in the late 1990s have widely divergent memories of these two decades after 1954. The very term "liberation" epitomizes this divergence. People of the Right continued to use the term to refer to the 1954 US-backed military coup and its aftermath; people of the Left emphasized the traumatic, violent interruption of democratic rule. Attitudes toward the prevailing racial hierarchy at that time are another telltale sign; depending on their current sensibilities, they recount these conditions with either nostalgia or chagrin. "High society" dances (*bailes sociales*) were exclusively for ladinos; the beauty queen of the municipio could only be a ladina; in Chimaltenango's plaza, if an Indian presumed to share the sidewalk with ladinos, he was fair game for verbal and physical abuse. Ladinos who were teenagers in Chimaltenango in the 1960s cannot name a single setting where ladinos and Indians interacted with each other on relatively equal footing.[10] In local politics, until the late 1960s, this ladino racial privilege trumped the formal principle of universal suffrage. Esteban López, an indigenous candidate for mayor in the municipio of Patzún, won the election of 1959, only to have outraged ladino *vecinos* (prominent townsmen) force him to resign, which he did to "prevent the murder of his race."[11] Those who in the 1990s still waxed nostalgic about this period—like Yolanda's father, Don Luis, and Don Miguel Angel Rayo Ovalle, governor of Chimaltenango in the early 1990s—portray a proper and insular ladino society, carefully bounded and set apart from the Indians, who in turn worked hard, stayed mostly in their own spaces, and displayed appropriately deferential behavior in mixed company.

Land tenure during this period followed the general pattern of ladino dominance, but also showed a few striking departures from this pattern, quiet signs of momentous changes to come. In general, after the 1954 coup, ladino land holders could invoke the power of the state to stop indigenous mobilizations for land in their tracks. Yet the short-lived land reform initiative in 1952–1954 did result in state purchase and *parcelación* (subdivision) of some twenty-two farms in Chimaltenango, in eight municipios, to the benefit of some 1,200 peasants.[12] The 1964 agrarian census, the only reliable source of baseline data of this sort, yields a calculation for Chimaltenango roughly similar to the well-known global figure: ten percent of landowners owned 70 percent of the land (see figure 2.1). When disaggregated by identity and municipio, however, the data reveal two significant qualifications of this global picture. First, a comparatively small but significant number of indigenous landowners had sizeable holdings: some 1,000 with 10 to 32 *manzanas*; 128 with 32 to 64; and 22 with 1 to 10 *caballerías*

	Total Property Owners	Area Owned (mzs.)
<1 mzs.	3,545	1,925
1 to 2	5,747	7,644
2 to 5	7,161	20,761
5 to 10	2,701	17,541
Subtotals	19,154	47,871
10 to 32	1,480	23,451
32 to 64	279	11,927
1 c to 10	232	40,924
10 c to 20	19	16,640
20 c to 50	8	11,933
50 c to 100	1	4,669
Subtotals	2,019	109,544
% Total	10%	70%
TOTALS	21,173	157,415

Source: Dirección Nacional de Estadística (1964).
Censo Agropecuario, Tomos I and II. Guatemala:
Ministerio de Economía.
Note: One manzana (mz) is equivalent to .7
hectares and 1.7 acres. One caballería (c) is
equivalent to 47 hectares and 114 acres.

Figure 2.1. Land Distribution in Chimaltenango (1964)

(see figure 2.2).[13] Second, the degree of disparity in indigenous and ladino land holdings varies greatly by municipio: from San José Poaquíl, where 7 percent of landowners are ladinos, who hold only 12 percent of the land, to San Martín Jilotepeque, where 17 percent of landowners are ladino and hold 71 percent of the land (figure 2.3). In both qualifications of the global picture, glimmers of indigenous empowerment appear. In such municipios as San José Poaquíl, Santa Apolonia, and Santa Cruz Balanyá, ladino presence either was never especially strong, or already had begun to fade. Throughout the department, a sector of advantaged indigenous land holders would have generated enough surplus to obviate the arduous migratory labor routine, to invest in modest ancillary activities such as commerce or services, and most important for politics in the years to come, to put their children in school. Among these schoolchildren of the 1950s and 1960s would be many future prime movers of the Maya efflorescence.[14]

Indigenous organization reemerged gradually after the trauma of 1954, often on

	Number of Property Holders			Total Land Area		
	Total	Indigenous	% Ind.	Total	Indigenous	% Ind.
<1 manzanas	3,545	2,677	76%	1,925	1,451	75%
1 to 2	5,747	4,604	80%	7,644	6,117	80%
2 to 5	7,161	5,782	81%	20,761	16,752	81%
5 to 10	2,701	2,107	78%	17,541	13,612	78%
10 to 32	1,480	1,015	69%	23,451	15,703	67%
32 to 64 manzanas	279	128	46%	11,927	5,307	44%
1 caballerías to 10	232	22	9%	40,924	2,629	6%
10 to 20	19	-	0%	16,640	-	0%
20 to 50	8	1	13%	11,933	1,382	12%
50 to 100 caballerías	1	-	0%	4,669	-	0%
TOTALS	21,173	16,336		157,415	62,953	

Source: Dirección Nacional de Estadística (1964). Censo Agropecuario, Tomos I and II. Guatemala: Ministerio de Economía.

Figure 2.2. Land Distribution in Chimaltenango by Area and Identity, 1964

an individual or family scale, with barely a hint of the mass-based strategies and cultural militancy that would later develop. In 1960 the Leonidas Mencos Ávila High School celebrated its first graduation of secretaries and accountants, and of the twenty-eight graduates only three were indigenous. The proportion grew steadily from that time, in a subtle but dramatic confirmation of individual indigenous efforts toward empowerment, well before they had an organized movement to back them (see figure 2.4).[15] In this period indigenous chimaltecos also devoted great energy to economic advancement, by organizing to increase the income that came from farming. They found support from the first wave of development funding connected to the Alliance for Progress, which sought to ameliorate economic conditions in the countryside in hopes of preempting agrarian radicalism, and they took great encouragement from the new agricultural technologies of the "green revolution," which increased yields as much as threefold, although at the cost of increased dependence on "up-front" inputs, and increased vulnerability to market fluctuations.[16] Between 1964 and 1970, peasant farmers—the vast majority indigenous—founded and formally registered a total of thirty-three cooperatives in Chimaltenango. In the late 1960s, a group of progressive ladinos, with funding from USAID, founded the Training School for Agricultural Cooperatives (EACA, later CENDEC), which brought hundreds of activists to Chimaltenango for workshops on the technical matters of cooperative organization and the "national reality," which eventually evoked fears that they were "turning Indians into guerrillas."[17] Rolando Fernández, Yolanda's uncle, was active in Comalapa politics at that time, including a term as mayor (1970–1972). He recounts having played a

	Number of Land Owners			Land Area		
Municipio	Total	Indigenous	% Indigenous	Total	Indigenous	% Indigenous
Pochuta	622	431	69%	8,827	189	2%
Yepocapa	741	477	64%	18,994	1,730	9%
Acatenango	976	561	57%	13,238	1,956	15%
Zaragoza	879	267	30%	4,041	1,003	25%
El Tejar	270	150	56%	1,108	319	29%
San Martín	3,302	2,740	83%	34,208	10,023	29%
San Andrés Itzapa	876	540	62%	3,586	1,524	42%
Chimaltenango	1,279	1,023	80%	5,906	2,700	46%
Parramos	707	364	51%	1,983	926	47%
Patzicía	1,687	1,346	80%	6,999	3,645	52%
Patzún	2,243	1,991	89%	15,755	8,407	53%
Tecpán	2,868	2,558	89%	22,267	14,826	67%
Comalapa	2,637	1,975	75%	11,378	7,891	69%
Santa Cruz Balanyá	488	440	90%	1,277	1,023	80%
Apolonia	519	474	91%	2,723	2,275	84%
Poaquíl	1,079	999	93%	5,125	4,516	88%
TOTALS	21,173	16,336		157,415	62,953	

Source: Dirección Nacional de Estadística (1964). Censo Agropecuario, Tomos I and II. Guatemala: Ministerio de Economía.

Figure 2.3. Land Holdings by Municipio and Identity, 1964

central role in the founding of cooperatives for potato growers, another for credit and savings, and yet another to buy agricultural land in the distant Petén department to relieve local land pressures. While the cooperative membership was overwhelmingly indigenous, they generally received support from the local ladino power holders, priests, or outside organizers of some sort. This reformist model of "community development"—influenced by USAID, the Catholic Church, and conservative NGOS—still had a tenuous grip on the region.

The Catholic Church provided much impetus for indigenous organization in these years after 1954, both in the secular areas of education and production, and more directly in the restructuring of religious activities. Soon after the events of 1954, the church implemented a sweeping program of renovation known as Catholic Action, designed to recapture control of the indigenous *cofradías* (religious brotherhoods), which had achieved considerable power and autonomy, and to bring the church into more direct contact with the daily needs of parishioners.[18] Although at first steeped in a highly conservative blend of anti-Communism and modernization theory, Catholic Action programs soon took on a different character, contributing to organization and politicization among the sector of indigenous parishioners open to the "modernizing" message. Catholic Action came on strong in Chimaltenango with these politicizing effects and, at the same time, provoked profound divisions between the *costumbristas*, or keepers of the cofradía-based customs of religious practice, and the *modernizantes*, whose modernizing agenda had both religious and secular dimensions. Divisions yielded to outright violent conflict in Comalapa in late December 1967, as costumbristas turned against the local priest, who sought to exercise control over one of their cofradías. Father Antonio Morales, who served a neighboring parish at the time, assumed the role of mediator. His description of the conflict paints a picture of contention between indigenous factions, with ladinos looking on:

> The father [that is, the priest in Comalapa] *hizo causa común* (found a common cause) with Catholic Action and all those groups, and went against the cofradías... In the end the cofradías got mad, and they rose up, and *fueron a sacar al padre a bolas* (they went to run the father out of town). The other groups found out because it was after prayer and they went to defend the father, and in that skirmish, they killed the *sacristán* (sacristan), and many other people; women ran out [of the church] with their heads beaten up, because it was a big fight. Some wanted to defend the father and others wanted to attack him. The father, when he saw all this, left town.
>
> There in the atrium of the church everyone gathered in a big assembly, and there's where we started to talk and to hear about all the problems, you know? We already knew, but we let them talk, you know? When the soldiers spoke, they calmed them down a lot, because the military calms people down with the threat of their weapons [Morales chuckles], and the indígenas were a little timid. They obey the priest out of faith, the soldier out of fear...that's how it used to be. Now all that has changed, but back then, no. So the military man talked to them and calmed them down.

While lacking a complete explanation, Father Morales's account provides a good descriptive feel for what happened, and a useful gauge of the dominant mindset toward indigenous people at the time.[19] He speaks of indigenous people as children—prone to fighting among themselves, bound unthinkingly to religious doctrine, and yet, easily subdued by the strong hand of a religious or military authority.

The pace and content of change in this period presented indigenous activists with a dilemma, which would reemerge repeatedly, in varying forms, in subsequent years. Demands for rights and advancement in a universalist frame had the greatest possibilities for success, but also often required an implicit conformity with ladino-defined notions of rights. Struggles for advancement through the establishment of separate indigenous spaces allowed greater expressions of indigenous cultural-political autonomy, but risked both backlash from ladino power holders, and inadvertent reinforcement of the very "separate and unequal" principles that these indigenous activists sought to contest. Father Morales, Rolando Fernández, and other ladinos of their ilk illustrate the first horn of the dilemma nicely. They worked, at times with great commitment, toward indigenous people's *superación* (betterment), through health educa-

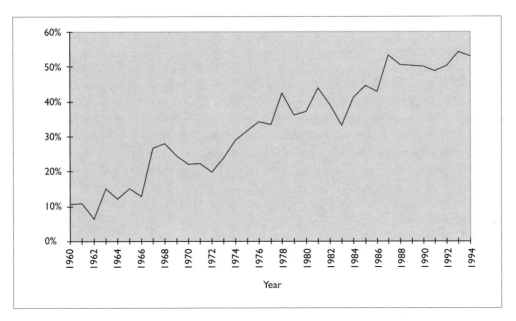

Figure 2.4. Indigenous Graduates from the Leonidas Institute, Chimaltenango. Source: Primary research in Leonidas school archives.

tion, cooperatives, and other forms of community development. Yet they rarely shook free from a deeply seated paternalism—an assumption that indigenous peoples needed help from benevolent outsiders—and a firm belief that indigenous culture had inherent deficiencies that would only be remedied when Indians became more like ladinos. The risks associated with the second horn of the dilemma are exemplified by the failed attempt to create an indigenous political party, as discussed in the next section. Finally, the *alcaldías indígenas* (indigenous mayoralties) are a good example of quasi-autonomous spaces that reinforced the separate and unequal doctrine. These institutions, a holdover from the separate and unequal ideology of the nineteenth century, were only partially eliminated during the revolutionary decade, and regained strength afterward. Pioneer indigenous activists such as Esteban López in Patzún, who organized to break the ladino stranglehold on local electoral politics in the 1960s, first had to eliminate the alcaldías indígenas, which ladinos defended as proper spaces for indigenous political participation.[20]

While indigenous activists in this period followed both the universalist and the cultural-political autonomy currents, the former seems to have prevailed. One exception is the beauty contests associated with the *ferias* (festivals): activists organized indigenous-only contests in response to their exclusion from the ladino-controlled activities, and most ferias still have separate events to this day. Another exception is the municipio-level organizations of indigenous students and intellectuals, which would exert an important influence on the subsequent emergence of the Maya movement. The preponderance of indigenous organization, however, especially in the political and economic realms, took place on the basis of universalist rights; activists contested ladino racism not in the name of autonomy but rather, through a fuller and more consistent application of universal citizenship. If the course of change had continued at a gradual and limited pace, in incremental steps toward realization of these ideals, one can imagine a scenario in which racial polarization and conflict might have been avoided. Instead, the pace of indigenous organization quickened, and ladino resistance, even to moderate universalist demands, deepened the activists' militancy and resolve. With the first hints of indigenous militancy, in turn, most ladino power holders shifted from hesitant support to outright fear, opposition, and resentment. Don Rolando's story of building cooperatives in Comalapa, for example, ends with characteristic bitterness: *"Todo ese trabajo, y la misma gente que ayudé se levantó en contra"* (After all this work, the same people who I helped rose up against me).

Social and Political Mobilization, 1976–1981

While in retrospect ladino power holders tend to describe politics in the second half of the 1970s as a gathering storm, culminating almost inevitably in armed conflict and violence, it must have felt very different at the time. The sheer diversity of activities, some overtly political, others ostensibly directed toward specific economic, cultural, or religious ends, must have left participants and observers alike bewildered, at a loss to find a single articulating principle.[21] Many of these activities had from the outset a specific focus on the affirmation of indigenous culture and identity; others, like cooperatives and municipio-level electoral activism, had a more pluralist cultural politics and often included ladinos, even in leadership positions. Even the dividing line between "guerrilla-aligned" and "independent" organizations, which would become so crucial from 1980 on, remained blurred and fluid for a few more years. Although most of the activists who survived into the early 1980s became radicalized—either toward indigenous militancy, revolutionary ideology, or some combination of the two—this process would have been just beginning in 1976. At this prior moment, one finds in most of these activities a strong echo of demands for universal justice and citizenship—ending racism, full inclusion in the political process, a fair chance in production and commerce—the basic promises of any liberal capitalist democracy. This section traces how movements with these relatively moderate political sensibilities, in the face of punishing racism and repression, turned radical, in some cases pushing demands for universal citizenship past their breaking point. My primary research focus on ladinos did not allow definitive answers to key questions about this period: How did indigenous people frame the rights and demands for which they struggled? To what extent did they consciously abandon an earlier cultural-political standpoint, in favor of a radicalized alternative? While future historians will certainly fill in some of the gaps, complete answers may well remain forever buried in the ashes of the violence and terror that culminated in 1981 and 1982.

The earthquake of 4 February 1976, with a Richter scale reading of 7.5 and an epicenter 75 miles northeast of Guatemala city, shook Chimaltenango society at its roots, and would become the primordial reference point for collective memories of the 1970s.[22] An estimated 27,000 people died from the impact and its immediate aftermath, many buried alive under the weight of heavy adobe walls and clay tile roofs. In the hardest hit municipios—Itzapa, San Martín, Comalapa, Tecpán, Patzicía, San José Poaquíl, Santa Apolonia, and Chimaltenango—the quake turned nearly every structure into rubble, including the most potent symbols of ladino society: the Casa de la Cultura of San Martín, the colonial- and liberal-era administration buildings of Chimaltenango, many of the colonial-era churches. Although the poor and indigenous majority clearly suffered disproportionately, the tragedy had a certain leveling effect, and ladino memories generally emphasize this egalitarian dimension: "*Agarró a todos parejo*" (It affected us all); for weeks we all lived in tents and collected food from the Red Cross; we pulled together to overcome adversity. The brigades of students and relief workers who poured into Chimaltenango, mainly from the capital city, both epitomized and contributed to the ladino victims' memories of the egalitarian ethos. The relief workers, mostly ladinos, including many with little knowledge of the indigenous highlands, were deeply moved by the suffering and squalor; to indigenous victims, this outpouring of ladino solidarity must have been a welcome relief from the indifference or disdain to which they were accustomed. The great flow of foreign aid, and the closely associated proliferation of NGO presence, also contributed to a general sense that in reconstruction, a more just society could be forged. Rumors that certain unscrupulous families (all or mostly ladinos) were getting rich from reconstruction aid must have begun to circulate early on; in any case, they later became standard in the more critical retrospective accounts. Yet at the time, evidence of such abuse and corruption would have been apt to provoke not cynicism but indignation and further impetus to organize. While nearly all the varied activities of social mobilization in the late 1970s have antecedents before 1976, in the aftermath of the earthquake the pace quickened, the sense of urgency deepened, and expectations soared.

Municipio-level indigenous electoral mobilization in Chimaltenango has its roots at least as far back as the revolutionary decade, and resumed in earnest in the late 1960s, but took a qualitative leap in intensity and effectiveness after 1976. While in 1970 indigenous people already had become mayors in six of the sixteen municipios, these were mainly the smaller locales, where ladino power and presence were already in decline. In the five most important municipios—Chimaltenango, Comalapa, Patzún, Tecpán, and San Martín—the first indigenous mayor after 1954 was Esteban López who, after suffering a stolen election in the late 1950s, won a second time in 1968 and came to power. In Tecpán, Basilio Cuá took office in 1970; in Comalapa an indigenous man of the last name Chalí won in 1972; and in 1978 indigenous candidates broke through the racial barrier in the two remaining municipios: San Martín (Felipe Álvarez) and Chimaltenango (José Lino Xoyón).[23] The Christian Democratic (DC) party played a major role in this transformation of local power relations—directing efforts specifically toward the indigenous majority, recruiting indigenous party activists, and putting forward indigenous candidates. In four of the five

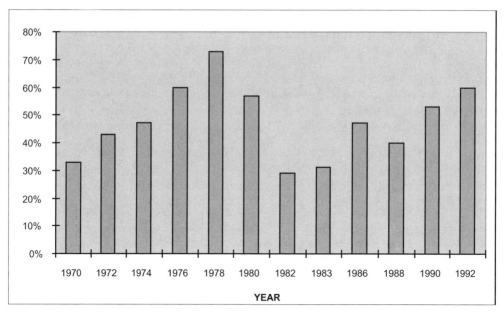

Figure 2.5. Indigenous mayors in Chimaltenango Municipios by Year. Source: Primary data collection (with special thanks to Silvia Barreno).

most important municipios, the first successful indigenous mayor came from the DC; Don Pedro Verona Cumes, a longtime DC activist from Comalapa, became the first indigenous member of Congress from Chimaltenango. By 1978 indigenous people had demonstrated their collective power as a voting bloc: setting aside the majority ladino municipio of Zaragoza, eleven of the remaining fourteen municipios had indigenous mayors, and the trend strongly favored a clean sweep (figure 2.5).[24]

National-level indigenous electoral mobilization gave this municipio-level trend even greater potency and impact. However disconcerting indigenous ascendancy in local government, it took place mostly under the aegis of national-level political parties—the DC and to a lesser degree the Partido Revolucionario (Revolutionary Party, or PR)—which remained solidly under ladino control. Not so for the Frente Indígena Nacional (Indigenous National Front, or FIN), an influential but ill-fated effort to organize an indigenous national-level political party. A group of indigenous professionals launched the initiative in 1974, and for support and guidance turned to Fernando Tezagüic, a teacher from Santa Cruz Balanyá, who had just been elected to the Congress for the department of Sololá. Under Tezagüic's leadership the idea caught on, and by 1976 the group had formed a Comité Pro-Partido (Committee to Form a Political Party), including an impressive roster of indigenous leaders, many of them from Chimaltenango.[25] Ladino power holders challenged the FIN in every conceivable way, from its name, to its alleged political immaturity and exclusion of ladinos, which, they claimed, smacked of "reverse racism," to the most inventive of criticisms—that it would cause other political parties to collapse by depriving all of them of indigenous supporters.[26] Although FIN's platform—remarkably moderate and pragmatic—contained very little to substantiate this hysteria, it was probably enough to hear the upbeat statements of leaders like Tezagüic, who predicted in March of 1977, as the country prepared for national elections, "[The FIN] will very soon have a million and a half affiliates, which will make it the political party of the future."[27]

An ostensibly separate flow of activities, though with many interconnections and areas of overlap, took place in the realm of Maya culture and identity. Every municipio had at least one organization, with strong youth participation and guidance from more established leaders, that promoted various forms of cultural-political *concientización* (consciousness raising). In each of the five major municipios, two or more of these organizations emerged and flourished simultaneously. Inevitably, they made the *ferias patronales* (festivals of patron saints) one of their first targets, challenging ladino-centric activities, insisting on an equal voice, often achieved through the establishment of separate Maya spaces: an indigenous beauty contest, an indigenous baile social, and so on. Other activities included the serious study of Maya culture and politics, support for indigenous students and professionals, and community development initiatives in rural areas. These organizations quickly developed department-wide networks of communication and exchange, enhanced by print media in newspapers such as *Ixim*, which heightened perceptions of a powerful movement in the making.

Activism revolving around the Catholic Church, though far from homogeneous, also contributed enormously to this upsurge of social action. Since the bishop of the diocese (which included the Sololá and Suchitepequez departments) during this period, Monseñor Angélico Meloto, had conservative leanings, the most far-reaching church activities emerged from outside the established sphere of influence of parish priests.[28] One such initiative—Programa Misionero Cakchiquel, or PROMICA—had its main offices in Chimaltenango and worked primarily in the municipios of Chimaltenango, Itzapa, and Parramos. Founded and directed by Ronald Burke, an American priest from San Francisco, PROMICA trained *promotores* (promoters), who carried out workshops on the Kaqchikel language, Maya culture, and identity. A second cluster of activities took place in the larger municipios to north—especially San Martín, Comalapa, and Poaquíl—under the leadership of Jesuit priests who worked out of the Zone 5 house.[29] Although in some respects overlapping with PROMICA, these Jesuit-led activities focused much more on action research, community organization, and political consciousness raising, influenced by the principles of liberation theology, with deepening ties to the largest guerrilla organization, the Ejército Guerrillero de los Pobres (Guerrilla Army of the Poor, or EGP). The language of these workshops was incendiary: encouraging indignation over the deep race and class inequities from which rural indigenous people suffered, supporting the inclination to organize and take action. Parish priests like Antonio Morales despised these Jesuit organizers—in particular Enrique Corral, who worked most in San Martín and later left the priesthood to join the EGP. Morales accused them of manipulating Indians who would otherwise have remained quiescent and loyal to his moderate, more strictly religious program for catechists. Given the enthusiastic response to the Jesuit workshops, however, it is more likely that the impetus for ever-greater militancy was mutual.

Although many details of this transformation toward greater militancy remain obscure, it seems clear that in Chimaltenango social mobilization followed a course, and developed a relationship with the guerrilla, with important differences from departments to the north and west. The original guerrilla organization, the Fuerzas Armadas Rebeldes (Rebel Armed Forces, or FAR) had a presence in Chimaltenango from the outset, in the mid-1960s. Some of the peasant syndicates—especially active in San Martín, Patzún, and Itzapa—had links to the FAR, as did one sector of the Chimaltenango teachers' union. An aggressive government counterinsurgency campaign dispersed these forces after 1967, and they would not regain a presence in Chimaltenango until the mid-1970s. In late 1977, a group of peasant leaders and other activists met secretly in a San Martín *finca* (large land holding) to form the Comité de Unidad Campesina (Committee for Peasant Unity, or CUC) and, from that time on, Chimaltenango remained one of the three major centers of CUC strength (along with the Quiché department, and the coastal plantation region). From the outset, the EGP exerted direct influence over the CUC and, as early as 1976, a handful of EGP militants like Enrique Corral introduced EGP-inflected political analysis wherever they could. But the EGP's strategy at the time was to promote popular-civic struggle, not generalized military insurrection against the regime; moreover, the depth and breadth of social mobilization in Chimaltenango far outstripped what a small number of EGP militants could hope to generate, much less control. In great contrast to widely circulating interpretations of other areas—especially the Ixil triangle—social mobilization in Chimaltenango preceded substantive guerrilla presence and influence, and may even have convinced the guerrilla to militarize the conflict prematurely, for fear of losing the political initiative.[30]

Although the heterogeneity of social mobilization between 1976 and 1980 defies easy summary, it appears that most initiatives that resumed or started anew after the earthquake took the universal citizenship frame as point of departure. The new indigenous mayors, many deeply influenced by the DC, kept a certain distance both from Maya-centered and revolutionary ideologies. Even the FIN, ladino hysteria notwithstanding, explicitly opposed more militant "mayanista" initiatives, whether on pragmatic or more philosophical grounds. While the seeds of an autonomous, collective rights–oriented politics probably were present in municipio-level organizations for Maya culture and identity, this was far from uniformly the case. Efforts to "de-center" ladino control of the ferias, for example, were most likely to be driven by an equal rights–equal time demand, to which ladinos could only respond by granting a separate space, because integration would have meant losing control completely. Similarly, many of the economic initiatives and most of the religious ones took moderate principles of cultural respect, fairness, and equality as points of departure. While guerrilla influence did increase in this period, and efforts of concientización like those of the

Zone 5 Jesuits did help to radicalize the indigenous population, the leftist political message emphasized universalist class struggle, and downplayed Mayan collective rights.[31] In any case, even when the influence of the revolutionary Left was still small, ladino power holders and local state authorities did not respond well to the rise of moderate, universal rights–oriented indigenous demands. Immersed in the separate and unequal mentality, these ladinos preferred to grant separate space to indigenous activists rather than to risk integration; immersed in a visceral anti-Communist ideology with racist underpinnings, state authorities took almost any political initiative, especially those with prominent indigenous leadership, as profoundly subversive. These two responses often reinforced one another, setting indigenous politics further apart and then lashing out with repression against them, which only deepened their revolve and militancy. Don Rolando, who worked extensively with indigenous farmers of Comalapa, captures nicely (though perhaps with a bit of self-serving embellishment) the mutual incomprehension:

> I talked with the people that were getting involved. I said to one of them: "*Muchá*, you are committing the mistake of your life." They responded: "But the ladinos insult us too much, saying indios this, indios that." I said, "You guys are not stupid, why can't you see that this thing is headed for disaster?" They responded: "You are different, more understanding, but the others, they just don't respect us."

As racial polarization deepened and indigenous mobilization met with increasing refusal and repression, the space for civic struggle in the name of moderate demands for equality and universal citizenship rapidly disappeared.

Disciplinary Assimilation, 1982–1991

The wave of repression that began selectively in the mid-1970s and reached a gruesome climax in 1982 had deep roots, both in the past century of state-society relations, and in the particular structure of racial dominance in Chimaltenango. Since the Liberal revolution of 1871 the state had ruled predominantly by dictatorship, with an established pattern—practiced even during the democratic interludes—of neutralizing or directly repressing political dissent. Even though Chimaltenango never became a principal theater of the guerrilla movement in the 1960s, selective repression against activists and opposition political leaders occurred steadily in the two decades leading up to the time of generalized violence. Rarely investigated and never fully clarified, these murders gave rise to abundant analysis and speculation afterward, which often implicated a powerful local ladino as informer, or even, instigator. In San Martín—and probably other municipios such as Comalapa—organizations of vecinos submitted petitions to the armed forces, pleading for a permanent presence to fend off the guerrilla threat. One can only imagine the levels of collaboration that followed, when the army acceded to these local demands. From the earlier years of the knock on the door by the feared *federales* (government soldiers), to the methodical killing of key activists after 1978, to the generalized army campaigns of 1981–1982, repression in Chimaltenango unfolded according to nationwide patterns. Local ladino power holders played key parts in this process, roles that most people knew or highly suspected, and that therefore live on to haunt subsequent efforts to achieve reconciliation or, at least, restore normalcy.[32]

By the end of 1980, Chimaltenango had become a focal point of the rapidly growing guerrilla movement. This strength lay not in the cumulative effects of political-military organizing, or for that matter in any extensive organized guerrilla presence at all, but rather, in an outpouring of radicalized social mobilization, which suddenly turned to overtly military tactics. In November 1980, the EGP took the fateful decision to militarize the CUC and other grassroots organizations under its influence, in response to vociferous demand from below and to additional pressure from an unyieldingly triumphal and impetuous field commander named Camilo. The decision to militarize—that is, to call for general armed insurrection against the regime—caused controversy among EGP commanders: they had a tiny number of armed regulars in the department, a few trained "irregular" units, and virtually no arms to distribute. The insurrection happened anyway, bolstered weakly in July 1981 with the opening of the Augusto César Sandino Guerrilla Front (FGACS), meant to direct operations in Chimaltenango and southern Quiché. Over the course of 1981, guerrilla-aligned forces attacked every center of municipio government except the city of Chimaltenango at least once, set up training camps, blocked the Pan-American Highway, charged war taxes, and began to mete out consequences for collaborators with the regime. Experienced with euphoria by some and horror by others, this revolutionary ascendancy did not last through the year's end. The state launched a counterinsurgency campaign on 17 November 1981, with a massive deployment of force from the capital city, and its first stop in Chimaltenango.[33] Armed guerrilla regulars of the FGACS quickly retreated to better fortified and more remote areas north and west, leaving the mobilized, militant, but largely defenseless indigenous multitudes to face an enraged and vengeful enemy. Over the next few months, the army established bases in every municipio, massacred suspected guerrilla supporters by the hundreds, and implemented draconian measures of vigilance among the civilian survivors, turning Chimaltenango into the testing ground for a counterinsurgency strategy applied with brutal uniformity throughout the indigenous highlands.

Although the army carried out this campaign with genocidal fervor, a different face of governance took hold once the worst of the torture, killing, and massacre had subsided. The brutality is well documented. The Comisión para Esclarecimiento Histórico (Commission for Historical Clarification, or CEH) of the United Nations officially named four regions where it could be proven that the army had committed genocide against the indigenous population; commission researchers amassed sufficient evidence for a fifth case of genocide in San Martín Jilotepeque, which they later set aside for technical reasons.[34] Abundant additional evidence clearly demonstrates the intent to "destroy the material bases of Maya culture"—physical settlements, crops, sacred sites, esteemed leaders—which may not meet the technical criteria of "geno-cide," but has been widely interpreted in this vein.[35] Independent ethnographic veri-fication that, well before the counterinsurgency campaign began, a significant sector of the Guatemalan national elite favored "extermination" as a means to resolve the "Indian problem," adds further credence to this interpretation.[36] Yet while it is highly plausible that a genocidal *tesis de exterminio* (extermination thesis) drove the counterin-surgency campaign in an initial phase, by mid-1982 it had begun to follow a differ-ent logic. The army sought not to eliminate but to control the indigenous population, not even to eliminate the material bases of indigenous culture, but rather, to reshape them, with the utmost violence if necessary, cutting out the cancer of subversion and dissent, affirming a space to be Indian within constraints imposed by a fiercely mili-tarized disciplinary state.[37] Far from contradicting this logic, massive state violence against so-called subversives and troublemakers served as its lynchpin: repression pro-vided a terrifying incentive to live within these constraints, while also advancing the perverse conclusion that dissenters were to blame for their own demise.

By the time I met Colonel Cifuentes in 1998, this brutal disciplinary assimilation had developed into a well-embedded, almost commonsense, centerpiece of the Armed Forces' self-portrayal. The first phase involved pacification and control of the civilian population that survived the massacres. The Ríos Montt government—installed in March 1982—called its first general amnesty on 24 May 1982, while the massacres continued. In Chimaltenango, over the following six months, thousands of belea-guered indigenous peasants turned themselves in, often after having fled their homes weeks or even months earlier. After weeding out those who had played leadership roles in subversive activities, the army assigned the "surrendered" civilians to resettlement camps, where they would live for the remainder of the decade under strict army vigi-lance. In San Martín the parish priest served as mediator in these operations, assuring civilians they would not be harmed, helping them adapt to the new conditions, but also, reportedly, helping the army distinguish the "subversives" from the rest.[38] The next phase involved the establishment of obligatory civilian patrols (called Civilian Auto-Defense Patrols or PACs), directly controlled by the army, and a network of sub-ordinates to supervise the system. The PACs had the ostensible purpose of turning sur-rendered civilians into the first line of defense against guerrilla intruders, and in the process served to oblige the community to discipline itself. While all forms of organ-ized political expression were prohibited during this period, the army did encourage the formation of public works committees (*Comités pro-Mejoramiento*), which quickly proliferated. At first the army controlled every facet of community life, from food dis-tribution to the rebuilding of homes; for many years to come, it would play a central role in the planning, financing, and execution of public works as a means to consoli-date its image as guarantor of peace and development.

Relief and development aid poured into Chimaltenango after the worst of the vio-lence had subsided. The first wave of these civilian organizations, handpicked and approved by the army, took a predictably partisan stance toward the conflict, even while cultivating an air of humanitarian neutrality. I spent the day with Zulema Cordero, the director of an NGO with projects in Chimaltenango, who worked in that first wave of quasi-governmental development aid during the Ríos Montt regime. She spoke at length about her experiences in those early days, arriving in government trucks to attend refugees and shell-shocked people throughout the central altiplano war zone:

> It was easy to convince them to join our relief efforts, because they had not
> joined the guerrilla out of conviction. They often could not even tell the two
> armies apart—guerrilla and ejército—or they simply distinguished one from
> the other by the type of boots they wore. The Indians are *muy sensibles* (very
> sensitive), like the quetzal [Guatemala's national bird], who has such a delicate
> spirit that if he is captured, he dies.

Seemingly oblivious to the power relations that structured her dealings with the indigenous communities, Cordero voiced a commonsense version of the "between two armies" ideology that would become the hallmark of the army's postwar role in Chimaltenango. Clothed in humanitarian empathy, disassociated from its own previous excesses in the armed conflict, the army reconnected with traumatized civilians who had little choice but to comply.

While people who had been subjected directly to army-inflicted terror were not likely to embrace this peace and development image right away, a number of factors made disciplinary assimilation especially powerful and persuasive. An unprecedented degree of penetration, control, and forceful restructuring of daily life left little space for organized thinking about alternatives.[39] The institution continued to figure prominently in such civilian activities long after it had no strictly military purpose; especially in the rural areas, well into the 1990s, military bases doubled as central government authorities. The army had a seat at the table in meetings of the departmental *Consejo de Desarrollo* (Development Council) and other important spaces of local and regional governance; it sponsored beauty queens and contributed to fiesta activities; local commanders made their presence known at every civic ceremony; and, more recently, they returned to the streets to help combat common crime and maintain social peace (figure 2.6). Equally important, the army carried out these activities with a discourse of basic respect for indigenous culture and affirmation of indigenous peoples as equals.[40]

The revived and fortified institution of *comisionados militares* (military commissioners) gave this army presence a local face, which contributed directly to its effectiveness.[41] During an initial phase of my fieldwork, I took lessons in Kaqchikel Maya from Chan, a Maya intellectual and cultural rights activist from Tecpán. Taking advantage of weekly trips to Tecpán, I also started conducting interviews there. Given my plans to collect political-economic data in each municipio, I thought it wise to visit the comisionado militar, both to get his approval of my research, and to interview a key ladino power holder in the community. I knocked on the door of the modest home of

Figure 2.6. Encounter of the Candles. Local army commanders at the culminating moment in the 1997 "Encounter of the Candles," a ceremony that initiates the yearly Santa Ana patron saint festival in Chimaltenango. Photo credit: Charles R. Hale.

Cristóbal, the head comisionado for Tecpán; his daughter answered, and reluctantly called her father. At first Cristóbal redirected my request for information to the military base and, to my dismay, for a moment it seemed that he might insist on taking me directly there. With assurances that I was already in communication with high-level authorities in Chimaltenango, he relaxed slightly and agreed to talk. His daughter remained involved in the conversation, and filled in the gaps left by Cristóbal's terse answers to my questions. She explained, for example, that Cristóbal had been an alcoholic, and implied that becoming a comisionado had been the key to his recovery.

Cristóbal spoke in a deep voice, which began quiet, and then turned eerily animated and vehement when we reached the topic of the Mayas. He provided a brief explanation of the previous period of violence, with a story line that followed closely that of his patrons, and ended with the ubiquitous assertion:

> There is no more separation between indigenous and ladinos, like there used to be. We come together to work, and we've overcome the days of separation. There are many mixed marriages now; it has happened in my own family. The indigenous people now are integrated with us; education is probably the most important factor.

The violent images that followed, in response to my seemingly bland question about Tecún Umán, left me almost speechless:

> There are small groups of Mayas who want to return to the old times, making sacrifices with animals and other things. They have followers. If it continues in this way, it could bring extremely serious consequences: they would kill the ladinos. They would kill us, as if we were Spaniards. This would bring on a war.

Cristóbal's mindset coincided with that of Colonel Cifuentes, though it was shocking to hear the prediction of a return to violent conflict come so spontaneously and viscerally from a resident of a Maya-dominant community with only a small monthly stipend from the army. His fears were focused not on an abstract, faceless enemy, but on people in his own town, his neighbors, people like Chan, my Kaqchikel teacher! The disciplinary thrust of these fears came through loud and clear: when indigenous people refuse the invitation to join ladinos "as equals" and seek collective empowerment instead, they must be preparing the ground for a race war; they can expect the army to respond accordingly.

Although one is tempted to view any army gesture toward equality as cynical manipulation, given its record of genocidal violence against indigenous peoples, this would miss the point. As my conversations with both the colonel and Cristóbal illustrate, horrific state violence and the vaguely populist endorsement of universal citizenship come as two sides of the same coin, which converge to produce the desired effect. Many indigenous people complied, whether because they had no choice, in anticipation of important benefits or, most likely, with a rationale that combined these two. Although disciplinary assimilation was a far cry from the utopian political imagery that circulated widely in the heat of social mobilization, a minimalist promise to eliminate overt racism, practice equality, and to end the living hell of state violence, must have come as a welcome relief. The principles of universal citizenship, after all, had provided many indigenous chimaltecos with the rationale to mobilize a decade earlier, whether out of conviction or a pragmatic sense that it would be impossible to achieve anything more.

In the aftermath of the armed conflict, important sectors of the Catholic Church reinforced this message of disciplinary assimilation. Although the church moved in the late 1970s toward a position of generalized opposition to the government, a sector representing very different views remained even at the height of the conflict, and grew stronger after the worst of state violence had passed. Father Roberto, the parish priest of Itzapa, epitomizes this latter position. An introduction by my Itzapa research assistant, a loyal parishioner, helped convince Father Roberto to open up immediately. An energetic and determined man under the age of forty, he greeted me in the parish house wearing a long, black robe; he spoke rapidly and with great confidence about the church's mission in the face of Maya efflorescence. He portrayed a conflict within the church on this issue, and insisted that his position—developed after sustained reflection on the "well-intentioned" but fundamentally mistaken efforts to accommodate Maya cultural-spiritual assertion—was ascendant. "We have three bishops—Flores, Cabrera, and Ramasini—who still support an Indian rights approach. It was four," he added dryly, "with Gerardi." Now, he assured me, clarity has emerged. In a long, wide-ranging conversation, Father Roberto went to great lengths to insist that, while remnants persisted, discrimination was in decline, and that the church had been at the forefront of this change. He was especially adamant on this point, perhaps because he comes from a prominent ladino family, with relatives in high positions in both government and the military:

> My principle is to treat everyone equal…I say, isn't it the case that the other has a nose and two ears, just like you? How much difference can the color of one's skin make? It is helping now that there are so many mixed marriages. I talk to them: what's the big deal about these differences? Skin color, wearing a *huipil* (Indian blouse): these are not fundamental differences.

Yet paired with this standard affirmation of equality, in remarkably frank terms that echoed Cristóbal, though in religious rather than military idiom, Father Roberto outlined "the church's" deep fears about the Maya:

> What worries me is the rise of neopaganism within Mayan religion. Elements must be separated. All their beliefs about the family, the earth—that type of thing—is fine; but this thing about adoring more than one God, we can't tolerate it…. It is important that the self-esteem of the indigenous people be achieved, but the big problem is how to do it without confrontation. Deep down what they're looking for is to create a Maya nation, and divide Guatemala in two countries. One state, with two nations; one indigenous, the other ladino. The Episcopal Conference fears that in Guatemala the next war will be a religious or a racial confrontation…I am certain about one thing: we must confront it now. Later, there won't be a chance. Don't forget that the indigenous already rose up once to kill the ladinos. We worry about the signs that there is no mutual tolerance.

Father Roberto ended our conversation with his preferred means to resolve the problem. Although emphasizing repeatedly the need to respect indigenous culture, avoid brusque and rapid change, and combat racism, at the end of the day he cast his lot with Christian universalism, a striking parallel to the profane ideology of disciplinary assimilation:

> I say that the only way to proceed is to forget about the indígena and the ladino. That happens in church work. In the [activities in my parish] it's half and half. I don't care who it is—faith isn't about asking that. All are God's children. Christian practice is capable of breaking that barrier. We're against class struggle, because it creates *divisionismo* (desire for divisions) among men. The same thing happens with the division between the races.

Besides the army and the church, a third variant of these universal-assimilationist principles can be found among left-leaning ladinos who trace their political loyalties back to the 1944–1954 decade of social reform. Although fervently critical of state violence and military control of politics, people in this group—epitomized by ladino schoolteachers—believe in the universalist promise of equality, and fear that an emphasis on indigenous culture and rights might undermine efforts to forge a unified Guatemalan national identity. A high school teacher expressed the sentiment this way:

> My point of departure is our identity as Guatemalans. If we do not have a strong common identity, then too many people want to be boss, and the government controls us more effectively. To me, multiculturalism boils down to a very simple principle: treat everyone as equals.

These teachers practice equality with conviction and consistency in the classroom, proscribing all overt expressions of racism and prejudice, and strongly endorsing universal norms, such as the obligatory use of school uniforms. For indigenous students to wear traje, or to exercise other rights to collective identity, would be to undermine the principle of unity through equality for all. While this position differs in important ways from that of the army and the church, the three converge on basic points: equality, cultural respect, and long-term assimilation toward a dominant (ladino-defined) norm of national unity. They all occupy powerful positions in the society, exerting deep influence over the indigenous majority, promoting the idea that universal equality is enough or, at least, all that dominant sectors could be reasonably expected to yield.

Although significant numbers of indigenous chimaltecos rejected this reasoning, the dissent almost surely has received disproportionate attention from analysts. Indigenous chimaltecos who continued to affirm their alignment with revolutionary politics, despite the enormous internal difficulties and external pressure, remained in radical dissent—at least to the extent that their left-inflected universalism placed them clearly outside the mainstream. Those who joined the Maya cultural activist movements dissented for different reasons: neither revolutionary politics nor mainstream state-centered ideologies acknowledged Maya culture as basis for rights to self-determination; the universalism of both implicitly favored ladino dominance. Reams of analysis have been dedicated to these two groups, especially the Maya cultural activists, at times with the assertion that their perspective converges with the consciousness and practice of the indigenous population in general.[42] Some analysts, however, are beginning to highlight the number of indigenous rural dwellers who identify with neither position, and defend instead a minimalist agenda of universal citizenship.[43] The fact that powerful ladino sectors supported this same position would certainly have helped close the gap between coercion and consent, increasing the attractiveness of this position, and making more expansive notions of rights appear unfeasible and dangerous.

Disciplinary assimilation, the ideology of governance that emerged from the period of intense political conflict, departed sharply from the preceding separate and unequal approach, even if its content, in other ways, remained ambiguous. Most important, after the worst of the violent repression had passed, the army's counterinsurgency tactics, like the conservative wing of the Catholic Church and the progressive ladino teachers, emphasized racial and cultural equality: respect indigenous culture, oppose classic racism, treat everyone as equal. Ambiguity emerged in the further refinement of this message, revolving around the character of the space for cultural difference and the reach of the equality principle. The latter had comprised, for some time, the key bone of contention between Left and Right: does the equality principle give license for transformation of the deep structural roots of inequality or simply equal treatment in the context of those existing conditions? In contrast, the former issue—how much space for cultural difference—did not fit so neatly within the well-established left-right divide. At least through the 1960s, the army may well have been ahead of the Left in harnessing a version of Indianness—the quasi-mythical Tecún Umán, for example—to its institutional interests.[44] In general, proponents of all variants of disciplinary assimilation preferred to keep the space for indigenous rights to a minimum: with basic respect, universal equality, and the additional influence of progress, they assumed, indigenous cultural difference would soon fade. Cristóbal and Father Roberto both shudder at the thought of Maya empowerment; they both envision, each in his own distinctive idiom, a Guatemala without "Indians or ladinos"—a classic assimilationist vision that implicitly favors people of the dominant culture. Yet even their support for bare bones equality and cultural respect opens spaces, giving indigenous rights activists with more expansive notions of rights a foot in the door. By the 1990s, however, in response to this activism from below and to external pressures, the state gradually began to acknowledge Maya cultural difference. The strict tenets of disciplinary assimilation began to give way, often in halting steps, to a new mode of governance that I have called neoliberal multiculturalism.

Neoliberal Multiculturalism, 1992–Present

In early November 1993, Yolanda invited me to accompany her on a day visit to the feria of San Martín. We soon found ourselves in the inner sanctum office of the mayor, Eustaquio Palma, along with other visiting dignitaries, all ladinos. Feted with rum and freshly cooked *chicharrón* (fried pig skins), we settled in for a relaxed, animated, if somewhat scattered conversation, on topics that ranged from the mundane and folkloric, to the substantive. The whole affair had a distinctly colonial feel, with ladinos comfortably segregated in a power-laden inner sphere, and large numbers of Indians milling around in the courtyard, waiting for the mayor's attention, or attending to some matter in their own, quite separate realm. Yet forces of change were equally evident. Palma had been engaged in a pitched battle with San Martín's ladino elite, Yolanda later explained to me, provoked by his policy of supporting the rural indigenous areas of the municipio, rather than the town center, with public works. He had conceived our gathering in the inner sanctum not as an unselfconscious expression of ladino dominance, but as a calculated political move to neutralize his (ladino elite) opposition. Moreover, one of the participants was the representative of *San Martinecos Unidos* (San Martín Residents United), an organization based in Los Angeles, which supports San Martín and confounds traditional lines of racial hierarchy.[45] In yet another sign of the changing times, I conversed with the vice-minister of Education, Licenciado Francisco Aguilar Sosa, and heard my earliest recorded statement from a government official, which explicitly abandons assimilationist orthodoxy. The vice-minister attached himself to me, presumably viewing me as someone of comparable status, perhaps angling for an invitation to the United States, repeatedly insisting that I note down this or that detail. The Education Ministry, he stated dramatically, had embraced wholeheartedly a new "multicultural" approach: "It is time for the colonial mentality that has guided education in this country to end."[46]

This change in state ideology did not come all at once in a grand act or declaration, but gradually, as the consequence of cumulative smaller initiatives, in response to an array of forces. Maya organizations were the most overt motor of change, especially effective in the late 1980s and early 1990s, when their moderate and pragmatic political strategy still made for a dramatic contrast with that of the Left. An array of international organizations—from small "solidarity" NGOs to the World Bank—also played key roles, by making funds available, exerting pressure on the Guatemalan state, and by taking action on their own. Bilateral aid programs of nearly all the important and powerful donor countries—especially Scandinavia, Western Europe, and the United States—took a special interest in lo indígena. Gradually and reluctantly at first, but unmistakably by the mid-1990s, national-level politicians adopted a proactive stance, paying attention to indigenous people as a distinct, collective political force, not only at election time, but also as official policy. The government of Vinicio Cerezo (1986–1990) consummated the first substantive step with the 1987 founding of the Academia de Lenguas Mayas de Guatemala.[47] Ramiro de León Carpio (1993–1995) named the first Maya to a cabinet-level position; as minister of Education, Alfredo Tay Coyoy was Vice-Minister Aguilar Soza's superior. During that same period, the "Maya sector" gained a prominent place within the Asamblea de Sociedad Civil, which attempted to influence negotiations between the state and the guerrilla, representing the interests of civil society.[48] By the mid-1990s, state initiatives, programs, and declarations in favor of multiculturalism had accumulated to the point where the basic principles stood beyond question: contemporary Maya identity merits recognition and respect; Mayas have collective rights grounded in cultural difference.

The great promise of this emergent multiculturalism, as well as its profound ambiguities and contradictions, come sharply into focus in the Peace Accords between the state and the guerrilla, finalized in December 1996. On 31 March 1995, the government of Ramiro de León Carpio and the URNG signed the Accord on Identity and Rights of the Indigenous Peoples, the most substantive of the seven accords if judged by degree of departure from existing state ideology and program. In the preamble this accord urges Guatemalans to acknowledge their country's history of "racial discrimination," and to work toward a change of "mentalities, attitudes and behaviors" to achieve its elimination. A series of specific commitments follow, putting the state on record in favor of Maya rights to language, to culture-specific religion, spirituality, clothing, education, management of internal affairs according to *normas consuetudinarias* (customary laws), and traditional lands important to subsistence and spiritual activities, all placed within the broader redefinition of Guatemala as a "multicultural, pluri-ethnic, multi-lingual" nation. These commitments grow more impressive when viewed in contrast to the Accord on Agrarian and Socio-Economic Affairs, which offers no substantive departure from existing policies and frames "solutions" largely within the neoliberal logic of economic incentives and market forces. Consistent with this contrast, the administration of Álvaro Arzú Irigoyen (1996–2000) combined an orthodox neoliberal approach to management of the economy—overt hostility to labor organizing; full backing for the interests of capital; development through investment in infrastructure and public works; scaling back of state commitments to social welfare, and so on—and a progressive stance on Maya cultural rights. Ostensibly in contradiction, these two strands of state ideology meld to yield a new mode of governance, on the rise throughout Latin America.

To claim that limited recognition of Maya cultural rights and economic neoliberal restructuring converge to constitute a single political project does not imply that governance proceeds in lockstep, nor that the project has unfolded free from contradiction. Some sectors of the ruling bloc conceived of their economic and political interests in ways that preclude any but the most trivial and folkloric recognition of Maya culture; even among those ladino elites who have embraced the multicultural turn there are substantive disagreements and ambiguities in their thinking about the line between permissible and "dangerous" Maya demands. The point is, simply, that neoliberal economic reforms have embodied great flexibility in regard to indigenous cultural rights; this follows because the key defining feature of neoliberalism is not strict, market-oriented individualism, as many contend, but rather the restructuring of society such that people come to govern themselves in accordance with the tenets of global capitalism. Compliance with the discipline of the capitalist market can be individual, but may be equally effective as a collective response; if civil society organizations opt for development models that reinforce the ideology of capitalist productive relations, they can embody and advance the neoliberal project as collectivities not individuals. As long as cultural rights remain within these basic parameters, they contribute directly to the goal of neoliberal self-governance; they reinforce its ideological tenets while meeting deeply felt needs; they register dissent, while directing these collective political energies toward unthreatening ends. It is no coincidence, for example, that high-level positions for Mayas in neoliberal governments have been reserved for ministries like Education and Culture, rather than Finance or Defense, or that the earliest restructuring of the state to reflect cultural rights would be the Academia de Lenguas Mayas. Yet even if these spaces emerge in conjunction with the neoliberal project, their outcome and trajectory is by no means fixed in advance. Neoliberal multiculturalism turns Maya cultural rights into a political battleground in the Gramscian sense: before, serious public consideration of such rights could not occur; now, all viable political forces endorse them as a social good, and the struggle ensues to shape their content and their reach.

In the decade of the 1990s, funding for Maya-oriented civil society organizations skyrocketed, sending a strong message that the international community not only respects Maya culture, but actively pursues "development with identity." Of the "special funds" established with World Bank donations, early on, the Fondo Indígena (Indigenous Fund) figured prominently. The United Nations Mission to Guatemala (MINUGUA) established indigenous rights as an important area of work, which heightened further when the Commission for Historical Clarification began its deliberations. USAID sponsored a major program to "strengthen civil society organizations," which focused primarily on the Maya. Funds from the European community and the Scandinavian countries poured in after the definitive signing of the Peace Accords in 1996, giving rise to a new coordinating body that was to be broadly representative of Maya interests, the Coordinadora de Organizaciones del Pueblo Maya (Coordination of Organizations of the Maya People or COPMAGUA), and channeling funds to dozens of smaller organizations.[49] One eloquent gauge of this shift in Chimaltenango was the intense discontent among ladino-run NGOs, which suddenly lost their privileged role as intermediaries between Maya communities and "international cooperation." Another is the rapid Mayanization of organizations that formerly had a ladino-run or multiracial character.[50]

Deep changes in Chimaltenango's political economy contributed further to this transformation, and to provincial ladinos' growing sense that neoliberal multiculturalism amounted to more than mere government rhetoric. New investment with capital from outside the department created important concentrations of economic activity— in maquila-type clothing assembly, and production and marketing of nontraditional vegetable exports—completely disarticulated from the networks of local ladino power holders. These local ladinos felt powerless and excluded in the face of Korean owners of maquilas along the Pan-American Highway, American capitalists who bought up vast tracks of land between Parramos and Itzapa for vegetable production, and Guatemalan entrepreneurs from the capital who controlled the vegetable purchase, transshipment, and export. These enterprises negotiate the terms of their presence at much higher political levels; they pay no local taxes and steer clear of local politics; their owners have little or no presence in local social relations. A few local ladinos find work in middle-level positions in these new enterprises, but most become dispensable, passed over altogether. While there was nothing explicitly multicultural about these macroeconomic transformations, they produced new labor relations and paths of capital accumulation in which provincial ladinos played no significant role, contributing to a general sense that the processes of change were completely out of their hands.

A parallel set of processes taking place at lower levels of the political economy reinforced ladino perceptions that change was in the air. Although census figures in

Municipio	1981 *Population*			2000 *Population*			*Change in indigenous population*	
	Total	Indigenous		Total	Indigenous			
El Tejar	4,264	1,873	44%	13823	5258	38%	-6%	3,385
Parramos	3,919	2,353	60%	9537	5053	53%	-7%	2,700
Chimaltenango	27,004	17,907	66%	74077	47768	64%	-2%	29,861
Yepocapa	11,330	7,369	65%	23509	16063	68%	3%	8,694
Acatenango	11,285	7,162	63%	18336	11848	65%	1%	4,686
Pochuta	9,920	7,369	74%	9842	5323	54%	-20%	(2,046)
San Andrés Itzapa	10,625	7,655	72%	21151	14730	70%	-2%	7,075
San Martín Jilotepec	36,566	31,690	87%	58578	51776	88%	2%	20,086
Patzicía	12,385	10,675	86%	23401	21335	91%	5%	10,660
Tecpán	29,555	26,706	90%	59859	55010	92%	2%	28,304
Santa Apolonia	5,701	5,150	90%	11859	11004	93%	2%	5,854
Patzún	23,429	21,740	93%	42326	40127	95%	2%	18,387
San José Poaquíl	11,556	10,855	94%	19982	19365	97%	3%	8,510
Comalapa	20,416	19,682	96%	35441	34428	97%	1%	14,746
Santa Cruz Balanyá	3,604	3,424	95%	6504	6324	97%	2%	2,900
TOTAL	221,559	181,610	82%	428,225	345,412	81%	-1%	163,802

Source: Instituto Nacional de Estadística. Censo Nacional de Población. Guatemala: INE.

Figure 2.7. Indigenous Population of Chimaltenango by Municipio, 1981 and 2000.

Municipio	Owners	Business Doctors	Lawyers	Commerce	Average
El Tejar	0	0	0	0	0
Parramos	0	33	0	0	8
San Martín	36	29	8	0	18
San Andrés Itzapa	3	50	33	NA	29
Santa Cruz Balanyá	0	33	NA	100	44
Tecpán	74	30	29	50	46
Comalapa	29	70	50	NA	50
San José Poaquíl	92	NA	0	67	53
Patzicía	100	50	50	33	58
Santa Apolonia	100	NA	NA	50	75
Patzún	76	100	75	50	75

Source: Primary field research (with special thanks to Silvia Barreno).

Figure 2.8. Selected Indices of Wealth/Privilege by Identity, circa 1998 (all numbers indicate percentage indigenous).

1981 and 2000 show a more or less constant percentage of ladinos (or at least "non-indigenous") in the department as a whole, this aggregate continuity obscures a trend toward bifurcation of the racial demography. In eight municipios that had at least 85 percent indigenous population in 1981, one finds a trend toward "mayanization": declining ladino presence (in percentages and even absolute numbers) in some cases approaching complete disappearance (see figure 2.7); and a corresponding Maya ascendancy in most or all positions of power, from local politics to commerce, services, and other professional positions (see figure 2.8). In a second set of seven municipios, where ladinos have long enjoyed greater demographic presence, the trend toward mayanization is markedly absent, and ladinos seem to have kept Maya ascendancy in local power structures at bay. Patzún might be taken as the paradigmatic case of mayanization, while El Tejar and Parramos illustrate the opposite trend of ladino reconcentration. Viewing figures 2.7 and 2.8 in conjunction brings into focus a dramatic pattern: demographic mayanization is closely correlated with Maya ascendancy, while ladino demographic growth correlates with entrenchment of ladino control of local power relations. The municipios of San Martín Jilotepeque and Tecpán are partial exceptions to this pattern: perhaps because of their large size and historic importance, ladino power holders have persisted to a greater extent than in the other locations. But given the overall strength of the pattern and the unmistakable demographic trend toward mayanization in these two municipios, one would suspect change in the same direction to be only a matter of time.

Ladinos chimaltecos often seemed to respond to this change—new political economic conditions and emergent state-backed multiculturalism—with perplexity, fear, and confusion. The problem of registering vital statistics—births, deaths, marriages, and other basic census data—illustrates this perplexity nicely, and also helps to dramatize the difficulties in collecting data on changing conditions of racial inequality, when the change in question affects the identity categories themselves. Prior to the 1980s, municipal secretaries and civil registries served as the cornerstone in the edifice of local-level ladino political power. They managed the paperwork of local governance, played key roles in the organization of local economic activities, and controlled the mechanisms that gave indigenous residents credentials as citizens. The civil registry recorded vital statistics, especially important in any effort to monitor changing relations between Indians and ladinos: Is intermarriage on the rise? To which identity category is the offspring of a mixed union assigned? To what extent do local functionaries enforce and reproduce the ideology of governance to which the central government is publicly committed?

From the mid-1990s on, apparently straightforward questions like these turned out to be nearly impossible to answer. Most civil registrars in Chimaltenango had stopped asking the identity question altogether, even though the form they use for vital statistics still has a line designated "raza" (race). How do they fill in that blank on the form, we asked ten civil registrars.[51] "The topic is too sensitive," one responded. The registrar from El Tejar elaborated:

People get upset. One time, I had a big problem with a woman who I thought was indigenous, because of her last names, and because I knew her family. I said to her, "You are indigenous, aren't you?" But she considered herself to be ladina, and took great offense, and *me dijo unas palabrotas* (began to yell angrily at me). Since that day, I never ask people whether they are indigenous or ladino, because I'm afraid of what they might say.

A third asserted, "The Constitution prohibits us from asking that question." Instead of asking the respondents' race, the civil registrars either provide an answer based on their own preexisting knowledge of the person in question, or they just leave it blank.

In the civil registrars' current practices of recording (or not recording, as the case may be) identity, we have an inventory of three distinct modes of governance: separate and unequal, universalist assimilation, and neoliberal multiculturalism. As local representatives of the state, these registrars have at different times been expected to enforce the first two; with the recent emergence of the third, which only partly displaces the previous ones, most simply have thrown up their hands. The registry form's original phrasing, "raza," is a vestige from the overt "separate and unequal" racism of times past: it portrayed a stark, almost unbridgeable chasm between Indian and ladino, and assigned relatively fixed racial characteristics to each. The registrars' inclination not to ask is emblematic of the shift to the universalist assimilation ideology of citizenship: people could continue to affirm indigenous culture and identity, but they are encouraged to move into the space of the dominant culture in order for the principle of equality to be fully effective. Instead of being disciplined or punished if they opt to "pass" in this way, they should be rewarded (at least by being relieved of the need to explain themselves to an inquisitive registrar). The "indigenous" woman's anger at having been called on her desire to pass reflects this powerful assimilationist ideology at work, and her anger must have been exacerbated by a sense that the registrar violated his own (that is, the state's) rules. The renewed inclination to ask reflects the influence of the Maya movement and the rise of state-endorsed multiculturalism, both of which reinforce the assumption that indigenous identity now connotes pride and self-affirmation.[52] One registrar's reference to constitutional prohibitions is especially ironic, since Maya cultural rights activists have been hard at work toward precisely the opposite end: giving the Constitution a multicultural content. They would indeed insist that the registrar ask the identity question, in hopes that respondents would use the "Maya" identity category with pride.

While multiculturalism emerged as the nascent mode of governance in the mid-1990s, it did not generate a strong and sharply defined project to be taken up and implemented by the state at all levels. In the diversified spaces of Chimaltenango regional politics, the shift left ample leeway for a range of sensibilities on questions of identity, including some that stood in direct contradiction with one another.[53] Maya organizations proliferated in Chimaltenango during this period, fully occupying the space opened by the promise of multiculturalism, and in many cases advancing demands for collective rights that pushed this promise beyond its limits. In contrast, among the indigenous mayors, whose rising prominence stands as another epitomizing symbol of Maya efflorescence, only a handful came to power with strong ideological and organizational ties to the Maya movement.[54] Other Maya mayors represented a range of political sensibilities, most linked directly to mainstream political parties, including the carefully scripted multiculturalism of the Partido de Avanzada Nacional (Party of National Advancement or PAN). Many indigenous chimaltecos do "vote indigenous" but seemingly without a burning desire to affirm cultural rights beyond the frame of universal citizenship—whether out of resignation, fear, or political philosophy. It is impossible to know the size of these two groups—one Maya-centric and the other indigenous universalist—because no one collects the relevant data, and the boundaries between the two categories are porous and fluid. It is clear, however, that the ascendant state-endorsed multiculturalism has only partly displaced the previous ideology of disciplinary assimilation, and together they saturate Chimaltenango with mixed messages: repudiation of racism, yet continuation of the same ideas in a more gentle guise; respect for indigenous culture, yet subtle ongoing disdain for things Indian; encouragement of respectful intercultural relations, yet deep skepticism about people's claims to being Maya. With access to modest resources, a supportive educational setting, positive role models, and organizational opportunities, indigenous chimaltecos can successfully negotiate these contradictory messages and follow the path of Maya empowerment. However, many others find a path of least resistance in practices of assimilation, made more attractive by the promise of universal rights.

With the rise of neoliberal multiculturalism in the 1990s, an inversion of racial ideologies in the making since the 1960s came into view. Before, most ladino power holders vehemently defended the separate and unequal ideology, while the state weakly evinced a discourse of universal equality. Today the state weakly promotes the notion of differentiated citizenship in the name of multiculturalism, while provincial ladinos express ambivalence: wanting to respect Maya cultural rights, but preferring the comfort of assimilationist politics that keep their own racial privilege firmly intact. The inversion is incomplete given the internal contradictions of neoliberal multiculturalism, including the state's lack of resolve for its own enunciated doctrine. Too many powerful ladinos remain unconvinced; the risk of a mobilized Maya population that overflows the carefully limited notion of multicultural rights appears too great; the ruling bloc is too divided to vigorously advance *any* single political project on cultural rights. Meanwhile, Maya efflorescence continues, partially backed by state-endorsed multiculturalism; these combined forces of change leave ladinos in Chimaltenango unsettled, apprehensive, and deeply ambivalent.

Ladinos Chimaltecos and Multicultural Governance

Disjunctures between central government and provincial ladino elites are a recurring theme in the past half-century of Guatemalan history. The architects of social democratic reforms during the 1944–1954 period promoted a left-inflected project of universal rights and cultural assimilation, only to meet with resistance from powerful sectors in places like Chimaltenango loath to give up either the "separate" or the "unequal" parts of the existing ideology toward Indians. The Guatemalan military, with ample backing from the United States, ended this experiment, and then became the unlikely heirs of a different assimilationist thrust, nominally egalitarian, and brutally authoritarian rather than democratic. At the end of the 1980s, just when a coherent mode of governance seemed to have emerged—emphasizing cultural equality, assimilation, and a universalist nation-building ideology—that project was eclipsed by the ascendancy of neoliberal multiculturalism. National-level proponents of multiculturalism could never have advanced this alternative alone: they received ample support from powerful donor governments and multilateral institutions. Similarly, Maya cultural activists would barely have been able to lift their collective heads, had it not been for the array of unlikely power allies, from "modernizing" national elites, to western embassies and development organizations, the same ones who, wearing other hats, have supported neoliberal economic reform across the region.

Finding themselves caught in the middle of these opposing currents of change, many ladino power holders in Chimaltenango have come to embody the ambivalence that the crosscurrents represent. They generally support a weak version of the multicultural ideal—mutual respect, equality, minimal concessions of rights to cultural difference—that papers over fears of the Maya efflorescence and seeks some form of assimilation that would dispense with the problem of politicized cultural difference altogether. Many express irritation and concern with the international community's ardent support and funding for Maya culture, identity, and rights. They might find reassurance in the likes of Father Roberto, Cristóbal, and Colonel Cifuentes, even while echoing critiques of the army and, to a lesser extent, the church. Although ladino power holders do continue to have privileged ties—of kinship, political, or economic association—to the state, these carry diminishing weight as Mayas become more prominent in local politics, and as the new sources of productive wealth draw increasingly on capital from outside the department. Concentrated in the municipios that have not thoroughly "mayanized," Chimaltenango ladinos continue to hold their own, but in pale reflection of their golden era of the 1960s, generally beleaguered by the changes thrust upon them.

Without discounting broader forces of change, in the chapters that follow I explore the fate of ladino-Maya relations focusing on local sensibilities and state effects in one locale. I demonstrate that most ladinos chimaltecos deeply wish to eliminate classic racism, without ceding racial privilege. The ideology of disciplinary assimilation that prevailed during the previous decade of counterinsurgency governance, and that remains pervasive in the likes of Cristóbal, Colonel Cifuentes, and Father Roberto, might well have provided a solution to their dilemma: a vision of a future Guatemala "without Mayas or ladinos," where the dominant culture norm would be smuggled back in as the universal standard. Yet as the decade of the 1990s unfolded, the credibility of this universalist vision steadily eroded. Maya activists had taken the principle of respect for cultural difference much further, with support and encouragement from powerful international forces. The transition was still incomplete by the end of the 1990s, but there was little doubt that multiculturalism would be ascendant. We might understand this coexistence of disciplinary assimilation and multiculturalism as an expression of "residual" and "emergent" tendencies, to use the terms that literary theorist Raymond Williams laid out in his classic Gramscian text (1977). From a different angle, we might also observe how these two seemingly contradictory ideologies combine to make governance all the more effective: multiculturalism opens space for cultural recognition and equality, while disciplinary assimilation helps keep that space strictly limited. This interpretation would certainly seem to apply when army spokesmen wax eloquent about respecting indigenous culture in one breath and emit frightening warnings of an imminent race war in the next. This awkward coexistence at the level of state ideologies, in turn, echoes and reinforces the racial ambivalence of ladinos chimaltecos: they embrace cultural equality, while harboring deep anxieties that all this change could go too far.

three
Reclaiming the Future of Chimaltenango's Past: Contentious Memories of Indigenous Politics during the Revolutionary Years, 1976–1982

> The claims of the [Haitian] revolution were indeed too radical to be formulated in advance of its deeds. Victorious practice could assert them only after the fact. In that sense, the revolution was indeed at the limits of the thinkable, even in Saint-Dominique, even among the slaves, even among its own leaders.
>
> —*Michel-Rolph Trouillot,* Silencing the Past *(1995)*

Héctor's mother Rosario was "disappeared" from their home in Chimaltenango, early in 1980. Armed agents of the state broke into the house, restrained his father, and dragged Rosario away as Héctor and his brothers watched, cowering from behind a half-closed door. Whether for fear of further retribution, anguish, or some other reason, Héctor's father abruptly closed down and banished the topic from the household. Héctor grew up never talking about his mother with anyone; years later, as a young adult, he learned of his father's tireless efforts to determine Rosario's whereabouts, documented in a stack of letters, petitions, and entreaties to government authorities, all in vain. It was not until the early 1990s, when Héctor met Elena and entered the warm, supportive, and unusually communicative inner space of the Valencia extended family that he began to talk freely of what happened, bringing suppressed memories into conversation, and breaking the imposed silence. The young couple had the tragedy of losing a parent in common. On 26 June 1984 Yolanda learned that her husband Alejandro had been abducted, badly beaten, and left for dead on the side of the road between Chimaltenango and Antigua. Alejandro died the next day in the Chimaltenango hospital. Although it was far from clear that the killing had been politically motivated, Yolanda had sufficiently left-leaning sympathies to assume and fear the worst. She gathered her three children and left immediately for the New York area to live with a relative. They returned less than a year later when the immediate danger had passed, but lived the next few years in the shadow of fear, uncertainty, disorientation, and grief. Even by the early 1990s when Héctor entered the family, talk of such matters only occurred around the kitchen table among family and friends; the thought of public "memory work" must still have seemed remote.[1]

During the period of revolutionary mobilization, marked roughly by the dates of these two deaths in the Valencia family, people in Chimaltenango saw their world turned upside down. State violence against civilian activists and leaders had begun in earnest by 1978, and would grow more widespread and brutal in this period; but in 1980 none of the many permanent army bases had yet been established, and none of the dozens of massacres carried out by the army had yet occurred. The rising tide of political violence had sown terror in the population, and had driven the most threatened into exile or to clandestine politics; but terror was still apt to give way to anger, repudiation, and greater militancy. Many in the departmental capital responded in this way to the news on the morning of 14 October 1980 that two armed men had killed their mayor. The next day they formed a massive funeral procession that followed the body of José Lino Xoyón—a young, charismatic teacher and psychologist, and the first Indian mayor in Chimaltenango's history—to the cemetery expressing "profound indignation" along the way.[2] Mobilization against the regime, by this time overwhelmingly indigenous, inevitably took on a racial character. Many ladinos feared a day of reckoning, when centuries of race and class accounts would be settled; indigenous participants, many deeply influenced by Catholic doctrine, had ample basis to believe that now, finally, the poor would inherit the earth.

The Ejército Guerrillero de los Pobres (Guerrilla Army of the Poor, or EGP) publicly announced its new military front on 19 July 1981, the second anniversary of the Sandinista Revolution in Nicaragua, and christened it with that revolution's namesake. A burst of political-military activity followed, including the brief occupation of most municipio town centers, the blocking of the Pan-American Highway, and military training (often without arms) in remote rural hamlets of the area.[3] Within eight months, the Frente Guerrillero Agusto César Sandino (FGACS) had been decimated. On 17 November 1981 General Romeo Lucas García, Guatemala's president, began a massive counterinsurgency campaign; some 15,000 troops marched northward on the Pan-American Highway and made Chimaltenango their first stop.[4] At that time the FGACS marshaled some 150 trained soldiers, loosely connected to the thousands of indigenous peasants who had organized to fight the army, had clamored for arms, but received none. After a very few battles the FGACS acknowledged defeat and retreated to the more remote and better fortified Quiché department to the north. This left the army free to establish bases in nearly every municipio of Chimaltenango, and to begin the carnage: the army committed some forty-two massacres in Chimaltenango over the next year.[5] By the end of 1982, thousands of chimaltecos had formally "surrendered" to the army, submitting to resettlement in "model villages," obligatory service in 24-hour civil patrols, and strict political quiescence on pain of death. In February 1982, when the four guerrilla organizations finally managed to put aside their differences and form the Unidad Revolucionaria Nacional Guatemalteca (Guatemalan National Revolutionary Unity, or URNG), the "revolution" in Chimaltenango was already over.

So brief was this episode of guerrilla-led mobilization, and so devastatingly brutal the aftermath, that contextualized oral accounts of what happened have been—until recently—very difficult to elicit. Fear, trauma, mistrust, disillusionment, and, perhaps most important, shifts in political consciousness have conspired to keep that year, and its immediate antecedents, shrouded in silence or dismissed in formulaic statements about "the violence."[6] Inside Guatemala, the government filled this void with its own "official story," which—at least in its initial blatantly self-justifying form—gained complicity but little credibility. Outside Guatemala, narratives of this period remained the province of guerrilla-aligned intellectuals and their iconic texts (most notably, *I, Rigoberta Menchú*[7]) and, equally important, of academics who wrote from within this narrative frame. Such accounts generally made scarce reference to the guerrilla itself, whether out of naïveté or security-minded prudence: they told a standard story of social mobilization, followed by selective state repression, followed by deepened mobilization, ending with a genocidal army rampage. Between these images— grassroots politics as streams leading inevitably to "*el gran caudal*" (the mighty river) of revolutionary fervor versus the government's bald assertion that indigenous supporters of the revolution had been manipulated by outside "subversives"—there was virtually no middle ground.

The imposed silence in Héctor's household, though perhaps extreme, formed part of this broader pattern. When I first visited Guatemala in 1988, two years after the "return to democracy," Rigoberta Menchú's testimony could not be found in the bookstores, the Left was still a taboo topic, and "la violencia" still lacked a boundary that separated it clearly from the present. Even in 1993, after the peace negotiations were well underway, people did not talk openly of their involvements during those critical years, especially if this included a guerrilla past. Although reticence was borne largely of fear, conflicted loyalties and outright perplexity came into play as well. Many ladino families I knew that included someone of strong affinities with the Left also included family members with sharply contrasting alignments. This often provided a safety net of sorts, a contradictory recourse to race-class privilege, generally disdained but still welcomed in times of need. Such advantages, unavailable to the vast majority of Indians in the line of fire, formed a standard part of many ladino families' survival strategies. At times perplexity could deepen these divided loyalties. To this day, the death and whereabouts of Héctor's mother have not been clarified. Conflicting theories abound. According to one rumor that circulated in the late 1990s, Rosario's disappearance had been staged, a dissimulated kidnapping to disguise her flight to join the guerrillas. The version of this rumor that I heard began with evidence suggesting that, "*esa patoja estaba metida en algo*" (that young woman was mixed up in something), followed by the report that, many years later, someone supposedly saw Rosario in a furtive encounter during market day in a highland Indian town.[8] Héctor still holds the government responsible, but for his older brother Tomás these seeds of doubt may have helped justify his starkly divergent political sensibilities and career path: as soon as Tomás had the opportunity, he joined the army.

By the end of the 1990s, with the Peace Accords signed and the "reintegration" of the guerrillas into civilian life near complete, memories finally began to flow more freely. There appeared a series of memoirs of time spent with the guerrilla, written by people who continue to have public profiles in the present.[9] In June 1998, at an event honoring Mario Payeras, Arturo Taracena Arriola, a prominent historian and former member of the diplomatic commission of the URNG, spoke publicly for the first time, with great eloquence, about his early years with the guerrilla. At around the same time, Chimaltenango received its own *reducto* (enclave) of demobilized guerrilla fighters, housed in a large open space belonging to a Maya NGO, trying to start their lives anew with pitifully inadequate assistance from higher authorities. The taboo finally began to lift, permitting uneven, guarded, but increasingly open discussion of previously prohibited topics. Epitomizing this new phase in Guatemalan history, the Valencia family took on a new member. Gerardo, a physician with a wry sense of humor, a gentle manner, and a bitingly critical analysis of Guatemalan society, had joined the guerrilla in the early 1980s and spent a good part of the decade dispensing medical care to guerrilla combatants and their civilian supporters in the jungle. Worn out and disillusioned by the growing chasm between his convictions and what the URNG had become, Gerardo left in 1994 and spent the next five years in three different countries, carrying on his vocation for politically engaged medical care. In 1997, Gerardo returned to his father's home in Chimaltenango; soon thereafter Gerardo and Yolanda, who had known each other as young adults twenty-five years earlier, fell in love and began to live together.

Although the taboo no longer reigns, chimaltecos—Maya and ladino alike—have barely begun the more substantive, empowering process of fully reclaiming their recent past. Homecomings, reencounters, efforts at documentation, and newly opened spaces for collective memories all contribute to this same end, but they face obstacles and limits. In large part, the limits are imposed by powerful forces that have begrudgingly allowed the memory work to proceed, on the implicit condition that it remains disarticulated from political organizing and action in the present. That message, transmitted loud and clear with the brutal assassination of Monseñor Gerardi in April 1998, was lost on no one. However, the limits also reflect the absence of alternative narrative frames, which could guide people's efforts to interpret their memories of thoughts and actions before the terrible period of political violence began, and to connect these with challenges and aspirations in the present. Even after the work of the two "truth commissions" at the century's end, most publicly legitimated and widely circulating interpretations of the crucial period in question were ones that had emerged from the violence itself. These interpretations have blocked people's efforts to engage in memory work because they offer so little access to processes *before* the worst of the violence began, and because they reproduce the very polarization that the violence wrought. These blockages, in turn, tend to reinforce the emergent mode of governance in Guatemala, which I have called neoliberal multiculturalism. If neoliberal multiculturalism prevails, it will do so not only by remaking racial hierarchies in the present, but also by keeping a tight grip on memories of cultural politics in key periods of the past.

The analysis in this chapter is intended to help loosen that grip, clearing space for fresh interpretations of one key period in Chimaltenango's recent history, and by extension, of Guatemalan society more generally. It draws on fine-grained empirical research, carried out jointly with Marcie Mersky.[10] As we worked together to reconstruct political events, processes, and sensibilities in Chimaltenango between 1976 and 1982, we came to the conclusion that people were engaging in politics in ways that existing accounts do not fully depict, much less explain. Our effort goes beyond the empirical, calling into question the narrative frames that emerged from this period of intense conflict, and which in turn have come to guide interpretations of what happened and why. Our central contention is that existing interpretations, produced from within each narrative frame, do not come to terms with the radical heterogeneity of political consciousness among indigenous chimaltecos who took part in the mobilization. To the contrary, each narrative frame rests on certain categories of consciousness (for example, a distinction between Maya cultural rights and popular or class demands) and certain political distinctions (for example, separating the Maya movement from the Left), which later came to appear entirely self-evident, but which had not yet come to predominate during the volatile and heady years between 1976 and 1981.

I use the term "narrative frame" without great theoretical pretension, in reference to the underlying premises that guide interpretations of the past, and to the material conditions that make a given interpretation possible in the first place. I juxtapose each of three narrative frames—provisionally named revolutionary triumphalism, *dos demonios* (two devils), and mayanista vindication—with a distinct phase of political mobilization between 1976 and 1982. I examine each narrative frame through an epitomizing text, taken not as a self-contained intellectual product but as a window on a general standpoint and, more specifically, as a guide to answering central questions: Why did indigenous chimaltecos mobilize so extensively in this period? What motivated their struggles, and what did they hope to achieve? Having explored the workings of these three narrative frames, I then examine their relationship to the political sensibilities of ladinos chimaltecos today. In particular, I associate the dos demonios narrative frame with ladino racial ambivalence, showing how this stance toward the past converges with the widespread desire to grant rights to cultural equality and recognition without eliminating racial hierarchy or ceding racial privilege.

Finally, I reflect on the relationship between efforts to rethink Chimaltenango history and the political conditions that might encourage a new narrative frame to emerge and flourish. Michel-Rolph Trouillot (1995) lays the groundwork for addressing this last question, but in my view stops short of the crux. Trouillot draws a basic distinction between "history" and the "narration of history" and argues that the former is only accessible through the latter. He urges us to devote systematic attention to how a given narration of history (or in my terms here, a narrative frame) comes into being, viewing it as a historical product in its own right. He does not elaborate on the corollary: one way to help imagine and defend an emergent political position in the present is to articulate its associated narrative frame, and give voice to the novel interpretations of the past that follow. Marcie and I explicitly conceived of our collaboration in this way. The more we examined the period in question, the more we found sensibilities parallel to those that have inspired our own political convictions over the past twenty years. The dead cannot be brought back to life and, in many cases, such as that of Héctor's mother Rosario, the details of their demise may never be clarified. What can be recuperated are the political sensibilities that led people into struggle in the first place, a past no longer subject to shame or suppression, a past that might even serve as a source of inspiration and guidance for the future.

Revolutionary Triumphalism

The history and central premises of revolutionary triumphalism, as a general, Latin American narrative frame, are well known. Nowhere in Latin America does this narrative frame have such a discrete and traumatic moment of inception than in Guatemala. The US-orchestrated coup in 1954 had a profound formative influence on the political calculus and content of what would become Guatemala's discourse of the national-popular: as reformist paradise lost, as definitive proof of US imperial designs, and also, increasingly, as touchstone in the argument that reform through electoral democracy could never prosper. The military-controlled, socially regressive state installed in 1954 would later be cited as the direct and immediate impetus for the initial formation of a guerrilla movement in 1961. This argument would be consummated in the late 1970s when operatives of the same repressive state brutally assassinated Manuel Colom Argueta and Alberto Fuentes Mohr, two immensely popular proponents of reform through electoral democracy. During the intervening years (1961–1979)—a period before the worst of state violence began—hundreds of activists, intellectuals, and advocates of reform lost their lives to state repression. From 1954 on, key political topics of the 1944–1954 "democratic spring"—agrarian reform, civil and labor rights, national defiance of US imperialism—remained at the margins of public discourse; in official accounts they came to be associated with subversive politics.

The specific place of indigenous people within this narrative frame—at least in Guatemala—remains understudied and hotly contested. Early statements by guerrilla leaders such as Ricardo Ramírez (whose nom de guerre was Rolando Morán) lend support to both sides in this debate. In 1969 Ramírez wrote:

> All these historically convergent conditions have turned indigenous peoples
> into carriers of an enormous revolutionary potential, which, guided correctly
> (with proletarian ideology) and with a sufficiently dynamic and unifying polit-

ical process (revolutionary war), will become the decisive element, not only in the liberation of our country in revolutionary triumph, but also in the future configuration of the Guatemalan nation.[11]

On the one hand, this statement shows how early intellectuals of the Left recognized the Indians' revolutionary potential. On the other hand, this same quotation dramatizes the remarkably unselfconscious assumption that Indians could only be emancipated under the leadership, and in accordance with the political vision, of more enlightened leaders.[12] In the narrative frame of revolutionary triumphalism, struggle around axes of cultural difference is pre-political, in need of an infusion of "perspective" and guidance to realize its full potential.[13] A purportedly eloquent example of this pre-political deficit among indigenous chimaltecos, with a disastrously reactionary outcome, is the Frente de Integración Nacional (Front for National Integration or FIN). A closer look at the FIN reveals both the analytical power of this revolutionary narrative frame and the alternative readings that it serves actively to suppress.

The Frente de Integración Nacional, 1976–1978

The FIN rose and fell just before the intense polarization began; indeed its very presence in the political arena suggests a pluralism and toleration of dissent that would soon become inconceivable. The 1974 election of Fernando Tezagüic Tohon as legislator from the department of Sololá for the Partido Revolucionario (Revolutionary Party or PR)—one of the first indigenous legislators—served as a catalyst for the FIN's creation.[14] Rafael Téllez, a leading PR politician, recruited Tezagüic as a counterweight to the rising success of the Christian Democrats (DC) among indigenous voters in this region.[15] According to one FIN activist, Téllez made no effort to disguise his disdain: "He said, this 'Fernandito' will be my 'gopher,' he will follow my orders...."[16] Tezagüic remained pliant until after the election, and then quickly proved to be no one's office boy. Using his legislative seat as a platform, he denounced abuses of indigenous labor and civil rights; in response to criticism from the political establishment (including his own party) in June 1976 he founded Patinamit, which began as a group of indigenous professionals formed to support his legislative agenda and by November had become a "committee to form a political party" with the name FIN. In April 1977, at the FIN's request in anticipation of the upcoming elections, Tezagüic announced his decision to resign from the PR and pledged allegiance to the FIN, "[For] the future of my people, who are the ones that elected me to the position that I presently occupy."[17] To the great dismay of most ladino politicians, Tezagüic promised that by the March 1978 elections, FIN affiliates would grow to a million and a half strong.[18]

Even adjusting for predictable hysteria and overreaction, the level of invective and opposition from the ladino establishment suggests that the FIN had become a serious political force. Moderates, such as Jorge Carpio Nicolle, and right-wing stalwarts alike weighed in with a curiously contradictory set of arguments: on the one hand, the FIN's likely electoral success would yield grave threats to the social peace, an upsurge of racism and ethnic conflict, and so on and, on the other hand, a party comprised solely of indígenas was not capable of managing its own affairs.[19] In the face of such intense opposition, which dashed hopes for an affirmative response to the legalization petition in time for the March 1978 elections, FIN leaders opted to negotiate with established political parties. They turned first to the DC, with two principal demands: seats for FIN leaders in the legislature, and swift action on legalization of the FIN after the election. Although promising at first, these negotiations soon foundered. In September 1977, in protest over the DC's lack of responsiveness, the FIN withdrew support and called on its affiliates to abstain from the upcoming elections.

In strange contrast to the nearly daily press coverage in the previous period, there ensued five months of silence, broken in mid-February with news of a contentious meeting in Chimaltenango to discuss a decision to support presidential hopeful General Romeo Lucas García. On February 18, in a rally at the Maya ruins of Iximché, FIN leaders made this endorsement public and, reportedly, received a promise for legal recognition in return. Lucas "won" the elections in March and the Electoral Commission formally denied the recognition petition in September; over the next four years state repression decimated the organization.[20] By 1982, of the twenty-two people whose names appeared in news reports on the FIN during its two years of activity, at least twelve would be dead or disappeared and three would be living in exile. As Maxia grimly concludes: "[Lucas] gave us full support in submitting our application to the Electoral Commission, to be recognized as a political party, and then used our lists to identify and kill us, one by one."[21]

A Revolutionary Reading of the FIN's Demise

In a late 1978 issue of the journal *Estudios Centroamericanos* devoted entirely to Guatemala, Ricardo Falla published an essay titled "El movimiento indígena" (The Indigenous Movement) and took the FIN as his primary focus of analysis.[22] A Jesuit priest and one of Guatemala's leading intellectuals, Falla received his doctorate in anthropology from the University of Texas in 1976. Until the late 1970s, Falla taught political science at the Catholic Landívar University and played a formative role in the Jesuits' research and social action program, conducted under the auspices of the Centro para Investigación y Acción Social (Center for Research and Social Action or CIAS), informally known as the "Zone 5 house" where the Jesuits lived. Much of the work of those associated with CIAS focused on the indigenous communities of Chimaltenango, especially after the earthquake of February 1976 devastated the area. Falla chose his topic well for this essay, which combined sustained theoretical reflection on the "ethnic question," with a powerful object lesson in how to achieve meaningful social change in Guatemala at that time. Although the FIN's fateful "pact with the devil" hangs over the analysis like a dark cloud, and imbues the central argument with an air of undeniability, Falla writes little about it. Instead, he proceeds to trace in methodical detail the FIN's every step, pausing periodically to draw from narrative evidence to substantiate a broader analytical point. The pact with Lucas serves only to seal an argument already carefully woven through this prior analysis.

Falla's essay poses a central question: given present conditions, is it politically practical and theoretically justifiable for indigenous people to organize separately as a group to achieve collective rights, fight discrimination, and generally improve their life conditions? He answers with a definitive "no," grounding his answer in both theoretical reflection and political analysis.[23] The indigenous people and culture that some portray as unified is actually rife with divisions, he argues; each competing faction had a distinct power base of its own. Indigenous peoples cannot be discussed while ignoring these factions, any more than one can speak of the Guatemalan nation without acknowledging class divisions that in practice leave the majority excluded. The FIN represents one such faction, which over the course of its existence opted consistently for struggle from within the dominant bloc. Another group of indigenous people opted for alignment with the subordinate bloc, consisting of "national organizations that represent the interests of the oppressed and struggle for their liberation" (1978:460). Falla's purpose in drawing this distinction—he repeatedly insists—is not to discourage indigenous collective action, but rather to argue that the content and efficacy of this action changes depending on broader political alignments. "In the strict sense of the word," Falla writes, "there is only one nation, which is Guatemala, which coincides with the State and the forces that oppose the State" (1978:460). However profound the chasm between the dominant and subordinate blocs, they share a single national identity. The FIN, in contrast, appears to orient its struggle "against the structure of the nation, as nation" (1978:457), which makes them vulnerable to attack from both sides. In the face of such pressure, it follows that the FIN would settle for a struggle for rights and redress from *within* the dominant bloc. This move, Falla concludes, is at best ill-conceived and futile and at worst incoherent and corrupt.

Finding a Place in History for the FIN

Falla's essay stood the test of time so well in part because of its persuasive acuity, and in part because the revolutionary narrative frame is so analytically powerful; but also, it has endured due to the closing of political space from which alternative accounts might have emerged. In the five years following the elections of March 1978, polarization grew acutely, and state violence took its toll even on those who attempted to stake out political ground in opposition to the regime but unaligned with the guerrilla. Guatemalan society, in short, took on precisely the dichotomous contours that Falla describes. Twenty years later, key surviving FIN leaders and others who remember have found their voices; scattered documents from the era have appeared; contemporary political sensibilities (for example, renewed interest in the formation of an indigenous political party) have posed new questions to existing materials. This reexamination yields data that does not fit readily into the overarching image of two dichotomous and bounded political groupings; it reveals more internal debate within the FIN, and less subservience to the dominant bloc, than Falla's portrayal would lead us to believe.

For example, in the interview cited earlier Marcial Maxia made a series of statements that do not fit well within the established picture. The group of urban-dwelling Indian intellectuals who later would form Patinamit apparently had been meeting informally for a decade, sizing up different possibilities for political action. They gathered secretly to listen with great enthusiasm to radio reports of Castro's advances in Cuba and they considered joining the Guatemalan guerrilla movement in the early 1960s but decided against it because, as Maxia put it, "they never take indigenous people into account." During that era Maxia met with César Montes, a leader in the 1960s guerrilla movement, and developed a friendship that continues to this day. In discussions of the CUC (which figured prominently in Falla's scheme as an organization that *did* struggle on the side of the *pueblo oprimido* [oppressed masses]), Maxia refused to acknowledge the political chasm: We had the same goals, he insisted, "the CUC leaders and the FIN leaders were one and the same."[24] Further indications come from news coverage of the FIN's public statements and demands. Although portrayed at the time, and remembered subsequently, as an *indianista*[25] (Indianist) party, the FIN consistently defended positions now associated with the "popular movement."[26] Tezagüic began his legislative career calling attention to abuses of rights among peasants of the Quiché, and demanding improvements in working conditions for migrant workers in coastal plantations. The FIN followed suit. Its inner circle included grassroots activists like Jesus Chacach of San José Poaquíl, and politicians like José Lino Xoyón, who ran successfully for mayor of Chimaltenango on a platform that included many elements of this pueblo oprimido discourse. Could it be that the great divide between these two political blocs had not yet fully taken shape?

Quite apart from relations with others, FIN leaders themselves evinced a diversity and complexity of political thought that belies their characterization as misguided indianistas. Participants engaged in serious and sustained internal debates over the role of militant Indianist identity and demands within the organization and, in most cases, moderates appear to have carried the day. Maxia remembers having to argue against the "recalcitrants" in the organization who wanted to exclude ladinos; Tezagüic still winces at the memory of severe criticisms he received in 1976 from hot-headed young Maya activists like Demetrio Cojtí, who considered him assimilationist for his moderate stance on Indian rights, and fainthearted for his inclination to rule out armed struggle. Genaro Xoyón recounts how his brother did battle with the "mayanistas":

> He told them, "are eyeglasses part of Maya culture? If we want to be Indians
> and true only to ourselves, very well gentlemen, let's take off our eyeglasses,
> even if that means we cannot see well, at least we'll be Indian...let's not use
> anything ladino, because the ladino is our enemy and let's take off our shoes
> and go barefoot." He really put it to them in a forceful way.[27]

Finally, and most directly in contrast with Falla's characterization of the FIN as struggling against the nation, FIN leaders themselves took great pains to end each and every stanza of political rhetoric with a nationalist refrain.[28]

At the level of public discourse, in response to a daunting volume of racist invective from the ladino establishment, FIN leaders maintained an unflinching pro-indigenous position, appealing to common human values, citing the Constitution, criticizing ambiguities in ladino identity, but always returning to the fundamental goals of affirmation and ascendancy of indigenous peoples: "Let us struggle in a unified way, to assign value to the most important group in this society."[29] Pressure from ladino politicians did constrain the fledgling organization, beginning with the name itself: in response to the argument that a party solely for indigenous people violated the Constitution's antidiscrimination clause, they changed the meaning of the "I" from *indígena* to *integración* (integration). Similarly, the decision to negotiate with traditional political parties followed from the refusal, almost surely on racial grounds, of accreditation as a political party. Given this pressure, it may not be warranted to conclude as definitively as Falla did that these moves reflected shifts in core principles.[30] Tezagüic claims that they changed the "I" simply to meet criticism, while their primary commitments to indígenas remained unchanged. Subsequent public statements meant to welcome ladino participation in the party usually came with a crucial qualifier, "but in keeping with indigenous ways."[31] Even the pact with Lucas had an underlying political logic, which had worked well for Tezagüic in 1974: "Our idea was that once in the Congress, the indigenous candidates could resign from the party and form an independent indigenous caucus."[32] They didn't take into account and, perhaps, could not have known that political conditions conducive to such a strategy in 1974 had all but disappeared.

This rereading of the evidence yields a considerably different portrait of the FIN than that of Falla: that is, as an organization that waged a consistent struggle against cultural oppression, through a strategy of electoral politics, at a time just before the dichotomy between reform and revolution had come into sharp relief. FIN leaders displayed a mixture of indigenous militancy and moderation, of loyalty to a multicultural nation and to indigenous ascendancy, of sympathy for leftist ideas with a specifically indigenous philosophy—mixtures that, a few years later, would be virtually impossible to sustain. Maxia characterized this heterogeneity nicely, in describing three of the principal FIN leaders: "Rolando Baquiax...always stayed involved with the cooperative movement...he was born with the cooperative on the brain; José Pinzón was born with worker syndicates on the brain, and I with Maya spirituality." The same goes for the electoral pact: without discounting the possibility of opportunism and corruption, it has a clear residual logic in light of conditions before 1978, even while appearing utterly irresponsible and foolhardy given all that followed. At the last formal meeting of the FIN, on 19 February 1978 in Chimaltenango, this very issue dominated the agenda. Members of a rebel faction led by Nehemias Cumes of Comalapa voiced dissent and accused FIN leaders of corruption.

In Falla's analysis, Cumes represents the path of political integrity and rectitude that the FIN did not take, and in light of subsequent events one can hardly dispute this conclusion. But in a longer-term historical appraisal, the FIN partly recovers from ignominy and assumes its place in history as an antecedent to the struggles that opened the political system to Mayas. While Falla turns out to have been right that such a struggle could not prosper within the political establishment, his prophetic understanding of history's future course may have limited his grasp of the complexities of the current moment. To focus on these complexities, in turn, casts a different light on the confrontation of 19 February 1978 in Chimaltenango. It offers a glimpse of the moment just before the revolutionary narrative frame acquired full strength: it had been in formation for two decades, of course, but mainly in theory. In contrast, for four years beginning in 1978, this narrative frame would have profound resonance in the actual course of Guatemalan history.

Dos Demonios

Although the meeting at Iximché in February of 1978 sealed the fate of the FIN, indigenous organizing and mobilization in Chimaltenango continued at a feverish pace. Divergent interpretations of this revolutionary period stake out their ground in relation to the key question: Under what conditions did indigenous chimaltecos turn so militantly and massively against the government? Analysts aligned with the regime, of course, have portrayed the mobilization as the direct result of guerrilla manipulation and treachery; their explanation, often laced with overtly racist notions that Indians are incapable of thinking for themselves, leaves no room for discussion.[33] Analyses from within the narrative frame of revolutionary triumphalism generally lacked nuance in their characterizations of indigenous politics. When the Armed Forces emerged victorious at the end of 1982, and began to talk of a return to democracy in 1983, political space for new interpretations began slowly to open. This space had two key defining elements: a cautious critique of Guatemalan Army "excesses" in the heat of the counterinsurgency campaign, and a central need to reconnect with a destitute and traumatized civilian population. Beaten into submission by an army rampage of genocidal proportions, taught that anything even remotely approaching a challenge to the existing political order would bring on horrible death and destruction, the survivors now sought to make sense of the nightmare of the previous few years. Religious mysticism (especially of the Evangelical variety) met that need for some; others took refuge in sullen cynicism. Many others found in the dos demonios idea a reassuring, effective, and convincing source of common sense: a conflict between two military forces, equally self-interested and brutal, both victimizers of civilians caught haplessly in between.

From Theology of Liberation to Teleology of Revolution

By the 1990s, the dos demonios narrative frame had acquired a more sophisticated and elaborate scholarly dimension as well. Among US-based academics, it is closely associated with David Stoll, whose book titled *Between Two Armies* (1993) received moderate attention and generally skeptical reviews. The same thesis attracted spectacular national media attention five years later when Stoll re-presented it as an exposé of Rigoberta Menchú (1999). Yet when the sound and fury around the exposé passed, it became clear that the second book made few empirical and analytical advances relative to the first. A more substantive and sophisticated version of the dos demonios analysis can be found in *La guerra en tierras mayas* (*The War in Maya Lands*), originally published in 1992 by French sociologist Yvon Le Bot (1995).

Le Bot's argument takes shape in four sequential steps, which in turn form the pillars of the dos demonios narrative frame. First, indigenous communities of the altiplano are not pristine or homogeneous; they are run through with divisions that produce constant tensions and periodic outright conflict. For Le Bot, the key division—between *costumbristas* (those loyal to long-standing indigenous cultural practices) and *modernizantes* (modernizers)—is ostensibly religious, but in fact involves core issues of indigenous culture and politics. Such divisions create opportunities for influence by external actors such as the guerrilla. Second, Le Bot narrates a complex story of elective affinity between community-based modernizantes and guerrilla-aligned religious workers; reasoning inflected with religious allusions gave legitimacy to the convergence of guerrilla and community.[34] The third element is brutal and massive state violence, conceived as a systematic effort to eliminate the actual and potential civilian bases of guerrilla support. This repression was indiscriminate. Architects of the scorched earth policy spared neither costumbristas nor evangelicals, and drew no distinction among modernizantes inspired by religious conviction, guerrilla-aligned religious workers, and guerrillas. According to the final step in Le Bot's argument, indigenous participants recoiled in dissent, with the pragmatic realization that the army was by far the stronger side in the conflict and, more important, that the guerrilla leadership never cared a whit for indigenous people in the first place. Le Bot emphasizes the racial dimension of this drama: "This war was imposed on the Indians; they did not want it…the commanders and the decision makers were always ladinos; the strategy, the objectives, and the logic of the revolutionary struggle was not formulated by the Indians themselves" (1995:288).

Beyond the Injerto (Graft): Probing Indigenous Agency

Le Bot's assertive conclusion that the war was imposed on the Indians encapsulates the great appeal of the dos demonios narrative frame, but also signals the anomalies that it brings to the fore. In the hands of Le Bot, the dos demonios narrative portrays indigenous community members as active, thoughtful agents—with their own political aspirations, and in control, at least initially, of their own destiny. Le Bot refers to this collective political energy as a "movement of modernization and emancipation of indigenous society" (1995:180), sharply distinguished from ladino-controlled revolutionary orthodoxy. He intends to vindicate this indigenous emancipatory vision, to advance a searing critique of ladino racism, and at the same time to echo contemporary community-level political sensibilities of fear, mistrust, and exasperation with all ladino outsiders, whatever their political-ideological affinities. The use of biological idioms to explain why this distinctively indigenous political vision lost its way, helps Le Bot to absolve indigenous actors themselves of responsibility for mistaken allegiances: the modernizantes underwent a "mutation" as their (local, indigenous) initiative became grafted (*se injertó*) to the (external, ladino-controlled) revolutionary movement. Yet this line of explanation leaves crucial questions unanswered. At what point in the mobilization underway does this injerto actually take hold? Where does one draw the line between a political initiative truly grounded in Mayan culture and one that has been hijacked by the ladino Left? A brief anecdote will help to ground this question. Enrique Corral, Jesuit priest turned EGP commander, describes an early encounter with an Indian catechist from Parramos, Chimaltenango, in 1976:

> First I had some contacts, but they were not organized. I started talking
> with a senior community leader in Parramos, a rural indigenous man. It was
> Christmas day, 1976, we were eating tamales, having some drinks, and enjoy-
> ing ourselves. After a while he said, "Look, when are you going to bring us
> weapons?" That's exactly what the man said; it was completely unexpected for
> me. He was a respected *catequista*, a man with great authority in his commu-
> nity. I said to myself, these people are expecting something to happen.

Although Corral's perspective remains firmly embedded within the revolutionary narrative frame, the anecdote speaks for itself. It would be extremely hard to discern whether this catechist was already subject to the injerto or whether he was still a protagonist of *"emancipación india."*

At least in Chimaltenango, this line of inquiry presents the dos demonios narrative with a major interpretive dilemma: either the widespread civilian mobilization prior to widespread militarization (November 1980) was already the product of guerrilla influence, or it was an expression of what Le Bot calls community-based initiatives of emancipación india. The former seems highly implausible. This would assign an exaggerated influence to a handful of radicalized religious workers and other cadre, and downplay the numerous settings where organizing occurred in the absence of guerrilla tutelage. Yet the alternative argument—that the militancy arose from "community-based initiatives of emancipación india"—leaves Le Bot no way to register the profound and multiple influences on indigenous political thought in the late 1970s: from radical *latinoamericanista* ideologies to classic liberal notions of citizenship; from economic communitarianism in the Marxist tradition to mainstream western models of cooperatives. In essence, the dos demonios frame obliges Le Bot to erect a rigid boundary between emancipación india and western-inflected radical traditions when the actors themselves repeatedly crossed this boundary, combined seemingly disparate elements, and pushed existing ideas to new forms, spurred on by a general and diffuse sense that radical political change was imminent.

Figure 3.1. Chimaltenango City Council, 1978. From the left: Jose Lino Xoyón, unidentified woman, unidentified man, Enrique Salazar, unidentified woman, Don Cheo Caná, unidentified man. Photo in the possession of Don Cheo Caná.

José Lino Xoyón (figure 3.1), who galvanized municipio-level politics in Chimaltenango between 1978 and 1980, illustrates the problem: local ladino power holders considered him a dangerous indigenous radical, while some indigenous activists claimed that he had abandoned Maya culture. He combined a discourse of indigenous rights and cultural pride with the populist rhetoric of class empowerment; by the time he was killed in October 1980, Xoyón had won rapt attention from all sides and the overwhelming support of the indigenous majority. Did Don José Lino embody the movement of emancipación india? Or did his populist charisma arise from an early case of the guerrilla injerto? Neither seems accurate, and the same goes for many other indigenous leaders of that period who defied the neatly bounded political categories on which the dos demonios narrative frame depends.

The case of José Lino Xoyón raises another question that cuts to the core of the dos demonios dilemma. Throughout his study, Le Bot conveys the impression that he can identify true and authentic expressions of Maya culture, which in turn makes him certain about when the injerto has occurred. In the community-level division between costumbristas and modernizantes, for example, Le Bot portrays the former as the true reservoir of lo maya, and the latter as walking a fine line between exploring new ideas and assimilation to the ladino. This is what makes the modernizantes so susceptible to "mutation" when guerrilla cadres come around. Whatever doubts such an assessment might provoke, they would magnify manifold if Le Bot had attempted to distinguish "Maya" from "ladino-like" characteristics among indigenous people who played influential roles in regional- or national- (as opposed to community-) level politics during the period in question. Curiously enough, these regional/national-level actors are completely absent from Le Bot's account. Neither the FIN nor the Centro Indígena and its newspaper *Ixim*, nor the wave of indigenous mayors elected in 1978, receives as much as a footnote. Although different in many ways, all three embodied distinctly *national* political processes, which at the same time had deep roots in Chimaltenango. All three also epitomized the fluid mixing of political ideologies that Le Bot's analysis keeps carefully cordoned off from one another. Take for example the newspaper *Ixim*. The editorial on the first anniversary describes the effort as "collective property of the indigenous population of the country...the first newspaper that publishes opinions related to the problems of political-economic exploitation and racial-cultural discrimination that the indigenous people suffer" (Coj Ajbalam 1978:366–367). It also insists on a pluralism that soon would become impossible to maintain:

> For the moment the Governing Body of the Newspaper believes that *Ixim* should not impose judgments and points of view, but rather, present the reader with all the possible alternatives in relation to a given problem and let the reader himself decide "HIS VISION AND CONVICTIONS." (1978:368)

Ixim's pages are filled with mayanista perspectives: denouncing the folklorization of Maya culture, insisting on girls' rights to wear Maya clothing in public schools, exposing racism in every facet of the Guatemalan political system. Yet it also regularly published CUC communiqués, and carried analysis with an overtly leftist inflection. The June 1979 editorial (#20–21), titled "Solidaridad con el Pueblo de Nicaragua" (Solidarity with the People of Nicaragua) made this ideological heterogeneity especially clear:

> The Indian peoples of America have risen up, and in this moment we express our solidarity with the struggle of the people of Nicaragua.... May the revolutionary and communitarian spirit of our ancestors become the guiding light in the war against oppression...only with political unity can we follow the path of authentic liberation of the Indian of America, arm in arm with the oppressed of the Third World.

As did the selection of poetry, such as this verse published in the second issue:

Oh! Patrón, pero no sabe	Oh! Patron, you do not know
Que es un miserable rico	How miserable is the rich man
Que se arrastra como la	Who crawls the earth like a
Serpiente que solo infunde	Serpent who only sows

Miedo.	Fear.
Y recuerde patrón que	And remember Patron that
el hierro se oxida.	Iron turns to rust

Analysis that remains within the dos demonios narrative frame ends up relegating political sensibilities like those expressed in *Ixim* to the realm of "nonindigenous" ideology. They are either too influenced by the Left or simply too far removed from community-level Maya existence to have a legitimate place among true aspirations of emancipación india. Although Le Bot does not mention these national-level Maya initiatives, that very omission, combined with generalizations about the character of Maya politics, make the point clearly enough. "As a group," Le Bot concludes, "Indians prefer to remain relatively withdrawn from the national political scene, and recent experience has only confirmed the wisdom of this prudence as a long term [political] strategy" (1995:308). By extension, when Indians contest power in national arenas and draw connections between themselves and non-Indian marginalized groups, they show signs of becoming unauthentic. For Le Bot, Maya culture and politics reside fundamentally and inexorably in the community.

The dos demonios narrative frame traps indigenous people in a fragmented and locality-bound political logic that is only partly of their own making. Its prevalence corresponds in part also to a legacy of colonialism, and to subsequent Republican-era strategies of political control. The more recent counterinsurgency campaign of the 1980s also rested on the none-too-subtle premise that upstart Indians, once reconfined to the community, could be subdued. Military strategists such as Hector Gramajo, and his civilian counterparts such as Vinicio Cerezo, saw in the dos demonios idea a means to disavow state violence and, also, to constitute a pliable community-based Indian subject with whom the state could reestablish political relations. Christian Democrats, ex-president Cerezo explained retrospectively, not only condemned the guerrilla, but also set out to create a

> consciousness [within] the military that their role had been *hipertrofiado* (excessive).... We noted the excessiveness of the army was because security had been converted into the national objective *por Excelencia.* [We said]…that if the army was an institution at the service of stability, it had to submit to the laws, beginning with its own laws. (Quoted in Schirmer 1998:192)

Affirming "excesses" on both sides of the armed conflict left the new regime free to establish a new relationship of democratic accountability with its citizens.[35]

That this new relationship would also affirm a more authentically Mayan subject—in contrast to the deviant who meddled in left-inflected national politics—made the idea all the more attractive. In this specific sense Le Bot, and others who worked within the dos demonios narrative frame, lent the crude reasoning of the National Security Doctrine an air of anthropological sophistication. In so doing, they may well have accurately reflected the widespread disillusionment, cynicism, and fear that had set in as it became clear that the revolution was a lost cause. Yet this emergent narrative frame has become an impediment to our understanding of the mobilization before the counterinsurgency campaign began, when indigenous chimaltecos faced extraordinarily expansive political horizons, and selected liberally from a wide range of ideas that all seemed to affirm the same conclusion: finally, after five hundred years of oppression, they had history on their side.

Mayanista Vindication

Political mobilization continued in Chimaltenango throughout 1981, but now with a distinctly military edge, and against a portentous increase in direct army presence and repression. Many municipio-level ladino power holders fled to the relative safety of Chimaltenango or Guatemala City; those who remained developed alliances, whether out of convenience or conviction, with the army, which had established permanent bases in every important *cabecera municipal* (county seat). Armed guerrilla detachments now commonly made incursions in the department and carried out highly visible actions such as stopping traffic on the Pan-American Highway, burning buses, and attacking police stations. By the end of 1981 the guerrilla had occupied, albeit briefly, every important cabecera municipal in highland Chimaltenango, except El Tejar and Chimaltenango proper. During the occupations of Tecpán and San José Poaquíl they killed the mayors who allegedly had right-wing affinities; in San Martín Jilotepeque they threatened the parish priest, known to have political sympathies with the ladino elite and the army. On the eve of the great counterinsurgency campaign of 17 November 1981, the guerrilla marshaled a tiny number of armed regulars but exerted vast political influence across the department. For the few months before November 1981, revolutionary triumphalism must have appeared wholly reasonable.

This was the period when the greatest number of indigenous chimaltecos joined, or at least developed active sympathies with, the guerrilla. It is virtually impossible to judge the extent of these sympathies since so many were killed, and since the tide turned so quickly. Evidence is emerging, however, to suggest both that many joined and that their loyalty to the cause, as defined by the guerrilla leadership, was far from complete. Hundreds of indigenous activists—organized, committed, and increasingly militant—were galvanized by mayanista analysis and attracted to the emancipatory discourse of the Left, and were just beginning to sort out the relationship between these two as they were swept up in a tidal wave of political-military mobilization. Once inside the guerrilla organizations, they began to probe the possibilities for achieving "Indian emancipation" from within, and met with discouraging results. Some left immediately, others buckled down and accepted the admonition "to wait until after we take power," and still others continued a beleaguered struggle from within. Consider, for example, this statement by a current leader of a Maya organization:

> There was negotiation [between the Mayas and the] guerrilla from the beginning. [The guerrilla] tended to respond: "After we take power." We wanted to

address concepts, raise issues. When the discussion became intense, they would bring up the Miskitu case, accusing us of being counterrevolutionary. There were people persecuted by the Left itself, especially after the document "Federalist Guatemala" of the Tojil Indian movement began to circulate. This document became our guide, together with the slogan "As indios they colonized us, as indios we will liberate ourselves." At some point, the Indigenous Revolutionary Front (FIR) was created; this was a dissident armed group that broke ties with the guerrilla. In response, a phrase emerged from within the Left: "FIR seen is FIR killed." Often we did not know where the repression was coming from. To raise issues we had to negotiate, but in general they did not want to talk. They closed ranks.

The constant "negotiation" points to an indigenous presence with the guerrilla, and an attendant political complexity that two decades later remains one of the great untold stories of Guatemala's revolutionary period.

Although the narrative frame of "mayanista vindication" took shape in response to disillusionment with the ladino Left and indiscriminate violence of the state, the key period of mobilization (1978–1982) does not figure prominently in its associated historical accounts. In striking contrast to both revolutionary triumphalism and dos demonios, the mayanista frame offers no novel interpretations of indigenous mobilization in Chimaltenango (or elsewhere) during those crucial years. In part, security considerations explain this vacuum: mayanista analysis emerged from and occupied the exceedingly fragile political space of Guatemala's return to democracy, in which the line between the acceptable and the "subversive" has been disconcertingly fluid. However, the vacuum also follows from a central premise of the narrative frame itself. Vigorous critique of leftist politics, and sharp differentiation from leftist organizations, became the hallmark of mayanista analysis, especially in the formative years of the late 1980s. This in turn made the period of mobilization—when indigenous political activity was so deeply entwined with the ladino-controlled Left—especially difficult to narrate. The mayanista solution to this dilemma, in general, has been to argue for the trans-historical validity of the key principle that grounds most contemporary (post-violence) organizing: cultural-political autonomy. This means calling forth two common threads in Guatemalan history: struggle, since early colonial times, for rights and resources that would guarantee Maya cultural-political survival; and victimization by a Euro-Guatemalan/ladino state, intent on breaking Maya resistance and imposing its will. The single phrase that most succinctly summarizes mayanista analysis of the period of mobilization and violence (1978 to 1982) is the "third holocaust."[36] In search for antecedents to current organizing efforts, mayanista analysts are much more apt to reach back decades, even centuries, to fix on clear-cut struggles for cultural-political autonomy, than to engage the more ambiguous cases of the FIN and the Indian mayors of 1978, not to mention the "*movimiento Indio Tojil*" (Tojil Indian movement) or the hundreds of indigenous rural dwellers who clamored for arms in San Martín.

The writings of leading Maya intellectual Demetrio Cojtí Cuxil, especially his work *El movimiento Maya* (1997), illustrate nicely the key premises of the mayanista narrative frame. The study unfolds against the backdrop of "internal colonialism," which evokes continuities in the political oppression of Mayas since the sixteenth century, and also defines "anticolonial struggle" as the privileged form of Maya cultural-political resistance. Analysis of the factors giving rise to the contemporary Maya movement follows. The fundamental factors are a Mayan "messianic nationalism" (which since the Conquest has harbored prophesies that one day "the Maya will equal the ladino and surpass him" [Cojtí 1997:56]), and the reality of everyday Maya resistance to ladino colonialism. External influences (for example, broader anticolonial, nationalist, and human rights movements) take on secondary importance, as do such conjunctural factors as democratization and learning from the crucible of the armed conflict. The account of the movement's emergence follows a similar logic. During the period 1972–1978, the movement grows and flourishes, and begins to develop "a well-defined ideology of [its] own, to unify Guatemalan Indians, making indigenous culture first priority, penetrating the high echelons of power" (1997:97). With the democratic opening of 1985 the movement reemerges from the ashes of a war in which "neither the army nor the guerrilla represented the interests of the Maya people," to vigorously denounce the persisting colonial mentality of ladinos of all political stripes, and to re-focus on the central demands of cultural-political autonomy. How, then, to make sense of Maya political consciousness and action during the intervening years from 1978 to 1982?

More than any other mayanista analysis to date, Cojtí does broach this question, tantalizing the reader, but ultimately stopping short of an argument beyond the twin themes of colonial oppression and anticolonial struggle. Cojtí presents the Maya movement and the guerrilla as two bounded and distinct political initiatives that eventually came face-to-face with one another on vastly unequal terrain. "The Maya movement," Cojtí explains, "was too incipient to take a strong stand in relation to one or the other side in the War (guerrilla and army).... Some were forced by circumstances to incorporate themselves into one of the four organizations that comprised the URNG" (1997:100).

Of those Mayas who did join, the narrative continues, some deserted early on over ideological differences; others developed this critical stance more gradually, as they became exposed to the influence of Maya organizations such as the *Movimiento de Ayuda y Acción Solidaria* (Movement for Solidary Aid and Action or MAYAS). Cojtí presents MAYAS as an autonomous, clandestine organization, presumably under the leadership of survivors from the previous moment of independent Maya organizing. As part of this effort, MAYAS circulated a series of "documents of political education," including the text that soon became the focus of clandestine debate, *Guatemala: De la república burguesa centralista a la república popular federal* (*Guatemala: From the Bourgeois Republic to the Popular Federal Republic*). This ideological struggle turned violent. "In Chimaltenango," Cojtí notes, "the guerrilla even reached the extreme of killing members of MAYAS" (1997:103). These conditions stymied the development of the Maya movement, Cojtí concludes, placing its leaders "between two armies, the guerrilla and the army" (1997:103; see also 105).

Despite this apparent convergence of mayanista analysis with the dos demonios narrative frame, the two diverge on crucial points, with consequences that would become dramatically clear by the end of the 1990s. First, from its very inception, mayanista analysis has been predicated on the existence and dynamic growth of a trans-communal Maya culture and political vision, in sharp contrast with the community-bound focus of the dos demonios narrative frame. The socioeconomic and spatial location of mayanista intellectuals themselves drives this point home forcefully. This national-level political vision and positioning leads directly to the second divergence: the mayanistas' strong inclination to reach across political differences within the pueblo Maya, differences that dos demonios analysis takes as definitive. Although mayanista organizations reemerged in the post-violence period under great constraints, "insularity" is certainly not a term that would characterize their trajectories ten to fifteen years later. In some cases, key figures in these organizations have joined forces with their counterparts in the Left; others (and at times even the same leaders!) have agreed to work in governments of the center-right. Coalitions have developed—for example, around the current campaign against racism—that cut across the standard categories of mayanista, left-aligned, and mainstream political actors; clusters of Maya leaders in favor of (and against) the proposal to form an indigenous political party are equally heterogeneous. Even if the stark dichotomy between "emancipación india" and the western-inflected injerto once had some validity—which I doubt—it has failed the test of time.

The mayanista vindication narrative frame leaves many questions unanswered in regard to the crucial years of indigenous mobilization in Chimaltenango. One set of questions revolves around the character of Maya intellectuals' political-ideological engagement with the Left—guerrilla and civilian—during those years. A specific empirical facet of that question is whether MAYAS represented an independent stream of Maya organizing, as Cojtí implies, or whether it emerged through the initiative of Mayas who served in and eventually broke with guerrilla organizations, as other accounts suggest. A deeper interpretive quandary follows. Cojtí's account may well understate the extent to which the post–1985 Maya movement took shape through an intense, contradictory relationship with the Left: at once attracted and repelled, at battle with ideas that already had been profoundly influential in the constitution of their own distinct cultural-political stance. A close reading of the brilliantly polemical text "*Guatemala Federal*," lends credence to this latter interpretation.[37] Its author(s)—whose identities have been kept secret to this day—write about the revolutionary movement with a combination of intimate knowledge and bile that could only come from sitting through hours of revolutionary political "education," and its proposed "federalist" solution clearly bears the stamp of the revolutionary politics it rejects.

A parallel set of concerns arises in relation to the dynamics of grassroots Maya mobilization. On this point Cojtí's analysis falls silent, leaving the reader to infer that Maya peasants followed the same course as the intellectuals: lacking the basis necessary to take a strong stand toward the guerrilla, forced to join, seizing the first opportunity to desert. Here the difficulty of using a mayanista depiction of its own political project to understand the antecedents to that project grows especially evident. The heterogeneity of grassroots Maya political consciousness during the heady years of 1978–1982 does not fit much better into the mayanista narrative frame than it does into the other two. Maya protagonists had motivations that were left inflected and pro-Maya, antiracist, and yet open to alliances with ladinos, pragmatic and utopian, in combinations that proved explosive, if at times mildly contradictory. The inclination to impose an ex post facto coherence on the process undermines the interpretive task at hand.

At one point in his study, Cojtí implicitly acknowledges this problem. Mayan "messianic nationalism," which predominates among "traditional and uneducated Mayan peasants," serves as his explanatory black box: inaccessible to anthropological analysis, in the well-guarded domain of collective memory, messianic prophesies sustain Maya political actions without conforming to any narrative frame (1997:56). Perhaps Cojtí's decision to pass over the mobilization of indigenous chimaltecos between 1978 and 1982 should be taken as an admonition: this was an outburst of messianic nationalism that it is best left unexamined. Perhaps the decision reflects his own perplexity.[38] Either way, despite the many evident and inspiring strengths of the mayanista narrative frame, it has yet to generate a full-fledged account of why so many indigenous people became involved in a war that was not their own, and how this involvement shaped the Maya movement that would emerge once that war was over.

Contemporary Reverberations

This chapter has outlined three narrative frames, each of which emerged from the period of intense political and military conflict and, in turn, guided subsequent interpretations of what happened and why. Each of these frames, I have suggested, came to be associated with a particular political space in the present: a past that could justify and give meaning to the here and now. I have devoted scant attention to the fourth narrative frame, the "official story," although it offers perhaps the most graphic illustration of this relationship between past and present. In the logic of the official story, indigenous opponents of the regime could only be hapless pawns of guerrilla manipulation, dispensable victims in an epic struggle against Communist subversion. In especially fervent versions, the official story also asserts that the massacres never happened, or that the guerrilla were the only real perpetrators of violence. Although this story lives on among true believers in the army and ultra-right sectors of Guatemalan society, it never enjoyed broad credibility, and lost much of its public resonance with the return to democracy in 1985. To make even minimal claims on legitimacy, democratic governments needed a buffer between them and the state-sponsored carnage of the preceding years, especially since the state apparatus had actually changed so little. How have the other three narrative frames fared in the subsequent two decades, in relation to the shifting contours of their associated political spaces? Brief consideration of each in this concluding section yields the following arguments: revolutionary triumphalism has lost its allure beyond a small cadre of activists; mayanista vindication remains vibrant among a growing sector of indigenous intellectuals and activists, but faces an unresolved dilemma regarding the crucial years in question; and dos demonios is powerfully ascendant.

I further suggest that the dos demonios narrative frame dovetails neatly with the racial ambivalence that most ladinos currently feel toward the Maya efflorescence. By extension, my effort to sketch an alternative narrative frame for guiding interpretation of Chimaltenango's recent history also entails an endorsement of an emergent political position in Guatemala today. This position is an amalgam of political sensibilities. It is antiracist, aligned with the Maya rights movement, critical of the revolutionary Left, and yet affirming of the revolution's most basic achievement, namely, to have mobilized great collective political energy that drew indigenous and ladino Guatemalans together in imagining and struggling for a new society.

Soon after the enclave of ex-guerrilla was established in Chimaltenango in 1998, I sought out Irene, a woman who identified as mestiza and who served as the group's leader. A number of ex-guerrilla tarried around the courtyard as I entered the large bunkroom where Irene and I would talk. Their casual manner immediately put me at ease—"*puro Ché Guevara*" (spitting image of Che Guevara) one burst out with a smile, in reference to my beard—and I was struck by what appeared to be a relaxed presence of ladinos and Mayas in the same social space. Irene spoke at length about her days as a teacher and clandestine organizer in Chimaltenango in the late 1970s, and she characterized social mobilization of those times in terms that resonate with my portrayal in this chapter: heterogeneous and militant, people often "took actions beyond what even the guerrilla leaders had in mind." She also offered thoughtful reflections about ladino racism, as a detonator of mobilization back then, and as a continuous, if more subtle, force in government practices toward Indians up to the present. Yet when we turned to her experiences within the guerrilla organization, and the challenges of forging egalitarian relations between ladinos and Mayas in the future, her answers turned surprisingly formulaic. Unable or unwilling to process the widespread accusations by indigenous ex-guerrilla of racism in the ranks, she affirmed that "in the struggle, everyone was treated as equals." She conceded at the end of a long interview, "Sure we are in for some rough times—because it is not easy to erase all this history, and start anew. That's why we have leaders who understand all these complexities." Whether by choice or reflex, Irene did not venture out beyond the authorized analysis of the Left, which assumed a stale and inflexible tone.[39]

To be sure, many basic tenets of the revolutionary narrative frame have withstood the test of time. The two truth commission reports confirm the basic story line, beyond doubt: numerous and repeated efforts at reform that met with state repression;

growing popular mobilization in support of radical social and political change; a ruthless counterinsurgency campaign that made no distinction between civilian and combatant. Yet except for a few stalwarts like Irene, the connection between this frame as a standpoint from which to interpret the past, and as a political space in the present, has been severed. With rising voices of internal critique, and the plummeting credibility of revolutionary alternatives across the region, the contemporary political space associated with the revolutionary narrative frame has all but imploded. Ironically, just when it has become possible to claim a past identity as "revolutionary" without risk to life and limb, to do so now one risks sounding out of touch, quaint, or faintly absurd. A telling sign of this implosion has been the rush by many former revolutionaries to embrace a narrative frame that they previously regarded with the utmost suspicion: mayanista vindication.

Maya intellectuals, who would play a growing role in the newly democratized national political arena, had a wide variety of relationships to the Left in the previous era, but developed a more unified stance as their movement gathered strength. Mayanista analysis cultivated a trenchant critique of guerrilla racism and authoritarianism, formed in many cases through the bitter experiences of struggle from within. It also endorsed, and further advanced, the central assertion that Maya civilians had borne the greatest human cost for an armed conflict they did not begin. This mayanista vindication narrative frame is widely endorsed by foreign scholars, some of whom followed the paths of the Maya activists themselves: from militant, if brief, endorsement of the ladino-led revolutionary movement, to disillusionment and eventual abandonment.[40] This narrative frame is most evocative of radical political alternatives for Guatemala's future, at a safe distance from the leftist imagery of socialism, agrarian reform, and worker justice, revolving instead around transformed models of citizenship, allowing for collective rights to language, identity, and culture, and demands for cultural-political autonomy.

In regard to the recent past of revolutionary mobilization and state-directed counterinsurgency, however, the mayanista vindication frame faces a serious, unresolved dilemma. It is exceedingly difficult, given the structure of human rights discourse and the correlation of political forces in the present, for Mayas to claim *both* their collective agency in the period leading up to the state campaign of terror, and their victimization in the events that followed.[41] When they emphasize collective agency back then, they inevitably portray themselves as aligned with the guerrilla, which in the minds of many obliges them to forfeit rights as victims of the violence. The recently formed Comisión de Resarcimiento (Reparations Commission), for example, embodies strong government and international backing for the proposition that victims of state violence deserve compensation. Emblematic of this political victory was the naming of Rosalina Tuyuc, a leading Maya human rights activist and founder of CONAVIGUA (an organization of Maya widows) to head the commission. It remains to be seen how people claiming compensation will position themselves in regard to this key period in the past. The clear tendency thus far, beginning with Tuyuc herself, is to downplay or disavow past affinities with the guerrilla, in order to dramatize victimhood. This leaves awkward gaps and silences in the historical record, starting with the impression that Maya collective agency and resistance, strong throughout preceding centuries and growing in the 1970s, suddenly recedes after 1978 as once active protagonists become civilian onlookers, pawns, and innocent victims of the terror.[42] This Faustian bargain with the past may well be the only means to resolve the dilemma, but there will be consequences that we are only beginning to perceive.

A brief anecdote illustrates this dilemma, and provides a glimpse of the consequences that may follow. In 1998 the mayanista press Cholsamaj agreed to publish David Stoll's monograph, *Between Two Armies*, in Spanish translation (Stoll 1993). Publication of this book, an interpretation of Ixil regional history, would have associated Cholsamaj directly with the dos demonios thesis: Ixil Mayas, according to Stoll, were not protagonists in the armed conflict but, rather, innocents caught in the middle, a fate for which they suffered immensely. When work toward publication was well underway, however, Stoll published his second monograph on Guatemala, which reiterates the earlier interpretation, but recasts the argument now as an exposé of Rigoberta Menchú: how her "testimony" misrepresents her own story and, by extension, how she helped produce a false and manipulative picture of willing Maya participation with the guerrilla (Stoll 1999). Almost unanimously, Maya intellectuals rallied around their iconic heroine, and Cholsamaj abruptly cancelled the publication contract. While mayanista intellectuals have no problem with sharp criticism of the Left, they could not stand for the implications of the exposé: that Menchú was either a victim herself or a traitorous ally of the ladino Left (or both), which would undermine her status as recipient of the Nobel Peace Prize. Yet while the cancellation allowed Cholsamaj to avoid immediate embarrassment, it left the broader dilemma unresolved. Menchú was an active participant in the guerrilla, as any careful reading of her testimony and elementary knowledge of the Guatemalan revolutionary experience makes evident. She also went on to become a major national-level political actor, as did many other Maya intellectuals and leaders, some of whom had their own entangled histories of involvement with the Left. If the Mayas-as-victims stance suppresses these entanglements, it runs the risk of undermining something of the credibility, complexity, and wisdom of these same Maya actors in the present.

The dos demonios narrative frame offers a different solution to this dilemma that goes a long way to explaining its ascendancy as point of reference for collective memories of the conflict. This frame revolves around the image of a traumatic conflict between two military forces, both of them self-absorbed, power hungry, and divorced from what civilians were up to at the time: neat mirror images of one another, each fueling the other's malevolence. Most emerging (or reemerging) civilian politicians since the late 1980s have endorsed this portrayal, which places a safe distance between themselves and the conflict and provides a means to reconnect with a traumatized and beaten down civilian population. Even within the army, the most astute intellectuals recognize the need to depict their own institution's past behavior as "excessive," if ultimately necessary. Many civilians—Maya and ladino alike—find in the dos demonios image a resonance with recent experience and a source of solace: as victims rather than protagonists, they have less burden of responsibility for the problems spawned by the violence, greater claim for redress, and more room for maneuver in facing present challenges. The dos demonios narrative frame resolves the "victimization" dilemma by asserting quite plainly that Mayas were victims in the armed conflict, and by implicitly questioning the authenticity of those who departed sharply from this pattern. Whether left aligned or otherwise, Mayas who became national-level actors, projected trans-communal identities, and forged interracial alliances were suspect because, as dos demonios analyst Yvon Le Bot puts it, Indians "in general prefer to maintain a relatively distanced stance in regard to the national political scene" (1995:308).

This assertion, in turn, provides a key link between the dos demonios narrative frame and the ambivalent response of ladinos chimaltecos to the Maya efflorescence. In general, the phrase "racial ambivalence" refers to political sensibilities that encompass both support for the principle of cultural equality and deep commitments to the social conditions that preserve ladinos' material and ideological advantage. By extension, the term applies to those who express solidarity with Indians, but as innocent victims rather than as protagonists, as acts of benevolence deployed from a higher rung in the social hierarchy. These sensibilities relegate indigenous politics to a carefully delimited space of civil society, where radical Maya demands and national-level Maya politics have little place. They express horror and condemnation toward the state's counterinsurgency violence against the indigenous population, yet in the same breath emit a quiet sigh of relief, at the thought of the indigenous empowerment that this very violence repressed.

Orlando Velásquez, a ladino teacher in Chimaltenango, exemplifies these sensibilities nicely. Working in Comalapa in the early 1980s, he remembers vividly the rising tide of state violence: "Those years in Comalapa were awful. The army questioned me every day, even though I wasn't involved in politics at all.... They killed a number of my students; when students went home to a rural hamlet, they were arrested as they returned; when the army found them with CUC membership cards, they killed them." Yet he also described the indigenous social mobilization with a shudder: "They had a well-armed organization, which covered both Chimaltenango and Sololá [the neighboring department]. A student of mine told me afterward, that the plan was all ready to go: they had already divided up the ladina women [as war bounty]." Don Orlando paused, to accent this last point, "*sí, era una cosa netamente racial. Es un problema serio que tenemos. Lo mismo que tienen ustedes con los negros*" (yes, it was a racial conflict. It is a serious problem that we still have. The same as what you have with the blacks).[43] Don Orlando abhors the army-instigated political violence, and yet also condemns the revolutionary mobilization, which he construes in racial terms. He applies the same parallel to the present: endorsing indigenous rights, while condemning indigenous radicals who "go too far." At times this radicalism is explicitly associated with the specter of a revived leftist adventurism and at times, even more effectively, it remains as an inexplicable excess, a serious racial problem, precisely what the return to democracy is meant to leave behind.

The analysis put forth in this chapter converges on an argument for paying greater attention to cultural-political heterogeneity. Indigenous people in Chimaltenango, like their ladino counterparts, mobilized with motivations too multiple and hybrid to fit neatly within the categories that later emerged: revolutionary subject, community-bound modernizante, autonomous Mayan. These protagonists expressed militancy with little fixed relationship to these now well-established political categories; they had hopes for broad-scale social transformation, linked to local and concrete material demands; they espoused goals of indigenous rights and antiracist struggle, not yet embittered by the racism of their would-be leftist allies; they had a chastened belief in utopias that brought forth abundant collective political energy, which refused the false choice between the pragmatic here and now and the vague, rough hewn, but resolutely emancipatory tomorrow.

Despite extensive organized memory work, the contemporary political space associated with this revisionist narrative frame has been slow to open. Mayanista analysis still largely finesses the past relationship of Maya activists to the guerrilla movement, while the dos demonios narrative frame insists that indigenous peoples at the time either were manipulated by guerrilla "demonios" or were hapless civilian victims.[44] The historical analysis of the UN Commission for Historical Clarification goes some way toward breaking out of existing narrative frames, although it never fully resolves the dilemma: how to portray indigenous people as victims of horrendous state repression, while insisting that they were collective agents of social change as well? As long as this victimization dilemma remains unresolved, the documentation of government atrocities will continue to have variable and ambiguous political effects. While such documentation does deepen awareness of the violence, and general outrage toward the perpetrators, those who seek to manage the problem without addressing its root cases can fairly easily appropriate these political sensibilities. Even the accusation of genocide against indigenous people, in many respects the most powerful finding of the commission's work, has the potential to exacerbate this victimization dilemma, portraying indigenous peoples as a separate class of victims, erasing images from past moments when Mayas and ladinos worked together toward common political ends.

The remainder of this book is devoted to probing the reverberations of this dilemma for ladinos. While for Mayas the dilemma revolves around a tension between agency and victimhood, for ladinos the problem is to achieve equality with Indians without renouncing racial privilege. Alignment with the political space in the making during those crucial years would entail an effort to confront this predicament head on, endorsing a notion of equality that would make ladino racial privilege impossible to sustain. Few are willing or able to go this far. The problem is not fundamentally one of individual volition, but rather, the lack of collectively forged political conditions. I found no organizations in Chimaltenango that practice the explicit ideal of ladinos and Mayas working together on substantively equal ground for common goals that include a systematic critique of ladino racial privilege. Throughout Guatemala, only a few organized initiatives meet this description. This absence is symptomatic of the rise of racial ambivalence and the broader ascendancy of neoliberal multiculturalism, which entail clear steps toward recognition and formal equality, while closing off deeper and more critical discussion of the problem.

For this very reason, efforts toward revisionist historical understanding of that crucial period, and toward spaces of antiracist political practice in the present, must go hand in hand. Just before completing this book, I spent the day with Genaro, to carry out a detailed interview about his involvement with the guerrilla, and to trace the evolution of his thinking about Maya-ladino relations from that time to the present. He offered a vivid description of life in the jungle as a guerrilla doctor in the early and mid-1980s, which serves as a touchstone for his thinking to this day. He described a steadily deepening cynicism toward the comandantes, combined with an abiding sense of wonderment for the new society that he, and his mostly Indian compañeros, imagined themselves to be creating. He did not remember a lot of talk about ladinos and Mayas, and the term "interculturalidad" had not yet even appeared. They forged relations of equality and respect based on the radical necessity of working together toward common ends, and based on quite literally having placed their lives in each other's hands. Was this "new society" grounded in a cultural-racial universalism that subtly erased indigenous culture in favor of a ladino-defined norm? Or was this a glimmer of the racial healing that true equality could engender? Even to ask these questions, invoking the image of revolutionary struggle and the era to which it belongs, may for some smack of socialist nostalgia. Yet to omit them completely would be worse still, an act of complicity with the historical forces at work since the mid-1980s to delegitimate these experiences and suppress their associated utopian imaginings. Our memory work in the present needs to recuperate these moments, in danger of being lost in cynicism and disillusionment, and to emphasize their connections—however faint the echo or dim the reflection—with the present. The point is not to uncritically recuperate yesterday's utopias—that *would* be socialist nostalgia—but to explore what people in struggle then understood themselves to be doing, to make sure that their past has a future from which we all can learn and take inspiration.

four
Ladino Racial Ambivalence and the Discourse of Reverse Racism

> "Individualism," "fairness," "merit"—these three words are continually misappropriated by bigots who have learned that they need not put on a white hood or bar access to the ballot box in order to secure their ends. Rather, they need only clothe themselves in a vocabulary plucked from its historical context and made into the justification for attitudes and policies they would not acknowledge if frankly named.
>
> —*Stanley Fish, "Reverse Racism, or How the Pot Got to Call the Kettle Black" (1993)*

> Ay indio, que por ser se enoja. (Indians! They are angry by nature.)
>
> —*Ladino saying*

The wave of social mobilization, intense conflict, and massive political violence that swept through Chimaltenango in the early 1980s, described in the previous two chapters, left no one unaffected, but took a predictably uneven toll. Like other urban middle-class ladinos, Yolanda remembers the first phase—from roughly 1978 when Romeo Lucas García became president, through the end of 1981, when the army began its brutal counterinsurgency march through the highlands—as the most terrifying. Multitudinous marches, protests, and meetings often turned angry and violent; news of guerrilla actions, including occupations of nearby municipio seats began to circulate; people disappeared after a knock on the door in the dead of night. With the November 1981 campaign, and especially when General Efraín Ríos Montt seized control of the state in March 1982, in this middle-class ladino view, the army restored a semblance of order in urban areas and reduced the unbearable tension of chaos and uncertainty. Memories from rural indigenous Chimaltenango convey precisely the inverse message: army control in the urban areas came paired with a rising tide of death and terror in the countryside. Methodical mass violence, torture, intimidation, and the militarized reorganization of everyday life caused collective trauma so deep and widespread that it remains, despite extensive documentation, impossible to fathom. These starkly divergent chronicles of the violence, in turn, stand as testimony to the pervasive racial divide in Chimaltenango society. Until the early 1990s, when Yolanda started to read about the massacres, she had no idea they occurred in such horrendous magnitude, so close to home. She genuinely believed that the political violence abated in late 1981, when for rural indigenous people 20 or 30 kilometers from the city the worst had just begun.

Yolanda's family suffered from the political violence in ways that would mark them forever, and yet, they also had the capital—cultural and material—that helped them fend off greater tragedy, and to recover relatively quickly. Like their responses to the earthquake a few years earlier, there was ample basis to affirm, as the saying went, "*nos agarró a todos parejo*" (it affected us all equally). The Valencia family was deeply affected by the loss of Yolanda's husband Alejandro and Héctor's mother Rosario to the political violence; many of their ladino friends and acquaintances in Chimaltenango have similar stories to tell. These experiences quickly dispel the notion that indigenous people were the sole victims of the violence. Yet ladino stories often had elements that their indigenous counterparts lacked: resources for quick flight; someone outside the country to take them in; a relative in the army to advise them when it was prudent to leave, and when conditions permitted their return. In Yolanda's family, the person who could have played this role of confidant-insider was *tío* (Uncle) Martín.

Yolanda spoke to me about tío Martín with hesitancy at first, always prefaced by allusions to the pitched ideological debates they had throughout the 1980s, but gradually a more complete picture emerged. Following a well-established family tradition, tío Martín had left Comalapa as a high school student, enrolled in the Politécnica (the military training school) in the early 1960s, and moved steadily up the ranks as a career officer. He studied in the United States for two years, and at another international officers' training school for a shorter period, rose to the rank of colonel, and stood poised to receive the jewel position of his career in 1992, when events surrounding the ousting of Serrano conspired against him. Rather than comandante of a base and promotion to general, he got an office job; soon thereafter he retired from the military, and started a private security business. I first met tío Martín in 1995 at a family party in Chimaltenango; after Yolanda made the introduction ("our anthropologist friend"), he mock frisked me for a tape recorder, and launched into a diatribe against the terrible effects of human rights, against Rigoberta Menchú ("she is an idiot with good advisors"), and, in reference to the presidential elections drawing near, saying, "What Guatemala needs is a good *gerente* (manager)." The best gerente-president in Latin America right now, he continued, is "Peru's Fujimori…he beat back inflation, and put Guzmán in a cage like an animal, while we have to negotiate with these *desgraciados* (miserable things)." A few years later, I accompanied Yolanda to tío Martín's house in Guatemala City for his birthday dinner party and heard more of the same: that the

United States lost in Vietnam due to political vacillation, that the Viet Cong used all kinds of unfair tactics—"I know because they [the guerrilla] did the same thing to us." The dinner guests consisted mostly of older-generation ladinos from Comalapa; a young indigenous woman served the food (not saying a word); tío Martín held forth throughout. The scene offered a rare, vivid portrait of the status quo ante: tightly knit ladino families, occupying a range of powerful positions; internally heterogeneous, but radically separate from indigenous people, whom they perceived as their inferiors.

Yet even at this dinner gathering, a seemingly safe bastion of ladino privilege, conversation also betrayed rumblings of change. It was the first anniversary of the signing of the definitive Peace Accords, and optimism about profound changes in Guatemalan society and feverish (if largely ineffectual) activities toward that end were at their height. On our way to the party that afternoon, we had tarried to chat with Yolanda's father Don Luis, who was too ill to make the hour's drive to Guatemala City. The Peace Accords became the focus of conversation, because indigenous rights activist Rosalina Tuyuc had just spoken in Chimaltenango's central plaza. After hearing a summary of her message, Don Luis shot off an angry salvo: "What I see with all this business about Maya, Garífuna, and Xinca rights is that they are forgetting completely about the rights of ladinos. Before you know it, we are going to be completely marginalized here." Various strands of the dinner conversation later that evening followed similar lines. Prompted by questions from a curious outsider, the dinner guests offered a chorus of bitter complaints to the effect that ladino society had all but disappeared in Comalapa; that even in San Martín Jilotepeque, a ladino stronghold, the inner circle of homeowners were "puros pixucos"[1]; conditions had deteriorated such that ladinos who stayed were obliged to marry Indians! "Like Oscar," someone chimed in referring to a young man they all knew. "The woman he married is not Indian, is she?" another exclaimed in dismay. Marielena settled the dispute dramatically, by raising her forefinger, and making a circular motion in the air: "Yes, she's envuelta."[2] Yolanda then interjected that someone had taken one look at the roster of Comalapa's soccer team and confided in her: "It pains me to see that the team is nothing but Indians. Couldn't you put at least one or two ladinos in there? I saw the name Roca and it gave me a moment of hope, but no! It turns out that Roca was pure Indian as well." Everyone laughed. Characteristically, Yolanda had introduced an element of collective self-parody into the conversation, distancing herself from the racial lament, while stopping just short of frontal critique. The most obvious rumbling of change, perhaps, was my own presence as an add-on dinner guest, an indication that Yolanda had no serious qualms about having this ladino-centric world observed, documented, and analyzed from within.

The next evening we went back to Guatemala City again, and a variation on the same topic continued to dominate the conversation during the trip. The occasion was the celebration of the anniversary of the Peace Accords, for which a large section of the central city had been closed to car traffic, and a symphony of church bells was giving a concert to the throngs who filled the streets. The evening engendered deep emotional feelings of pride in everyone; Héctor said it was times like this that he truly loved his country. Yet while sipping hot chocolate afterwards, it was noted that indigenous presence among the multitudes was minimal, and this evoked Marielena's discomfort with Rosalina Tuyuc's speech the previous day. She referred to us as "no-indígenas," Marielena reflected, "it's a negation; it leaves us with nothing." Besides, she added, in what seemed at first like a non sequitur, "I really don't think it's a good idea to officialize so many languages. It would be an *atraso*, a step backward."[3] Others defended the proposal, and a heated debate ensued. Elena argued that "ladino" was not an accurate term, since "we all really are mixed, mestizos." Héctor added caustically, "But hardly any Guatemalan ladino would admit to having indigenous descent," and if you look up "ladino" in the dictionary, you find it means all kinds of bad things, so "no-indígena" is all that's left. This image of "identity-less" ladinos brought to mind one of the family's favorite topics: the Italians. Sometime in the 1980s, an Italian solidarity group had connected with Chimaltenango, initiating aid programs and mutual visits. Yolanda's family became involved. Even after they had visited Chimaltenango, however, the Italians seemed not to grasp the ladino-Indian divide, and apparently continued to believe that everyone was Indian. When a group of Chimaltenango children—including Yolanda's son Alfredo—received an invitation to spend a month in Italy, the group leader, in hopes of satisfying their benefactors' fantasies, insisted that the children—mostly ladino—dress in indigenous clothing. After we all laughed at the Italians' woeful ignorance, Héctor turned serious: "Part of the problem is that there's nothing there. Indígenas have lo maya, but for us, it is only imitation."

Ladino Anxiety and the Remaking of Racial Common Sense

While this diffuse anxiety surrounding topics of race and identity is typical of Chimaltenango ladinos, the open, critical, self-reflective demeanor of Yolanda and her offspring is not. Leaving aside those of the older generation, like Don Luis, who express an overt and close-to-the-surface classic racism, most ladinos play down the anxiety and assume a more discerning stance: criticizing excesses in the name of Maya cultural-political activism, while at the same time espousing a principled antiracism. One specific, and especially revealing, dimension of this antiracism is the central focus of this chapter: the move from the critique of overt racism of the older generation to a more specific repudiation of certain ideas and acts of Indians themselves. My argument, simply stated, is that this antiracist discourse of ladinos, while representing a step away from the classic racism of times past, also serves to reconstitute the racial hierarchy, producing new, more subtle, and perhaps more durable rationales for keeping Indians in their place. While counterintuitive at first, this argument grows more plausible in light of close parallels in other realms. The larger problem is a disparity between stated intentions and social effects, between lofty claims to have eliminated the bases of racial inequality and the powerful forces that contribute to the reproduction of racial hierarchy.

Guatemalan Racism: Anthropology's Benign Neglect

An echo of this disparity, which I explore among ladinos in Chimaltenango, can also be found in anthropological discourse on race and culture. In their determination to repudiate racism and reiterate that race as a biological given has no scientific validity, anthropologists often have trouble focusing attention on the deep substrata of racial formation, which in turn leads to generally racialized understandings of the world.[4] This awkward record—of ostensibly antiracist academic production that misses the persisting commonsense bases of racism—has been abundantly evident in the anthropological scholarship on Guatemala. Until recently, the position of near-consensus in North American anthropology held, quite simply, that in Guatemala racism does not exist.[5] In an early statement along these lines, Sol Tax (1942:46) baldly asserted, "since the criteria of 'race' difference are cultural rather than biological...race prejudice as such is, by and large, absent." His assertion rested fundamentally on the observation that people socially defined as Indians could, in the course of their own lifetime, "become" ladinos. For an intellectual raised and trained in the United States, where the folk model of race stipulates that one drop of black blood makes one immutably black, it is perhaps understandable that this possibility of identity change would have made such an impact. Essentially, Tax and his cohort used the US folk model as a universal means of defining features of racism and, finding in Guatemala a different folk model, logically concluded that racism did not exist. Some Guatemalan social scientists contested these conclusions beginning in the late 1960s, while others endorsed and repeated them.[6] The ladino and Euro-Guatemalan elite could only have welcomed this well-credentialed scientific cover for (what most everyone would now recognize as) the miserably widespread and deeply ingrained racist underpinnings of their own society.

I begin with this historical note not to establish a safe distance from the early writings of North American anthropologists on this topic—a move so mechanical and de rigueur these days that it has been stripped of meaning—but rather, because it brings a crucial analytical point to the fore. The primordial emphasis that Tax and his cohort placed on identity change draws attention to a key defining feature of Guatemala's folk model of race and, by extension, of Guatemalan racism: the evolving, but always entangled coexistence of cultural and biological reasoning, the conundrum raised initially in chapter 1. The omnipresent elite discourse of the "redeemable" Indian, rooted at least as far back as the 1870s, directly contradicts any notion that race in Guatemala has rested exclusively on the precepts of inherent biological inferiority.[7] At the same time, this very cultural discourse paves the way for entanglement. It associates "lo indígena" with a series of attributes, situated in the blurred middle ground between the mutable and the inherent. Indians can "improve themselves" but their success is measured largely in the extent to which they manage to distance themselves from indigenous culture and, ultimately, indigenous identity. "Improved" Indians shake free from the shackles of their culture, but doubt remains regarding the biological attributes, and the distinction between the biological and the cultural is never that clear to begin with. The prevailing mindset, then, endorses and encourages cultural "improvement," yet harbors skepticism that full "redemption" can ever really be achieved. Even as it has become proper for such skepticism to be handled discreetly, it remains near the surface, epitomized by the still frequently heard admonition, *"Te salió el indio"* (The Indian in you is showing).

Racism in Guatemala over the last century, in short, has been grounded not in exclusively biological nor in exclusively cultural precepts, but rather, in a subtle fusion of the two. We are deeply indebted to Marta Casaús Arzú (1991) for having demonstrated that strong currents of strictly biological reasoning persisted among white/ladino elites into the 1980s. As for the legacy of Tax and his cohort, the disturbing unanswered question is not why they insisted that cultural reasoning could not add up to racism but, rather, why they left the overtly biological precepts unreported, unexamined, and untheorized. To juxtapose Tax's 1942 article with the interview material provided by Casaús Arzú engenders the bizarre sensation that they could not possibly be talking about the same country.[8] Regardless, the unfinished business in both lines of argument is a systematic analysis of the entangled relationship of these two distinct logics—one cultural the other biological—in the racial discourse of one historical moment, and over time.

This chapter responds directly to that challenge. Among elite and middle-sector ladinos in Chimaltenango a predominant and clearly ascendant condemnation of racism has taken hold. Nearly everyone embraces the principle of equality in some form, and most take pains to mark the contrast with "before" when discrimination prevailed. The same is true in national-level public discourse. This was evident, for example, in a heated exchange among newspaper columnists in July 1995, stemming from an accusatory recounting of Miguel Ángel Asturias's plan—developed in the 1920s—for miscegenation with white Europeans to solve Guatemala's "Indian problem."[9] Even Asturias's ardent defenders did not attempt to justify his eugenics-inspired proposal; rather, they explained it as a phase, quickly superseded and even renounced before the "mature" Asturias came to the fore.[10] Perhaps more substantively, the preamble to the agreement on the "Identity and Rights of Indigenous Peoples," signed by the URNG and the government on 31 March 1995, affirms that indigenous peoples continue to suffer from "discrimination and oppression." Sharply distinguished from economic exploitation, the connotation of this phrasing stops barely short of the term "racism."[11] Those inclined to imbue humor with social significance will be further convinced by how Filóchofo, caricaturist for the daily newspaper *Siglo XXI*, could mercilessly lampoon columnist Luis Enrique Pérez's assertion that "there is no racism or machismo in Guatemala" (figure 4.1). We can best understand this shift both as a step toward the elimination of classic racism, and as a form of rearticulation. Before, in the entangled fusion of biological and cultural reasoning, biological precepts provided the articulating principle, the ideological glue, and source of provisional coherence; after the shift, biological precepts have receded to the substrata, giv-

Figure 4.1. "There is no machismo or racism in Guatemala." —Columnist Luis Enrique Pérez, Libre Encuentro, August 27, 1995. Son: "My god! I think this gentleman has a brain the size of a pea." Father: "Yes, and what's more, it has been swollen."

ing way to a new articulating principle that refers largely to indigenous people's culture. To restate the argument more fully: widespread denunciations of racism in Guatemala today focus largely on the assertion that Indians are biologically inferior, but have barely begun to exorcise the densely woven cultural precepts that underlie the image of the redeemable Indian.

On this terrain of the substantial remaking of racial dominance in Guatemala—which entails substantial openings as well as serious threats—the ladino discourse of *racismo al revés* (reverse racism) has taken root. Briefly, reverse racism involves a claim that indigenous people: (a) use racial reasoning to define their own identity and to mark their difference from others (mainly ladinos); (b) assign deprecatory or inferior characteristics to ladinos; and (c) employ these racial distinctions to their own advantage, and to the unfair disadvantage of ladinos. There also has emerged a more theoretically elaborated version of this claim, which I will consider briefly later on. The main empirical focus of this chapter, however, is the discourse of middle-class ladinos in the department of Chimaltenango, and their use of reverse racism and similar phrases to express dissatisfaction, criticism, and fear in response to the changing social conditions around them. The chapter devotes a separate section to each of four questions. How is the discourse of reverse racism expressed—by whom, in what contexts, with what underlying meanings? Why has this discourse gained such prominence in the present historical moment? What consequences does the discourse of reverse racism bring to Guatemalan cultural politics? Finally, where does reverse racism fit with efforts to theorize racism and to conceive paths forward toward racial equality and social justice? In keeping with the overall ethnographic focus of this book, I frame these questions almost exclusively around ladino discourse and practice—attempting to counterbalance two widespread problems in the existing literature: ladinos are either rendered invisible or reduced to a caricatured role of oppressor.[12]

My central argument, which encompasses all four sets of questions, begins with the observation that the discourse of reverse racism is deeply contradictory. Except in its most cynical and opportunistic variants (which I believe are relatively rare), it embodies considerable progress toward a societal consensus in the repudiation of classic racism; the person who claims to have perceived or experienced reverse racism is apt to be especially adamant in this regard. A central motivation behind the discourse is an expressed desire for "equality" that has been frustrated, or perhaps actively rejected. These sensibilities—of endorsing equality and being a victim of racial animus—help to explain why people commonly imbue this discourse with such indignation and emotional force. At the same time, the accusation of reverse racism is a direct response to the multifaceted indigenous challenge to ladino power and privilege, which has arisen gradually since the 1960s and especially since 1985. One need only step back from the details to bring a suspicious coincidence into focus. Just as indigenous people are beginning to transform, through collective and individual actions, the deeply racialized structural inequities of Guatemalan society, ladinos respond by asserting that equality has already been achieved, and that those who persist in this political quest are themselves divisive and racist. This facet of the discourse has the effect of delivering a preemptive strike against indigenous ascendancy, a move for closure before "their" power grows any further, and ultimately, a newly conceived attempt to shore up ladino dominance. The central challenge in understanding reverse racism is to assign proper analytical weight to both the egalitarian ideal and the preemptive strike, not as discrete alternative meanings that a given group or individual might espouse, but as constitutive parts of a full-fledged racial ambivalence.

Don Antonio and the Waves of History

To avoid committing the error of creating theory that overlooks everyday consciousness and practice, I want to begin by considering how people actually express these sensibilities. Early on in my fieldwork, I befriended an elderly parish priest who was stationed in the municipio of San Martín Jilotepeque. He took me into the inner sanctum of the parish house, talked with me at length about his work, his life, and the municipio's tumultuous history. Padre Antonio (PA below) played an especially powerful role in San Martín because he had been stationed there for so long and, perhaps especially, because his family was originally from there. Although steeped in a ladino mindset and social milieu, the padre assigned great importance to his priestly responsibilities and expressed genuine pride at his achievements with his predominantly indigenous parishioners over the past three decades. This unselfconscious pride and confidence, combined with some measure of vanity, led him to agree with enthusiasm to my suggestion that we conduct an interview to document his life history as a priest.[13] The project grew into a multisession endeavor, yielding many hours of taped conversations. What follows is a brief fragment from that interview, beginning with my question:

> CRH: Would you say that the legacy of the period of violence is that there is more unity between indigenous and ladino? Or have the two become more polarized?
>
> PA: *Mire usted* (Listen my friend), there is no disunity. Now we look at everyone as equals. That is, Indians have overcome their complexes...they are not burdened by complexes as they were previously. The Indian has heard, and knows very well, that he has rights, and that's it, *¿verdad?* (you know what I mean?). There is no separation, to the contrary, now they both gather in public spaces without problems, without complexes. That racial division, you know, has been overcome. Everything is equal. The only thing that is happening now is that the Indian now recognizes that he is equal to the others, and now it seems that he's a little lacking in culture. It is alright that he knows he's equal to the others but often what happens next is that he doesn't know how to distinguish his rights from the rights of others....
>
> Mire usted. Groups are appearing, I see them, especially among the youth. As long as they do not enter into conflict with the others groups, there is no problem. The problem would come when these other groups start to protest. But the ladinos normally do not protest. Now it is the reverse. The ladinos look on, let things happen, ¿verdad? They do not protest. As long as there's no protest, there is coexistence, but it is a disastrous coexistence, because cultural values get lost, many good things get lost....
>
> CRH: These groups of youth, what are their motives?
>
> PA: Before, perhaps, they had no culture, but they were docile, well behaved, more human, that is, more obedient. Now, these groups still do not have culture, the culture you are supposed to receive in school, ¿verdad? But now they are rebels, they do not respect anyone, ¿verdad? [They say] "I have freedom, we live in a free country." That is freedom: do whatever you like, even if it affects the principles of the collective good.
>
> I am not sure if you have noticed, the indigenous movement is appearing, and becoming strong. They want their identity recognized, and they even

want...at times I've thought they even want...to achieve a state within the state, because the tendency of the Indian now is almost to separate more from the ladino. They are the ones now who are insisting that there are two races, and in doing this, they are creating the bases for a new conflict.

CRH: In what sense?

PA: Because they are raising up the Maya race, ¿verdad? They want to put the Maya race on top. They have realized that their identity is worthy. They want to put it on top, and, it is almost as if they want the others to disappear....
They are struggling for their own identity. What comes next, we do not know.
If they handled the whole thing prudently, there would be no problem, because we all have to recognize that Guatemala is a multiracist country, ¿verdad?

CRH: Multi...multi...what?

PA: That is, we have many ethnic groups, and we have to accept this reality.
But this reality should not divide us.

CRH: Do you think that this movement could lead to great division?

PA: I think so, I may be making a hasty judgment, ¿verdad? I think it could be dangerous, if they do not know how to manage it prudently.

CRH: Does it have elements of discrimination, or racism, toward ladinos?

PA: I suspect it does. I cannot judge because I do not have a good understanding of the leaders' tendencies, ¿verdad? I do not know how they are thinking, but I fear—it could be a prejudice—but I fear...[a long pause follows]...if the movement continues, it could produce exactly what our history produced, except in reverse. Now it would be them who would discriminate against us, against the ladinos, ¿verdad?

For centuries, indigenous people were discriminated against, and now they are rising up. These are the waves of history. The wave moves in one direction, and then, it moves back the other way...such that those who before were last become the first, and the first become the last.... We have seen this happen in the history of all peoples.

How Is the Discourse of Reverse Racism Expressed?

Census data create a deceptively straightforward picture of Chimaltenango's racial demographics: roughly 80 percent indigenous inhabitants, a ratio that has changed little since the nineteenth century, with greater proportions of ladinos in the municipios bordering Sacatepéquez to the southeast, and in each cabecera municipal.[14] In 1970, the distribution of political-economic resources fit the standard highlands pattern: a ladino monopoly on power except in its most local manifestations; a great social distance between indígena and ladino in every realm of daily existence. Profound forces of social change since that time have fundamentally altered this picture, creating new conditions that, while to some extent unique to Chimaltenango, fit generally within national-level trends. Analyzed at length in chapter 2, these forces can be summarized in four points. The first is the growth and consolidation of a small but highly visible indigenous middle class—people who are educated, at times with professional degrees, holding positions of relative authority in organizations, state bureaucracies, and the private sector, and enjoying modest economic security. Second, the indigenous vote has become a major factor in departmental electoral politics, and often decisively so at the municipio level. Third is the widespread emergence of Maya NGOs, whose work is broad and heterogeneous but can be glossed with the phrase "cultural rights activism."[15] Finally, largely as a result of these other conditions, the social distance between middle-class ladinos and upwardly mobile indígenas has narrowed considerably, yielding a proliferation of spaces in which the two interact on relatively equal terms. This last observation must not be overstated. The increased quota of power that indígenas have acquired is not remotely proportional to their numbers; their interaction with ladinos is often superficial and rarely includes the more intimate spaces of family and friendship; efforts to dismantle institutionalized racism and its cultural-political underpinnings have barely begun. Nonetheless, most Chimaltenango ladinos frequently come into contact with indígenas of equal education, economic resources, political power, or bureaucratic authority. However limited in relation to Guatemalan social structure more broadly, this quotidian space of racial equity is completely unprecedented and, for some, deeply troubling.[16]

Ladino responses to these changes come in a variety of registers, from rational analysis to visceral emotion. The theme of reverse racism at first emerged unsolicited, and for me quite unexpectedly: in response to my stock question—"Is there racism or discrimination in your daily social environment?"—people repeatedly inverted my intended meaning and presented *themselves* as the victims. Later, I began to ask the question more directly, as I did in the interview with padre Antonio. Although responses varied, padre Antonio's sensibilities are broadly representative of middle-class ladinos I interviewed—although his are an increment more candid and detailed than most.[17] With his rich narrative as the point of departure, in this section I describe the discourse more fully, placing it in social context, exploring its heterogeneity, drawing out its key precepts. This undertaking lends itself to the tendency—at times tempting—to vilify the speakers, portraying them as driven solely by the need to fend off challenges to their privilege and power. My insistence on presenting another, more egalitarian side as well stems not from a disengaged commitment to balance, but from the contention that this second dimension is so analytically crucial. This egalitarian sensibility is what makes the discourse of reverse racism so disarming, and ultimately so deeply influential and effective.

Although a common context for talking about reverse racism is the present-day Maya efflorescence, the topic often brings to mind historical antecedents. The most important of these, which almost invariably emerges from spontaneous free association on the topic of "Indian racism against ladinos," is the Patzicía conflict of 1944. These events have been indelibly etched in the collective memory of ladinos, especially of the older generation, and they are not reluctant to talk about them in the least.[18] For these informants, the events of Patzicía seem quite explicitly to symbolize what could happen, as padre Antonio puts it, "if they [Indians] do not manage things prudently." Two specific characteristics of these memories stand out. First, no doubt through repetition and the quasi-intentional editing that occurs as collective memories take shape, the rendition has become highly stylized and remarkably uniform in its key details. When I interviewed Don Edgar Garrido, an elderly and ailing chimalteco, he jumped to his feet and dramatically enacted the story line:

> The Indians had a carefully worked out plan to kill all the ladino men; they
> already had the ladina women divided up among themselves! Defenseless, the
> vecinos (townspeople) hid their children in the closet. Indians entered through
> the windows and the roof, discovered their hiding place and killed them then
> and there. If the people of Zaragoza, and later the army, had not come to their
> rescue, it would have been a blood bath.[19]

The second characteristic is the striking contrast between the lurid detail in this first part of the story and the absence of commentary on the events that followed. That lack of commentary seems less about conspiratorial coverup than disinterest. Army killings of between four hundred and nine hundred Indians, compared to the estimated fourteen ladinos that died, is simply not important to the narrative's take-home message.[20] "*Muchos ladinos murieron allí*" (Many ladinos died there) they conclude with a shudder; and though some mention land problems or manipulation by politicians, they all describe the motives behind the Indian assault, fundamentally, as "racist."[21]

The second historical antecedent, equally emotionally charged though less uniform in its rendition, is the political mobilization and violence of the late 1970s and early 1980s. Some interviewees claimed the mobilization was about economic differentiation, not race. Padre Antonio, for example, explains:

> Quite apart from race, it was a question of achieving equality for everyone. I
> say this because there were cases in which the guerrilla killed Indians who
> were relatively well off. One boy would have a pick-up truck, some cattle, and
> slightly better economic conditions, and he was a "rich person." The struggle
> was against the rich, whoever that might be. The period of violence...was not
> racist, but rather, an economic conflict.... We all have to be equal. That was
> their goal.

Others, however, place the same events in an explicitly racial framework. Don Rolando, Yolanda's uncle, who used to wield considerable power in his municipio, vividly remembers the racial overtones of the mobilization, and cites them as the reason he withdrew from politics and moved his family to Chimaltenango:

> There was a night when the indígenas wanted to kill all of us. That's why the army had to spread out everywhere [to protect people]. That was 19 October 1979. Someone who had been in the meeting went to inform us, and the army came. So, the other group [the guerrilleros] attacked the army and that's how it started. The nineteenth of October 1944 there was an uprising of the indígena against the ladino in Patzicía. They wanted to do it in Comalapa, too. The army showed up to protect us then, and they had to do the same thing in 1979.[22]

Don Orlando, a teacher introduced in the previous chapter, reiterated the contours of Rolando's account, and went on to dwell on the problems of his father in the late 1970s, when the municipio elected José Lino Xoyón as their first Indian mayor. Although his father had served forty years as the town's registrar, weathering all sorts of political storms, Xoyón reportedly made life miserable for him and forced him to resign. "No power is eternal," the mayor was reported to have remarked haughtily, a clear allusion to ladinos in general, with the added sting of biblical backing.[23]

These collective memories place current accusations of reverse racism in historical context. They demonstrate the existence of a deeply embedded historical memory that portrays Indians as inclined to direct collective actions against ladinos. How inclined? Under what conditions? These are questions that the memories do not ask or purport to answer. Regardless, they substantiate a diffuse but potent image of indigenous retribution, and they draw explicitly on racial precepts to do their work. While generally quick to insist on the prevalence of intragroup divisions, and on indígenas' tendencies to mercilessly exploit "their own," in the context of these memories, ladino informants nearly always affirm the foundational premise that, in the last instance, "*la raza indígena*" (the indigenous race) is unified for itself and against "us." The entanglement of cultural and biological reasoning is evident in this assertion: it is neither merely a contingent historical response to oppression, nor solely a natural feature of la raza indígena, but both at once. The image of collective Indian retribution, led by people bound together by a deeply seated (tending toward natural) racial unity is instrumental to the resonance and emotional charge of the discourse of reverse racism. Well beyond the realm of academic theorizing, this concerns the future of "*la raza ladina*."[24] As Don Rolando put it, echoing Don Luis's outburst cited earlier:

> Now it is the Maya who have power, and we ladinos who are marginalized. It would be a grave error to give them any more [power] because they want to divide the country and expel the ladinos. If the foreigners don't start helping the ladinos, we are not going to survive.

This grave warning brings us back to the present, and its hyperbole serves as a reminder that individual experience is a crucial factor in the content and intensity of the discourse. Don Rolando, for example, is especially bitter because he portrays himself as having played an instrumental role in the advancement of indigenous people in his municipio. As mayor in the early 1970s, he founded a high school, supported the formation of cooperatives, and worked hard to increase the quota of central government funds invested locally. "Now I regret having founded the high school," he concluded. Perhaps this sentiment could be read as an early expression of the racial ambivalence that would become so widespread later on.[25]

Quite apart from the impact of revolutionary mobilization, the rise of Maya electoral clout spelled the end of Don Rolando's career as a municipio-level politician. However laced with paternalism, his efforts to "raise the indigenous people's cultural level," in his own mind, were profoundly *"malagradecidos"* (ungratefully received). Consequently, his perception of reverse racism takes on the additional emotional charge of having experienced personal rejection. Although somewhat unique to older chimaltecos, a variant of this same response can be found among the younger generation. Liliana, a woman of perhaps thirty-five years, worked in various government entities that put her in daily contact with rural indigenous chimaltecos. Liliana proudly portrays herself as someone who has overcome racial barriers, and who is explicitly committed to the principle that everyone deserves *"un trato de iguales"* (treatment as equals). The anecdote that follows is one she told me took place a few years earlier, but it continued to bother her because it invoked a persisting problem: Indians who give her no credit for having changed.

> When I was in the University extension in Chimaltenango to earn my degree
> in pedagogy...we were a small group of ladinos among a majority of Indians,
> and they discriminated against us. [CRH: In what way?] For example, the first
> day the professor told us to form working groups. None of us knew one
> another, but even so, all the Indians formed their own groups, leaving us out.
> This division lasted even in the coffee breaks; we always did everything
> separately.[26]

There is a clear difference between Liliana, who believes deeply in the principle of a "race-blind" society, and padre Antonio, whose commitment to equality barely conceals a nostalgia for times gone by when Indians were "docile, well-behaved, more human, more obedient." The two converge, however, on the perception of discrimination against ladinos and, behind this, the fear that *"se podría voltear la tortilla"* (they could turn over the tortilla).

These fears come most sharply into focus among those ladinos whose work significantly overlaps with that of the Maya NGOs: people involved with cooperatives, community development, education, or other grassroots activities.[27] Members of this "progressive" subgroup frequently refer to the "Mayas only" policy of many Maya NGOs as racist; one tellingly quipped that behind this policy was the philosophy "they came in boats, so let's send them back the same way." Exclusion carries an extra sting for them, because they see themselves as having devoted large parts of their lives—at times risked their lives—to work with and for indigenous communities. Consistent with that stance, they are deeply critical of typical ladino racism. Gregorio Sánchez, a young ladino who heads a development NGO that works largely with rural indigenous communities, prefaced his long self-justificatory account with adamant references to the older generation: *"Mi abuela era muy racista...trataba a los indígenas como esclavos, como que no fueran gente"* (My grandmother was a real racist...she didn't treat indígenas like people, she treated them like slaves). Yet his own story was laced with impatience at what he called the "racist tendency" in the Maya movement:

> The financial agencies often ask us, "What are you doing about the Indian question? How are you confronting racism?" We always respond that we don't make any distinction between Indian and ladino, we treat them both with complete equality. To do anything else would be discrimination.
>
> Some Maya leaders tell us that our work is discriminatory. We do not speak the language, we do not pay attention to people's customs, or their *cosmovisión* (spirituality). This anger is much more common among the intellectuals, perhaps because they are more aware of historical conditions. They retain these conditions more.... They speak a lot of Mother Earth, how great it is to sleep on a *petate* (woven mat) on the ground, because the petate has magical qualities. But don't you believe that the intellectuals actually do this! These customs are getting lost. They don't use sandals, they use computers. There are elderly men who wear traditional clothing with tennis shoes, or with Lee jeans. They have lost the pure version of their culture.
>
> I have read the writings of Demetrio Cojtí. He argues for a regionalization of the country along linguistic lines. Each ethnic group would be a small government. If this came to pass, what would happen to those who are mixed? What would happen to ladinos? The ladino, technically speaking, is a cross of pure Spanish and Indian. We are mestizos. I identify as ladino by tradition, but we are mestizos.
>
> The funding agencies like everything Maya. They always ask for this, and for anything having to do with women. This is because of the Peace Accords. They support anything Maya, and worse if it has to do with Maya women. But I think that with globalization, the Maya will soon fall out of style.... With economic advancement, the cultures will mix even more. Indigenous people cannot isolate themselves; the indigenous of the US have demonstrated that. Everything is growing more and more mixed. The indigenous girls are using their traditional clothing less. They wear bikinis, shoes, and makeup. Their identity is fading.... Only the elders use the clothing. I would venture to predict that, before long, we'll have only one type of person in Guatemala.[28]

The stance of Gregorio Sánchez cannot be conflated with assimilationist fantasies of times past; yet any Maya cultural activist who heard these complaints would be deeply suspicious. Sánchez betrays a series of anxieties, borne in pressure from both his "base" and his donors. These anxieties are the stuff of accusations that the very people they are trying to help have now turned racist toward them.

The discourse of reverse racism is pervasive among Chimaltenango ladinos, spanning the political spectrum and crossing generational lines.[29] Moreover, this is not a case of people using the same phrase with substantively different meanings.[30] Inherent in the perception of reverse racism is a critique of the classic racism that used to prevail. At times this critique encompasses a healthy dose of self-criticism, and other times an insistence that, as Don Rolando put it, "What happened, happened. Why should we take the blame for what took place five hundred years ago?" Either way, self-exoneration logically follows: to accuse someone else of reverse racism implies that the accuser him or herself has embraced the principle of equality, and thereby transcended the problem. This, in turn, gives rise to what Etienne Balibar (1991) calls the "turnabout effect." Though in the past "we" may have been racist, now "they" are the ones using racial precepts, deepening racial divisions, and committing acts of racism against "us." Finally, the discourse of reverse racism draws on deeply seated biological precepts that contradict the affirmation of cultural equality. Lurking behind the still frequently used term "raza indígena" is the specter of collective Indian retribution, rationally explained as the product of an unfortunate history of oppression, but in some degree sustained by the biological precept that, when push comes to shove, the Indians "naturally" ally with one another against ladinos. Don Caralampio, an older ladino man, once a key player in municipio politics that Indians now control, elaborated on this theme, echoing Héctor's sentiments noted at the beginning of this chapter:

> The Indians will always dominate politics here in the future. They have a great
> advantage in relation to ladinos: we have neither race nor culture. Ladinos are
> of mixed descent; we are *mistados*, that is, mestizos. To the extent that we have
> culture, it is pure imitation. The Indians' culture is ancestral, and that pro-
> vides them with a basis for unity.

Why Now?

At the beginning of the year 1970, within one month of each other, two books were published that galvanized the debate among ladino intellectuals regarding class, culture, and revolutionary politics in Guatemala.[31] To simplify considerably, in the first book, *Guatemala: Una interpretación histórico-social*, Carlos Guzmán Böckler and Jean-Loup Herbert (1970) argued that the fundamental structural division in Guatemalan society—encompassing class relations but not reducible to them—was between Indians and ladinos. Consequently, they reconceived the rising wave of revolutionary mobilization as an indigenous, anticolonial struggle.[32] In the second book, *La patria del criollo*, Severo Martínez Peláez defended an orthodox materialist interpretation of Guatemalan history. For Martínez Peláez, the social category "indio" was a colonial creation, and racism existed "*en función de la discriminación social*" (as a function of social discrimination). References to "*lucha racial*" (racial struggle) between indio and ladino, he argued, were misconceived, diversionary efforts to slow the development of the indios' "true" identity as "*explotados*" (exploited people), to derail their growing participation in the revolutionary struggle defined strictly in class terms.[33] In a 1973 essay, Martínez sternly (and revealingly) warned of consequences that could follow if Guzmán Böckler's thesis won the day: "It would not surprise me if this road carried us right back to racism (although this time, it would be a reverse racism, favoring the Indian, but just as irrational and out of keeping with science as any other)."[34] This is the earliest Guatemalan reference I have found in published text to the generalized discourse of reverse racism today. In at least one public forum Martínez reiterated the warning, even drawing a parallel between the lucha racial thesis and fascism.[35]

As some of the previously cited memories suggest, conditions of popular mobilization from the mid-1970s onward could well have given rise to more widespread use of the phrase "reverse racism." Narratives from at least three municipios of Chimaltenango suggest that some ladinos in the cabeceras (county seats) perceived the threat of revolutionary mobilization in explicitly racial terms, echoing the sentiments of Don Rolando. Apart from the guerrilla movement, the myriad civil initiatives underway in Chimaltenango in the 1970s, described in chapters 2 and 3, all precursors of contemporary Maya efflorescence, could also have engendered such a response. By 1978, Indian mayors had come to power in many of the majority Indian municipios. Indigenous leaders from Chimaltenango played important roles in the formation of the Frente Indígena Nacional (FIN) in the late 1970s. Despite its short duration and disastrous end, FIN served notice that Indian electoral strength would have to be taken seriously.[36] There are no doubt many other cases of grassroots organizations —from cooperatives to Christian-based networks to peasant leagues—with predominantly indigenous participants, which ladinos might have perceived as dangerous portents of reverse racism.

The ladino discourse of reverse racism did not flourish in the 1970s, however, for a number of reasons. The Guzmán Böckler and Herbert thesis raised many of the critical issues, but the absence of indigenous voices in the ensuing debates probably muted accusations of reverse racism. Early Maya intellectual leaders, such as Don Adrián Chávez, reportedly received the Guzmán Böckler and Herbert book with enthusiasm; more widespread discussions of the book's contents among indigenous groups followed.[37] But these effects were minimal compared with its impact among the overwhelmingly urban and ladino students of the San Carlos University (USAC). For many of these students, the book encouraged introspection, critique of the (ladino) power structure, and a strong impulse for solidarity with indígenas. In the charged "pre-insurrectionary" atmosphere of the mid-1970s, such responses often led students to the guerrilla and, more specifically, to the Organización Revolucionaria del Pueblo en Armas (Revolutionary Organization of the People in Arms, or ORPA).[38] This raises the second obvious reason that the discourse of reverse racism did not catch on in the 1970s: however important the autonomous indigenous mobilization in those years, at some point it was overtaken by the revolutionary movement, which defenders of the regime portrayed as Communist. While it has become increasingly clear that racism infused and amplified this anti-Communism, and played a formative influence in the army's genocidal counterinsurgency campaign, in one important sense the virulent repudiation of "Communist subversion" was not compatible with the discourse of reverse racism. It ultimately asserted that Communist organizers had cajoled, coerced, manipulated, or fooled Indians into joining the rebel cause. The accusation of reverse racism requires a perception of autonomous, premeditated initiative on the part of indigenous peoples themselves—a condition that defenders of the regime portrayed as a serious future threat, not a present feature, of the conflict.

Though extensive indigenous participation in the revolutionary mobilization of the 1970s did not evoke widespread use of the discourse *then*, this history is a central factor in people's use of the discourse today. The experience of the 1970s proved that indígenas were capable of massive, disciplined mobilization, even if this time non-Indian outsiders ultimately directed it. Memories of this experience, still only a decade old, underlie the fears of reverse racism today. If they went that far fighting for the interests and ideals of others, the reasoning goes, imagine what would happen if the leaders, interests, and ideals were their own! Faced with a movement with a coherent, dynamic program by and for Maya themselves, people like padre Antonio immediately suspect the worst, and fear deeply what might happen if they are right. Lessons drawn from the mobilization and violence of the 1970s, then, have become one key facilitating condition for the emergence of the discourse today.

A second condition is the shift in national political culture, which has discredited overtly racist justifications for indigenous subordination, and given rise to a discourse that champions equality amid cultural difference. Far from opportunism or empty rhetoric, this new egalitarian discourse engenders in most Chimaltenango ladinos a strong endorsement, a deep sense of self-satisfaction and a sigh of relief. No one believes that indígenas suddenly have achieved equality in structural-institutional terms, but simply that the principle of "trato de iguales" is a major step toward defusing the potential for violent conflict. Few take the next step, to systematically explore the cultural precepts subtly fused with remnants of biological reasoning that emanate from and justify persisting inequities. Rather, ladinos endorse and, to varying degrees, attempt to follow the equality principle with the implicit assumption that they have done what is necessary and ethically required to remedy the problem. This leaves them situated on the antiracist high road, further inoculated by the faintly ironic report that *"nos civilizamos"* (we became civilized); that is, "before" we discriminated against them, but not any more.[39] From this standpoint, a challenge or slight by an indígena will logically elicit indignation: just as we ladinos have shaken free from this racist ideology, the reasoning goes, just as we ladinos have affirmed that all Guatemalans, though culturally different, are equal, the indígenas have turned racist against us.

The rise of an indigenous middle class constitutes a third underlying condition because it gives the discourse of reverse racism further empirical substance. Applying the principle of trato de iguales is possible, but a good deal more difficult and ambiguous, when an enormous chasm of class difference separates the people in question. That is, when Chimaltenango ladinos claim to be living by the equality principle, they are referring not to interactions, say, with the *doméstica* (servant) in their home, but rather with someone who is more or less their socioeconomic equal. Two decades ago, such zones of equal status interaction were relatively rare, except among the most impoverished. Today they have proliferated, giving Chimaltenango ladinos ample empirical basis to assert that the equality principle now reigns.[40] Yet these relatively high-status indígenas, the same ones who ladinos (begrudgingly or otherwise) now treat as equals, are seen as more likely to display reverse racism. Lower status indígenas, by contrast, are more inclined toward the docility and servility that animates padre Antonio's nostalgia. What better evidence that upwardly mobile indígenas want not merely equality, but a racist, vindictive "flip of the tortilla"?

This brings the argument back to Maya efflorescence, which directly or indirectly provides the fundamental answer to the question "Why now?" Maya organizations have brought about a series of concrete changes in Guatemala's political culture—from the perceived need for indigenous presence in public institutions, to multiple spaces for serious discussion of Maya demands, to the critique of deprecatory or racist ideas. Yet more than the specific impact of cultural activism, the Maya efflorescence affects Chimaltenango ladinos as a diffuse and general reminder that the actions of individual indígenas are linked to a well-elaborated, well-funded, national-level collective program. Without this reminder, there would be a strong tendency to attribute changes and challenges to the individual characteristics of the perpetrator—an especially resentful, unruly, or maladapted individual. These individualizing tendencies still occur, but one cannot take them far without confronting the individual's articulation with the collective. The reflections of padre Antonio illustrate this point nicely. His main concern is the "groups of youth" in San Martín, who he vaguely associates with the "the indigenous movement." He admits not knowing who the leaders are, or what they profess, beyond a desire to "raise up the indigenous race." But this, combined with their youthful "rebelliousness" is enough to generate the image of a momentous inversion in Guatemalan social relations. Maya cultural activism is the key facilitating condition for the discourse of reverse racism, because of what it has achieved, but more importantly, for what it represents, and what ladinos imagine it could do.

Cultural-Political Consequences

Building on the analysis of the previous two sections, I contend that the ladino discourse of reverse racism is symptomatic of the broader cultural-political sensibilities that, throughout this book, I call racial ambivalence. In the face of an increasingly evident crisis of dominance, ladinos have fashioned a dual response: substantive concessions to Maya ascendancy on the one hand, and an underlying drive to retain a disproportionate quota of power on the other. Granted, most of these concessions amount to little more than ex post facto recognition of spaces that indígenas have opened and occupied through their own struggles, without asking anyone's permission. They are crucial nonetheless because they form a constitutive role in the new arrangement. To confront the crisis successfully, ladinos must do more than simply reassert toned-down claims to political-economic dominance: they must persuade a significant sector of indígenas that the new commitment to equality is for real.

The contest has the makings of a full-fledged struggle for hegemony, with the rising tide of Maya pride and cultural-political assertion pitted against ladino efforts to defend their long established position of dominance and privilege. While the redistribution of material resources—whether by preemptive concession or in response to frontal demands—plays a key role in this contest, the discursive struggle over the meaning of this redistribution is crucial as well. The lynchpin in this latter struggle, in turn, is the assertion that "trato de iguales" among culturally different Guatemalans has become a widely endorsed, if still not pervasive, guiding principle. Indigenous activists contest this assertion on multiple grounds, from everyday experience to a more generalized skepticism about the real motives that lie behind the discourse. By far the most radical and rigorous contestation comes from intellectuals of the Maya movement, who reinterpret the very principle of equality as a homogenizing, assimilationist move: they read the phrase, "a Guatemala without ladinos and indígenas" as a direct threat to their own existence, as if its underlying purpose were to achieve "a Guatemala without the Maya movement." Here the discourse of reverse racism enters the equation. If Maya critiques of the dominant society are discredited as racist, they can be refuted with the same original assertion: there is no place for *any* form of racism in a newly egalitarian Guatemala. This parsimony goes a long way toward explaining the efficacy and appeal of the reverse racism idea: the very principle of antiracism that has won the day, in a "turnabout effect," now is deployed to halt the movement's advance. One clear consequence, in short, is to bolster ladino power holders in the current phase of their struggle for hegemony.[41]

Yet given the nature of any such struggle, and the complexities of this one in particular, the consequences are likely to be highly variable. The discourse of reverse racism may advance the bid for ladino hegemony, but not without exacting a price. Predicated on the repudiation of classic racist precepts and the reinforcement of an egalitarian ethic, the discourse helps to rule out certain well-established modes of ladino dominance, and makes ladinos in general more vulnerable to critique than ever before.[42] Although apparently superficial, such changes in form are themselves significant, and they can lead to further changes in substance. Don Édgar Garrido, the man who dramatically recounted the conflict in Patzicía, later on in the interview offered his comportment on public buses as an example of how he practiced the new ethic of equality. Before, Don Édgar explained in great detail, to sit next to an indígena would have been uncomfortable and unpleasant. Now, he sits down and converses abundantly without a second thought. Although at first bewildered that his example could be so revealingly trivial, on further thought, I reconsidered. That a man of seventy years, raised on values steeped in colonial subordination of the Indian, has taken this step is an indication of how far the shift has reached. Who knows what new patterns of consciousness this "conversation between equals" on a bus might produce. The analogue in a younger generation might be Gaspar who, against his parents' protestations, married an indigenous woman and now severely criticizes the racist milieu in which he was raised. Or it might be Yolanda's children, who give the critique of ladino dominance consistent and acute attention. The ethic of equality is infectious and, especially among youth, can motivate changes that reach beyond the original conservative, hegemonic effects.

Those who level the accusation of reverse racism generally do not engage in a careful, systematic effort to distinguish between the facets of Maya assertion that are remedial—that is, clearly directed toward the elimination of existing inequality—and those that are unnecessarily provocative. Rather, ladinos use the discourse with a more elemental calculus: indígenas are gaining power at ladinos' expense; an important vehicle of this change is the critique of ladino power, both past and present; their efforts are well organized, conceptually sophisticated, and well financed. I describe the resulting critique as "preemptive" because its main purpose is to fend off a threat, to build a defensive case against an anticipated outcome. Racism or discrimination become code words, meant less to discern specific excesses associated with an ideology of racial or quasi-racial superiority than to stake out ground against an upcoming political challenge. Committed Maya activists are all too familiar with this line of argument, and are very unlikely to find it convincing. The most immediate consequence, instead, is further polarization. Mayas accused of reverse racism respond by turning more resolute, more distrustful of ladinos who espouse an ethic of equality. The accusations of reverse racism appear to confirm that behind even the wholly progressive-sounding term "equality" there lurk efforts of delegitimation. Among the causalities in this polarization are the ladinos solidarios: even their practice of equality becomes suspect and, by extension, the Maya activists themselves lose potential friends and allies.

Finally, we must briefly consider the proposition that a critique of what ladinos call reverse racism could be constructive. If this discourse focused solely on rigidity or authoritarianism in Maya consciousness and practice, could it not generate useful dialogue and help to engender what padre Antonio refers to as "prudence"? The answer should be yes. Only a zealot or a romantic would seriously claim that such problems do not exist in Maya cultural politics, or oppose dialogue about them. Yet these preconditions for constructive dialogue generally have not been met. As noted earlier, ladinos rarely back the accusation of reverse racism with an informed effort to discern the reasonable from the excessive. It tends to come in blanket form, with a strong whiff of defensive posturing, which undermines the invitation to dialogue. Moreover, even the more discerning critiques rarely expand to include parallel critical scrutiny of ladinos themselves.[43] The complex of cultural and biological precepts that constitute ladino identity and guide ladino attitudes toward indígenas is a topic that has just begun to surface in public discussion, and that cries out for further attention. Analysis that sidesteps this hornets' nest altogether to focus exclusively on indígenas, remains seriously incomplete, and can be expected to deepen mutual perceptions of polarized difference.

The discourse of reverse racism also raises a basic conceptual problem: is "racism" the appropriate analytical term to use? I have saved this question for last because, in many cases, it is not compellingly relevant. If ladinos use the phrase without theoretical pretensions, it is counterproductive, if not foolish, to respond with theoretical critique. I have taken pains to understand the discourse in its own terms and in its sociohistorical context precisely to avoid this problem, alluded to at the outset, of the theorist's conceit. However, the discourse of reverse racism does have a more theoretically elaborated expression, which in turn exerts influence on the commonsense discourse that I have analyzed thus far. Constructive *theoretical* dialogue on this issue has also been largely absent, owing to conceptual ambiguities in the very phrase "reverse racism." Substantiation of this point requires a more strictly theoretical discussion, which brings us to the fourth and final section of this chapter.

Reverse Racism and Racial Ambivalence

Admittedly, the analysis of reverse racism put forth here rests on an understanding of racism that not everyone shares. In my own usage, racism refers to settings of institutionalized power inequalities, where the systematic disadvantage of one group is justified and reproduced on the grounds of their alleged inferiority.[44] This usage by definition precludes the possibility that Indians could be racist toward ladinos, until a time when Indians occupy a position of institutionalized dominance in Guatemalan society. My usage also allows for the shift from classic to new or cultural racism: when persisting structural-institutional inequities are justified in largely cultural rather than strictly biological terms, and when "perpetrators"—that is, individuals or institutions with explicitly racist discourse—play a role of declining significance in reproducing racial inequalities. Racism, in this line of analysis, focuses our attention on socially produced consequences, rather than the specific content or intent of discourses or practices.

Those who use the term "reverse racism" as an analytical construct adhere to a very different definition of racism: any discourse or practice predicated on the inherent biological difference between two groups of human beings. This definition is widely deployed in both specialized intellectual and everyday settings, which gives rise to strained and often confusing dialogue about the topic at hand. Adherents of the first definition—racism as a certain form of structural inequity—and adherents of the second—racism as a certain form of cultural practice—cannot engage in meaningful dialogue as long as they use the same term to refer to such radically distinct social processes. This is precisely the situation that prevails in Chimaltenango, as the discourse of reverse racism has grown more prominent. Theorists such as Mario Roberto Morales, deploying the second definition, decry certain tendencies within the Maya movement as racist, and Maya intellectuals, using the first definition, point to these very criticisms as evidence of persisting ladino racism toward indígenas.[45] Both are probably right, given the particular understandings of racism they deploy. Perhaps padre Antonio's Freudian slip, affirming that Guatemala is "a multiracist country" is not that far off the mark after all! This conceptual confusion not only becomes an impediment to constructive dialogue but in addition has more specific political consequences. Despite the definitional gap, nearly everyone involved agrees that racism (however it is defined) is negative and needs to be stamped out. Once the accusation of racism is pinned on significant tendencies within the Maya movement, delegitimation inevitably follows. Quite apart from the speakers' intent, the discourse of reverse racism has consequences that must be taken into account: conveying the message that the Maya movement has lost its way, gone too far, turning innocent ladinos into its victims.

That being said, I do not endorse a position that in effect prohibits all such criticism of Maya politics as a safeguard against delegitimation. It is inconceivable that Maya cultural political activism would not suffer from problems, both circumstantial and endemic, which merit critical attention. Whether the problems are internal—for example, rigidity, authoritarianism, gender inequality—or external—for example, an overly dismissive or homogenizing stance toward ladinos—to stifle critical scrutiny would be a serious mistake. For the same reason, those who wish away such problems with a flourish, arguing that the essentialism of subaltern peoples is "strategic" and therefore exempt from negative effects, have little defensible ground to stand on.[46] The question is, rather, what role does the idea of racism have in this critique? Theoretical work in other settings may help to clarify this matter.

For some time now in Europe, and to a lesser extent the United States, theorists have analyzed the emergence of what they call "new" or "neo" racism.[47] A bare-bones description of neoracism, drawing on an essay by Etienne Balibar, includes three key features. First, its proponents repudiate biological reasoning in favor of the premise that people are culturally different, and that all peoples/cultures are formally equal. Second, they assume that these cultures are bounded, with core features that are quasi-immutable, yielding "racism without race." Balibar elaborates:

> At the cost of abandoning the hierarchical model (though the abandonment is more apparent than real…), culture can also function like nature…in particular, [by] locking individuals and groups a priori into a genealogy, into a determination that is immutable and intangible in origin. (1991:22)

The third and final premise comprises the "turnabout effect" mentioned earlier. The mixing of these cultures, because of their irreducible differences, leads "naturally" to polarization, mutual antagonism, and conflict, which then (lamentably and mistakenly) get understood in racial terms.[48] Given these latent tendencies, the logic continues, efforts to unify, to demand cultural rights, or denounce racism on behalf of subaltern groups merely fan the flames of an inherently explosive situation. These antiracist efforts are portrayed as causes of racial strife, because they exacerbate existing inclinations to divide people along cultural/racial lines. These activists, in effect, become the racists.

Although the differences between Balibar's neoracism and the emergent conditions in Guatemala are important to explore, I want to focus here on two instructive parallels. First is the shift from an emphasis on biological reasoning toward its cultural counterpart, with the possibility that something rigorously understood as "racism" can persist nonetheless. The second is the chain of logic that flows from this shift, resulting in the conclusion that activists who combat institutional conditions of inequity between culturally distinct groups could themselves be construed as racists. These two parallels comprise a strong case for thinking in terms of a distinctly Guatemalan variant of neoracism. Its key characteristics include the repudiation of social analysis or public policy grounded in biological or hereditary notions of indigenous inferiority; the persistence of deep structural-institutional inequities between most ladinos and most indígenas; and the reproduction of cultural precepts that justify and reinforce these inequities. These precepts, which affect *all* indígenas (not just the impoverished), include straightforward, deprecatory stereotypes, associations of the indigenous with immutable traditionalism, paternalism, and also an abiding fear that cultural difference tends inevitably toward vengeance and retribution.

This prior analysis of Guatemala's neoracism would provide the proper and indispensable context for critical engagement with the Maya movement. That is, I would be much more comfortable with critiques of Maya "racism" (preferably using a different term) if this *systemic* connection were clearly addressed. This proposed response to the problem posed at the beginning of this section has added the advantage of redirecting the discussion back to my principal analytical concern, not the consciousness and practice of theorists but rather of middle-sector and elite ladinos. A theoretically "correct" usage of the term "racism" would take into account these predominant understandings, critically situating the analysis within Guatemalan history and social process. This would require not just protestations of support for the principle of equality, but a self-conscious analysis of the relationship between the critique of the Maya movement on the one hand, and the broader social formation of neoracism on the other. It would require use of the term to be fully situated in relation to the dilemma of racial ambivalence that all ladinos—especially progressive ladinos—confront.[49] A theorist who accomplishes this prior step will have made a valuable contribution to the decolonization of ladino identity in particular, and of Guatemalan society in general. Credited with such a thoroughgoing critical and self-reflexive analysis, who would deny him or her the prerogative to advance a critique of the Maya movement as well?

Reverse Racism and Ladino Hegemony

I presented a few of the ideas in this essay to Héctor, whose brother joined the army after the traumatic disappearance of their mother Rosario and now works in the army public relations office. He focused especially on my account of the rising Maya challenge and the fearful ladino responses. "Army analysts are aware of all these changes,"

Héctor said, noting his brother's boast that "the next conflict in Guatemala [would] be an ethnic war." I replied: "Then why isn't the army doing more about it now?" Héctor did not hesitate: "Their strategy is to sit back, let the Maya organizations do their work, and wait until the conflict gets really serious. Then the [ladino] citizens will have to call the army in as their saviors." It would be easier to dismiss this exchange simply as one more example of people's profound cynicism toward the army, except that the vice-minister of Defense, in an interview, made a very similar statement.[50] I offer the anecdote as a sobering reminder not to let our analysis of ladino discourse overstate the Maya challenge and direct attention away from the brute realities of political-economic and military power. It is as if Héctor were saying, "all this analysis of discourse is interesting, but there are enormously powerful sectors in this country who will *say* almost anything, but they'll never actually give up their power." He is of course partly (even largely) correct. My only response to his critique (which in effect reduces my analysis here to window dressing) is that the dichotomy is misconceived. The contest over relations of coercive power is simultaneously a struggle over representations, waged in the realm of discourse. No political actors are more aware of this fact than army analysts themselves, which I suspect explains why they are allowing the image of an impending "ethnic war" to emanate so freely from their ranks.

For precisely this reason, it is crucial to understand discourses like that of reverse racism in all their complexity. My first, perhaps more obvious, contribution toward this end has been to associate the discourse with ladino responses to the multifaceted Maya challenge and, more specifically, to the expression of ladino racial ambivalence. This is a defensive response, based in part on what already has occurred, but more importantly on anticipated changes to come. Consequently, accusations of reverse racism feed directly on key elements in the ladino political imaginary—the focus of analysis in the next chapter: indigenous treachery, the specter of the insurrectionary Indian. My second conclusion focuses on the egalitarian sensibilities present in most renditions of this same discourse. These sensibilities—expressed as a commitment to trato de iguales—are a key source of efficacy and appeal, because they connote ethical rectitude, and because they offer indígenas real hope for improvement of their situation. Moreover, these sensibilities make racial ambivalence contradictory and unpredictable: both a preemptive strike against Maya cultural activism and a genuine opening where more substantive forces of change might enter and take hold.

This multivalence lies at the heart of the discourse of reverse racism, precluding any definitive, singular conclusions about its social effects. But the argument does have a more practical and, to some degree, urgent message. Analysts must be able to distinguish between the two guiding premises in the discourse—preemptive strike and egalitarian coexistence—and find ways to wrench them apart, encouraging the latter to develop and flourish. This same analytical effort must critically scrutinize the egalitarian sensibilities, separating the formal and homogenizing meanings from the transformative ones.[51] Granted, this task is much easier to conceive in theoretical terms than to implement in practice. Most important, it runs the risk of giving the theoretical formulation the lead, leaving everyday expressions of ladino racial identity and consciousness in the shadows. To at least mark my own awareness of this risk let me conclude by returning one last time to padre Antonio. Where might a dialogue begin that affirms the egalitarian ethic present in his reflections? Could that same dialogue also generate a critical acknowledgement of how his discourse of reverse racism has the effect of a preemptive strike? The following chapter is devoted to answering this question—exploring the tightly knotted set of premises that serve as the mortar, keeping the fearful, polarizing response to indigenous collective assertion cemented into place. Although often barely perceptible, these premises come to the surface with the phrase "la raza indígena"; they underlie the deep resonance of the specter of the insurrectionary Indian; and they are present in Don Antonio's image of the "waves of history." I find this last image especially haunting. In one sense, it merely signals the resignation of an elderly man, who even admits, after all, that justice would be done. At the same time, the image makes the impending conflict appear inevitable, which impedes dialogue and prepares the ground for blind reaction. The distinctly Guatemalan variant of neoracism, I fear, will increasingly rest on images like this one—ostensibly cultural and historical, but linked to remnants of a deeply racialized view of the world.

The power of this image lies, let me reiterate, in its cautionary not its predictive message. Especially since so many people like padre Antonio anticipate a major ethnic conflict in the near future, it would be unwise to rule out the possibility. It would be even more negligent, however, to assign the prospect as much credence as they do, when concrete evidence is so lacking. In my own appraisal, the prospect of a new ladino hegemony is much more likely. This would be achieved through the concession of formal equality as enticement, the discourse of reverse racism to fend off the most effective counterarguments, and repression of an upcoming ethnic war as the ever-present threat of coercive force that assures disgruntled conformity.

f i v e
Exorcising the Insurrectionary Indian: Maya Ascendancy and the Ladino Political Imaginary

> [Fantasy is] a major component of political life and a key factor structuring power relations. [I understand fantasy not]…as a purely illusory construction but as a form of reality in its own right, a scene whose structure traverses the boundary between the conscious and the unconscious…. [Fantasy] is not opposed to reality but constitutes its "psychic glue."
>
> —*Begoña Aretxaga, "Maddening States" (2003)*

> Al indio hay que invitarle a comer, y después tirarles los platos en la cara.
>
> (You have to invite the Indian to dine, and then throw the dishes in his face.)
>
> —*Ladino saying*

By the 1990s Don Luis, well into his eighties, had come to represent the ladino mind-set of past times, which subsequent generations had left far behind. The oldest of eleven siblings, Don Luis had come of age during the Ubico dictatorship (1933–1944), and already had a job with the state-owned liquor store when the October Revolution began. A tall man with a heavy frame and a deep voice, Don Luis held forth on Guatemalan history and politics with an air of great authority, and seemed to relish the role of the contrarian. Although they often disagreed with him, Yolanda and others of the younger generations had long since stopped arguing, whether out of deference or simply assuming that he was too old and obstinate to listen. As soon as Don Luis had retired from the conversation, deference would fade into a stance of distanced bemusement: his extreme positions on nearly every topic served to highlight how much the younger generations had changed. Yolanda could recount, nearly verbatim, Don Luis's thoughts on a series of topics, from Ubico (whom he deeply admired), to the decade of social democratic reform (which he detested), to constant

137

threat of Communist subversion, to ladino-Indian relations, often using them as a means to frame, by contrast, a position of her own. The contrast conjures an image of steady progress, especially through intergenerational change, toward increasing open-mindedness, self-reflection, and egalitarian respect for cultural difference.

One afternoon I settled in for a conversation with Don Luis and his wife Doña Maribel, about life in Comalapa in the old times. Doña Maribel seemed to have substantially different views on many of the things we discussed and occasionally interjected commentary, only to have Don Luis summarily silence her and resume the role of narrator. As expected, on the topic of "agrarian reform" during the reformist decade (1944–1954) Don Luis grew especially exercised:

> There wasn't much land reform in Comalapa. They hardly took any land. But people [that is, ladinos] were really worried about Decree 900. The Indians said they were going to turn everything upside down, take land, make the plantation owners work like peons. They told the ladinos that they were going to take over their houses and steal their wives. They thought they were gods back then. But in that era, we didn't hear anything about "Mayas." Nothing. We didn't even know they were Kaqchikeles. That came much later, with the Nobel Prize they gave to Menchú. Before, the Indian was Indian; and the ladino, ladino.

Here and throughout the conversation, in a common pattern among those of the older generation, Don Luis made a seamless bridge between "then" and "now." Conditions have changed, they readily grant—Indians now call themselves Mayas, and have a public political voice that before would have been unthinkable; but for Don Luis the basic racial antimony remains.

Although much of the analysis in this book is predicated on an endorsement of Yolanda's contrasting frame—between the classic racism of Don Luis's generation and the substantially different sensibilities of younger ladinos—here I want to revisit and critically examine that dichotomy. There is considerable heterogeneity among Chimaltenango ladinos of the younger generations (that is, those who were not yet adults during the 1944–1954 period)—from the outliers who still echo Don Luis, to the majority who embody and express what I have called "racial ambivalence," to a small but growing number who take an active stance of solidarity toward the Maya (the subject of chapter 6). These differences have substantive and empirically detectable consequences for Maya-ladino relations, which I do not wish to overlook. At the same time, I found that even the ladinos solidarios, in moments of unusual candor, often reveal a substratum of feelings toward Indians that sound disturbingly akin to the more explicit discourse of Don Luis. Although these inner feelings could perhaps be explained away as remnants of a superceded mindset, it is not at all clear that, so explained, they actually *go away*; to the contrary, this chapter documents the deep influence they continue to have. Characteristically self-reflective, Yolanda immediately thought of an example when I presented her with this line of inquiry. After all these years, Yolanda admitted, she cannot bring herself to leave the house after a shower with her hair still wet. Doing so brings forth a scolding voice, ringing in her ear, *"Aquella parece india bañada el sábado"* (She looks like an Indian after her Saturday bath).

This seemingly trivial anecdote goes to the heart of the central problem I explore here: to what extent do premises about Indians, shaped during the previous era, live on in the imaginaries of people who explicitly disavow classic racism? In numerous interviews and informal conversations, I gathered considerable evidence that points to this "afterlife" of classic racism, which clustered around one especially powerful epitomizing image: the insurrectionary Indian. Far from an isolated case of hyperbole, the composite picture that Don Luis invoked in our conversation is remarkably widespread: an Indian rabble, descending from the hinterland, to seize ladino property, kill the men, capture the women—in short, to turn the racial hierarchy upside down. Why has this image of the insurrectionary Indian proven so resilient? Under what conditions does it come to the surface and influence ladino daily thoughts and actions in the present, even among those ostensibly intent on building *relaciones interculturales* (relations of mutual respect for cultural difference) with Mayas? The problem grows more complicated still in contexts of social interaction: the ladino image of the insurrectionary Indian must draw on a series of assumptions about how Indians view ladinos, about Indian people's "true" intentions as they pursue collective means to better their lives and contest anti-Indian racism. Meanwhile, Indians must strain to make sense of what lies beneath the veneer of civility and mutual respect, to understand what ladinos' "true" intentions might be. Although this Indian side does not receive systematic attention here, the problem still must be framed in reciprocal terms: the ladino political imaginary feeds not only on stubborn premises about Indians, but in addition, on what ladinos imagine Indians to be thinking about them. My central argument follows. Within the ladino political imaginary, the insurrectionary Indian has become a flashpoint, ignited not by physical threats, which are rare and generally implausible, but rather, by acts that call ladino people's relations of racial dominance with Indians into question.

Indios Bochincheros *(Unruly Redskins)*

Two brief stories will help to give this problem ethnographic grounding, and to specify the stakes of the analysis. Soon after the 1995 presidential elections a Maya friend told me the first story. Self-confident, sharply analytical, and strongly Maya-identified, my friend had returned recently from a number of years outside the country. These elections would be the first ever for him and his wife, and they registered to vote with a sense of guarded anticipation. On election day they waited in a long line, and when they reached the table a problem arose: the election official claimed that his wife could not vote because she had not registered correctly. Though convinced that the official was in error, and seething inside, they did not persist. "I looked at the line of people—

mostly ladinos—behind me," my friend explained, "and I knew that if I protested they would take me for an 'indio bochinchero.'" Though at first I did not assign this story special importance, it came back to mind in the following months, as I became involved in a project called La Franja para el Diálogo Intercultural (Space for Inter-cultural Dialogue, or for short La Franja) that was conceived to encourage intercultural dialogue between national-level Maya and ladino intellectuals. Initiated by ladinos concerned with the critical absence of spaces for such dialogue, the project's first phase, which I helped to facilitate, involved a discussion solely among ladinos about their own identities and their relations with Mayas. As I began work with La Franja, the election story served as a constant reminder of the daunting complexity of the task they (and I) had undertaken. Looking back at the line of people behind him, my friend responded not to anything specific that one of them did (or had there been a momen-tary glare of disgust?), but rather, to what he imagined that they would imagine him to be.

At first, the scene seems to fit nicely with Michael Taussig's provocative image, a parable of sorts for the colonization of the Americas. Seeing the colonizer approaching in a canoe the "native" mocks him with obscene gestures, and in return the colonizer mocks the mockery, taking it as definitive evidence of barbarism.[1] Yet Taussig's play-ful image stops short of the crux in relation to contemporary Guatemala. Especially with the new wave of more systematic analysis of the revolutionary epoch (1961–1996), we are now beginning to understand the extent to which racism—as distinct from the anti-Communist counterinsurgency doctrine—comprised the brutal logic of the army's rampage against rural Indian communities.[2] To have the wrong person per-ceive you as an indio bochinchero well into the 1980s was a deadly serious matter. The previous era had been characterized by massive state violence against Indians, includ-ing abductions, disappearances, torture, massacres, and shockingly widespread sexual violence against women. As Don Luis's comment cited earlier suggests, this tight clus-ter of associations—racial polarization, violent conflict, and sexual violence against women—hark back to experiences that took place long before the internal armed con-flict of the 1980s. For precisely this reason, ladino people's deep and urgent desire for interculturalidad, and their widespread fears about racial polarization and conflict are far from transparent. They correspond not only to what ladinos and Mayas are saying and doing, but also to the political imaginaries of each, and to the way these imagi-naries influence what each assumes the other is up to.

The second story begins at Yolanda's workplace, a house converted into the regional office of DIGEA. The DIGEA office, which I visited frequently, was apt to be full of técnicos (staff teachers) who organized literacy classes in each of Chimaltenango's sixteen municipios, and came periodically to check in, gather mate-rials, or attend meetings. Since the técnicos were a mixed group of Indians and ladi-nos, and since I had gotten to know them fairly well, the DIGEA office seemed an ideal setting to gauge the tenor of daily relations between the two. Enthusiastic about the study, and proud of the intercultural sensibilities of her staff, Yolanda encouraged me to interview them all, and directed me especially toward Igor, a ladino teacher in his mid-twenties, who lived in a lower-middle-class neighborhood of the city. Igor stood out in Yolanda's mind, because he departed sharply from the ladino norm. In addition to the regular job with DIGEA, he volunteered with a fledgling effort to establish a nearby bilingual-bicultural elementary school, especially for Maya children whose parents want them to value their culture and (the occasional) ladino parents who also supported those goals. I arrived one afternoon at Igor's home for an interview, which began with a visit to the school and a long talk with the Maya woman, a university teacher, who heads up the effort.

Afterward, in the privacy of Igor's front porch, I began to probe the premises underlying his solidarity.[3] When I asked about ethnic conflict in his workplace, he quickly affirmed that "there is much discrimination against the indígena, so much that it has become part of Guatemalan culture." I pursued further the issue of conflict. I asked if indígenas were "doing anything to bring this on?" "Yes," he answered reflectively, "they practice many forms of provocation." When I encouraged him to elaborate, he responded with a from-the-gut catalogue of grievances that began as a trickle, and ended in a torrent:

> Perhaps this is a product of resentments brought on by the Conquest. But also, they think that one day they are going to dominate us and they want to let us know. One of the things they do is what we call the "re-Conquest." They spread the word that it is good to have ladina women, so that they can exterminate the ladino people more quickly. They want to dominate in everything—industry, commerce, and even in matters of the heart. The fact is that the indigenous race is stronger, predominant, and for that reason, when they mix with ladinos the Indian defines the outcome. We know they would be extremely drastic if they came to power. *Sería una matanzinga* (It would be a massacre).

This brought to mind a further reflection on his own identity:

> It is not fair that they have so much resentment against us. If we were Spaniards, they would be completely right. But we are a product of the Conquest too. We are not to blame. Throughout history, the ladino has been deprecated by those of both sides. Neither the Spanish father nor the indigenous mother loved them. They were kicked around by both.

Perhaps this image of mestizaje reminded him of another troubling pattern of identity politics in the poor barrios of Chimaltenango: Mayas are living there in increasing numbers, taking on many allegedly ladino cultural attributes, yet remaining Maya-identified:

> Those from the rural areas have much more basis to make claims as indigenous because they maintain the purity of their culture. But I think of the boys of

this alleyway. They are completely alienated from the indigenous culture—language, clothing, customs—they even wear earrings! But they still make claims as indigenous. I think that in a confrontation these would not have the right to speak. Yet they are the ones who jump up and down, while the ones from the rural areas, *ni fu, ni fa* (they are indifferent). What happens is these guys manipulate the others.

What really irks Igor is not that they are urban-dwelling youth wearing Reeboks and earrings, but rather that they would claim to be Maya as well! But there is an even more serious and sobering recurring theme in what by this point had become more a soliloquy than a conversation: the specter of racial violence.

The strongest ones are the Maya priests. A movement is growing, of those who practice the Pop Vuh. We could never get involved in this because they practice magic—some white magic, others black, but they do it. This is not compatible with our ways. The Maya priests are the most warlike.

By this point in our conversation I was thoroughly perplexed. If the Maya efflorescence had consequences that bothered him so, if Maya cultural activism was indeed fanning the flames of racial polarization, why on earth was he offering his time as a volunteer in support of an educational project steeped in the philosophy of Maya cultural pride and self-affirmation? For precisely that reason, he responded, without missing a beat. "In the moment of a confrontation, I want to be able to say that I am neutral, that I have helped both sides. I do it to have a little more security for my family." He then recalled what his grandmother had told him about Patzicía: "The indigenous people wanted to exterminate the ladinos." If the ladinos had not suppressed the uprising, they would have "finished us off." He then returned to my question: "I do not support the school to promote Maya culture, but rather to show that I respect it. That way, I will be able to claim neutrality, *cuando viene el cuentazo*" (when the day of reckoning comes). Igor ended our conversation with a recommendation: "The international donors, perhaps without knowing it, are promoting the conflict. They do not know that the organizations they support want to *sacudir a nosotros* (wipe us out). It would be good, Carlos, if you did a thorough investigation of this." Caught off guard by the intensity of Igor's feelings, I subsequently tried a number of times to continue our conversation. We never managed to arrange a follow-up meeting, and his lukewarm response to my entreaties left me with the vague sense that he felt he had said too much, gone too far.

It is possible, of course, that Igor believes in the cuentazo's imminence because of specific evidence that he sees and I somehow have missed. If so, it is striking that he did not cite this evidence, even when I pressed for details. The closest we came were some cases of minor tensions in the workplace. Instead, he portrayed the logic for and imminence of a confrontation between ladino and indigenous as almost self-evident, unnecessary to explain, a natural outgrowth of the past five hundred years of history and, more concretely, a direct sequel to the relatively isolated outbreak of racial violence fifty years ago. I want to be careful here not to overstate the case. Many ladino informants bring other factors into play, especially those who provide more analytically elaborated versions of their thinking. Nevertheless, Igor's story does contain a basic insight. Something is happening that makes the image of the insurrectionary Indian so ubiquitous, even among people whose more circumspect political analysis tells them otherwise. This "something" does not come directly from daily relations with Indians, nor does it obviously guide ladino conduct in, or perceptions of, those relations. Rather, it has a more complex logic: unspoken, though ready to surface in response to probing, and capable of providing a semantic bridge between seemingly disparate thoughts and observations. It is this semantic bridge, for example, that turns adolescent boys who wear earrings, seek ladina girlfriends, and yet identify as Maya into agents of "racial extermination."

From Identity Politics to the Political Imaginary

For a brief period during the mid-1990s, interculturalidad was the keyword of the day. The newly elected government of President Alvaro Arzú had taken moderate—though unprecedented—steps toward curbing and punishing military abuses. In 1996, his government consummated and began to implement the Peace Accords with the URNG, ending the internal armed conflict that had framed politics in the country since the 1960s. Emblematic of this achievement, and of the surety that a new political era was imminent, Arzú recruited two men with long histories of involvement with the revolutionary movement for key posts in his cabinet.[4] Government policies toward the majority indigenous population also underwent a sea change. Son of a prominent oligarchic family, closely aligned with the country's modernizing business elite, Arzú and the party he led epitomized the wave of neoliberal politics that swept Latin America in the 1980s and 1990s. Though intransigent toward labor, unfavorable toward state-supported social services, unwilling even to broach issues of the distribution of wealth and resources, the Arzú state generally encouraged political activity focused on the rejuvenation of civil society and the rights of citizenship. This created a favorable climate toward Maya cultural activism. Even compared to the previous two (ostensibly more centrist) governments, the opportunities for significant advance of Maya cultural and political rights were clearly greater under Arzú.

Although the Arzú administration created a conducive atmosphere for Maya efflorescence, Mayas already had achieved great momentum of their own in a process that began much earlier—in the mid-1980s, the early 1970s, or perhaps the early 1500s, depending on how one reckons. These achievements ranged from rising power in local (municipio) elections and commerce to majority Maya presence in schools that were previously ladino dominated; to the dramatic, largely spontaneous growth in the nationwide practice of the "Maya religion"; to the proliferation of Maya voices in the public sphere; and to the spread of "intercultural" desires throughout the society's ruling and dominant institutions, such that having visible Maya presence is a source of legitimacy. A rising level of financial support from multilateral organizations, international NGOs, and many governments of the West, strengthened the material basis for this efflorescence and heightened a general awareness that Maya cultural activism has powerful allies. My analysis of redistribution of power away from ladinos toward the Maya majority shows these achievements to be moderate, in some cases meager (see chapter 2). Such analysis might well understate, however, the profound change in Maya-ladino relations that has come with the gradual *mayanización* of civil society. It would certainly miss the charged reverberations of Maya efflorescence in the minds of many ladinos: sensibilities that include fear and indignation, guilt and right-eousness, often in bewildering combinations. A ladino intellectual with left-leaning politics summed it up succinctly, if inadvertently, with a revealing metaphor: "The future of Guatemala is in danger," he told me, "we are in danger of ceasing to be a unitary country. The indígena is a [political] actor who is knocking at the door." The metaphor offers a more intuitive, even homey, way to describe this chapter's central analytical question: How do ladinos respond when they awaken to find Indians knocking at the door?

My analysis thus far has focused on two general observations, which converge to yield what I have called racial ambivalence. The first ladino response involves the endorsement of a new ethic of equality and an explicit renunciation of the classic racism that holds Indians as inherently inferior. "There used to be racism here," most ladinos chimaltecos will admit, "but those days for the most part have passed. We are equal now, we do not make distinctions." The second response involves various efforts to constrain, or even to carry out a preemptive strike against, the most assertive expressions of this efflorescence. The same person who espouses egalitarian principles, as noted in previous chapters, will often add, "The problem now is that *they* are being racist toward us." Racial ambivalence reshapes social relations along the lines of a new cultural racism: a shifting cluster of discourses and practice that affirms the principle of racial equality and recognizes cultural difference, but at the same time singles out certain "Maya" cultural attributes that prevent harmonious coexistence and criticizes most forms of Maya organization as "clannish" self-marginalization, a cause of conflict rather than a response to inequality.[5]

This cultural racism, in turn, has a loosely articulated relationship to a new strategy of governance, which began with the democratic opening of 1985 and emerged in fuller form with the Arzú government. For the first time in Guatemalan history, the state adopted a strategy toward the Maya majority that allows the role of brute coercion to fade into the background, replaced by a concerted effort to rule through hegemony. One crucial ingredient in this new strategy is concessions by the state in the form of affirmative responses to Maya cultural-political demands. Another ingredient involves the setting of limits for such demands and spelling out the consequences if those limits are passed. The rise of a neoliberal economic model provides the infrastructure for this new mode of governance: considerable rewards for collective organization around demands for cultural recognition and great encouragement for efforts to strengthen civil society, combined with formidable barriers to any Maya initiative that would seek to proactively transform the societal distribution of resources or the political arrangements that would confer the power to make such transformations. This "neoliberal multiculturalism" constitutes significant openings and menacing closures that have fundamentally redefined the arena of contention between Mayas and the state.

Probing Atavistic Fears

While this analysis has considerable explanatory power, it also has rough edges, which are the focus of my attention in this chapter. It helps to situate the dual sense of vulnerability that many ladinos in Chimatenango feel: challenged from below by Maya upstarts, and destabilized from above by government and global multiculturalists who emit a steady flow of disconcertingly pro-Maya discourse and policy initiatives. It also provides a useful broader context for thinking about many ladinos' ambivalent response to the Maya efflorescence: hearty support for the new ethic of equality combined with sharp critique of many of the organizations and efforts that are working hard to bring those conditions of equality into effect. Yet this more linear and logical analysis of cultural politics is less helpful in making sense of the specter of a serious racial confrontation. Such fears could be portrayed as part of Machiavellian state actors' strategy of governance: a not-so-subtle warning to Maya activists and their followers. However, an instrumental explanation along these lines cannot account for why some variant of this image of *guerra étnica* (ethnic war) is also on the minds—albeit just below the surface—of many ladino chimaltecos like Igor. The spontaneity, depth, and surety of expression make it unlikely that this would simply be an echo of the warning from above. Besides, middle-class ladinos like Igor have their own reasons to be deeply resentful and suspicious of the state. Why, then, is this image of the insurrectionary Indian so ubiquitous and powerful?

Although the revolutionary mobilization and counterinsurgency campaign of the late 1970s and early 1980s had clear racial dimensions, at the level of national political discourse the conflict was cast primarily in standard Cold War binaries. Local understandings were more varied and complex. Some ladino chimaltecos speak of the insurgency as an Indian rabble, which had the specific objective of rising up against ladinos. More generally, the mere fact that large numbers of Indians took up arms, even if under the direction of ladino commanders, adds a charged immediacy to the question of what they are up to today. Still, the recent guerrilla insurgency is not the most common point of reference when ladinos chimaltecos cite historical antecedents for their fears. They are much more likely to skip over the revolutionary period altogether, focusing instead on a relatively isolated outbreak of "racism" some fifty years ago in the municipio of Patzicía—exactly what happened in my conversation with Igor, cited earlier. Amid all the current facets and expressions of Maya efflorescence, Igor was hard pressed to cite evidence that Mayas incite violent political confrontation of this sort. My guess is that such evidence would be difficult for *anyone* to find. Yet the image lives on. Without really understanding—much less accounting for—its ubiquity, at first I simply added this image awkwardly to my analysis, letting it serve as a general reminder of how charged relations between Mayas and ladinos had become.

My experience with La Franja led me to reevaluate that resting place, to pursue more vigorously the meaning and analytical status of this specter of the insurrectionary Indian. I do not report on that project here, out of commitment to the integrity of a political initiative whose participants insisted that the data not be used for any purpose other than the project itself. Suffice it to say that La Franja involved lengthy discussions with about eighteen national-level ladino intellectuals and political leaders who were deeply concerned about the future of relations with their Maya counterparts. Far from typical of their broader class-race milieu, participants in La Franja were generally left leaning, intensely analytical, and in principle favorable toward most facets of the Maya efflorescence. They were highly motivated and dedicated participants in the interviews I conducted individually with each, not out of deference to someone else's research objectives, but because the interviews formed part of a project of their own conception, an effort to create a forum for dialogue with Mayas. As a result, the probing and reflective frankness of our discussions achieved a depth that I rarely achieved in my own interviews with ladinos chimaltecos. Two broad conclusions from that experience had a major impact on my analysis and subsequent research. First, I was struck that fears of a serious racial confrontation were also prominent—albeit not unanimously so—among the members of this group. The image of the insurrectionary Indian is not, I was forced to conclude, merely a nightmare of provincial middle-class ladinos who cling to power and privilege amidst an increasingly restive indigenous majority. Second, through discussions of this image and related ones, I became convinced that interculturalidad cannot be properly conceived as an ideal, much less implemented as a process or practice, until people directly confront the work that the ladino political imaginary does.

At this point, let me simply use the phrase "political imaginary" to refer to thoughts, premises, and images that are set apart from the explicit analytical and sensory realms, though potentially present in both. It does not form part of the "unconscious" in any simple sense; the political imaginary can be conjured up, expressed, drawn on to inform a given line of analysis. Yet, like the unconscious, it can lie dormant and live on without direct discursive and experiential reinforcement. My inclination is to remain as inductive as possible: the political imaginary refers to the cluster of intense emotions—fear, desire, guilt, anger—that come to the fore in frank, unguarded discussions with ladinos about Mayas. The need to explore this level of analysis came up immediately in preliminary discussions about La Franja, but often initially in the third person. If this project was to advance, one participant told me, we would need to address the ladinos' "*miedos atávicos*" (atavistic fears) that Indians would come down from the mountains with machetes and chop them to pieces. "But Franja participants are middle-class ladinos from the capital city," I probed, "…their daily social existence involves few interactions with Indians, except perhaps domestic workers and market women." In response to this line of inquiry, some delved deeper, to identify fears, feelings of collective guilt, childhood experiences; to articulate ideas, premises, and memories that did not form part of their explicit political analysis but, nonetheless, were there. This, in turn, drove me to delve into my research in Chimaltenango with a more critical lens.

The idea of the political imaginary, even in this raw and untheorized state, helps to demarcate the analytical stakes of talking about ladino responses to Maya efflorescence. It is not only a question of how ladinos can simultaneously affirm equality and defend racial privilege, but also about deeply seated flashpoints that turn moderate expressions of Maya cultural assertion into threats of violence. It is not only about burying once and for all that sterile debate between primordial and instrumental theories of ethnic conflict, but also about acknowledging that some factor is at play, more closely akin to what used to be called "primordial sentiments" than most analysts would like to admit.[6] It may even bring us closer to understanding that most horrifying enigma in the study of ethnic-national relations: how people of different ethnic groups, living side by side with one another in apparent harmony, could one day suddenly take sides in a conflict and brutally attack one another. This of course is not primordialism in the term's original meaning, despite what the mainstream media often would want us to believe. Granted, a large part of the causal weight must be assigned to opportunist, authoritarian leaders and social inequities, as David Maybury-Lewis has pleaded that we understand.[7] But this plea to identify the "rational" interests at stake, taken to its logical conclusion, risks bringing us back to some redressed form of instrumentalism. A notion of the political imaginary, in contrast, might help guide a deeper search for what makes the call to arms ring true.

The Butcher Shop and the University

One afternoon not long after I had learned my "lessons" from La Franja, an unusual opportunity arose to explore this problem further. It emerged from a more linear research objective: to talk, with an elderly man from San Andrés Itzapa, about vague recollections I had heard from others of an Indian uprising in the making there, at the same time that one actually occurred in Patzicía. I settled into the living room with the man and three others from a younger generation, only to find my original objectives completely frustrated. They remembered the event and knew a lot about it, but kept directing the conversation elsewhere, connecting the memory of what happened a half-century ago with conditions that worry them in the present. This makes the conversation useful to recount for a different reason: it highlights an association between ladino identity, the current conditions of Maya efflorescence, and the image of the insurrectionary Indian. This conversation is also revealing because it is one of the few occasions in many hours of taped sessions, when the dynamic shifted from "interview" to free-flow conversation.[8] This yielded a spontaneity which I experienced frequently in informal conversation, but rarely managed to capture on tape.

The conversation itself has important antecedents. The first is a prior interview with Guillermo, a teacher originally from Itzapa, who now lives in Chimaltenango. As I had grown to expect, at a predictable place in my roster of interview questions, Guillermo mentioned the events of Patzicía in 1944, when the Indians rose against the ladinos. But Guillermo added a detail that I hadn't heard before, which interested me immensely: something similar, though with less dramatic consequences, had happened at the same time in his own community. I pressed for details but Guillermo had none; he suggested instead that we talk with his uncle Miguel, in his eighties, who had always lived in Itzapa and was a grown man in 1944. Stimulated by my enthusiasm, Guillermo proposed a plan: we would go to Itzapa on Sunday afternoon and talk with Don Miguel at the home of Hermelindo, another family member. Hermelindo would be sure to be there because every Sunday afternoon he convened classes of the "university"—sessions where friends gathered to drink rum and talk over the problems of the day. Guillermo referred to "university" repeatedly as we worked out the plan's details, amused by the additional meaning it took on given that I worked at a university. "The university has a *matrícula* (entrance fee), though, Carlos: some meat to put on the grill."

To buy the meat I visited my butcher, Don Rigoberto, who also happened to be a ladino from Itzapa. Though I had talked with Don Rigoberto a number of times, I had never been inside his shop, located in the heart of Chimaltenango's central market. Since the end of the morning business was not heavy, I decided to sit inside for a while, talk with Don Rigoberto, and watch him dispense meat. Although he had a few pieces of electrical equipment, he did most of the work with sharp knives of various sizes and a large hatchet; vigorous use of the hatchet, I soon found out, accounted for the bits of meat and bloodstains that covered the walls. We struck up a conversation, which Don Rigoberto stopped abruptly to dispatch clients who came to the counter, and then continued right where he had left off. Many clients were indigenous women, whom he attended with a jocular familiarity that comes with long-term commercial relationships. He generally addressed them with the familiar "*vos*," while they responded with "usted" but otherwise the exchanges were relaxed, filled with friendly give and take, and mutual repartee: "*Dáme un pedazo bien chulo, como usted*" (Give me a really pretty piece, as pretty as you are), one woman said; "*No seas mañosa*" (Don't get fresh with me), he responded, as he cut and weighed her order. And so it went, with well-worn jokes that played on the double meanings of the many descriptive adjectives of the trade (fat, tender, tough, juicy).

The somber and deadly serious tone of our conversation, carried on in the spaces between clients, could hardly have been more different, and the contrast bewildered me. I set that tone, perhaps, by telling Don Rigoberto of our plan to spend Sunday in Itzapa at the "university" talking about what happened in 1944. "Oh yes," he responded, "there was a confrontation. Two ladinos died, and some twenty Indians. They wanted to rise up, to take over our lands. The government sent troops to help." But beyond that statement he mustered few details, and turned quickly to connect that historical event with conditions in the present:

> This does not go away easily. It is a profound anger. What happens is that
> the ladinos have exploited the indigenous for many years. Now they are rising
> up, and they want to do the same thing to us. There are some who are more
> well behaved, better educated, more ladino. But as for the majority, you cannot
> trust them. They are treacherous, with evil intentions. When they kill a
> ladino, they cut him up in pieces, as an expression of their anger.[9]

My mention of Don Hermelindo's university also brought to mind the woeful
state of local politics in Itzapa. Before, ladinos always controlled the mayor's office,
with token presence of Indians despite their demographic majority. Since 1985 that
formula has been reversed, leaving ladinos relegated to the sidelines. Don Hermelindo,
a long-time local politician, had been the only ladino member of the previous *corporación* (town council), and had resigned in frustration. Don Rigoberto remembered the
problem with great bitterness:

> I told him to leave there, because they would eat him alive. They would speak
> in their language [Kaqchikel] and Hermelindo didn't understand anything.
> He was the only ladino among that horde of Indians. The problem is their
> anger: when they get into positions of power, we suffer. And there are so many
> of them, they will always win the elections. Now it has gotten even worse
> with this girl that always comes out in the newspapers, what's her name?
> [CRH: Rigoberta Menchú?] Yes, that Menchú. Now that Menchú wants to be
> president. [CRH: And if she wins?] It would be hell. There are lots of them
> who want to seize power, and if they do, they would proceed to kill us off.

I think it was the interlude of a jocular exchange with another client that brought Don
Rigoberto to change the subject and focus on the chasm between the two sets of interactions:

> We always maintain the appearance of good relations. I get along well with
> everyone. If I pass the indigenous boys on the road to Itzapa, I give them a
> ride into town. Everyone greets me, "Adios Don Rigo,"—a sign of affection.
> But you cannot trust them completely. We get along well, but you cannot
> have a deep trust, because you never know for sure what they are thinking. I
> have good relations with them because, in the moment of a conflict, I'd be
> well situated. This is a way to take care of myself, you see? If we get along
> well maybe they won't fuck me over.

With that Don Rigoberto sent me on my way, plastic bag of his best *lomito* (beef
shoulder) in hand, and an appropriately butcher-like popular saying to sum up our
conversation. "Remember, Carlos, *mascamos pero no tragamos*" (we chew but we don't
swallow).

The university convened in the early afternoon in Hermelindo's living room,
with plenty of rum and, a little later, meat, fresh tortillas, and *chiles chiltepes* (habanero

chiles). It is a comfortable, spacious home, with all the expected amenities characteristic of the rural ladino middle class. At first we were six people, but some drifted in and out of the conversation, including Hermelindo himself who was called away on an errand. The three who participated most actively were Angelina—Hermelindo's sister, a woman of about fifty years who teaches elementary school in Itzapa—my friend Guillermo, and Don Miguel, his uncle. Don Miguel was lucid but quite deaf; he would remain quiet until someone shouted a question directly at him, and then take off on a detailed response. At first, I directed every question at Don Miguel, and everyone listened attentively. But the focus of the conversation gradually shifted toward Angelina, as it became clear to all that Don Miguel had relatively little of great importance to say. I started with the Ubico era, which immediately preceded the events of 1944:

> CRH: In Ubico's time, here in Itzapa, did indigenous people live in the center of town, or only ladinos?

> Don Miguel: Look, in general, very fortunately, only ladinos have lived in the center of Itzapa, few Indians…. It is not like Chimaltenango, where the ladinos are in the outskirts and the indigenous dominate the center. All the houses that you see in the entrance to the bus terminal are owned by Indians. It is even worse now than before, two-story houses owned by indigenous, stores owned by indigenous, pharmacies owned by indigenous.

Disconcerted by how focused this octogenarian was on indigenous ascendancy in the present, I tried again:

> CRH: In that time, how did you bring in the harvest?

> Don Miguel: Look, before there were workers, but today it is becoming difficult, now that humanity has grown…work options have expanded, and the Indians have become civilized. Something strange is happening with the workers. I have a bit of coffee, no big amount, but the foreman says to me, "Don Miguel," he said, "it is 15 minutes after four." I respond, "How could that be, it is four o'clock sharp." He says to me, "No, look at my watch." He is uneducated, doesn't know how to read and write, and now he carries a watch? Now even the little kids have watches. Civilization is advancing too much.

I tried once more, and with the help of some prompting from the other two, finally got some modest results:

> CRH: When Ponce came in, on the 20th of October, how did the conflict start?

> Guillermo: When Ponce came in on the 20th of October, Carlos says, how did the problems begin? Can you tell about the massacre in Patzicía?

Angelina: The revolution of October 20th of 1944....

Guillermo: People say that the indigenous men wanted to take the ladina women....

Don Miguel: Ah! Of course they did, they had a plan to finish off the ladinos, and each one of them already had a woman picked out who would stay with the men.

CRH: Really? How did this happen? Why did they rise up?

Don Miguel: It turns out that the Indians were prepared.... I remember the central plaza, where the church is now, they had gathered there with rifles to wait. One ringing of the bell and they all would have risen up against the ladinos. But thank God in that time the local commander was there, gathered with his men; he took charge and confronted the problem head on.

In some three hours of conversation, Don Miguel never provided much more detail than that. As far as I could make out, it wasn't that he didn't know more, but rather that recounting details would add little to the main conclusion already drawn. I fished for specifics, using a piece of information that Guillermo had given me previously:

CRH: I was told that the father of the present mayor was involved, with his own organization.

Guillermo: Yes, he was a leader.

CRH: And what did he do?

Don Miguel: Lead.

Guillermo: Stirred the people up.

Don Miguel: It had to do with interests in land, the lots where the houses were built, they wanted to take our houses away....

Guillermo: They are the equivalent of the guerrillas today, Carlos.

CRH: Was land the central issue?

Angelina: Back then, the indigenous people were all in agreement, in all the departments, not just here. They were going to rise up that night in support of Ponce Vaides. They supported him, and he endorsed the idea that the Indians should get their lands back.

CRH: Lands that were mainly in ladino hands?

Angelina: Exactly. It was a land problem, which people died for. When Ponce Vaides fell, and Ubico entered, Ubico sent lots of reinforcements to Patzicía right away, when the news spread that they had killed Señor Mata. Señor Mata was a butcher. They beheaded him, and hung his head in the butcher shop. They say the indigenous people entered people's houses through the roofs: they ripped off the tiles, took everything. Don Neto Avila hid his 14-year-old son in a closet, and they found him. Using a hatchet, they cut him into little pieces.

Although she had the sequence of presidential succession backwards (Ponce came after Ubico), Angelina recounted the events in Patzicía in the precise phrasing that I had heard many times before. The conclusion of all this Guillermo delivered with a stern nodding of his head: *"Era a nivel racial, puro racial"* (It was a racial thing, purely racial).

These excerpts comprise a very small part of what amounted to perhaps the first third of the conversation. Yet in that entire time, few other important details about the events of 1944 surfaced, and those that did came from what Angelina remembered having been told by her mother. It seemed important only to reiterate the basic conclusion—summarized vividly by the events of Patzicía and the tragic fate of Don Neto's son—in order to address its current implications. This was especially evident in Don Miguel's repeated efforts to use my historical questions as an entrée for commentary on the present, and in the way the conversation grew more animated as it moved toward contemporary topics:

> CRH: After the 1944 revolution, after that uprising, were there other events in Itzapa, or did things calm down?
>
> Guillermo: Yes, something that I can tell you, Carlos, is that the Indian's resentment runs in his veins, and when they acquire power, they take advantage…
>
> Angelina: They marginalize themselves; I don't know why they do it.
>
> CRH: How does that happen?
>
> Angelina: Because, take for example in the workplace: they always go off by themselves and, if they get a new position, it goes to their head.
>
> Guillermo: It's as if they are taking advantage of the situation to get vengeance.
>
> CRH: And do they treat their own people poorly too?
>
> Guillermo: No, they favor some over others.
>
> Angelina: Haven't you seen how Don Vicente Reyes [school supervisor in Itzapa] is with the Vice-Minister of Education? They are compadres. Some get help, others don't.…But this is none of our business here.

Angelina's last comment expressed discomfort, as if she felt she had gone too far by naming people in the Education Ministry who were the objects of her critique, but who also were her superiors. Guillermo filled the awkward silence that followed by directing the conversation back to its original objectives: "Carlos: What important information are you interested in? Tell us."

In deference to Angelina's sensibilities, I shifted back to safer historical terrain, and asked about intermarriage between indígenas and ladinos. An intriguing exchange followed, in which Angelina sought to disabuse Guillermo of the common ladino lament that Maya culture has claims to purity that leave ladinos hopelessly behind:

> Guillermo: They still have an identity, their race is still pure, we're the ones that don't have either any more.
>
> Angelina: How could they have a pure race after five hundred years?
>
> Guillermo: But they have been able to conserve it. For example, in Itzapa, how many ladinos are there who have married Indians?
>
> Angelina: But they were already mixed.
>
> Guillermo: OK, but how many?
>
> Angelina: Yes, but there is no such thing as a pure Mayan. They say they are Mayan, but this is a lie. When the class of *señoríos* (nobility) was founded, the Mayas already had disappeared. There are no authentic Mayas. Now, why don't they just call themselves indígena? Indian is not a bad word, but rather an indication that they were from India. In error, they were disdainfully called "Indians." Authentic Mayas no longer exist, and this business about teaching people Maya culture is a pure lie. It really bothers me when they refer to themselves as Mayas.

I probed further:

> CRH: But what about those who have recovered the Maya religion?
>
> Angelina: They do not have the right, historically or culturally...they have no right to call themselves Mayas.
>
> CRH: Why not? When did it disappear? With the Conquest or before that?
>
> Angelina: The Maya Empire had long since disappeared when the Conquistadors arrived. The Conquistadors found only the nobility that developed after the Mayas. There had been much mixture; the noble class had mixed with the Toltecs and the others that came from Mexico. By then the Mayas had disappeared completely.
>
> CRH: So what culture did they find?
>
> Angelina: A mixed culture.
>
> Guillermo: And the nobility, how did it form?

Angelina: The nobility formed with Toltecs, Chichimecas, and other tribes, all of whom came from Mexico. They migrated here. The Mayas had disappeared. Only vestiges remained, but the pure Maya race already had disappeared.

CRH: Then how do we explain the fact that Mayan culture is emerging with such strength these days?

Angelina: Look, it's a pretext, how can I say it...?

Guillermo: A battle horse.

Finally, Guillermo gets with the program and begins to work the issue in tandem with Angelina:

CRH: Then it is an invention of certain people?

Angelina: That's it, a charisma that is being imposed on the current conditions.

Guillermo: I remember that in Xela they crowned the Rabina Ajau[10] and they were all kneeling down on their woven mats with their indigenous paraphernalia, and they interviewed one of them, and she said the same old thing, that we have to struggle for our Mayan race, and this, that, and the other thing. Then they said, "Very well, Miss, could you give a message in your dialect to the public?" She responded, "I'm sorry, I don't remember."

Angelina: It is, how can I say it, a shield (*coraza*) that they are using to say, we are Mayas.

Guillermo: Anywhere you go there are leaders that manipulate the situation and look for an opening.

CRH: Has there, in response, been a recuperation of ladino culture, or isn't there a concern about this?

Angelina: For us ladinos, we are interested in having the indigenous take on our ways. That's what I told you, Carlos. We did a survey in the primary school, to see [what people think of] all these bilingual education programs, and the indigenous people are not interested. The survey showed that what the parents really want is for their children to learn to read and write in Spanish.

CRH: And what about Maya culture?

Angelina: They do not talk about the Maya, any more than what the history books might tell them.

Guillermo: Look: to maintain all that is a step backward for us, that is, progress for them is to change their customs.

Angelina: Look, now, at how many indigenous people study English, French, and have lost interest completely in their own languages.

CRH: What about Kaqchikel?

Angelina: For what? It is not an international language; it is a tiny dialect.

In this conversation, speakers' concerns revolved around three main themes, which combine to make a powerful, if not altogether coherent, critique of the Maya efflorescence: Maya people have no claim to modernity, except through ladinos; Maya cultural rights activism is dangerous and threatening, due in part to quasi-biological tendencies toward resentment and retribution; and Mayas are attempting to bolster political legitimacy in the present, with spurious assertions of cultural continuity with the classic Maya civilizations of times past. Don Miguel is miffed and perplexed by the idea that Mayas would make these claims on modernity: building two-story houses on a main road in town, using wristwatches to measure the working day on their own. In more subtle versions of these same concerns, Angelina and Guillermo insist that Mayas believe their own languages are inherently backward. Angelina sums up the matter with arresting frankness: "We want the indígenas to become more like us." Here the idea is that "they are invading our space, assuming roles that legitimately belong to us." Confirmation that this ascendancy is ill-advised comes from observations of how Mayas behave when assigned positions of authority: headstrong, authoritarian, vengeful, playing out age-old resentments. Rising use of the term "Maya" bothers Angelina because the claims it implies are so potent: we have been here all along; we have an ancestral culture; we have much more to contribute to an authentic Guatemalan national identity than ladinos do. The assertion of Maya cultural continuity from time immemorial brings the entire argument into focus: Mayas are both authentic and modern, politically ascendant in local and national arenas, looking toward the future yet with vivid memories of the past five hundred years—so vivid that the memories "run in their veins."

Political Imaginaries and Racial Formation

The problem stretches Gramsci—my usual source of theoretical inspiration—nearly to the breaking point. Something more is going on than the creation and reproduction of hegemony, if for no other reason than because the images that I seek to understand are so permeated with visceral fear, so divergent from what one would expect watching these same ladinos' daily social and political interactions with indígenas. Michael Omi and Howard Winant's much cited and recently updated classic text, *Racial Formation in the United States*, for example, invokes clearly identifiable "social, economic and political forces," which shape racial categories and in turn are shaped by racial meanings.[11] They move closest to the problem we confront here in their discussion of the new Right's use of "code words," to invoke race and generate powerful racialized political effects, while remaining within the bounds of antiracist democratic ideals (1987:120). Yet this observation still begs the question: how do we understand

and explain the powerful effects that these code words have? A similar limitation applies if one tries to think of images like that of the insurrectionary Indian as a "private transcript," in the sense developed by James C. Scott (1990): a rational, clear-headed analysis carried out "off-stage," carefully hidden from the public exercise of power. Such images are part analysis, but also part fantasy; part historical reflection, but also part shuddering memory of a grandmother's admonitions. Most important, the political imaginary as I use it here refers to ideas that people feel deeply, that at times influence how they think and act, but do not necessarily guide their daily interactions with Mayas. This is precisely the realm of ideas that would not be apt to arise, for example, in an effort at intercultural dialogue. They are too dangerous, too excessive, too raw.

In response to this analytic challenge, some have turned to the psychoanalytic notion of the unconscious. One example is Žižek's (1993) Lacan-inspired analysis of ethnic-national conflict, which mocks both political science banalities that rely on a premise of rational interests and anthropological notions of key public symbols around which identities are constructed and contested. In a similar vein, my late colleague Begoña Aretxaga also pushed herself and her students toward ever deeper and more complex explorations of the "psychic glue" that constitutes social reality and gives it cohesion (or at least, the appearance of cohesion).[12] The analytic projects that motivate this emphasis on fantasy, political imaginaries, psychosexual processes, and the like vary from the (in my view, less useful) full tilt critique of the "master narratives" that have preceded them to projects that grapple with discrete analytical problems, showing how they cannot be fully understood if these psychic processes are neglected.[13] Aretxaga, for example, asked broad questions about the political—the ambiguous position of women in ethnic-national resistance movements; the compulsions of the antiterrorist state toward precisely the kind of terror that it purports to be fighting; the predominance of sexualized violence under late capitalism—and deployed analysis of psychic processes to yield insight that other explanations have lacked.

This latter approach is especially valuable, in my view, when the analyst engages and enhances other analytical frames, rather than attempting to displace them completely. Stuart Hall, for example, has acknowledged gaps in his own Gramscian framework, and has taken on the task of making it more attuned to the nonlinear facets of political consciousness. In response to a challenging dialogue with Homi Bhabha and Jacqueline Rose, Hall affirms the need to analyze identity, looking beneath the surface of a group's self-ascribed key symbols, toward "a domain of discursive operations in which extremely important forms of social and political action take place, [actions] connected to…psychosexual processes, [actions which] cannot be understood without reference to the imaginary or to the unconsciousness" (1995:64). Hall directly acknowledges that his analysis—of Thatcherist politics and ideology, for example—would have been enhanced by greater consideration of these psychic dimensions. Yet even Hall, who surely is unparalleled in his ability to digest complex bodies of theory in comprehensible prose, seems incapable of actually bridging this gap, of showing how we might draw on both Gramsci and Lacan in a synthesized way.[14] Just after the passage cited above, he adds a crucial qualifier: these discursive actions do not simply consist of "repetitions or reiterations of psychic processes. *They also have a reality and acquire a social logic in the world*" (1995:64, emphasis added).

Taking guidance from this qualifier, I attempt to strike a balance, or perhaps to maintain a creative tension, between two inclinations: to give "psychic processes" a full hearing, while also examining their "social logic," which I take to mean how they are historically constituted and structured in society. My rationale for this dual approach is both theoretical and political. Theoretically, while I affirm the importance of psychic processes to the problems at hand, I find it difficult to generate a convincing account of their provenance and effects unless they are located squarely within the flow of the social. Politically, I contend that this "social logic" provides not full answers, but rather an indispensable point of departure for confronting the "what is to be done." An analysis of racial hierarchy in Guatemala, in terms of historically structured inequities between Indians and ladinos, yields a straightforward principle for how anti-Indian racism, in both its ideological and material manifestations, might be eliminated. Consideration of psychic processes—and for that matter, other aspects of how members of both groups live and understand race—is bound to complicate and disrupt this clear-cut principle. That, after all, is the main conclusion of the present chapter. Yet without this initial premise the analysis could easily fall victim to the most common of academic conceits: reveling in complexity and multiplicity, allowing them to overshadow or suppress basic political realities. The balance I attempt to strike, then, seeks the analytic closure that any form of political engagement requires, while remaining open to psychic and other cultural processes, which reopen and wreak havoc on those very political-analytical conclusions.

Despite interpretive disputes on many substantive points, cumulative historical research in the last decade has converged on the idea that the contemporary identity category "ladino" took shape in the course of the nineteenth century, and especially in the aftermath of the Liberal revolution of 1871.[15] This transition marks the period when, for the first time in Guatemalan history, self-identified "Euro-Guatemalans" joined with ladinos to govern the country together.[16] Ladinos made concerted efforts to exclude Indians from this historic bloc, and in the process transformed what it meant to be ladino. Deep divisions and intense political struggle could occur within the bloc, even while certain basic premises, now part of the common sense shared by all who belong, remained intact. These premises not only served as the psychic glue that kept the bloc together, but also became foundational elements of ladino identity itself: that ladinos are starkly dichotomous from Indians despite the possibility of Indian ancestry; that indigenous culture (despite an illustrious pre-Columbian past) is fundamentally at odds with modernity; that ladino culture, though perhaps lacking in authenticity, offers a secure bridge to modernity; that the national culture, whatever its other attributes, must be thoroughly modern in conception, making ladinos the only ones with "national potential" and leaving indigenous people with little to contribute to the nation beyond the "feathers and flourish" associated with their distant Maya past.[17]

According to this logic, indigenous people's persistence itself is not threatening; what provokes atavistic fears are changes that call into question the racial hierarchies on which ladino identity rests. The persistence of indigenous peoples, especially when they remain relegated to the traditional space of rural communities, offers economic advantages, and has added an aura of authentic cultural material from which to build Guatemalan national identity. Even the halting integrative efforts to draw indigenous people more fully into this society and polity, to grant greater equality and basic rights of citizenship—though certainly disconcerting to some—would not directly threaten the discursive chain linking ladinos to political-economic privilege. A problem of a very different magnitude arises when Maya political mobilization and other less intentional processes of social change place these links in doubt: either when indígenas bypass ladinos altogether on the road to modernity, or when it becomes clear that the national project can only result from a direct negotiation between Maya and ladino. The self-assured, historically grounded, culturally rich, and yet also modern contents of Maya identity begin to make ladinos, by contrast, appear to be without identity, like crass imitators without convincing claims on the nation. These challenges—associated with identity, modernity, and national pretensions—shake the foundations of ladino political dominance. These are precisely the issues that so preoccupied Guillermo, Angelina, and Miguel; they are the very embodiment of Maya efflorescence in the present.

These challenges also bring the image of the insurrectionary Indian to the fore. The premises of ladino political dominance have rested on a series of binaries, which have kept the hierarchical ordering of the two firmly in place. Ladinos view themselves as modern, national, and if not "authentic" at least culturally dynamic and forward looking, and they view Indians as backward, local, untrustworthy, vindictive, and capable of great collective violence if provoked. A key feature of this dichotomy—the embodiment both of the allegedly Indian characteristics, and the brute force on which the dichotomy was founded—is the Indian rebellion. Actual occurrences of such rebellions (or perceived threats) certainly evoke the image most directly. Much more important, however, is the symbolic and sensory resonance, especially given the striking infrequency of rebellions after the late nineteenth century. They recapitulate the very distinctions through which the Indian-ladino dichotomy was constructed from the start. My assertion, in sum, is that over the last century the image of the insurrectionary Indian has become an epitomizing symbol around which ladinos have organized a sense of who they are, and who they are not.[18] The few historical instances of such rebellions have taken on such enormous resonance in this light because they serve as anchors for collective identity, and self-evident rationale for the overarching, racially hierarchical organization of society.

The ubiquitous sexual imagery that accompanies discourse about the insurrectionary Indian provides the other crucial piece of this broader argument. The ubiquity is beyond question. As exemplified in the conversations above with Don Luis, Igor, and Don Miguel, and in material cited elsewhere in this book, in my experience with La Franja and in numerous informal conversations, ladinos rarely express fears of Indian ascendancy without reference to the sexualized violence and sexual conquest that would result. This evidence may be most convincing when the conversation is informal, and the association completely matter of fact. For example, while waiting for an interview with an engineer, to talk about economic development in the department, I engaged in small talk with his secretary, a young ladina woman from Patzicía. There are two cemeteries in Patzicía, she said, one for ladinos and one for Indians. In general, though, these old-time divisions between the two groups were breaking down; many Indian *patojos* (young men) were going out with ladinas. The ladinas accept, she continued, because so few ladinos have remained in town. Then, to my surprise, she made a mental leap from this front office small talk, to the revolutionary years. At that time, she continued, the Indians rose up and their plan was to kill the men and take the ladina women. The plan was foiled, but they never lost the desire to carry it out. Now the patojos are doing the same thing, achieving conquest through romance rather than revolution. This seemingly self-evident connection between interracial romance and violent (racial) revolution is widespread in the minds of ladinos chimaltecos; as such, this connection is another source of the psychic glue that has sealed relations of racial dominance.[19]

In this line of argument, sexualized fears of retribution are so strong precisely because sexual predation has been so integral to ladino-Indian relations in the past. Indeed, everyday practice in Guatemala is so saturated with transgressions of this supposedly impermeable boundary that transgression and boundary might be thought of as mutually constituting. Sexual predation is ubiquitous, if rarely talked about openly, following the familiar pattern of dominant culture males viewing lower status women as fair game. Although I found it difficult to collect first person accounts—probably more due to my own residual Puritanism and fear of descending into anthropological voyeurism than to their inhibitions—I recorded enough third person descriptions of cross-racial sexual relations to be sure that in Chimaltenango it has been commonplace. A number of ladino men expressed sexual fascination with Indian women: their earthy exoticism, their ignorance of sex and love beyond the animal-like physical acts of reproduction. According to Samuel Montoya, an economics professor in a local fly-by-night "university," the *faja* (cloth belt) presses an Indian woman's sexual organs downward, so that the man, when he penetrates, feels the vagina much closer to him, which increases his sexual satisfaction.[20] Guillermo told me that during his year-long experience in a rural Indian community as a young man, he discovered with great surprise that Indians do not know how to kiss.

> I taught them how to express this form of affection, and it had an enormous
> impact in the community. I explained to the community *cacique* (village
> leader), you have to *acariciarles* (show physical affection). "I'm going to talk

with my people," he responded. Developing the ability to show affection
became my main concern.

Guillermo's story flowed seamlessly into third person accounts of sexual relations with Indian women:

It is common for the young man to have relations with the domestic worker.
He would be a horny and persistent boy, waiting until the muchacha was
alone, when the adults went out to go shopping or something. Then, he'd tell
his friends, "that Indian is really good, *bien ajustadita* [nice and tight]..." and
the others would be dying to try.

Rounding out the topic, Guillermo switched to a didactic tone, explaining Indian women's behavior in trysts with ladinos. "The Indian is very cold and passive," he began. "In general, she will never show emotion. But if she responds with passivity, that sends a message that she is willing."

Whether from outright rape, or some other point in the power-laden continuum of coercion and consent, when the Indian woman became pregnant, she would generally withdraw to raise the child in an Indian milieu, without the benefit (whatever that may be) of the father's recognition, material support, and surname. A conversation about this problem of "outside children" in the coffee growing municipio of Acatenango yielded detailed descriptions of the practice and a summary phrase that elicits a wry smile of recognition from people of Yolanda's generation: "*Ah si, aquella es hija de la molendera*" (Oh yes, she is the daughter of the tortilla maker). These Acatenango ladinos then sang a Mexican *corrido* (folksong), which summarized the resulting predicament: "*Yo soy hija de nadie*" (I am no one's daughter)—a reference not to being orphaned but to lacking a proper last name.[21] Unrecognized, and denied entry into the ladino world (but quite possibly preferring it that way), these "hijos de nadie" ended up reinforcing the ideological precepts of the racial hierarchy, even while presenting bodily evidence of their transgression. Yolanda confirmed this point with a story about Felipe, a childhood friend from a neighboring municipio. Felipe's doting mother would make a special effort to bring young indigenous women home as domestic workers so that he could have sex with them. Sexual predation of this sort generally strengthened racial boundaries, by reinforcing the central precepts of ladino patriarchy. These transgressions would have the opposite effect only under exceptional circumstances, when they pierced the protective coat of the unspoken, through the development of genuine mutual affection or the Indian's public claims of legitimate status within the ladino family.[22]

From the assumption in ladino households that adolescent boys would practice sex with young domestics, to the *finquero*'s (plantation owner) traditional rights to the "first night" of an Indian woman employee, to the commonplace occurrence of rape whenever Indian women come into unprotected social contact with ladino men, the tightly intertwined character of racial and sexual inequality is beyond doubt.[23] In times of intense conflict this relationship receives further confirmation. The UN Commission for Historical Clarification (CEH) report on political violence during the revolutionary period includes a series of testimonies, recounting barbarous sexual violence against women, which amply substantiates the study's conclusion that "the army used [sexualized violence]…as habitual, even systematic, practice, as a weapon in the counterinsurgency struggle" (Comisión para el Esclarecimiento Histórico 1999:29, 55).[24] Even given ladino chimaltecos' highly uneven knowledge of specific acts, it seems reasonable to assume a cumulative historical understanding, a social memory of sorts, that reinforces this basic association of anti-Indian racism with sexual dominance and predation. With the rising contestation and self-critique of this racism of times past, one can only expect that fears of in-kind retribution would be rife.[25]

Let me reiterate: the image of the insurrectionary Indian is always there (somewhere), but it does not govern the meanings and patterns of quotidian relations between Maya and ladino. Instead, it recedes into the background, only to grow salient in times like the present when the foundations of the social formation are being called into question. According to this logic, the image comes to the surface as part of ladino responses to displacement and insecurity for reasons largely unrelated to the actual likelihood of a racial confrontation: it shores up the founding premises of ladino identity, breathing new life into worn out answers to the question "Who are we?" It helps to place the bewildering diversity of challenges and exceptions to the once more or less stable, predictable racial divide back into a familiar framework: if all this change is really about an imminent guerra étnica, then, however frightening and horrible the prospect, at least it now is comprehensible. Even this, however, suggests a much more linear reasoning than I want to portray. I would like to think of the insurrectionary Indian as a flashpoint, an image that jumps suddenly to mind, and in so doing summarizes and reiterates what it means to be ladino.

This formulation, though preliminary and far from fully elaborated, yields a specific proposition regarding the question posed at the outset: why the ubiquity of the image of the insurrectionary Indian? I propose that this image becomes prominent in the discourse of ladinos whenever they perceive the founding premises of their identity to be under attack. One impetus for ladinos to draw such a conclusion would be to uncover evidence that Mayas are indeed preparing ideologically and militarily to launch a collective assault against them. Some do make such allegations, though the evidence they cite is scanty and nearly impossible to verify. The proposition is meant to highlight other types of challenge as well, including those that have little to do with political-military confrontation, which might evoke the image in much the same form. When Mayas make strong, independent claims on modernity; when the assumption of isomorphism between ladino culture and national culture is called into question; and when doubts regarding the substantive content and "national potential" of ladino identity come to the fore; these cultural-political conditions alone, I contend, are enough to evoke the specter of the insurrectionary Indian as a self-evident conclusion, a potent symbol for everything else that is going on.

From Political Imaginary to Practical Politics

If this notion of the ladino political imaginary stands the test of analytical scrutiny, it should be useful not only for making sense of specific features of ladino discourse and practice, but also broader comparative questions that Guatemalan cultural politics bring to the fore. I raise three such issues briefly here: the relationship between globalization and the rise of Maya cultural activism; the evolving forms of ladino racism and the work that it does; and, the challenge of efforts to build relations of interculturalidad in various facets of Guatemalan society.

To emphasize the ladino political imaginary is to generate, in the first place, a straightforward empirical reminder regarding the global dimensions of indigenous movements in Latin America. Even highly sophisticated theorists of global-local articulations (for example, Arif Dirlik [1996]) tend to portray a stark confrontation between global corporate capitalism writ large on the one hand, and local resistance on the other. Though there certainly are cases where indigenous peoples directly confront globally constituted entities such as multinational corporations, and while they certainly do operate in a globalized public sphere, these interactions are often played out as confrontations with equally "local" adversaries like the ladinos of my account. These relatively dominant local actors are engaged actively in the construction of their own identities, imbuing them with political-discursive contents that may stand at odds with the gist of academic theory making. Participants in my conversation at the "university" in Itzapa, for example, defended their claims to dominance with references to the always-already "mestizo," hybrid, and evidently constructed character of everyone's identities: Mayas had mixed with Toltecs; just as Spaniards mixed with Indians (and before that, Moors). Such a string of associations flies directly in the face of images provided by theorists such as Michael Shapiro (1994), for whom a "post-sovereign" and "hybrid" ethics of indigenous politics stands neatly juxtaposed to the universalist, western "Cartesian," state-centric notions of sovereignty. My conclusion goes well beyond the obvious point that "sovereignty" (whether conceived with Western philosophical groundings or not) is crucial to most indigenous movements. More important still is the striking theoretical inversion. Ladinos are using a form of "hybridity theory" to bolster their own claims to modernity, and to de-legitimate competing Maya claims, made allegedly in an essentialist discourse of cultural continuity from time immemorial.[26]

In addition to tracking and theorizing connections between indigenous politics and global processes, therefore, I want to call attention to the impact of these broader forces on how indigenous people's local adversaries think and act. A prime example is ladinos' visceral reaction to the most visible presence of "global forces" in local power relations: international support for and recognition of Maya cultural activism. This was Igor's parting recommendation to me for further research. A prominent novelist and former leftist, Marco Antonio Flores, makes the case even more explicitly. He begins with the now-familiar prediction: "The indigenous have been exploited forever, and they are now preparing their cadre, at all levels, for the 'great confrontation.' We are at the edge of an abyss, jumping rope and painting ourselves with *achiote* [a brightly colored substance]." But he then continues with a pointed diagnosis of the problem:

> But those who are stoking the flames of this Balkanization are the same old colonizers: from the United States, Spain, Germany, and so on. This rotten crew, maintained by their governments and by international organizations…have arrived to Guatemala with the colonizer's paternalism, bad conscience and a Christian guilt complex to "save the Indian," and the only thing they're doing is generating a conflict of incalculable proportions.[27]

Leaving aside the rich ironies of his hyperbole, I want merely to note how the analytical framework offered here helps to explain the logic underlying this frequently repeated diagnosis of the problem. Multilateral organizations and Anglo-European governments represent the pinnacle of modernity, and they are the very ones showing a pointed preference for the Maya. This reinforces independent Maya claims on modernity, while at the same time making it all too clear that Maya can negotiate in the national and international realms without working through (or even with) ladinos. Such challenges alone, quite apart from what the Mayas and their supporters plan to do with their newfound power, constitute self-evident proof that a "great confrontation," of "incalculable consequences" is imminent.

This analysis of the political imaginary also generates a deeper, and more troubling, portrait of ladino racism. What comes through in all the interview material that I have cited, but especially the conversation at the "university," is a set of judgments about Indians that combine, or alternate between, standard assertions of racial inferiority, and visceral anxieties that just do not seem to fit. In the public discourse of younger ladinos and important sectors of the state, these assertions of Indian inferiority have receded, replaced by the affirmation that now "we are all equal." Far from putting people at ease, this new discourse could well provoke new rounds of anxiety. The epitomizing symbol of such anxiety is the insurrectionary Indian, which reinforces the very premises of "otherness" and inferiority that the public discourse of equality ostensibly seeks to renounce. This problem becomes even more acute in the realm of the psychosexual. Given the pervasive history of how racial inequality has played out through sexual coercion and violence, what appears as the prime expression of reconciliation—consensual sexual relations between Mayas and ladinos—can take on jarringly contrary meanings. The semantic slippage between sexual intimacy and racial conquest, documented with numerous ethnographic examples in this chapter, speaks to this inversion, reminding us of how the past continues to weigh heavily on any attempt to dismantle a given racial formation in the present. Unless these contradictions are addressed, progress toward racial equality in the name of intercultural relations could be deceptive, leaving an underlying antagonism in place. Even more disturbingly, practices of intercultural sociability could have the perverse effect of bringing to the surface the very fear that they are supposed to assuage.

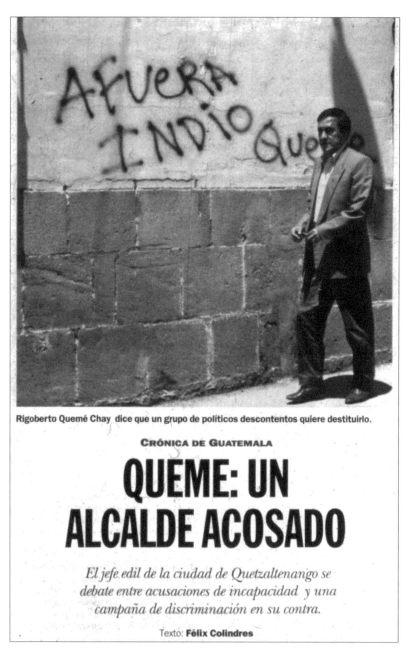

Rigoberto Quemé Chay dice que un grupo de políticos descontentos quiere destituirlo.

CRÓNICA DE GUATEMALA

QUEME: UN ALCALDE ACOSADO

El jefe edil de la ciudad de Quetzaltenango se debate entre acusaciones de incapacidad y una campaña de discriminación en su contra.

Textó: **Félix Colindres**

Figure 5.1. A Mayor under Seige, Quetzaltenango.

Despite these risks, there are good reasons to insist on bringing this analysis of the ladino political imaginary to light. This focuses much-needed attention on the question "Who are the ladinos?" and suggests that the question must be addressed by ladinos themselves as a prior step to intercultural dialogue. If their answer points to elements deeply engrained in ladino identity that are corrosive to such a dialogue—as the material in this chapter suggests is the case—then focused work toward the decolonization of ladino identity becomes an urgent priority. The urgency lies, at least in part, in demonstrable political consequences. As long as the specter of the insurrectionary Indian retains a prominent place in ladino consciousness, it will continue to generate a visceral receptivity to political initiatives seeking to shore up ladino power and privilege. Mention by government elites of the coming "race war" tends to articulate with ladino racial ambivalence against the emergence of egalitarian political cooperation between ladinos and Mayas. One obvious example of these effects is the way opponents to the constitutional amendments of 1999 (known as the Consulta Popular) generated a loyal following. A second example is the way the presidential race of 2000 between the PAN and the FRG became racialized, especially when campaign officials with the PAN referred to the latter as the party of the "*xumos*."[28] Yet a third example is the way political opposition to Rigoberto Quemé, the first Indian mayor of Quetzaltenango, was so often expressed in viscerally racial terms (see figure 5.1).

Finally, and perhaps most important, it seems likely that ladino fears about the specter of the insurrectionary Indian have become part of the Maya political imaginary as well. These fears form part of what Mayas imagine ladinos to be thinking. Here lies the deeper point behind the indio bochinchero anecdote presented earlier in this chapter. Behavioral changes and new initiatives that move Guatemala toward the practice of interculturalidad are crucially important, but they may have limited effect if the mutually reinforcing contents of these two political imaginaries remain intact. They would allow cordial interaction, even dialogue, but always within limits, always "without swallowing" as Rigoberto the butcher advised. They would produce a practice of interculturalidad subtly undermined by gnawing doubts, sparked by images that come to mind in a flash, in moments of uncertainty, evoking powerful mutual fears of treachery and betrayal.

six

Racial Healing? The Limits of Ladino Solidarity and the Oblique Promise of Mestizaje from Below

> Healing is a process that has many steps. Yet we try to move too quickly from the traumatic even to the day the bandages are removed. In our zeal to avoid inflaming the wound, we fail to clean it properly. We rush to close it and do not check to see if our stitches have held. We ignore the possibility of infection, and convince ourselves that the occasional oozing is nothing to worry about.... And so our racial wound festers. And eventually, like Langston Hughes's dream deferred, it explodes.
>
> —*Harlon Dalton,* Racial Healing *(1995)*

> *No tiene la culpa el indio, sino el que lo hace compadre* (It is not the fault of the Indian but of the person who makes the Indian his fictive kinsman).
>
> —*Ladino saying*

Although I shared the results of my research with Yolanda regularly—at times almost daily—enlisting her to help interpret a key phrase or to fill in background information, I did not ask her for a formal interview until late in my principal fieldwork year. By the time we actually did the interview, as part of an animated conversation over lunch in Pollo Campero, she could anticipate every question. Still, in response to the standard, "Do you have indigenous descent in your family?" she hesitated before responding yes. "How do you identify?" I continued. Even more tentatively, she answered, "Mestiza." Both this move to endorse mestizaje and the hesitancy are common among ladinos of Yolanda's political sensibilities. By affirming indigenous descent in the family, she directly contested a central pillar of the prevailing racial ideology: that ladinos are a tightly bounded social group, subject to no significant

167

cultural or biological influence from Indians for many generations. By answering "mestiza," she further undermined ladino claims to racial-cultural separateness, and gestured toward a common ground of interests and identity with Mayas.

A variety of factors contributed to Yolanda's hesitation. Her own shift was a little too recent and self-conscious to sit comfortably; she and I often had criticized the hypocrisy involved when others suddenly claimed an identity different from what everyone knew them to be. Moreover, even as she spoke, Yolanda surely imagined the counterarguments of relatives and friends, especially of the elder generation. She did not have long to wait to hear them directly. A few days later, Yolanda accompanied a group of relatives to the feria in Comalapa, and told them about the interview. Horrified, they proceeded to set her straight with a lengthy genealogy lesson and adamant reminders of the strict racial divide in Comalapa when they all had lived there. A sense of loss amplified the emotion behind their history lesson: ladino society had all but disappeared in Comalapa. After a short time walking the streets that day at the feria they had concluded with disdain: *Solo indios hay aquí, ¿hasta donde hemos llegado? Vo'nos*" (Only Indians here; what is the world coming to? Let's get out of here). That evening, around the kitchen table, Yolanda recounted these events with characteristic bemusement, marking a critical distance from her relatives' racist grumblings, but then assumed a more serious tone: "I've changed my mind, Carlos. Please record me in your study as ladina."

Yolanda's fluctuation between mestiza and ladina frames the central analytical questions of this chapter. Why have some ladinos come to endorse a position of solidarity with Mayas, given all this implies for dissent from the existing racial order? Why does this solidarity so frequently come in the idiom of mestizaje? What consequences do these challenges bring? A good part of the evidence that I bring to bear on these questions comes in the form of "identity talk"—how people express attachment and dissent in relation to the identity categories to which they belong, and how these categories themselves are constituted. Underlying this dual focus is a preferred understanding of identity, as the meeting ground between the creation of identity categories and people's constant maneuverings within and against them, what theorists call the convergence of subject formation (or "interpellation") and self-making.[1] The third facet of analysis here—in addition to subject formation and self-making—is political process. Too much literature on identity politics, I contend, focuses on the complexities of identity formation, while neglecting the broader flow of social interactions that produce specific political effects and consequences. In contrast, the central objectives of this chapter are not only to understand these diverse, changing expressions of identity among non-indigenous peoples (ladinos and mestizos alike) but, equally important, to trace the material consequences of these transformations in their relations with Mayas.

This broadened line of inquiry raises an analytical problem from the outset. When ladinos express a desire to remake their historic relations with Indians, how much importance do we assign this critical self-making in relation to the structural dominance that the ladino identity category in general continues to exercise? Answers that understate this self-making capacity risk a fatalistic determinism, portraying dominant actors as already constituted, unable to depart from their structurally prescribed scripts. Answers that overstate this capacity, however, risk turning a blind eye to the workings of racial privilege. Yolanda's fluctuation between mestizo and ladino is symptomatic of this analytical dilemma. Her inclination to embrace mestizaje signals a deep process of social change underway, in which critical ladino/mestizo self-making has played a crucial role. Her ambivalence, coupled with the variable consequences of both mestizo and ladino solidarity, alert us to the limits of ladino self-making as catalyst for change. If racial privilege adheres to identity categories, and people accrue this privilege simply by occupying the category in question, then solidarity requires a double move: critique of racism in active alignment with the Maya, and dissent from the very identity category that makes such alignment possible. Without the latter move, critique of racial inequality could come to little more than rhetorical flourish, or even an implicit affirmation of racial privilege. Without the former, this analysis could be interpreted as encouraging hopelessness or political paralysis. My analysis in this chapter follows how ladinos and mestizos themselves confront this dilemma, tracing both their "identity talk" and its political consequences in relation to the racial hierarchy that they purport to challenge.

I use the phrase "ladinos solidarios," as an umbrella category, which encompasses diverse groups of non-indigenous people who have relations with Indians that embody a desire for, and an active attempt to practice, interracial equality. I initially found some twenty-five people, all living in the department of Chimaltenango or with a significant presence there, who fit this description and agreed to formal interviews. Further analysis led me to divide these ladinos solidarios into four groups, clearly differentiated from one another both in their identity talk and in the consequences that follow. *Mestizo universalists* are those who, deeply influenced by the October Revolution (1944–1954) and the ideal of universal citizenship, identify as mestizo and fervently promote an egalitarian, race-blind society where there are no Mayas or ladinos, only Guatemalans. *New mestizos* are inhabitants of generally poor neighborhoods in Chimaltenango and other municipios, who have taken on a mestizo identity in quiet denial of the Indian-ladino binary: mestizos by default because they are not accepted, or do not fit, anywhere else. *Mestizo militants* also identity as mestizo, but as an explicit gesture of solidarity with Mayas; they seek to acknowledge their Indian ancestry, to renounce association with ladino racism and oppression, and to forge a new identity that expresses these ideals. Finally, I consider *ladino dissidents* such as Yolanda: people who share a penetrating critique of the ladino identity category, for all the familiar reasons, but who identify as ladino or ladina nonetheless and wage a struggle to transform ladino identity from within.

In an attempt to examine these distinct modes of identity talk in relation to their political effects and consequences, I juxtapose an episode or series of interactions with each. I associate mestizo universalism with the ideology of the October Revolution, which at one time posed a progressive challenge to racial hierarchy but now has lost its allure and appears increasingly out of place. I associate the new mestizos with an ephemeral protest movement and with the formation of youth gangs in Chimaltenango's poor neighborhoods. Although ostensibly quite different, both illustrate nicely the contradictory sensibilities of this identity category. They are energetic and creative, but diffuse, with little ability to move from critique to collective political alternative. To provide a context for thinking about the other two modes of identification (militant mestizos and dissident ladinos), I follow the path of a religious ritual—*el Día de Guadalupe*—and its protagonists' attempts to mediate between the received and transformed meanings of their activities. These mediations highlight the differences between these two modes of identification, the significant departure of each from the dominant ladino mindset, but also their limitations as catalysts for the deep process of racial healing that conditions require.

While this chapter is filled with examples of individual ladino acts of dissent from the prevailing racial order, and solidarity with Mayas, my overall conclusions are not especially sanguine. I emphasize limits to solidarity that derive from two basic conditions. As individual acts, these sensibilities have important contextual and aggregate effects, but they generally lack the transformative power achieved through organized collective political action.[2] Once these acts turn organized and collective, however, they are hindered by the very legacy of racial dominance that they purport to contest. It is telling, for example, that so many of the ladinos solidarios in this study went through a phase of involvement with the revolutionary Left, which provided the opportunity for extensive interaction with politically active Mayas, and which pursued an organized, collective vision to resolve the problems afflicting Guatemalan society. It is equally significant that most of these same interviewees have broken ties with the Left for a range of reasons, including the Left's inability to shake free from its own universalist failings: continued patterns of racism and ladino dominance, thinly veiled by the discourse of universal equality and working-class ascendancy. Yet this analysis also dramatizes how easily the demise of these utopian visions for collective action gives way to political atrophy: shifting and unstable identities; fragmentation and internal conflict; and widespread dissent, which never quite congeals as an effective political challenge. To some degree this dissipation is to be expected, an inevitable symptom of the racial ambivalence that I have documented throughout this book, a reminder that substantial and durable transformation of Guatemala's racial hierarchy can only come through the struggles of the Maya majority. Yet this reminder, taken to its logical conclusion, leads to another specious form of (Maya) universalism, which condemns ladinos as eternal prisoners of their inherited racial subjectivities. In contrast, I hold out for a transformed ladino-mestizo identity: collective and politically directed; differentiated from but closely aligned with the Maya; conceived not as pure antiracist subject but as expression of solidarity—where divestment of racial privilege is achieved incrementally amid constant efforts to acknowledge and work through the pervasive limits of this very endeavor.

Ladinos, Mistados, and the Decline of Mestizo Universalism

Ladino identity has been constructed, at least since the nineteenth century, in constant dialogue with the specter of racial contamination. The "agent" of contamination has generally, but not always, been the Indian. References to blackness are uncommon in ladino race talk in Chimaltenango, but that very infrequency makes the stereotypic associations with blackness all the more striking when they do emerge: stories about a black predator in Indian communities; jokes playing on shared assumptions about black sexuality; invocations of blackness with commonsense negative attributes.[3] Ladinos in Chimaltenango live with the onus of denigration by Euro-Guatemalans, people with "powerful" family names that connote *abolengo* (blue blood racial lineage), and who deploy a map of social boundaries that conflates ladinos and Indians on the same side of a great white/non-white racial divide. According to this map, ladinos are the Euro-Guatemalans' blacks, or at least subject to contamination by proximity, spatial and genealogical, with Indians. Ladino responses over the years to this contentious mapping of Guatemala's racial hierarchy have been far from uniform, and the workings of the racial divide between the two are the subject of considerable debate.[4] Amid this complexity, however, it is certain that what Ramón González (1999) calls an "ideology of *blancura* (whiteness)," has continued to exert deep influence: keeping self-identified Euro-Guatemalans in an ambivalent relationship to ladinos, shaping internal distinctions among ladinos, and keeping the divide between ladinos and Indians intact. This last psychic investment is perhaps the most remarkable. Even while engaged in rebellion against the Euro-Guatemalan oligarchy, few ladinos could fathom an identity politics that put them on truly equal footing with Indians.

In Chimaltenango, ladinos still regularly use the curious term "mistados," which illustrates the deep, persistent influence of the specter of Indian contamination. I first came across the term in the course of data collection in the Leonidas Mencos Ávilos high school. With the help of Don Timo, who had held administrative positions in the school since its founding, I was able to record the identity of each student and, in so doing, chart the rising proportion of Indians in each successive graduating class (see figure 2.4). Although Don Timo confidently placed most students as Indian or ladino as we went down the list, occasionally he would hesitate: "*Ah, usted, aquél es mistado*" (Ah, that one is mixed). Perplexed at first, I persisted, "OK, but where then should we place him?" Timo hesitated again, as if he wanted to say "nowhere," and then answered weakly, "I imagine he would take hold of the father's side." After this I heard the term with some frequency. In long, early morning taxi rides to the airport, I would often engage Don Efraín, my regular *taxista*, in discussions of my research. During one trip, he launched into bitter complaints about Chimaltenango's governor, whom he described disparagingly as a mistado. To pursue the issue, I asked him about the identity of the taxi drivers whose flotilla gathers daily around the park in the center of town. "Eight Indians, and the rest (some fifteen) ladinos, except for four mistados," he responded without hesitation. "What happens to the identity of these mistados?" I queried. Their identity is volatile, he replied, and mixed marriages in general were not advisable "because the two bloods do not mix. It is better, as we say here, to marry within your own class." On the way back a week later, it occurred to me to ask Efraín about indigenous descent in his own family. To my surprise he responded, "Yes, I am mistado also. It doesn't matter how you identify, the evidence stays in the blood."

Although mistado and mestizo sound like synonyms, they key into distinct ideological precepts. To refer to someone as a mistado is to foreground an infelicitous mixture of starkly different racial types, with the implication that the two sets of characteristics are destined to be at war with one another, jockeying for dominance within the hybrid body, the "ladino" side fending off contamination by the Indian. Adolfo Sandoval, a long-time activist in the cooperative movement, richly illustrated this logic as we discussed the consequences that follow for offspring of mixed unions:

> Ah! I think that there could be a clash of characters in the child…there
> could be qualities from the father and others from the mother, which logically
> would be different, ¿no? This could produce a lot of instability…although it is
> difficult to know for sure, because very intelligent children also have resulted
> from the crossing of indigenous and ladino…I think we'd have to study this
> question further…we'd enter another realm, perhaps, we'd have to study
> biology.

Sandoval imbues the offspring with a volatile character and an indeterminate identity and, in so doing, reinforces the image of an impermeable divide between ladinos and Indians. Ideologies of mestizaje came about throughout Latin America as a direct challenge to this image of the contaminated mistado, although racial terminology varied: mistados are outcasts, anomalies, racial by-products, while mestizos are the harmonious and hardy product of racial fusion.[5] Consequently, whenever ladinos have seriously contemplated an inclusive *proyecto de nación*" (project of nation building) references to the mistado disappear and metaphors of mestizaje come to the fore.

Transgressions of the boundary between ladino and Indian were common, of course—so common that it becomes a puzzle to explain how the ideology of the mistado could have been so tenacious.[6] The answer lies, at least in part, in the constant efforts on the part of ladinos to shore up the ideology, whenever everyday practices conspired to blur the boundary. Yolanda portrays older generation ladinos like her father as constantly busy policing the boundaries of ladino identity, even (or especially?) within their own family. For example, Don Luis never stopped grumbling about his sister, Doña Leti, who married "that son of the indio Florindo"; he expressed repeated indignation toward an indigenous teacher who presumed she could pass as ladina just by exchanging her traje típica for western clothing; he participated actively in scandal mongering whenever a solid member of the "raza ladina" got too close to someone suspected of being Indian.[7] Arguments about the particulars (for example, how much contamination would result from contact with so and so?) could be won or lost, yielding a wide diversity of actual practices, without challenging the basic precepts. Doña Leti eventually overcame her family's resistance, but paid a high price. Yolanda told me that when Doña Leti's daughter chose a boyfriend perceived as "too Indian," Doña Leti chastised her in much the same terms that Don Luis had used a generation earlier.

This prevailing racial ideology of the mistado, although broadly endorsed by ladinos, did not go unquestioned. Indians challenged its precepts in myriad ways, both by various forms of racial border crossing and by insisting on equality within the separate realm that the ideology prescribed for them.[8] Ladinos also mounted challenges and expressed solidarity, although with notably partial effects. Most of these prior challenges can be traced to the October Revolution.[9] Reforms promulgated in the 1944–1954 period on behalf of the Indian majority carried a large dose of paternalism, framed within a nascent national ideology of mestizaje that followed the standard Latin American pattern: offering Indians full citizenship, conditioned upon assimilation to the mestizo norm. A telling marker of the limits of these reforms was the deep and abiding fear of an Indian uprising, even among the ladino reformers themselves.[10] The coup of 1954 truncated both the reforms and the internal racial strife, which allowed left-inflected collective memories of this period to become canonized with scant reference to racial hierarchy or racism. Subsequent generations of ladino intellectuals who came of age in the aura of the October Revolution espoused an egalitarian universalism, antiracist in opposition to indigenous people's exclusion and exploitation, but unable to fathom Maya cultural rights as a means to assure political inclusion and empowerment.

Mestizo universalism, a direct outgrowth of the reformist decade, rose to prominence during the 1960s and 1970s in Chimaltenango. Many participants in this early wave of solidarity were influenced by the social doctrine of the Catholic Church, especially its vision of gradual transformation through consciousness raising and through organization in the form of cooperatives and other community development schemes. Edwin Morquecho is a quintessential example of these pioneers of ladino solidarity. Coming of age in the 1950s, by the early 1960s Morquecho already had become active in agrarian issues. He worked in various development and social service related endeavors before founding CENDEC (formerly EACA), devoted to training and technical support for the burgeoning cooperative movement. When I interviewed Morquecho in 1998, he still served as director of CENDEC, a large training center that, in keeping with the neoliberal times, now hired out its facilities to a wide and disparate range of activities. Morquecho talked with me at length about the organization's travails during the years of state violence and the 25,000 persons, 85 percent indigenous, whom CENDEC has trained since its inception. A man of humble origins who married a woman of "pure Spanish descent," from a family of abolengo (high race-class lineage), Morquecho identifies adamantly as mestizo and offers scathing commentary on his high-class ladino neighbors in the capital who might have become his primary race-class cohort. They are racist—*"Piensan que los inditos {están} solamente para servirles"* (They think Indians are only here to serve them)—ignorant of indigenous realities, hypocritical, and prone to maintain their privilege through violence. Morquecho, in contrast, had logged thirty-five years working for indigenous betterment, befriending and becoming the godfather of many, traveling to isolated rural areas, suffering persecution, defending the principles of the cooperative movement throughout.

Perhaps such an impressive record of commitment inevitably breeds disdain toward more recent initiatives; still, Morquecho's views on contemporary Maya organizing bear clear markings of a version of solidarity forged in a bygone era. Although disdainful toward the ladino elite, he reserves criticism of comparable emphasis for Maya activists who came into the limelight during the 1990s. "They are divided among themselves," he says, and *"Promueven la segregación, y eso es discriminación"* (They promote separatism and discrimination); they are devoted to specious ideas of Maya cosmovisión and spirituality. "In relation to real development, with these ideas they would stay behind."

Morquecho's mestizo universalism informs these criticisms and gives substance to his solidarity: he identifies as mestizo, construes this identity as a direct challenge to ladino privilege, and then projects this challenge onto Guatemalan society as a whole. "The ladinos are going to have to accept a Guatemala without Indians or ladinos," Morquecho asserts, and Indians will have to as well:

> Relations are becoming more polarized but, with the passing of time, Indians
> and ladinos will unify…I identify as mestizo, and I think Indians will eventu
> ally come to this same identity. We are not two, three countries, we are one!
> We all are equal, and in any case, we are all mestizos. There should be no
> privileged classes…the powerful class will have to share more, show more
> solidarity.

As compelling as Morquecho's principled egalitarianism may be, his call to assimilation sticks like a bone in the throat of contemporary Maya rights activists, who have made Maya cultural rights their primary rallying cry. Morquecho is far from alone, even if the power and prominence of his generation has faded.[11] Persisting mestizo universalism goes a long way in explaining pervasive Maya distrust toward *any* assertion of mestizaje, especially when it invokes a "we" that speaks for Mayas without consulting them first.

Guatemala is unusual in Latin America for the limited influence of mestizo universalism.[12] While the mid-century reformist state did forge an inclusive, egalitarian, and assimilationist alternative that would become a touchstone for Edwin Morquecho and others of his generation, this state-making experiment ended with the coup of 1954. As I argue in chapter 2, mestizo universalism returned in the 1980s with a distinctly right-wing inflection, as part of the army's strategy for stamping out the guerrilla insurgency and winning over the civilian population. While some ladinos in

Chimaltenango do still express strong support for these ideas, the combination of Maya efflorescence and a global shift toward multiculturalism have conspired to displace mestizo universalism in favor of recognition for rights grounded in cultural difference. The Guatemalan state consummated this displacement in 1995 with the signing of the indigenous peace accord, which opened the way for negotiation of collective rights for each of the four "peoples" that make up Guatemala's multicultural, pluriethnic society.[13] By the mid-1990s, history had left mestizo universalism behind.

New Mestizos and "Mestizo" Anti-Politics

Two flows of experience marked my fieldwork in Chimaltenango during the first months of 1998. A protest movement erupted in February, ostensibly against a nationally mandated property tax, but motivated as well by a deepening dissatisfaction with Chimaltenango's mayor. I followed the movement closely, attended its meetings, interviewed its leaders, and analyzed their evolving strategy. At around the same time, I began to explore, in affiliation with an NGO called Solidardidad con la Niñez y la Juventud (Solidarity with Children and Youth, or SNJ), questions of identity in two poor barrios of Chimaltenango. My objectives in these two sets of activities were separately conceived. I expected the protest movement, the most prominent expression of organized politics during the years I lived in Chimaltenango, to provide insight into how grassroots politics had been infused with new racial meanings now that Mayas had become important national-level political actors. In the two poor barrios, by contrast, I hoped to make sense of the changing expressions of identity, especially among youth, in spaces that were neither "ladino" nor "Indian." Barrio dwellers were not prominent in the protest movement, and movement leaders made no special effort to address the issues that mattered most to the barrio youth. Yet upon closer examination, striking similarities between the two emerged. Both spaces had a deeply ambiguous politics of identity, seeming to have moved beyond the Indian-ladino binary and yet plagued by the persistence of racism; both had creative potential, and yet both were stymied by an "anti-politics" of disaffection, fragmentation, and ambiguity. I refer to both as mestizo spaces, in hopes of drawing attention to a particular facet of late-century Guatemalan identity politics (or anti-politics), often obscured by the dramatic rise of Maya cultural activism.

Ambiguous Protest

The story of the protest movement begins with the announcement of President Arzú, in January 1998, that his government would implement a new property tax called the Impuesto Único Sobre Imuebles (Unified Property Tax, or IUSI).[14] Any talk of new taxes strikes a raw nerve in Guatemala, both for the rich, who are used to getting away with murder, and the poor majority, who live on the brink. Indian communities throughout the highlands exploded in protest (although the media reported, quite plausibly, that wealthy opponents of the IUSI and opposition politicians of the

Guatemalan Republican Front or FRG helped to stir passions).[15] Within a few weeks the protests forced Arzú to withdraw the proposal. When the anti-IUSI protest spread to Chimaltenango, it congealed around a movement against the mayor, who belonged to Arzú's party. They named it "February 27 Movement," to mark the day protests first erupted. A number of prominent community leaders joined, and the movement's focus broadened to include the dismal administration of the city water system, misuse of funds, and lack of accountability, which all converged in a call for the mayor's resignation. In April 1998, the movement generated intense meetings, marches, demonstrations, and fiery speeches—the stuff of local politics.

By the time the movement collapsed in mid-May, however, I had grown utterly mystified by the whole affair. The movement's leadership defied easy characterization and, to some extent, commonsense political logic. Two of the prime movers were older middle-class ladinos with histories of involvement in right-wing political parties, and proven (in private conversation) to be profoundly racist toward Indians. Another three or four were indigenous activists, including the brother and nephew of José Lino Xoyón, the charismatic Indian mayor of Chimaltenango who was gunned down by the death squads in 1980. The mayor, although a member of the PAN, was an indigenous merchant with little political experience. In private, ladinos of all political persuasions derided him as an incompetent drunkard elected solely because the PAN wanted an Indian figurehead, and because he had offered to pay the most in return for the nomination. The movement's demise was equally mysterious. We awoke one morning in early May to the news that, the night before, gunmen had fired on the houses of both the mayor and the councilman most supportive of the movement to oust him. The mayor, claiming the mantle of a courageous politician who stands firm in the face of violence, gained the upper hand; the councilman resigned and fled, and the movement collapsed under the onus of association with a return to political violence. Even while in full swing, the movement had no clear ideological message. It combined rhetoric reminiscent of the revolutionary Left (epitomized by the ubiquitous slogan, "the people united will never be defeated"), exhortations of good government, allusions to Mayan rights (especially when the indigenous leaders spoke), and abundant criticism of the mayor. At least, I mused at one point, ladinos had kept racist thinking to themselves; the movement might therefore exemplify a new intercultural sensibility in local politics. Then, after one of the last demonstrations outside the mayor's office, I found graffiti spray-painted on his door: *Queremos agua, no seas ladrón, negro hijo de puta* (We want water, don't be a crook, black son of a whore) (figure 6.1).[16]

Since Yolanda still held an elected post as city councilwoman at the time, she had access to much information, which fed constant discussion of these events. We had many a kitchen-table session during that period, drinking rum, mulling over the events of the day, assessing explanations and analysis, in discussions laced with humor chapín, a morbid, cynical, self-deprecatory genre all its own. In our session after the shooting at the two homes, conspiracy theories abounded; according to the one that gained the most support among those assembled that evening, the mayor hired gun-

Figure 6.1. A mayor under siege, Chimaltenango. Mayor's office door, spray-painted after a demonstration. The writing says: "We want water. Don't be a thief. Black son of a whore." 29 March 1998. Photo credit: Charles R. Hale.

men both to fire on his own house, to renew his faltering political capital, and on the house of the opposition councilman, to scare him off. Other theories, however, seemed equally plausible; no one even investigated, much less resolved, the mystery. Yolanda shared and readily voiced the scathing depictions of the mayor, but she troubled over the thin line between these depictions and anti-Indian racism, concerns that my snapshot of the racist graffiti only amplified. She also criticized the movement's pretensions to oust the mayor through extra-democratic means and bemoaned the wanton opportunism of movement leaders, both ladino and Maya. With the shooting incident as catalyst, and the general absence of viable political options as rationale, Yolanda soon decided to resign from her position in the city council and withdraw from local politics.

As the movimiento gathered strength, the multiple currents of racial sensibilities—some residual others emergent—came together to overload the spaces from which ladino solidarity might be expressed and cultivated. When ladinos respond to these conditions with ambivalence and perplexity, in part they surely are struggling with the dilemma created by the desire for both equality and privilege; in part, also, their perplexity reflects the contradictory social conditions of the times, where every potential space of racial solidarity is compromised by cross-cutting meanings, which imbue local acts of solidarity in particular, with unstable contents, mixed messages and unintended consequences. It is these mixed messages, rather than the identities of those involved, that give the movement a "mestizo" character. This in turn suggests a parallel with another type of space, created not by active protest, but rather by cumulative disaffection and marginality. Inhabitants of this space are poor, with few prospects of upward mobility; they are of Indian descent, yet with scant identification as Maya; they forge their own identities in adamantly local ways, largely disengaged from Guatemala's ladino-Maya binary. These mestizos—in the more conventional sense of the term—have a politics that is curiously resonant with that of the February 27 Movement.

Oblique Subversion

Yuri fascinated me. About twenty years old, diminutive, full of energy, and utterly uninhibited, she had a quick smile and sparkling eyes. She arrived forty minutes late to our first interview, soaked from a sudden downpour that caught her between the bus and Pollo Campero. We greeted, and before taking a seat she suggested that we move to a quieter corner and before I answered proceeded to pick up my papers scattered on the table. Never losing her poise, she launched right into our discussion, talking about her job search and about Buena Vista, the poor barrio in Chimaltenango where she lived. At one point, she interrupted me in mid-sentence to direct our attention to the music playing over the sound system: "That's Merengue House, one of my favorite groups." A few weeks later, following Yuri's suggestion, I showed up at a ramshackle disco where the Cholos, the *mara* (youth gang) with which she associated, were supposed to be gathered. I stuck out like a sore thumb on the sidelines of a dance floor full of dark-skinned, slightly tough-looking youth dressed in baggy clothing, until Yuri sauntered over, asked me to dance, and pulled me out before I had the chance to answer. In a memoir titled *Brown*, Richard Rodriguez celebrates the intrepid, irreverent creativity of mestizo sensibilities.[17] If *Brown* has a Guatemalan counterpart, Yuri would be its personification.

I met Yuri through Ramón, who worked as a youth promoter for SNJ, which had just received a sizeable grant to administer youth programs in two poor barrios of Chimaltenango, Buena Vista, and El Esfuerzo. As part of the project, they were to carry out (in typical development jargon) a "Diagnostic" of the two sites. Equipped with two new computers, a dreadfully long and mundane survey instrument, a legion of temporary interviewers, and very limited social science training, they collected mountains of data and began to "systematize" the results. With the grant deadline fast approaching, SNJ director Herman Santos sought me out for help and, especially, to ask advice on the "identity question": the survey results were a mess, full of answers and non-answers that wreaked havoc with the survey's binary (that is, Indian-ladino) approach to identity categories. I agreed to write the section on identity, provided that I could do my own research to complement the survey. Herman agreed with relief, and assigned Ramón as my research assistant.

During one of our preparatory sessions I peppered Ramón with questions about Chimaltenango's maras and about one gang in particular, the Cholos. I had been interested in the Cholos for some time, on the hunch (derived mainly from their name) that they might epitomize an emergent third space of identity in Chimaltenango, distinct from the established two. My middle-class ladino friends knew little about the Cholos, and warned me away with stereotypical images—Cholos as delinquents, *vagos* (lazy bums), prone to violence, and involved with drugs—which only piqued my interest. Although Ramón had a lot to say about this world, when my questions persisted he demurred: "You should talk with Yuri, she knows everything." Yuri lived with her sisters and parents in a precarious house in the heart of Buena Vista barrio, set back from a mud and gravel street. When Ramón took me there to propose an interview, she launched right in talking about the Cholos and their defining passion, a particular kind of break dance. They call it the *mortal*; you have to learn to *mortalear* if you want to gain status among the Cholos. Previously an active member, Yuri had grown more distanced from the Cholos since she finished high school and started looking for a job. But she still wore the signature *ropa tumbada* (baggy clothing) and joined the Cholos on Sunday afternoons at the disco.

Although questions about Buena Vista as a "non-Indian, non-ladino" space were foremost on my agenda, young residents like Yuri had other concerns, such as money, music, and maras. They found this "identity talk" uninteresting and off-topic, even if the underlying issues did seep back in. During our initial interview, Yuri spoke at length about her frustrating day of interviews in the capital city; she had put aside her ropa tumbada for the short skirt, blouse, and heels that are standard for entry-level jobs. Many employers required two years' prior experience, she complained; also "they told one of my girlfriends no, because she wasn't *de corte* (indigenous). That's discrimination!" These jobs offered the paltry entry-level salary of 800Q, roughly US$100 a month, 200Q less than the salary at one of Chimaltenango's maquilas.[18] Given this differential, I asked why she still sought an office job. She had tried the maquila, but could not tolerate the "exploitation." Besides,

> working as an accountant, one acquires experience and new knowledge. In the maquila, on the other hand, human rights and labor rights are not respected. When you're sick, they don't give you time off; when they're angry or unsatisfied, the Korean managers yell at you. They also feel up the girls as they pass by. They do this more to the indigenous girls, who do not know their rights. Some of these girls even think the managers are demonstrating affection, falling in love with them, and all that. So they don't resist.

Having finished high school makes Yuri a great anomaly in Buena Vista; most residents her age could not remotely consider working in an office and can aspire to little more than dead-end jobs in the maquila. She is also unusual for having continued to hang with the maras while advancing in school. "Raza 18, Fatal Fury, Salvatrucha, Whitefence, Escorpiones, Cholos, Caras, Diablos 13"—she rattled off nearly a dozen groups, their internal characteristics, and relations with one another. Part of what attracted Yuri to get involved with the maras was to challenge the "erroneous ideas" that others had about them:

> At times I dress as they do, with baggy clothing, earrings, and all that. I even put an earring in my nose. Not permanently, just when I went out with them, to show that even though I am an intellectual, I don't think like the others. This mere act [of solidarity] generates a great reaction in people. My mother told me, "Be careful about what you're getting into," but she lets me do it. I had a mara boyfriend too, named Coyote. I did it mainly for curiosity. I had the idea that they were only interested in sex, in the woman's body. I wanted to know if that was true. To my great surprise I found him to be very affectionate, with many feelings—and he still is to this day.

I defend the maras, she concluded, and others too. "I even defend women who work as prostitutes. I am very feminist in this sense. My sister is even more so."[19]

Yuri insistently describes Buena Vista and the maras as spaces of mestizaje, where the ladino-indígena dichotomy has no place. Among barrio muchachos:

> Some are indigenous, but mixed…Not directly indigenous, but a mixture of indigenous with ladino, and they deny their own origins…Here people just do not conserve indigenous culture…because there is so much mixture…. We cannot define this neighborhood as either indigenous or ladino race, only as mestizo.

Consistent with this description, Yuri feels no particular need to resolve the ambiguities surrounding her own identity. We sat in her bedroom during this line of questioning, and Yuri was showing me her favorite articles of ropa tumbada. I asked, "Are you of indigenous descent?" After an uncharacteristic hesitation, Yuri yelled to her mother, who was washing dishes in the kitchen: "*Mami, tenemos de maya, ¿verdad?* (We have Maya in us, don't we?)" Her mother responded: "*Si, mi'ija. Soy indígena de Cobán*" (Yes, child, I am indigenous from Cobán). Yuri continued, now with more confidence:

> Well then, yes...because we are Guatemalan and Maya...I consider myself
> Maya and I like it....My mother used to wear traje típico from Cobán, but
> that traje is too expensive. This factory-made clothing is much cheaper. Many
> people do not admit that their grandparents were indigenous...I say I am
> Maya, because that is our descent and we will never denigrate our origins.

Even apart from the question of cost, Yuri likes ropa tumbada more than both skirts and indigenous clothing, because it connotes rebellion against the attempt of others to control her. The *chavos* (neighborhood peers) show her more respect, she insists, when she wears ropa tumbada. Whether on the topic of race, gender, sexuality, or youth culture, Yuri epitomizes the border crossing, candid social criticism, and dynamic cultural creativity that many have associated with mestizaje.

This picture, however, leaves the question of solidarity with Mayas largely open. How do people like Yuri, and the mestizo spaces they occupy, relate to the racialized social hierarchy all around them? Yuri describes relations within these spaces as egalitarian:

> I do not see much discrimination in Buena Vista. The chavos are a great mix-
> ture. Everyone gets together, and no one says anything. I follow the principle
> of treating everyone with equality, to value who they are. The maras follow the
> same principle. They treat each other as if they were brothers, from the heart.

Yet in the same breath, Yuri portrays Indian maquila workers as gullible and ignorant, and generally views ladinos as more imaginative, less shackled by tradition. Yuri treads a fine line between healthy (if irreverent) critique of Indians and racist disparagement.

A principal force that keeps Yuri from unreserved solidarity with Mayas is the prevailing anti-Indian racism, from which people like her also suffer. Ramón lives in the barrio adjoining Buena Vista, identifies as mestizo, and talks more explicitly than Yuri does about these questions of solidarity, racism, and identity. He describes the reaction from others in the barrio, if they view the association as too close:

> If you hang out with an indigenous girl, the others begin to bother you. For
> this reason, I don't like to go out on the street with someone de corte. When I
> was in high school, I would walk an indigenous girl home. When I passed by
> a group of ladino guys they would taunt, "Look who he's hanging out with."

Quite apart from visible acts of affinity, however, this racism also affects Ramón directly:

> If you are dark skinned, you are denigrated. My brother is taller and whiter

than me. He has much more influence among the ladinos for this reason. One day we went to the group and he introduced me to them. "You don't look like him," they said. They were judging the color of my skin. By looking at the color of your skin, they judge which society you belong to. If two guys ask for the same job, the white-skinned person will always be favored. The *canche* (light-skinned person) is always advantaged. Even if I have better ideas, experience and everything, it doesn't matter.

Yuri and Ramón are in a weak position to contest this racism, because it is not exactly directed at them. They experience racial insult as admonition: "You appear too close, too aligned, too contaminated." When entire barrios receive this treatment, as Buena Vista regularly does, it could provoke collective acts of defiance. Much more commonly, however, it brings forth contradictory individual responses: Yuri distances herself from the denigrated category, even while, in another register, she affirms it as her own.

Ramón has explored more actively an identification with indigenous culture, but with mixed results. His work with SNJ generated an invitation to a workshop on Maya culture, his first exposure ever, which he found exciting and empowering. He also had daily contact with Juana, a young indigenous woman who worked in SNJ as the computer expert, attended college with a Maya fellowship, and was headed toward a professional career within the widening space of opportunity for upwardly mobile, educated, Maya-identified youth. Still, it remains extremely difficult for Ramón, and many like him, to deepen their articulation with Maya identity. In the first place, it takes considerable capital—social and material—to "become" Maya in the way that Juana has. This is an essentially middle-class position, with all the associated attributes: disposable income, education, familial support, high aspirations. Ramón lacks this capital, both cultural and material. Second, in part due to racism, in part to other forces of change, indigenous culture has thinned out in the poor barrios of Chimaltenango, making Indian identification a stretch. I explored this problem with various people as Ramón led me through the neighborhood. Indigenous language? You almost never hear it any more. Clothing? We stopped using it. Practices of significance, like cofradías, or harvest festivals? When we were young, not anymore. Values, like veneration of the elders? Yes, but some of us practice them and some don't. Maya cosmovisión? Maya what? When presented with these responses, Juana coined the epitomizing phrase: "Yes, you're right. Indigenous culture in the barrio has become *aguada* (watered down)."

The contrast with Cholos—rooted in barrio life, inciting desires, connected with global culture, on the move—could hardly be sharper. To a large extent, Maya cultural rights activists have given up on barrios like Buena Vista, associating emergent mestizo identities with ideologies of mestizaje that induce "alienation" of indigenous identity. Whether ill-advised or prescient, this stance has become a self-fulfilling prophecy. Mestizaje from below connotes fluidity, and openness to a range of possible articulations, while *mayanidad* (mayanness) prefers the closure that collective mobi-

Figure 6.2. Yuri and her children, June 2002. Photo credit: Charles R. Hale.

lization requires. Maya activists define mestizas like Yuri, who feel only partly Maya, as part of the problem.

The space of mestizaje from below has great transformative potential, which remains largely unrealized. Engendered by the breakdown of the binary racial formation, with a strong egalitarian ethos, these political sensibilities could pose a formidable challenge to traditional ladino dominance. The mere fact that new mestizos do not yearn to be accepted as ladinos delivers a stinging blow to the previous racial ideology, a sign that new mestizos have shaken free from the crippling epithet "mistado." New mestizos seem to defy or cut through any orthodoxy that stands in their way. Yuri epitomizes this potential: her confident irreverence, her ability to reach across various cultural boundaries, taking and leaving as she chooses. Yet while Yuri disapproves of the racism that Ramón (and no doubt she herself) experiences, she finds no way to make that critique collective, and tends to edge away from all that connotes "indigenous" within the mix. Strangely enough, the prospect of "becoming Maya" for these barrio dwellers seems almost as remote as becoming ladino. As new members of the workforce, their trajectories lead directly to the maquila, the quintessential economic space of mestizaje from below. Even Yuri, smart as a whip, with a high school education, has not yet broken through to the next stratum. A few years after our 1998 encounters, I found Yuri on her own, with two small children in tow, content but more subdued, less extraordinary, blending in with all the other new mestizas at her stage of life, hard at work just trying to get by (figure 6.2).

Militant Mestizaje: An Ambiguous Gesture

Until recently, it would have been inconceivable for people like Yolanda, a respected and well-known member of Chimaltenango's ladino community, to consider calling herself mestiza. Today, all her children, her son-in-law, her compañero Genaro, and a handful of others like them claim the identity term, as a gesture of solidarity with indigenous Guatemalans, and a repudiation of ladino racism, past and present. One telling indication of the depth of this shift is the experience of ladinos in the previous era who dared to cross the line. Soon after I settled into Chimaltenango, and began to talk with people about my research topic, they invariably directed me, often with a mischievous smile, to Dr. Américo Heredia. A physician in the community since the late 1950s, a special guest each year of the cofradía festivities, he is married to an indigenous woman with numerous children whom he claimed they were raising as Indians; this man, people assured me, could explain anything I wanted to know about indigenous-ladino relations. The waiting room to Dr. Heredia's clinic, at the front of his sprawling three-story brick house on the Pan-American Highway, immediately dispels the notion that he is a conventional doctor. Desks and tables are piled high with books and papers—Rushdie's *Satanic Verses*, a French-Spanish dictionary, a pediatrics reference book, the Popol Wuj; medical instruments are strewn here and there. The walls are adorned with pictures of him together with mainly indigenous figures— a Maya priest from Chichicastenango, elders from Chimaltenango who first oriented him to the region thirty years ago, his *compañera de vida* (lifelong companion), and a picture of the *corporación municipal* (city council) from the time when he was *síndico* (head councilor). Behind me another man entered, bottle of rum in hand, speech slightly slurred, and greeted the doctor as his compadre. A bottle of coke appeared, along with crackers and tidbits; the doctor served his two guests highballs and *bocas* (appetizers) as the conversation began.

When he arrived in Chimaltenango from the capital in the late 1950s, Dr. Heredia remembered, he felt like "*un turista en tierra ajena*" (a tourist in alien lands). There were "two societies," completely separate from one another. In an attempt to understand the world of his indigenous patients, he solicited the help of Don Manuel Xuyá, "*un gran cacique de los Kaqchikeles*" (a great leader of the Kaqchikels). With instruction from the cacique, extensive medical trips to the countryside, and an indigenous wife, he learned about and eventually came to see Maya culture as the way of the future. "Ladinos are destined to disappear," he confidently asserts, "because they have no history. They have no spiritual or historical foundation." At that point he takes out the *Enciclopedia Universal* and begins to read the entry for ladino: "*Astuto, sagaz, pícaro, taimado, zorro, fistol, cazumo....* The most despicable man on earth," he concludes.[20] "For this reason, we cannot speak of ladinization, but only of Indianization." In addition to studying Maya calendrics and things spiritual, Dr. Heredia has elaborate theories about everything from Mayan politics, to interracial sexual attractions, to the spread of AIDS through nasal inhalation, to coming global catastrophes due to "entropy." Admittedly, he is idiosyncratic, if not mildly deranged. At one point in the course of pontification, he assures me, "these points of view are eminently scientific and with full backing in the Bible." Yet before coming to a dismissive conclusion, one must consider idiosyncrasy in relation to racial opprobrium. "When ladinos found out that I had married an indígena," the doctor remembers, "they were scandalized. I lost all my ladino clients. They wrote me off as crazy. They would have killed me if they had been able to." When Dr. Heredia crossed the race line in the 1960s, he took on a persona that made him a cross between prophet and court jester; since then, he has lived both parts with a vengeance.

Although it would be misleading to present Dr. Heredia as typical of the recent move among ladinos toward an endorsement of mestizaje, certain features of his experience are instructive. Ladinos solidarios I interviewed often recounted stories of disapproval, if not scandal, caused by their having crossed the line—more so if they were from elite families and more so still if they identified as mestizo, thereby calling into question the purity of the family line. "*¿Seguís trabajando con los inditos?*" (Are you still working with those little Indians?) is all Ignacio Pérez's father would ever say for years about his work with an indigenous NGO. Bruno Calvo remembers a world where racism formed an unquestioned part of his family's common sense: "Like in the majority of Guatemalan families of the middle class, in our household people would always say, 'stop being indio, you look like an indio, that's pure indio' and things like that. I learned all this growing up." At first Bruno would avoid family and friends in Antigua rather than face the ridicule of his "affection" for indigenous people. Whether in anticipation of this admonishment or in response to a deeper internal conflict, many ladinos solidarios face identity as a struggle between the "bad" features of the ladino that Dr. Heredia enumerates and the awkward task of exorcising the past through an identity shift.

Ignacio Pérez, one of the sharpest analysts and most committed solidarios I know, inadvertently dramatizes this internal struggle, in an utterly convoluted response to my straightforward question, "How do you identify"?

> That's a very good question, vos...I identify as...I'd say Guatemalan, perhaps...I'm not sure...how could I say it...that my identity as Guatemalan stands in relation to a very heterogeneous reality, you see? Even more so because I have a social conscience...I say Guatemalan, and I love my country, I am committed to my country, but I recognize that...this identity is not...or what I mean to say...since I work mainly with indigenous people, who think of Guatemala very differently than I do...this makes for all kinds of contradictions, you see? It makes for many Guatemalas in one, you see?

To endorse mestizaje does help guide one through this thicket, to make a clean break, to carve out a space. The solution is necessarily gradual, however, as mestizo "converts" imbue the new identity category with meaning, and then negotiate the gap between "their" understanding and the multiple alternative meanings that others attribute to it.

Berta Monjardín, a mestiza sociologist who formed part of the AVANCSO *equipo género* (gender analysis group) that I worked with for a period, expressed exasperation at this problem, both in her daily practice, and within the equipo itself. Supportive of (though mildly impatient with) the rising prestige of lo Maya in leftist circles, asserting in jest that she had indigenous descent too and would soon begin a speaking tour as "the last Xinca," Berta vividly remembered the trauma of a few years earlier, when she had carried out research in Patzún and indigenous townspeople had treated her as if she were the oppressor. Now, she felt even more hurt by more subtle versions of the same rejection on the part of her indigenous co-workers. Another member of the equipo género, an indigenous women named Marta, had made a comment the previous day, straight faced, but with a hint of mischief in her voice: "He is ladino, but he's a good person." "But…?" Berta sputtered. A discussion of racial categories and relations ensued, beginning with the two indigenous equipo members recounting the numerous times that ladinos had hailed them on the street with the deprecatory *"vos María."*[21] "That's exactly the problem," Berta countered, "If I use 'vos' with an indigenous person, it brings to mind the racism of the 'vos María.' If I use 'usted,' it connotes formality and distance. Either way, the hierarchy remains."[22] The same dilemma applies, in a general way, to mestizo militancy writ large: reaching out with egalitarian intent, mestizo militants cannot quite shake free from the "vos María" that lurks behind the gesture, the experience of mestizaje as violence and appropriation.

Even in the face of this dilemma the shift to mestizo identity advances, as a consequence of the growing space of egalitarian relations between Mayas and ladinos, and the growing critical self-consciousness of ladinos.[23] It often includes a painfully searching exercise in personal genealogy, which imbues the process with additional depth. Flor provides an especially thoughtful explanation of this chosen identity:

> Personally, I am inclined to identify as mestiza. I have affinities with the
> Maya, an identification with the Maya, a tendency to value Maya culture.
> Ladino for me refers to a different sort of people: the "proper" families of
> Guatemala…Mayas maintain a strong sense of cultural difference, through language, clothing, religion, and other things. These are not mestizo characteristics: there are clear differences between them and me. I have no maternal
> language, for example. I could engage in Maya spirituality, but it would be
> different, because it would not come through descent (*herencia*), but rather
> through choice. To be mestiza means having a specific position on the current
> [political] situation.

She goes on to explain the personal dimension of this shift, a still unfinished exploration of a hidden and suppressed family history:

> I grew up in a ladino setting. My father never told me about his background.
> He is dark skinned, but does not acknowledge any indigenous descent. My

mother is white. She is extremely proud of her *abolengo* (elite family line), her Spanish descent. My father was involved in a magazine that had a section called "yesterday's people." One time he wrote an article on my maternal uncle. He wrote about the ladino side of the family but never the other side. I asked him why once, but he didn't respond. I am very curious to learn my family history on my father's side.

In the racial ideology of his day Flor's father would probably have been considered a "mistado." He became a teacher, a position of considerable social status, "married well," and managed to break into ladino society. Ironically, in her home as a child, Flor remembers an atmosphere of discrimination against Indians, especially when they put on airs as "*igualados*" (acting as if they were equal) dressing and acting like ladinos. Flor's embrace of mestizaje includes an inclination to explore this suppressed history of igualados in her own family, to know the indigenous ancestors that her father felt compelled to deny.

This intimate dimension of mestizaje must go a long way toward explaining why the term itself has become the metaphor of choice for expressing an emergent form of solidarity, despite its baggage and ambiguities. When reflecting on their own identity, it is fairly common for ladinos solidarios to make half-joking references to "*la indígena que mi abuelo encontró en el camino*," (the indigenous woman who my grandfather encountered on the road) as a counterpoint to the ideology of strictly bounded separation reaching back to the very origins of family memory.[24] Even if they are not inclined to pursue the matter further, to recuperate the family member about whom no one talks, the metaphor of "mixed bloods" already has suggested itself. Given the vivid power of this metaphor, people regularly press it into service even when its usefulness is dubious. I sat with a focus group of high school seniors from the Leonidas, who the previous week had provided an intriguing spread of answers to an anonymous identity question: 45 percent indígena, 38 percent mestiza, 17 percent ladina. I asked what factors determined this range of identifications. Biological composition served as the touchstone for the animated discussion that followed:

> I think that the majority understand mestizo as persons...persons...at least this is the way we've understood it...those who are mixed, between indigenous and ladino. The pure ladino doesn't really exist anymore, like my compañero said, they would be descendants of the Spanish, people who don't have anyone in their family line who has worn indigenous clothing.

As long as these biological premises remain prominent—remnants of the ideology of the mistado—it will be difficult for the new meanings of mestizaje as solidarity to make headway. There will always be a residual tendency to view mestizaje as fate, indigenous blood that runs in your veins, suppressed, hidden, overcome, but prone to come out at the least expected time. Flor's key insight that mestizaje is an option, a constructed position, loses ground in spite of her own intentions, turning her new identity into a "human interest" story, a personal encounter with heretofore suppressed racial destiny.

Yet even if Flor's intended meaning were to prevail, if mestizaje could indeed be understood as a constructed position of conscience, yet another predicament would emerge. By its very nature, this identity choice could be quite ephemeral—a youthful fit of idealism, a passing phase. As Robyn Wiegman (1999) has cogently argued in the case of white "race traitors" in the United States, the option to endorse particularity is the prerogative of those who enjoy a privilege of universality: racialized peoples, by contrast, do not have the power to do and undo their identities at will. The greater the flourish and confidence with which mestizos wish away their birthright, creating a less compromised identity category with a wave of the hand, the more suspicions are aroused, the more arrogance the gesture connotes. While Flor's low key, unassuming manner allays such concerns, the new identity category is a collective space whose features are established through processes that are not ultimately determined by the intentions of individuals. The great political promise of mestizo militancy is a decolonized non-Indian identity, distinct from, but existing on equal terms with, indigenous Guatemalans. Its contribution toward this end, to date, has been to help break the racial ideology that underpins ladino dominance, emphasizing the fluid boundaries between (some) ladinos and Indians, creating the language to imagine alignment without appropriation. Yet while that break is evident and the new language stands ready to deploy, corresponding social and political alignments remain incipient at best. Indigenous mistrust, and the weight of alternative meanings carried forward from the past, conspire to slow the transition. Militant mestizos have to differentiate themselves both from mestizo universalists like Edwin Morquecho and from new mestizos like Yuri and Ramón, whose irreverence could drain from the militancy its earnest sense of purpose.

Ladino Dissidents: Waging the Struggle from Within

Another group of ladinos chimaltecos, including some with long histories of close alignment with indigenous struggles and deeply critical stances toward their own, argue adamantly for transformation from within. In part their adamancy is grounded in skepticism toward the main alternative, "militant mestizaje," whether out of distaste for perceived opportunism, fear of repercussions within their own family, principled critique, or, more likely, some entangled combination of all three.[25] Yet it would be easy to overstate the differences between these two stances, reading extravagant conclusions into the varying preferences of an identity label. For example, although Yolanda and Gerardo argue constantly about whether to use the "mestizo" or the "ladino" identity category, they agree on most questions of substance related to race and identity politics. The same is true of Araceli Danton and Blanca Gálvez, two protagonists of the rejuvenated Día de Guadalupe festivities, which I followed with interest in December 1997.

From Penitence to Solidarity: "Guadalupanismo" in Chimaltenango

Influenced by Mexican traditions of folk Catholicism, ritual homage to the Virgin has deep roots in Guatemalan Catholicism, among both ladinos and Indians. Beginning in the 1920s these rituals assumed the character of a public festival, influenced by the rise of the tourist industry and the first rumblings of Guatemalan indigenismo, as well as by internal forces within the Catholic Church. Elite and middle-class ladino participants in the ritual would do "penitence" before the Virgin Guadalupe by dressing their children as Indians and parading through the city streets to the church. This festival had its most loyal following in the capital city and the central highlands, including Chimaltenango.[26] Adherents to these original meanings would not have been completely disappointed in 1997: they could still dress up their kids, striking the balance between authentic clothing and key markers (for example, makeup on light colored skin) to reassure the curious observer that the crossover was not for real; children could still march down Chimaltenango's *la calle real* (principal avenue) to the church, where they posed in wood and thatch crèche-like structures to be photographed; and they could still gather afterwards among family and friends, in settings that reinforced cultural distance and racial dominance. Yet since the early 1980s participation had been in decline, and if it were not for Araceli and Blanca, the ritual would probably have stopped altogether.

The quiet campaign of Araceli and Blanca to transform the Día de Guadalupe ritual began in the early 1990s. They had been instrumental in recuperating the tradition, reversing its decline since the 1950s and, in so doing, had fused its original religious content (veneration of the Virgin) and its traditional racial meanings (Indians as separate and unequal) with something new. Araceli explains:

> Blanca and I started to do some research, because behind each religious act there must be a message, an underlying context. Through study, reflection, and a dose of spiritual maturity, we came upon this idea of racial equality. We believe that there should be one day when were are all equal...a day free from racial conflict. This is the new meaning that we have given to this day.

Blanca Gálvez, a lay Catholic activist in her early thirties, led the church service that preceded the procession. Although non-Indian herself, Gálvez wore indigenous clothing—an anathema to adult ladinos. This cross-dressing, she explained, was a gesture of solidarity with indigenous people, in recognition of their immense suffering. Speaking to the children and parents gathered at the outset, she re-presented the Virgin of Guadalupe as symbol of ladino-Indian racial unity. Although indigenous chimaltecos did not participate in the procession, they watched from the sidelines with bemusement. In this ritualized racial mimicry, where Indians watched ladinos dress up as Indians, older meanings commingled awkwardly with the new (figure 6.3). Did the ritual still entail an assertion of ladino dominance? Had that message been displaced by a faintly absurd nostalgia for the racial boundaries of times past? A vague envy of indigenous authenticity? Had the newly imbued gesture of racial solidarity, at least for

Figure 6.3. Día de Guadalupe procession. Ladinos are dressed as Indians, and Indian shop workers look on. Photo credit: Charles R. Hale.

some, taken hold? Whatever the answers to these questions, the very indeterminacy left no doubt that the ideology of strict racial difference, once a point of reference for all, had begun rapidly to unravel.

Yet the ambiguous consequences of this unraveling are equally striking, especially given differences in perspective between Araceli and Blanca. Both want the Día de Guadalupe to link "adoration of the Virgin" with an expression of racial solidarity, but beyond this they disagree. Araceli explains:

> She uses indigenous clothing. She says there should be a neutral day, when we are all equal. If we all use indigenous clothing, then we all are equal. I agree, but I cannot bring myself to dress that way. I feel uncomfortable doing it. Blanca's idea is that we should all identify as one race. She would say to me, "You should dress this way too, to express your identification and your same-ness." Her idea is that we lower ourselves, that we show the ultimate humility for one day. She definitely goes further than I do.... This is our disagreement. But we always get along well, and we keep talking about it.

Although Araceli attributes their disagreement to taste and temperament—"*Lo que pasa es que a Blanca le gusta lo indígena.... Yo, en cambio, soy mucho más recatada*" (You see, Blanca likes things indigenous.... In contrast, I am much more reserved)—it also maps neatly onto identity politics. In response to my direct question, Araceli claimed an identity as ladina; Blanca's sensibilities, in contrast, are unmistakably mestiza.[27]

As with Yolanda's identity fluctuation (noted at the outset of this chapter), it would be mistaken to associate these two positions with fixed and singular political consequences. Blanca's mestiza sensibilities do appear more assertive and potentially transformative. She wears indigenous traje herself, an act of transgression that few ladinas (Araceli included) can bring themselves to make; she takes the lead in making the link between religious symbolism and racial politics; Araceli even revealed at one point in our interview that Blanca had expressed a desire to marry an indigenous man. Araceli, in contrast, is more cautious on all these counts. She disagrees with Blanca's "one race" egalitarianism ("Indians and ladinos are equal, yes, but we have different characters"), and still shudders remembering her father's admonishments when an indigenous boyfriend began coming by the house. Araceli is ultimately loath to forsake the identity category in which she was raised, even while acknowledging that most ladinos, her own parents included, persist in their racism toward Indians. On the other hand, Blanca's vision of racial politics treads a fine line between solidarity and appropriation, between critique of ladino dominance and assertion of a mestiza identity to which all Guatemalans should belong. Her egalitarianism is dangerously close to a call for assimilation, an act of appropriation. In this light, Araceli could emerge as the more respectful and sage of the two: crossing into the realm of lo Maya with no pretense of staying there, shouldering the challenge to transform ladina identity from within. Both positions could act to transform the racial hierarchy—Araceli by retaining ties as ladino and waging the struggle from within, Blanca through a more frontal attack. Both also risk having precisely the opposite effect.

This multiplicity should discourage the inclination to expect a particular set of political consequences to flow from a given idiom of identity—whether ladino or mestizo. Especially in the United States, and in other former European colonies that inherited rigidly bounded ideologies of racial difference, mestizaje has been associated with transgression, cultural creativity, and expansive political horizons. Feminist critiques of the first wave of anticolonial and racial vindicationist struggle imbued these associations with additional strength and specificity. Mestizaje, along with its theoretical affine "hybridity," offered a means to dissent from both the dominant scheme of racial categorization and the patriarchal, authoritarian character of resistance movements, showing how they remained captive to the very forces of oppression they sought to resist. Postcolonial theorists such as Homi Bhabha (1990) carried these arguments further: the dialectic of colonial relations yielded a "third space," which could become the seed of an alternative politics, beyond the mimicry of local resistance to colonial domination.[28]

These multiple meanings, in turn, go to the heart of the analytical problem of racial solidarity in Guatemala today. To express solidarity as ladina, as Araceli opted to do, preserves a direct articulation with the legacy of ladino oppression of Indians, with present-day ladinos who actively carry on that legacy and, perhaps most important, with a racial category that Mayas perceive and experience as "the dominant." To express solidarity as mestiza, Blanca's chosen course of action, ostensibly avoids these articulations, and yet brings forth others that Mayas could well find equally threatening. It sounds very similar to the discourse of mestizo universalism; even the more theoretically resonant notions of "third spaces" and hybridity sound like redressed calls for assimilation, threats to indigenous people's emergent power and legitimacy.[29] When I queried Yolanda further on her reaffirmation of ladino identity, this was the gist of her argument. The embrace of mestizaje, she claimed, wishes away the experience of having been raised ladino a little too easily. Yet the struggle from within has its own traps and ambiguities as well.

Between the Rainbow and the "Mancha Mongólica"

At stake in the debate between the ladino and mestizo identity labels is the basic question of how best to encapsulate an antiracist politics that both groups presumably share. For example, Jorge Solares, director of the Instituto de Estudios Étnicos of the San Carlos University, defends ladino identity with reference to abhorrent meanings that he assigns to mestizo identity:

> Mestizo has no place in Guatemala; ladino does. The Indian is mestizo, because
> if this were not the case, we would be talking about one mixed population and
> another pure one. It is racist to speak of [racially] pure groups; by extension,
> the very term mestizo is, in the worst of cases, racist—an echo of Hitler's dis-
> course. Ladino and mestizo are different terms and we should not use them as
> synonyms. (cited in Carrillo 1993:12)

A more nuanced position defends ladino identity as a broad, internally tolerant, and multiracial alternative. "Ladino encompasses more than mestizo," one ladina dissident told me, "because mestizo necessarily brings up the race question. Ladino, in contrast, is a cultural concept. Ladino-ness is more capacious." The image here is a rainbow of racial phenotypes—white, Indian, black, and everything in between—all of which are included and affirmed. Proponents of this image do not deny the history of racism toward Indians; rather, they argue that because ladinos have been so intent on policing the Indian-ladino boundary to keep Indians out, they are especially accepting, even egalitarian, toward all those who have made their way inside. The challenge of transforming ladino identity, in this view, is to affirm this pluralist tolerance *within*, and then to extend the same principle toward Indians who historically have been excluded.

This image of the phenotypic rainbow, and the argument it supports, is difficult to assess in Chimaltenango. From social settings to public institutions and even within single families, ladinos display a strikingly wide range of phenotypes. On the one hand, when the focus of attention is the boundary with Indians, this phenotypic diversity seems to fade in significance. On the other hand, whiteness does correlate closely with status, with the usual exceptions where money, education, or another source of prestige can "whiten" an individual, who then often marries or mates with someone lighter skinned, giving rise to socially whitened progeny.[30] Moreover, scratching lightly beneath the veneer one finds this phenotypic diversity to be the subject of constant discussion and biting commentary, especially difficult for those of darker complexion who are accepted as ladinos and yet disparaged for being too close to Indians. Even those dark skinned ladinos who do achieve a secure place within ladino society seem to have paid a high price to get there.

Upon arrival in Chimaltenango in search of a house to rent I met Don Rigoberto, a short, stout man of distinctly Indian phenotype, who I naively assumed was Indian. I soon found out not only that he is adamantly ladino, but also espouses an especially virulent anti-Indian racism. Don Rigoberto "married well" (that is, a lighter skinned, unquestionably ladina woman) and will leave a solid middle-class inheritance to his children, who all have married ladino as well. In one sense, Don Rigoberto could stand as evidence of the "racial democracy" among those who claim ladino identity. Yet Yolanda remembered well the scandal that resulted when Don Rigoberto's sister married a ladino. "*¿Se casó con aquella india de Itzapa?*" (He married that Indian from Itzapa?), Don Luis had exclaimed in horror.[31] In face of similar opprobrium, Don Rigoberto might have found virulent racism toward Indians to be the price of acceptance: a begrudged welcome, once marriage had been consummated, as long as he slammed the door behind him.

Ladino dissidents, then, face a two-fold challenge. They must keep that door open, taking a forceful and explicit stand against racism toward Indians, while at the same time affirming the value and particularity of ladino identity. Under current conditions, they face an uphill battle. Euro-Guatemalans, always skittish and ambivalent about being considered part of the rainbow, are now increasingly inclined to defect.[32] As noted earlier, Euro-Guatemalans regularly disparage ladinos in places like Chimaltenango as "*choleros*" or as bearers of the "Mongolian spot" (a patch of dark skin on the lower back of a newborn), which supposedly proves Indian blood. Ladinos' resistance to this disparagement has always involved, at least in part, an internalization of the critique, that is, an assertion of proximity and affinity with whites. As the ladino identity category becomes more open, ladinos lose the ability to exclude Indians and, by extension, they grow more susceptible to the Euro-Guatemalan assertion that they are contaminated.

Meanwhile, lower-class ladinos, at the "Indian" end of the phenotypic spectrum, appear to be defecting as well. Many of them would have remained outside in any case, condemned by their proximity to the Indian. Instead of persisting against the odds, as Don Rigoberto did a generation ago, they are now apt to affirm an identity as mestizos, whether out of resignation or active refusal. Some might even be attracted to the idea of becoming (middle-class) Maya, on the grounds that educated Mayas seem to have more prerogatives in the global economy than ladinos. Paradoxically, the more open the ladino category becomes, the less hegemonic appeal it has for those at the margins, hoping to be allowed in. Dissident ladinos must also contend with the growing numbers of militant mestizos who, in search of a forceful statement of solidarity with Indians, or a forthright encounter with their own mixed heritage, or both, have defected from the ladino identity category as well. All this leaves "ladino society" with strong remnants of its previous dominance, but increasingly vulnerable and tension ridden. Under these conditions, the earnest struggle to transform ladino identity from within often turns ironic: a self-critical but also vaguely self-justifying reflection on the predicaments of racial dominance.

Ladino Dissidents and the Janus-Faced Discourse of Lo Guatemalteco

Analysts have tended to neglect generic assertions of Guatemalan identity, and their influence on Maya-ladino relations, because interest in Maya cultural politics has been so strong. By opting to collect data on resolutely "Maya" cultural spaces, or by focusing exclusively on how people engage in identity talk, they tend to gloss over the many contexts where issues of race, culture, and identity are self-consciously absent, or perhaps present through their very absence.[33] In Chimaltenango it is striking—given the proliferation of Maya NGOs, and the rise of state-backed multiculturalism—how frequently topics related to ladino-Indian relations or Maya cultural rights (not to mention racism) are utterly absent from public discourse. This is especially true in local politics where candidates seeking support across racial lines sidestep the issue completely, perhaps assuming that an appeal to one group would alienate the others, or perhaps remaining unsure how popular such an appeal would be, even with their own base constituency. Early in my fieldwork I attended a three-hour-long mayoral candidates' forum in Chimaltenango, listening earnestly, pen and notebook in hand, to the speeches of an array of indigenous and ladino candidates, but unable to record a single reference to race, ethnicity, cultural rights, or identity.

A while later, I went with Yolanda and family to the neighboring town of Sumpango to attend the annual Day of the Dead kite festival and competition, a resolutely Maya cultural space. Crafted for months by youth groups and neighborhood associations in this predominantly indigenous town, the kites often feature deeply felt Mayan images, epigraphs, and political aphorisms. Typical inscriptions that year included "We weave our own history," "We are part of the nation," and "We identify as the Mayan people." Yolanda's brother-in-law Abelardo, a teacher at the Leonidas high school, expressed great enthusiasm for this Maya efflorescence. He directed my attention to the writing on one kite that he especially liked: "They killed our people, but they could not extinguish our culture." Civic minded, deeply egalitarian, constantly exercised about the corruption and hypocrisy of the political class, Abelardo embraces the values of the 1944–1954 reformist government, and imagines a future time when Guatemala's national dignity might be recovered. This is not, however, simply an expression of political nostagia. Abelardo's outlook has been sensitized and shaped by official multiculturalism and by the political thrust of the Maya efflorescence: affirming Maya cultural pride, applauding the rise of Maya political leadership, joining in the critique of anti-Indian racism. In these respects, Abelardo fits the description of a ladino dissident.

In other ways, however, Abelardo confounds this analysis. Acutely aware of the changing racial composition of his classroom, now obliged to make his curriculum explicitly multicultural, Abelardo still favors color-blind pedagogy: rules that students wear uniforms, resistance to race-based data collection and other forms of recognition, the same standards and treatment for all. Abelardo told me proudly how he crossed out "ladino" and "indígena" boxes in forms the Ministry of Education sent to his school, and wrote in "Guatemalan." While applauding Maya efflorescence, he also worries how he would implement the principle of equality for all if the emphasis on cultural difference grew too prominent. He favors Maya rights, but the specter of Maya separatism leaves him unsettled. The problem with identity in Guatemala, Abelardo believes,

> is that people do not feel Guatemalan. Quite apart from everything else, they should feel this identity. It doesn't matter what you are. Mexico doesn't have this problem: as they say, "Mexico first, Mexico second, Mexico third." We are not that way: here there is no loyalty...if we all identified as Guatemalans, the problem would disappear because we would accept one another. This is difficult for those of Don Luis's generation. [Guatemalan identity] has to be based on mutual acceptance.

This appeal to a common Guatemalan identity cannot be collapsed with the mestizo universalism of the previous generation. Although Abelardo highlights what all Guatemalans have in common, he leaves plenty of room for cultural difference. He pointedly notes that the fiercest resistance to his ideas might well come from "traditional" ladinos like Don Luis, bent on defending privilege and dominance.[34] Coming from people like Abelardo, the appeal to lo guatemalteco constitutes another expression of ladino solidarity: offering a rigorous standard of equality, without the accompanying presumption of assimilation. Yet even among ladinos who strongly support Maya cultural rights, discussion often returns to the questions of national identity that Abelardo posed: What unites us as Guatemalans? What should the new national project look like? How do we create safeguards against the "Yugoslavia" scenario? Beyond the bromides that call for "unity in diversity" few answers emerge; into this awkward space the premises of ladino dominance, disguised as a universal Guatemalan identity, can easily seep back in.

The religious counterpart to Abelardo's embrace of lo guatemalteco can be found in many organized churches of Chimaltenango. Although specifics vary widely between Catholic and Evangelical, and within each, a general rule prevails: forging a religious identity that rises above all others, that bridges the divide between Indian and ladino. I spent many hours in conversation with the congregation of the Alfa & Omega, the most ladino-identified evangelical church, and with its head pastor Rubén

Zavala, a thoughtful man from Patzún who a generation ago ladinos might have disparaged as a mistado.[35] At my request, Zavala gathered his deacons on two separate occasions to engage in a group discussion about religion, race, and identity. Their contributions were formulaic and suspiciously uniform, but revealing nonetheless:

> As soon as one enters the church community that [cultural difference] stops being a problem. There is a very simple rule: love thy neighbor [cites Ephesians 4:3].... The foreign countries, Europeans, the MINUGUA people, are correct when they say that the Maya have been marginalized. But there is a danger of going too far, letting them do whatever they want. We have to deposit our faith with Jesus Christ.

> In the rural areas, those who attend [our] church do not lose their identities. We wear traje. There are many families who speak their language. Outsiders accuse us of promoting the loss of Maya culture, but this is not so. What really happens is that Maya culture just begins to take on a lesser importance. This is natural.

> I think the Mayas are right. In El Salvador, seven families control the country's wealth. There are reasons for this. Who offers the peasant retirement benefits? We are not Mayas, and we are not Spaniards. We are a mixture. We are mestizos. Revolutions are necessary. Otherwise, only the powerful will have a voice. But to strengthen indigenous identity is not our priority. This is not a matter of racism inside the church—we are unified. Cultural difference doesn't matter much—what matters is Christ.

The Alfa & Omega Church embodies a formidable challenge to the Maya efflorescence, not because it discriminates against Indians, but because it purportedly does not. Granted the elite ladino image of the church does already constitute a form of institutionalized racism, and earnest affirmations of equality surely veil subtly discriminatory practices. Granted, one deacon did utter the telltale assimilationist line, invoking a mestizo Guatemala without ladinos or Mayas. In general, however, the church does seem to assign more importance to creating Christians than to reinforcing a dominant identity, which makes its implicit racial ideology run parallel to that of lo guatemalteco: leaving space for cultural difference while changing the subject, as it were, to a preferred topic. While the deacons of Alfa & Omega do at times go head-to-head with Mayas, especially when it comes to the religious dimension of Maya efflorescence, they prefer to finesse discussion altogether. They do smuggle a ladino-mestizo subject back in, but not in the traditional guise of outright assimilation. Rather than opposing Maya identity, they simply move discussion to a "higher plane." Ladinos become de facto leaders in these efforts, in the name of Christ; in so doing they both renounce ladino dominance and reclaim it; they both insist that Indians are welcome and create standards of Christian practice that Indians strain to follow and ladinos find it much easier to keep.

This, in different variants, is the basic predicament of the Ladino dissident: they affirm Maya cultural difference and rights, critique ladino dominance, and use this as the groundwork for respectful, egalitarian relations with Mayas. Yet because they also affirm the identity category "ladino," they tend to be aligned or at least passively associated with other ladinos who seek to forge egalitarian relations with Mayas through recourse to a higher principle of unity (lo guatemalteco, *lo cristiano*, and so on). It is fairly easy to dismiss this latter move on theoretical grounds: hegemony of the particular, under the guise of a supposed universal. It is often more difficult to draw that line in practice. As expressed by people like Abelardo, recourse to lo guatemalteco creates a conducive setting for the ladino dissident position to grow: a standard of social justice to which all can appeal as they negotiate the terms of coexistence in a multiracial society. Yet once ladino dissidents affirm some such notion of lo guatemalteco, they perch themselves on a slippery slope, implicitly endorsing (or at least being perceived as endorsing) a single standard of unity that in reality privileges ladinos.

The "Ladino Problem" and the Challenge of Racial Healing

By the late 1990s, in the Guatemalan political sphere, critique of classic anti-Indian racism, calls for intercultural dialogue, and respect for Maya cultural rights had become commonplace. The preamble to the Accord on the Rights of Indigenous Peoples set the tone, and most politicians, public institutions, and civil society organizations fell into line. Gradually, and at times begrudgingly, most ladinos in Chimaltenango came to endorse this seismic shift in race relations, while at the same time attempting to limit or discipline the Maya efflorescence under way. This limiting action often began with the enumeration of stubborn cultural features that prevented indigenous people from fully realizing the fruits of their newfound equality, emphasizing distinctions between moderate and radical Mayas, and expressing shuddering fears of "reverse racism." In keeping with the rise of neoliberal multiculturalism, these sensibilities and practices confronted Maya cultural activists with strategic dilemmas: when to occupy the newly opened spaces and when to reject them as too compromised; whether to continue defending so-called radical positions, or to moderate them; how to contest the racism that comes in this newly modulated, cultural form. These dilemmas, I contend, contribute directly to the impasse that the Maya movement currently confronts.

The present chapter, in contrast, has focused on ladinos (or mestizos) who in some respects have pushed beyond this impasse, showing active solidarity with Maya efforts to transform their society, toward racial equality and social justice. I defined "solidarity" in terms of a simple criterion: people who had substantive relations with Mayas, under conditions that embodied both their desire for, and their active attempt to practice, relations of interracial equality. This criterion yielded a sizeable and diverse group in Chimaltenango, from mestizo universalists like Don Edwin to those like Yuri, who practice a "mestizaje from below," from "mestizo militants" like Flor to ladino dissidents like Yolanda. They are fascinating and, at times, inspiring people who occupy a wide range of positions in Chimaltenango society: cooperatives, NGOs, public institutions, youth gangs, an enclave of the recently demobilized guerrilla. Those who work closely with politicized Mayas almost inevitably relate painful episodes of rejection; those who live within the gray area between indigenous and ladino identity generally experience a certain amount of anti-Indian racism, which complicates their solidarity. In some cases, these are spaces that people are working explicitly to forge; in others, they are the unintended consequence of basic efforts to get by or to get ahead. They all are spaces without guarantees, neither clear-cut nor contradiction free.

To explain the emergence of ladino solidarity in all its multiple facets, it is crucial first to give the Left its due, even while noting in the same breath the limitations and contradictions of this influence. The revolutionary movement, though disastrous in its eventual outcome, helped mightily to break the stranglehold of a small group of ladino power holders on Chimaltenango society, to create a context where indigenous chimaltecos could imagine a radically different society, and mobilize toward these ends. It also brought many politicized ladinos into intense long-term relations with indigenous peoples, forging a broader cultural-political setting where critique of racism and ladino dominance became de rigueur. Most of the informants who fit my description of ladinos solidarios, with the exception of the new mestizos, confirmed the deep formative influence of the Left, whether as militants or simply as participants in this leftist political culture. At the same time, most had become painfully aware of the limitations of this left-inflected racial solidarity: recourse to formulaic answers that pale before the complexity of the problems addressed; righteousness born in commitment and struggle, which creates a chasm between the "enlightened" and the rest; submission to authority, rather than trusting insights borne in direct experience and self-reflection. Of the qualities that seemed best to counterbalance these ills, capacity for self-reflection stood out. Those who clearly went beyond the limitations of the Left had a notable capacity for introspection, for viewing oneself through the eyes of others, recognizing the contradictions of their own position, without yielding completely to cynicism or despair.

Although I sought a political process in Chimaltenango, where ladinos solidarios might be playing especially prominent roles, during the years of my research I found none. The most significant political mobilization during 1997–1998 was the February 27 Movement, which turned out to lack a significant challenge to Chimaltenango's prevailing racial hierarchy. In general, local politics in Chimaltenango play out in racially ambiguous discourse: invoking chimaltecos, Guatemalans, popular classes, or various more specific collectivities with clear-cut interests (merchants, widows, human rights victims, city water users). The dozens of Maya organizations with home offices in Chimaltenango do not directly challenge this pattern. They have a strong presence, felt in many ways, but their following is not large, and they exert minimal influence in conventional politics or even public sphere political discourse. This means that ladinos have a limited range of options for enacting solidarity: within predominantly Maya organizations, in mixed institutional contexts where explicit discussion of indigenous-ladino relations is rare, and in social interactions where etiquette dictates avoidance of conflictive topics. The most dense and significant intercultural dialogue may well be going on not as self-conscious border crossing but as relations within the ambiguous spaces of mestizaje from below, or within the capacious umbrella of lo guatemalteco, with consequences that are as difficult to trace as those of the February 27 Movement.

Expressions of solidarity through mestizaje from below are the most novel, and the most theoretically resonant. Yuri challenges orthodoxy; she straddles, plays with, or simply refuses the standard identity categories in Chimaltenango. She epitomizes the intrepid creativity that so many theorists have associated with mestizaje and its synonyms. At the same time, despite her engaging intelligence and unusual fortitude, as of 2002 Yuri had no job and few prospects for upward social mobility. Being adamantly "mestiza" did not help. It connoted a rebellious indifference toward the norms of proper ladino society, a respect for Maya resistance, but mild disdain for Maya cultural affirmation as too controlled and tradition bound. This stance surely expresses an element of solidarity, based in part on the recognition that, even though she identifies as mestiza, she is not immune from that same racism herself. Yet this same oblique racism acts to nudge Yuri away from Mayas, encouraging distance rather than commonality. New mestizos have enough problems trying to get by, without adding solidarity with Indians to their burdens. While the transformative potential of mestizaje from below would seem to depend directly on this bridge to strongly identified and politicized Mayas, it is a bridge that neither the new mestizos themselves nor Maya cultural activists show much interest in building.

The situation is very different for militant mestizos, whose signature is an assertive gesture of solidarity toward the Maya world. People in this category almost always have jobs, or reasonable prospects of getting one; they are generally well educated, thoughtful, politically engaged, and solidly middle class. Their moves to mestizaje may also include a personal odyssey, an effort to uncover, recuperate, or revalue a suppressed indigenous ancestor, someone who physically embodies the bloodline that the new identity evokes. Militant mestizos inevitably carry with them a faint whiff of the convert, since the category itself is so new: a bit more self-conscious than is generally the case when people talk about their identities, a little more hesitant, awkward, and earnest. The majority of my sample of solidarios claimed this militant mestizo identity and saw it as crucial to the work they were doing. This work, in many cases, was important and admirable, on the front lines of struggle for indigenous rights against ladino racism. Yet the crowded semantic field that this militant mestizo identity occupies also acts to undermine the clarity of its message. They cannot be confused with mestizo universalists who harbor visions of an overarching mestiza national identity, inclusive and egalitarian for all; they certainly need to distinguish themselves from iconoclastic intellectuals such as Mario Roberto Morales, who deploy the mestizaje idea as an offensive weapon against all claims made in the name of Maya culture.[36] They tend to disavow the space of mestizaje from below as well; it is too fluid and irreverent to be hospitable to the political project that militant mestizos embrace. These multiple, ambiguous meanings of mestizaje are apt to be lost on Maya cultural activists, who are more likely to see *any* mestizo discourse as a threat of appropriation, or a surreptitious bid for assimilation.

While ladino dissidents shake free from such suspicions of concealed motives, they have problems of their own. Their great achievement is to remain positioned at the center of the dominant identity category that they seek to decolonize. The ladina dissident, in this case with anthropologist on her coattails, could partake in the "ladinos only" baile social (high society dance) in San Martín Jilotepeque and amply record the racist banter at extended family gatherings, while maintaining an ironic, highly critical stance toward it all. Ladino dissidents generate such critical insight into ladino race privilege, in part because their break with that privilege is partial. Their solidarity comes in small acts, yielding incremental not revolutionary change. Often laden with irony, at times shrouded in chingadera, these small acts are always mildly compromised; ladino dissidents embrace this ambiguity and do not expect anyone's identity to be contradiction free. The source of their authority as ladinos makes their dissidence edgy, partly imbued with the dominance they vow to contest.

Yolanda fits this description precisely and, strangely enough, this made her the ideal touchstone for my research. Yolanda made no topic taboo, and seemed to genuinely enjoy hashing over the contradictions in the very social positions she occupied, the identity she espoused. Even if this awkward balance of complicity and critique is not a comfortable resting place, it does generate a sharpened analysis of what the Maya are up against, and delivers a pointed reminder of how contradictory all these diverse expressions of solidarity turn out to be. This same reminder, I readily admit, applies fully to white anthropologists, who fancy ourselves to be working in solidarity with subaltern peoples, and in the process move a little too easily from solidarity to erasure of race privilege. The message is not despair or paralysis, just a reminder, best delivered with a touch of humor chapín, that solidarity grows more effective as it becomes more cognizant of its own limits.

seven

Racial Ambivalence
in Transnational Perspective

Seldom has whiteness been so widely represented as attuned to racial equality
and justice while so aggressively solidifying its advantage.

—*Robyn Wiegman (in reference to contemporary United States),*
"Whiteness Studies and the Paradox of Particularity," (1999)

I see discrimination, in any case, as something natural: we all discriminate, by
sex, color, etc. If it is not exaggerated, it is normal. It is normal, for example,
that you would not want your daughter to marry some big lazy black man (*un
gran negro, que no quiere trabajar o nada*). The conflict is natural. But it doesn't
happen to any great extent here: it is not a life and death matter.

—*Frederico Melgar, ladino chimalteco, June 1998*

I have struggled with the odd sensation, since about 2002, of being only in sporadic
touch with Guatemala, and inevitably relying on a lens shaped by conditions closer to
home to take stock of what I hope this book has conveyed. During the spring of 2004
we in the United States marked the fifty-year anniversary of *Brown v. Board of
Education*, in what can only be described as a deeply discouraging remembrance.
Although much could of course be said about how much has changed for the better
since those pre–Civil Rights Movement days, media reports and in depth analysis alike
focused much more attention on racial equality's enormous unfinished agenda.[1] The
University of Texas played its part in the remembrance by inviting John Hope
Franklin to deliver a public address. A ninety-year-old eminent historian who had
worked with Thurgood Marshall on the Brown case, Franklin talked mostly about the
shocking racism he had encountered as a young man before the ruling, and about the

intense conviction, idealism, and esprit de corps of Marshall's legal team. Then, in the final moments of his speech, in a subtle and soft-spoken manner that might have led one to downplay the devastating critique, Franklin reflected on the chasm between conditions today and the new society that his generation of activists imagined themselves to be building. The problems are serious and getting worse, he concluded; they await a new civil rights movement that has yet to be imagined.

Parallels between Franklin's retrospective assessment and the central analytical problem of this book weigh heavily on my mind. Since the mid-1980s, Guatemalan society has undergone an extraordinary transformation. Rising from the ashes of a brutal and traumatic, state-directed counterinsurgency campaign, Maya collective actors have seized the moment. From barely perceptible grassroots organizing, to high profile national-level negotiations, to a dense web of relations with "global" civil society, Mayas have claimed rights and challenged racism with impressive results. Although the feverish energy and excitement associated with the first round of struggle—similar, perhaps, to how Franklin characterized the spirit of the Marshall legal team—largely has faded, this reflects at least in part a consolidation that brings its own advantages. This book has taken these impressive achievements, well documented by others, as a given in order to pose a different series of questions: How have ladinos, the relatively powerful actors in the drama, responded to the challenge? How have they shaped, and been shaped by, these transformations? Are there ideological and institutional limits built into this process of change and, if so, what effects do they have? Even without the three decades of additional hindsight that Franklin had, I contend that it is crucial to begin this assessment, abandoning the "wait and see" standpoint, moving beyond sterile debates about whether the glass is half full or half empty.

The arguments presented in the preceding pages, beginning with the observation that Maya cultural rights activism currently faces an impasse, are sober and cautionary. My understanding of the impasse does not, however, draw on extensive interviews with Mayas. While this research project grew out of a multifaceted dialogue with Maya activist-intellectuals, those very conversations led me to focus primarily on ladinos and to avoid making Mayas the direct subjects of ethnographic scrutiny. My analysis is grounded in the assumption that much could be learned about the reach and limits of Maya rights activism by examining the people and structures of power that this activism has been directed against. In this sense, to draw a more specific parallel between the problems Franklin identified and my project here, one would need to focus on white people and the structural positions we occupy. How have different sectors of whites responded to the rising, if still limited, power of African Americans and other people of color since the beginning of the Civil Rights Movement? Although the full-fledged comparative analysis that this question demands will have to await another occasion, even to frame the question in this way has been illuminating. The following section substantiates this assertion, suggesting how this study draws from, and might contribute to, analysis and political engagement focused on the dominant actors in racial entanglements.

Ladinos, Mayas, and Whiteness Studies

Influenced by theoretical work on whiteness and racial formation, I decided to write this book using the conceptual apparatus of race, where others might have deployed ethnicity.[2] The reader will search in vain in the preceding pages for ethnic terminology—because race worked better in many cases and, where it did not, because I opted to substitute another term. In part, the rationale for this decision goes beyond the particular analytical mandate of this book. A close association in recent years with African Diaspora scholars has engendered a commitment to analyzing and working on issues of indigenous and Afro-descendant Latin Americans in a unified, comparative frame.[3] This endeavor calls forth the curious observation that, in the past thirty years, scholarship on black Latin Americans has tended to remain "racial" while their indigenous counterparts have been converted wholesale into "ethnics." Even after registering all the internal cultural processes that might have contributed to this divergence, it must also be attributed in part to the differential effects of racial ideologies, which presented Indians as a font of authentic national culture and blacks as alien, impossible to assimilate, non-national. This generates a gnawing sense that ethnicity theory emerged in complicity with state projects of nationalization, and with the differential subordination of black and indigenous citizens. Critique along these lines has been amplified by indigenous activist-intellectuals across the hemisphere, who overwhelmingly reject "ethnic" as a term of collective self-appellation. It would make us appear woefully out of step with the political sensibilities of our allies (and embarrassingly "unanthropological") not to follow suit.[4]

There are more specifically analytical rationales for this decision as well, which in the case of this book must be gauged not in relation to black and indigenous peoples, but rather, to the study of dominant culture ladinos or mestizos. I am far from alone in this move to re-center race in the study of inequality in Latin America; indeed, the steady flow of recent literature makes it appear to be something of a trend.[5] This is race as cultural construct, of course, sharply differentiated from its pre-Boasian biological meanings, remnants of which persisted in social science into the 1950s, when they would be pushed aside by ethnicity theory.[6] Indeed, the contrast with this antecedent literature reveals a telltale difference as racial analytics have returned to the fore: previously scholars used the term in reference mainly to racially marked peoples themselves, with scant concern for the workings of racial hierarchy, and no attention to whites and ladinos-mestizos as the dominant actors in their countries' unfolding sociopolitical dramas. The rationale for the return of race to Latin American studies, in contrast, is that it generates insight into these broader social relations, and redirects the spotlight of analytical scrutiny toward those who are racially dominant.

There is much to be gained from the study of ladinos in Guatemala, and mestizos in other Latin American countries, in comparative and theoretical dialogue with US-based studies of whiteness.[7] One principal catalyst for whiteness studies has been to analyze and contest the way white racial dominance has been reproduced through assertions of universality, or more subtly still, by making white particularity stand as the unmarked, yet ubiquitous standard of social organization. Anthropology has been complicit with this racial hegemony in our consistent preference to study subordinate peoples, with ample respect for cultural particularity, but also with the implicit premise that difference from the dominant racial norm is what makes people into attractive subjects of study.[8] Whiteness studies ask that we reverse the lens. A further contribution of whiteness studies has been to defer questions about whether a given individual, or a given utterance or practice, is "racist." Instead, proponents have defended a more structural conceptualization of racism—as an ideology of racial inferiority articulated with race-based power inequities. By focusing on whites as a dominant racial group, this work redirects attention to a wide array of social forces that keep white people collectively in a higher position on the racial hierarchy, quite apart from individual white people's attitudes, practices, and discourse. Ladinos, I argue here, constitute a dominant racial group in Guatemala; as such, many of the theoretical insights of whiteness studies have been useful for guiding my analysis of ladino-Indian relations.

Let me name and address the objections to this assertion from the outset. Can this phrase—ladino racial dominance—hold its own, given that boundaries among groups in Guatemala are so porous and hierarchies so heterogeneous? Negative answers to this question tend to rest on three principal objections. First, to think of ladinos as a dominant racial group immediately raises a question about their relationship to Euro-Guatemalans, who generally occupy a higher position in the racial hierarchy. How dominant is dominant? Second, the boundary between ladinos and the diverse peoples who occupy lower rungs of the racial hierarchy is also porous. A third objection focuses on the relationship between ladinos and the colossus to the north. If ladino political sensibilities, identity, and practice are shaped in part by the history of subordinate relations between Guatemala and the United States, then ladino racial dominance (toward Indians) and racial subordination (in relation to US imperialism) become two sides of the same coin; this is an especially challenging point, given that I am white North American. All three objections might be combined and summarized as follows. The very term "racial dominance" invokes a generalized, transhistorical condition, which gives way under scrutiny of the great variability, fluidity, and particularity of ladino-Indian relations in Guatemala.[9]

These objections key directly into a major debate in the literature on race in Latin America. To simplify considerably, this debate is between those who defend the usefulness of a general "racial formation" framework and those who emphasize particularity, fearing that any generalized notion of racial formation would do violence to the rich and extensive heterogeneity in the ways that race is signified across space and time.[10] Although played out largely on conceptual grounds, the debate takes on an additional charge in cases where proponents of the racial formation approach themselves belong to, or are closely aligned with, a subordinate racial group. Critiques of racial formation, in these latter cases, extend to include the allegation (explicit or otherwise) that the analysts in question have failed to differentiate between their political agenda (for example, some form of transnational or diasporic racial unity) and their analysis of how race is lived in a given context. The counterallegation (explicit or otherwise) is that the "particularists" underestimate transnational racial inequities and discount the racial unity that the protagonists themselves have found so crucial to their struggles for rights and redress. In the logic of this counterallegation, analysts who are reticent in naming and analyzing racial hierarchies run the risk of complicity with the ideologies that legitimate racism.[11] Perhaps a closer look at ladino-Indian relations in Guatemala will help to move this debate forward.

The approach I have taken here views ladino racial dominance and the contextual particularities of racial meanings in Chimaltenango not as opposing perspectives, in tension with one another, but rather as key pieces of the analytical whole. The basic conditions of ladino racial dominance imposed themselves so forcefully and consistently in my daily experience as an ethnographer that they often could have faded into the unremarkable background of the normal. I remember walking outside our house one morning to find a group of three young ladino boys playing in the street with a puppy. They egged the puppy on to jump and nip at them, scolded the puppy in feigned anger, and then coaxed him to jump again. "*Chucho de mierda*" (You shithead dog), one yelled gleefully; "*Chucho indio*" (You Indian dog), another chimed in. I found this commonsense ideology of indigenous inferiority, this pervasive idea that ladinos are "*más que un indio*" to be ubiquitous in everyday settings, although often suppressed in "civilized" public discourse. Persisting race-based political-economic inequality also was a fact of life, despite incremental changes in some realms. Yet even amid this ubiquitous evidence of ladino racial dominance, one could always find fluidity and ambiguity as well: individuals and whole families whose very existence defied the assertion of racial boundaries; inversions of the standard inequalities; layers of complexity; exceptions to the rule. My approach to this juxtaposition of seemingly contradictory observations—racial dominance and disruptive ambiguity—has been to place them in dialogue, insisting that each can be properly understood only in relation to the other.

The relationship between ladinos and Euro-Guatemalans is a revealing case in point. In Guatemala and throughout Latin America, there is a long and rich intellectual tradition of critical scholarship on white (or "Creole") elites, their subservience to western imperial ideas and interests, their inability to fashion an inclusive national identity, their racist precepts toward non-white members of their own societies.[12] While this critique was at first advanced with the mestizo ideal as explicit alternative, more recently it has gone further, acknowledging how the celebration of mestizaje generally came paired with an ideology of *blanqueamiento* (whitening), which separates the constituent parts of the mix and assigns greater value to the parts that are racially white and culturally Anglo-European.[13] These very critiques, in turn, highlight the key question: how to think about racial dominance in Guatemala? In some respects ladinos and Euro-Guatemalans belong in the same loosely composed racial category: most ladinos endorse the ideology of blanqueamiento, and (in keeping with that ideology) a ladino who accumulates substantial wealth and marries well might even be accepted in the elite stratum. In other respects, however, the division between these two groups remains analytically crucial: Euro-Guatemalans' general insistence on marking their racial difference from ladinos exerts a deep influence on how ladinos think about themselves and, by extension, on ladino relations with Indians. Combined, these two observations point to the same conclusion—it would not be analytically sufficient to focus solely on the structural relationship (ladino and Euro-Guatemalan as a racially dominant bloc) or solely on the particularity (the porous boundaries and contradictory internal relations between these two). The particularity disrupts any straightforward notion of racial dominance, while this very notion remains crucial to making the particularity intelligible, and to situating ladinos as a group in Guatemalan society.

A careful look at the relations between ladinos and those at the lower end of the racial hierarchy informs a parallel argument. As emphasized in the preceding pages, ladinos in Chimaltenango, and throughout the highlands, typically feel deeply invested in the stark boundary between themselves and indigenous people. While individual and even collective transgressions always have occurred, in the past their consequences have been managed to reinforce this basic distinction and to relegate Indians to spaces that are separate and unequal. In chapters 2 and 6, I provided evidence to suggest that the incidence of these transgressions is increasing, and that the line between (lower-class) ladino and Indian is growing more blurred and porous. In the past offspring of mixed unions between ladinos and Indians often were called "mistados," a term with the connotation of instability and an assumption of inevitable assimilation to one group or the other. Today, in contrast, the counterpoint to the mistado are the new mestizos, who refuse identification with either side, and who seem to be forging a distinct collective identity. This increasing presence of new mestizos, in turn, complicates my assertion that ladinos are a dominant racial group: do the new mestizos partake in ladino racial dominance? Or are they best understood as a distinct sector of non-Indian subordinates? Drawing on the ethnographic scrutiny summarized in chapter 6, my answer is "some of both." Middle-class ladinos chimaltecos typically view new mestizos as Indians who have lost their culture, and racialize them accordingly; new mestizos themselves, though defiant of ladinos, often explain their distance from Indians by drawing on the same racial ideology that these middle-class ladinos espouse. The notion of ladino racial dominance that I deploy here does not screen out this complexity, but rather highlights it: new mestizos are racially ambiguous precisely because they are subject to ladino racism, while lacking clear recourse to Maya identity and cultural resistance. Structural analysis situates new mestizos as members of the racially subordinate bloc, who have internalized the ideology of racial inferiority directed against them. However persuasive this view, it does little to help us understand how new mestizos also have constituted themselves as a distinct social group. Ethnographic scrutiny fills in this gap, but the portrayal becomes fully intelligible only when framed in reference to the structural position that the new mestizos occupy.

Finally, the notion of ladino racial dominance also directs useful attention to the global racial hierarchy and, more specifically, to relations between my ladino subjects and the United States. I could not focus on ladino racial dominance without evoking questions about my own racial position and its effects on this study. One facet of this problem is the way white racial dominance might have influenced how ladino informants responded to my inquiries. The quotation from Frederico Melgar that serves as an epigraph to this chapter is an extreme version of a common cultural-political sensibility. My field notes record numerous instances where ladinos, in the course of an interview or informal conversation, drew a parallel between "our" Indians and "your" blacks, in what I took as a misplaced gesture of racial solidarity. This suggests that the ladino discourse analyzed here could contain a strained or overstated assertion of racial dominance resulting from their effort to connect with imagined mappings of my racial position and sensibilities as a white North American. Another facet of the problem is the triangle of relations among ladinos, Indians, and white foreigners. Many ladinos resent what they perceive as a growing bond of solidarity between white foreigners and Mayas, which precludes ladinos' traditional role as intermediaries between Indians and the outside world. Sensing this resentment, white foreigners deepen their ties with Mayas and develop an overly trenchant critique of ladino racism. Stated bluntly, the critique is that my emphasis on ladino racial dominance could be in part a manifestation of my own romanticized affinities with Mayas, which downplays the broader power inequalities that constitute all Guatemalans—ladinos and Mayas alike—as subjects of North American ethnographic scrutiny.

While the approach adopted here offers no easy response to these challenges, it has the distinct advantage of placing them centrally on the analytical agenda. After the first few times of experiencing the misplaced gesture of ladino racial solidarity, I had my antennas permanently raised for these racial eruptions, making sure to include them in my ethnographic renderings of the encounters (for other examples, see chapters 3 and 6). Making whiteness visible, contesting its unmarked status, is a first modest step toward addressing the problem of how white racial dominance might have affected the methods and conclusions of this study. Awareness of this problem also led me to listen with special attention to ladino histories of struggle to transform the Guatemalan national space, in opposition to both US imperialism and the Euro-Guatemalan oligarchy. It heightened my receptivity to many ladinos' skepticism of white North American solidarity with the Maya; in some cases, I came to endorse their analysis that this solidarity rested on a longstanding fascination with exotic peoples that has formed part of the culture of imperialism. At the same time, a keen awareness of the racial hierarchy engendered careful scrutiny of these ladino visions of Guatemala's *national* liberation, with special attention to how these political sensibilities so often have been conceived and deployed through the prism of anti-Indian racism.

The approach I have developed here, in sum, deploys the notion of ladino racial dominance in constant juxtaposition with ethnographic particularity. This approach yields no ready-made conclusions about racial processes in Guatemala, and imposes no self-evident clarity on the ambiguities, internal tensions, and blurred boundaries of the racial identities that are the subject of study. To the contrary, the approach directs us precisely to these rough edges, obliging us to confront them in all their complexity. The basic theoretical principle, though at first counterintuitive and never simple to practice, has proven to be a reliable guide in working through the topic at hand: ladino racial dominance, a notion grounded in social structure, becomes more useful when it is disrupted by ethnographic particularity. Such disruptions, in turn, make the notion of ladino racial dominance all the more indispensable. This principle is a first step in the effort to draw conclusions from the extensive accounts of ladino responses to the Maya efflorescence presented in the preceding chapters. The next step is to situate this approach in relation to the theoretical ideas that framed the research, and to explore how my conclusions might help us challenge and refine the theory.

Guatemalan Racial Formation

Racial formation theory has an eclectic intellectual genealogy. To simplify considerably, we can portray it as the convergence of two principal flows of theoretical work. First, racial vindication scholarship, which (following the lead of W. E. B. Du Bois) places racial meanings and hierarchies at the center of social analysis.[14] Second, cultural Marxism, in the tradition of Antonio Gramsci, which loosens the structural determinism common to Marxist thought, and redirects attention toward what we now call cultural politics. Gramscian analysis retains a Marxist emphasis on political economy, while assigning equal importance to how structural inequalities are signified, how political struggles are played out not just in the realm of material resources and coercive power but, in addition, often fundamentally, as struggles over meanings and representations. Building on these key interventions, racial formation theory directs our inquiry *both* to the structured relations of political-economic power and to how people signify these inequalities. It calls for a balanced consideration of structure and signification; directing attention to how racial categories and meanings change in the course of political struggle; but also insists that, amid this change, racial hierarchy and racism can persist, taking on new forms while producing strikingly similar consequences. Conceived in this way, racial formation theory provides a powerful guide for the narration of racial processes: how race is constitutive of the social order; how particular racial meanings congeal to represent the common sense of the moment; how these structures and meanings gradually fade, giving way to new ones; and how this change both conditions and is propelled by political struggle.[15]

My ethnography makes use of and generally endorses this framework, while also drawing attention to the need for further elaboration. The building blocks of structural inequality and signification serve well to guide my analysis, but they remain wooden and "experience-distant" in relation to the specifics: how people live with, reproduce, and contest racial categories and their associated cultural meanings. Racial formation theory does not preclude, but nor does it explicitly encourage, ethnographic and theoretical work in the realm of what we now call political subjectivities. Ethnographically, this means being more attentive to people's thoughts, feelings, fears and desires, precepts and elements of common sense, forged in the course of everyday practice. Theoretically, racial formation analysis focuses primarily on how political subjectivities are constituted by powerful external forces (subject formation), and needs to devote greater attention to how collective and individual actors actively give meaning to the world around them (self-making). This, in turn, would help connect racial formation theory to the often perplexing everyday racial politics that I encountered in Chimaltenango: where racial categories were both ubiquitous and absent, where racial meanings saturated social relations in routine (often highly normalized) ways, but also disrupted those relations with unpredictable and unintended consequences. Racial formation theory, enriched by these ethnographic disruptions that challenge and de-center the general story line, can play a crucial role in explaining why racial hierarchies are so resilient, and how social change occurs. Below I elaborate on the first part of this argument, reviewing key elements of racial formation theory that have guided my analysis of relations between ladinos and Mayas in Guatemalan society. This discussion revolves around three key concepts: racial hierarchy, racism, and racial privilege. In the following section, I explore the "ethnographic disruptions"— when ladino practice interrupts, overflows, or otherwise messes with the structured processes that racial formation theory brings to the fore.

I have used the phrase "racial hierarchy" throughout this study in reference to a general feature of Guatemalan society: sharp differentiation among distinct strata along the lines of power and privilege, with ladinos generally occupying a higher stratum and Indians a lower one. In the past one strong tendency has been to characterize these strata primarily in class terms; indeed, reams of analysis on Guatemalan society and politics have been written using standard class categories (peasant, worker, oligarch, bourgeoisie, and so on), rendering Indians, and the role of Indian-ladino relations, nearly invisible. The most important impetus for critical revision of such analysis has been the rise of collective Maya claims for rights and empowerment, which called into question, at the very least, the salience of class as the primary basis for political identification. Class relations, of course, remain central in understanding how all strata of the racial hierarchy are composed, and in probing differentiation within any given stratum. To cite two examples: a small but important group of Mayas has reached the middle class and the class categories of worker and peasant include large numbers of ladinos. Even after fully registering such complexities, the notion of racial hierarchy is still indispensable to an understanding of how material inequality is experienced, contested, and reproduced. Historically, ladinos have claimed the prerogative to occupy a higher stratum than Indians, and they have tended to justify the resulting differentiation in racial terms. This racial differentiation lies at the heart of innumerable institutional arrangements and practices, which keep the Guatemalan social formation in place. Similarly, Mayas generally understand their disadvantage as a function of ladino dominance, and their resistance often (though certainly not always) proceeds along racial lines. These basic empirical observations provide an initial rationale for using the term "racial hierarchy" and, once adopted, the term itself opens the way for further scrutiny.

My analysis also casts critical light on the transformation of racism in Guatemala, contributing to a growing literature on this topic. I have documented a shift, from the classic racism of times past to a new cultural racism, associated with the rise of neoliberal multiculturalism. This new racism comes embedded in a central and ubiquitous disavowal: those who preceded us were true racists, while we have overcome these problems. This disavowal flows directly from the "perpetrator" model, whereby racism only exists when we can identify an individual agent who espouses and acts on the assertion that people who belong to a given social category are inherently inferior. While Guatemala is still full of perpetrators who fit this description, they are decreasing in numbers and prominence, and increasingly subject to direct contestation by Mayas, and even other ladinos. The new racism, then, focuses not on perpetrators, but on consequences: the routinized reproduction of social inequality organized along racial lines. While overt biological justifications of inferiority are on the decline, ladinos still regularly note cultural differences between themselves and Mayas, and often point to these differences in explaining why Indians have remained in inferior social positions. Although ostensibly sensitive and respectful, this cultural discourse often is deployed to place limits on future Maya ascendancy (for example, pointing to proper cultural attributes that they lack) and to blame Maya for their own subordination (for example, Maya culture is poorly adapted to the rigors of modernity). I use the term "cultural racism" to mark this shift, and to trace how the rise of official multiculturalism, paradoxically enough, has made racial hierarchy more resilient. This claim at times has been misinterpreted to mean that racism was once all about biological inferiority, whereas now it revolves around (inferiorized) cultural difference. To the contrary, my research echoes others in demonstrating precisely the opposite: that racist ideology in Guatemala always has muddied the distinction between biology and culture, in commonsense understandings, political, and even academic discourse.[16] We can affirm the longstanding character of this race-culture conflation, while at the same time noting a pervasive shift: references to inherent biological traits, animal analogies, and quasi-Lamarckian reasoning, once unselfconsciously center stage, have now receded to the discursive margins, living on as ambiguous metaphors or in terms of benign and fungible cultural difference.

This argument for cultural racism, in turn, invokes the ethnicity question. Especially since ladinos increasingly conceive of themselves, and their differences from Indians, in cultural terms, the argument goes, this is an obvious moment to adopt the theoretical language of ethnicity, precisely to register and fully explore that shift. An extension of this argument points to the rising currency of the self-appellation "mestizo"—bringing Guatemala in line with most of the rest of Latin America—which also draws centrally on this same cultural logic. Yet ethnicity theory, precisely because it is predicated on the strict dichotomy between cultural and biological reasoning, turns out to be a poor guide for exploring how these two get entangled, or how ostensibly cultural reasoning can subtly take on inherent, quasi-biological properties. Moreover, while ethnicity theory certainly does not imply the absence of hierarchy, its use is associated with the era of state recognition of cultural difference; by extension, it is also associated with increased possibilities for subordinate groups to improve their status through assimilation or upward mobility. Race-centered analysis, in contrast, emphasizes continuities between past and current forms of racial hierarchy, tracing the particular entanglements of cultural and biological premises that justify each. These are elements that analysis guided by ethnicity theory would be likely to overlook.

A third and final key notion in my analysis is racial privilege: a historically imbued set of symbolic and material advantages that come with having a dominant position in the racial hierarchy.[17] These advantages are not earned or actively worked for; rather, they are attributes of the dominant position itself, the cumulative benefits of long-term patterns of racism. The consideration of racial privilege is crucial because it turns our attention away from specific practices—for example, a ladina employer's treatment of an Indian domestic servant—toward analysis of general relations—a social structure predicated on the fact that in the past century Indians generally have been servants to ladinos. Moreover, assertions of racial privilege make no recourse to explicit attitudes or ideologies of racial superiority. Instead, a subtle assumption of superiority permeates—not automatically, but as strong, diffuse propensities and patterns—the entire range of life experiences, from job and career, to sex and marriage, to most other social relations and sensibilities. The diffuseness is crucial, because racial privilege is not defended through action in a specific context, but through a general inclination to keep existing institutions and social relations in place. When I contend, as I have throughout this book, that ladinos affirm the principle of cultural equality and yet are generally unwilling to cede racial privilege, this diffuse, enduring sense of superiority is the point of reference. People effectively defend racial privilege not through arguments for racial entitlements or prerogatives but, rather, through a general disposition toward a wide array of taken-for-granted material props and cultural values; in effect, an entire way of life. This notion of racial privilege directly informs what I have called racial ambivalence, the fusion of affinity and refusal that characterizes ladino responses to the Maya efflorescence.

Ethnographic Disruptions

This very image of ambivalent ladino responses to Maya ascendancy opens another line of inquiry, for which racial formation theory is necessary but insufficient. It does not encompass a fine-grained analysis of political subjectivities: How is racial ambivalence constituted and how does it feel? What kinds of practices does it engender? To what extent, and in what ways, is racial ambivalence acknowledged as such and, by extension, contested and transformed? The ethnographic approach taken in this book provides some answers to these questions, focusing special attention on the "affirming" dimension of the ambivalence, that is, the widespread ladino affirmation of the cultural equality principle and the range of everyday practices that follow. This principle has generated a wide variety of political positions toward Mayas, from the mestizo universalism inspired by the October Revolution to the multiculturalism of the present, and a variety of everyday expressions of ladino solidarity. Indeed, the cultural equality principle is one force (though certainly not the only one) behind the increasingly popular move to abandon ladino identity altogether, in favor of the collective self-appellation "mestizo." The effects of this affirming dimension are not preordained and cannot be understood solely with reference to overall continuities in the racial hierarchy. Even if the inclination to maintain racial privilege generally acts to limit, derail, or partially neutralize the egalitarian impulse, there are countervailing possibilities and ample space for unintended consequences. The notion of racial ambivalence, in sum, must encompass both the imposing structural-ideological weight of racial formation and the open-ended variability of cultural-political practice and, most important, the interaction of these two.

This analytical focus puts me in critical dialogue with two major currents in the theoretical literature on race and identity. The first is the move "against race" and "beyond identity," which comes in a wide range of guises, some driven more by theoretical interventions, others by ethnographic preoccupations with complex cultural analysis of social process.[18] While these diverse emphases yield very different kinds of intellectual products, they share a series of basic attributes. Their insistence on a Foucault-inflected notion of power—fluid, capillary, diffuse—generates skepticism toward, and general neglect of, the political-economic structuring of racial hierarchies and racism. Their insistence on the contingent and multiple character of social boundaries engenders skepticism toward the idea that ideological processes and lived experiences of racial subordination might yield consistent patterns of racial identities and politics over space and time.[19] These "against and beyond" theoretical commitments have given rise to a bewildering proliferation of quotation marks around race, identity, and other such terms, to mark their contingent and constructed character; more substantively, they have produced work that is sharply critical of identity-based racial politics, unconvinced by antiracist analysis overly tied to the notion of racial dominance, and skeptical of overgeneralization of racial meanings from one site (generally the United States) to other settings.[20] While salutary in many ways, especially in their constant reminder to keep class, gender, and other crosscutting axes of inequality present in race-centered analysis, these approaches generally neglect the structural-ideological dimension of racial processes. The consequences of this neglect are especially evident when the dominant racial group is the focus of analysis. In regard to ladinos, for example, this neglect would lead notions of racial hierarchy and privilege to fade into the background, giving ladino racial ambivalence the status of a sensibility or an aesthetic. This would seriously understate the distribution of political-economic power that allows most ladinos to remain in a position of dominance, and it would reinforce the commonsense idea that the persistence of this hierarchy has nothing to do with racism.

Yet my close ethnographic reading of ladinos' defensive moves in Chimaltenango also disrupts any notion of a straight causal flow from structural-ideological conditions to political outcomes. A second strand of work on race and identity, much of it explicitly antiracist in focus and intent, tends to reproduce this problem. In part the problem lies in the deep allure of "racial interpellation," which allows little space for self-making within and against already constituted racial categories.[21] Another telltale sign is a rigidly scripted analysis of racial formation, where individuals stand in for, and predictably play out, their preassigned positions in a racial hierarchy.[22] Yet another is the legal studies contingent of critical race theorists who produce sophisticated, critical readings of racism in textual, legal, and institutional contexts, with scant attention to the day-to-day workings of racial politics.[23] My particular concern with ladino racial politics again helps to specify the key point of divergence. While I found no organized ladino-led movements of direct opposition to racism in Chimaltenango (and very few nationwide), there were many instances of individual disruption or transgression, and a general sense of instability in the emerging mode of governance. My ethnography does not mistake individual transgression for transformative politics, but I do insist on examining the reach and effects of the former, exploring the tension between ladinos' defense of racial privilege and their embrace of cultural equality. The theoretical point follows. These disruptions are not incidental or inconsequential noise in an otherwise stable racial hierarchy; they hold the key to understanding how the racial hierarchy is reproduced and challenged. Making sense of political process, in its unruly and open-ended complexity, is indispensable to my application of the racial formation approach.

These two lines of analysis—one emphasizing structural-ideological conditions and the other open-ended political subjectivities—themselves stand in partial tension with one another. Although reminiscent of the structure-agency conundrum, which animated so much thought in the 1980s, a number of developments have injected new energy into our thinking in this realm.[24] One is a much greater sophistication in theories of the subject—replacing previous assumptions of the sovereign, autonomous individual with the idea of subject formation. Another is a broadened understanding of the structural, toward an appreciation of the irreducibly multiple character of social inequality—what has come to be known as "intersectionality."[25] More generally, there is a much greater inclination to live with the tension in this binary, abandoning the quest for a synthesis. I have incorporated each of these developments into the general approach taken here. Throughout these pages I have traced the structural-ideological dimensions of racial formation in Guatemala, and used the notion of racial privilege and related concepts to formulate my analysis. At the same time, I have allowed my argument to develop ethnographically, tracing the subjectivities of ladino and ladina chimaltecos in the flow of everyday practice. In some ways, this ethnography directly substantiates the structural analysis, while in other respects troubling and disrupting it. Rather than take the resulting tension as a problem to resolve, I have cast it as an achievement. These spaces of disjuncture—where the structural-ideological conditions and political subjectivities confound one another—are the generative sites of the most important findings of this study. In the following section I briefly note three such findings, both to encapsulate the book's contributions and to further specify my theoretical approach to the study of racial politics.

Racial Dominance and Political Process

Much recent work on racial identities and politics has neglected fine-grained, political-economic analysis in favor of an emphasis on the discursive. In contrast, I have assigned considerable importance to tracing the race-based distribution of political-economic power, in order to juxtapose ladino anxieties about losing ground to Mayas to separately derived data on this same question. These data, summarized in chapter 2, paint a complex and differentiated picture. Ladinos are indeed losing ground to Mayas in some areas, but also to powerful outsiders (both foreigners and elite Guatemalans) who exert increasing control over the local sources of economic dynamism. Moreover, the spatial distribution of racial hierarchy is changing. In some municipios (for example, Comalapa) ladino presence is minimal to nil, while in others (for example, El Tejar) non-Indians are consolidating power and demographic predominance. This consolidation, however, depends crucially on ladinos' ability to strengthen political affinities with the growing numbers of new mestizos who populate these spaces. Ironically, although the new mestizos pose no collective political challenge to ladinos (at least for the time being), their indifference toward, even scorn for, the prospect of becoming ladino could make them appear just as threatening as the Mayas. Political-economic analysis, in short, both confirms the basis for ladino perceptions of displacement, while also showing how ladinos exaggerate the threat, and tend to reduce a multiply constituted process to a single cause.

If political-economic data exerts a grounding influence on ladino discourse about and practice toward Indians, the reverse is true as well: attention to political subjectivities engenders welcome skepticism toward this very data. One great problem with political-economic analysis of this sort, a principal reason that studies of racial formation often look elsewhere for substantiation, is that the data themselves come in ideologically charged, racialized categories. By marshalling the data as if they provided a transparent account of a given social formation, the analyst can divert attention from the politicized interests at play in their creation, and even yield conclusions that are complicit with those very interests. Careful attention to how racial categories are constituted, by broader societal forces and by the daily practice of people who occupy them, offers a partial antidote to this problem. In this study, such attention has revealed anything but neatly bounded categories: there is no consensus about who is ladino, about how to think about the emergent, multifaceted category "mestizo," nor about what meanings follow from these designations. Racial categories are subject to deep flux, perplexity, and contestation. More specifically, there is no state-endorsed category for, no official means to count, an estimated 30 percent of the population in some municipios of Chimaltenango who identify as mestizo. Most civil registrars have simply given up recording identities in birth and death records to avoid running afoul of one current or another in the charged emotions surrounding the politics of naming. Under these conditions, to call forth race-specific political-economic data without thorough scrutiny of how racial categories are made and contested would be at best an exercise in futility. Yet to use this fluidity as a rationale for abandoning the effort to map changing patterns of race-based political-economic power, would be capitulation to ideologically driven assertions that racial hierarchy and racism do not matter anymore. My response to this dilemma is to do both, and to embrace the tension that results.

The same goes for a second major finding of this study: ladino racial dominance persists, but under conditions of increasing indigenous irreverence and resistance, and a decreasing ability to represent racial inequality as natural or legitimate. The evidence presented here for Chimaltenango, combined with accounts from elsewhere in Guatemala, leaves no doubt that the racial composition of Guatemala's class structure is changing. The steady flow of indigenous upward mobility and the dismantling of the separate and unequal racial ideology of times past have yielded a proliferation of middle-class spaces that ladinos and Mayas share. Important as this diversification is, as a base for Maya movement activism and as general evidence that indigenous people are gaining ground, its limits are equally evident. In comparative demographic terms this class mobility is still miniscule, and drops off rapidly with each ascending rung in the economic hierarchy. Moreover, a significant portion of upwardly mobile Mayas still attempt to distance themselves from indigenous culture and identity, to blend in at the cost of affective ties and political affinities with the majority—although pressures for such assimilation are less intense than they were even a decade ago. In any case, more important than these transformations in the class-race hierarchy is the rise of myriad forms of contestation. Indigenous Guatemalans have acquired individual and even collective voice to contest racism and to challenge the injustice of their continued marginalization, even if, thus far, this voice has resulted in fairly marginal change in their structural relations with ladinos.

Daily interactions that I observed in Chimaltenango are full of examples of this disjuncture between increasing contestation of racial inequality and relatively marginal change in the racial hierarchy. Most ladinos I interviewed focused on the contestation, which had changed their daily relations with indigenous people in important ways: domestic servants who refuse to show the deference and humility that their employers deem proper; Indian youth who talk back to the parish priest; Maya intellectuals who miss no chance to denounce racist discourse in public settings. Yet since this contestation has advanced a blistering critique of racial meanings with a relative neglect of political-economic relations, the disjuncture remains. This generates marked instability in the present arrangement, with a rising sense of ladino anxiety that further change is in the air. One day, for example, I accompanied Guillermo Álvarez to San Andrés Itzapa, because he wanted to show me his land, in past generations a small plantation, now rented out to an indigenous family. As we drew near the homestead on foot, a man on horseback approached; he was Valentín, the elderly father of the tenant family. As Valentín began to greet us, Guillermo cut him off brusquely: "*Vos Valentín, bajáte, queremos hablar contigo*" (Hey boy, get down, we want to talk with you).[26] Valentín slowly dismounted, and now stood a full foot shorter than the two of us. As we walked the rest of the way to the house, Guillermo talked down to Valentín (in both senses of the phrase) in a steady chatter. That brief "vos Valentín, bajáte" vignette vividly encapsulates the colonial race relations that have characterized Guatemala for so long and that in many ways persist, some blatant like this, others much more subtle. Our brief interactions with Valentín's family at the house, however, left a very different impression. Far from cowed by Guillermo, the assembled family members found him risible, perhaps even more than usual given his endeavor to impress a white North American friend with his now tawdry landed wealth. They almost seemed to mock him, staying just within the bounds of etiquette, but sending a clear message that the old patterns of ladino authority, which Guillermo imagined himself enacting, had long since lost their power of persuasion.

It remains to be seen how destabilizing this disjuncture will turn out to be. In some respects, of course, it is nothing new: another example of the age-old pattern whereby subordinate people defer to authority they cannot directly contest and then mock the very basis for this authority's legitimacy, up to the limits of what political conditions permit. Yet any disjuncture of this sort reaches a point where the claims to legitimacy grow so fragile, and the spaces of contestation so difficult to suppress, that the hierarchy becomes impossible to maintain. According to one scenario, Guatemalan society is moving steadily in that direction: toward a breaking point when the systemic basis for longstanding racial hierarchy would be directly and massively transformed. However, analysis in these pages points to a second scenario, whereby persisting racial hierarchy finds a substantively different basis for continued legitimacy: change generated in large part by the cumulative political force of indigenous resistance, but directed by the more powerful forces at play. Indigenous people are not inferior, but affirmed as equals; indigenous culture is to be respected, even celebrated; the few who make it to the middle class are welcomed, as bodily evidence of the new ethic of equality and as proof that something other than racism must explain why racial hierarchy remains virtually unchanged for the vast majority. Based on research in Chimaltenango, I have offered evidence that this sobering alternative scenario already has begun to unfold. At the same time, this analysis suggests that the disjuncture—between rising Maya contestation of racism and persisting racial hierarchy—continues to provide fertile ground for those working to give the transformative alternative a fighting chance.

Another dimension of the "vos Valentín" vignette provides an entrée to the final illustration of the analytical tension that I have sought to embrace. Ladinos chimaltecos, in loose articulation with dominant sectors more generally, have begun to fashion a new mode of governance, a combination of substantive concessions to Maya cultural activism and preemptive strikes against more expansive demands. At the same time, deep forces at work in the ladino political imaginary threaten to disrupt and derail this arrangement, just as it begins to take hold. Even if Guillermo did get Valentín to dismount, even if he could still carry on a condescending conversation with his family as their *patrón*, he cannot have been pleased by their poorly concealed irreverence. It is precisely interactions like these, I argued in chapter 5, which provoke deep fears of treachery and betrayal. I have attempted to encapsulate this anxiety, documented with some consistency among a range of ladino informants, as a flash of intense feelings focused on the image of the insurrectionary Indian. The image comes to the fore, I argued, when ladinos feel that the premises of their position in the racial hierarchy are being called into question. This notion of the political imaginary complicates my central conclusion that a new mode of governance has begun to emerge. The emergent structural-ideological conditions, that is, the combination of concessions and preemptive strike, carries much more pent up, highly charged, emotional energy than it can contain. The fear of Indian men taking ladina women as bounty, a standard component in the insurrectionary Indian nightmare, is just one example of many. Whatever the explanation for this particular embellishment—and admittedly, my hypothesis presented in chapter 5 barely scratches the surface—its very existence points to a fundamental instability that will be difficult to overcome. The new mode of governance requires substantive ladino discourse and practice toward Mayas to be characterized by equality—a principle that most ladinos endorse but, deep down, in moments of danger, feel compelled to contradict. My insistence on keeping the political imaginary present in the analysis, without attempting to contain this "overflow," stands as a call for further research on this topic, as a warning against facile solutions of "intercultural dialogue," and as a reiteration of my theoretical approach. This emphasis on the ladino imaginary brings political sensibilities, in all their complexity, into the picture, noting their destabilizing influence on the new mode of governance, which otherwise seems to be gaining momentum and sinking roots.

These three instances of disjuncture between structural-ideological conditions and political subjectivities, drawn, roughly speaking, from chapters 2, 4, and 5, all play a part in giving shape to racial ambivalence, the central concept in this study. I use the concept to emphasize how ladinos both affirm the principle of cultural equality and set firm limits on its reach, how they both critique racism and cling to racial privilege as the guarantee that Maya ascendancy will not wreak havoc. By extension, this notion of racial ambivalence directs attention both to the increasing contestation of ladino dominance and its stubborn persistence. Especially by attending to the political imaginary, I explore the force of feeling of racial ambivalence, making it something deeper than merely an instrumental response to a collective predicament, giving it an intensity and volatility with unpredictable consequences. Indeed, my exploration of the political imaginary shows how ladinos themselves end up disrupting their own carefully articulated commitments to the principle of cultural equality with Mayas.

Constituted in this way—with attention to structural-ideological conditions, political subjectivities, and the tensions between these two—the concept of racial ambivalence encapsulates ladino responses to the Maya efflorescence. This position—a local, untheorized collection of political sensibilities and practices—contains the essential building blocks of an emerging mode of governance, which I call neoliberal multiculturalism. Not all forms of ladino (or mestizo) identity and political practice fit this description. As I argued in chapter 6, some ladinos/mestizos work actively to contest or overcome racial ambivalence, even while continuing to embody it. These individuals—whom I refer to as ladino dissidents and mestizo militants—push the equality principle beyond its comfortable resting place and subject the powerful allure of racial privilege to critical scrutiny. I have argued that in general this equality principle exerts a stabilizing influence on the racial hierarchy, absolving ladinos from any further responsibility for persisting racial inequity. Yet this same principle, pushed to its logical conclusion, can also generate the opposite effect. Here, then, lies the paradox: the newfound affirmation that Mayas and ladinos are equal is both constitutive of, and a constant threat to, the dominant racial order in the making.

This paradox takes a broader sociopolitical form as well. I do not argue that middle-class ladinos in Chimaltenango neatly epitomize broader processes, nor that the "global" exerts an impact on this particular corner of the "local" in irresistible and determinate patterns. These influences certainly do take place, and to neglect them would be to fall back on one of the most notorious anthropological fallacies: the bounded community study. I argued in chapter 2, for example, that part of the squeeze that ladinos chimaltecos feel comes from the state's newfound enthusiasm for multiculturalism and from the changing productive relations, both of which directly correspond to the globalized logic of neoliberalism. I extended this argument in chapters 4 and 5, pointing to how burgeoning flows of international aid to Maya civil society became a thorn in the side of ladino dominance. Yet the thrust of the study has not been to trace such global connections, but rather to argue that the problem of racial ambivalence and the paradox of cultural equality have been global from the start. We should be able to break into the global from any given site in this web of local-global relations and gain considerable (if ultimately partial) insight from that vantage point. In this case, the insight focuses on neoliberal multiculturalism, an emergent mode of governance throughout Latin America, of which ladino racial ambivalence is one local and idiosyncratic variant.

Neoliberal Multiculturalism: The Paradox in Global Context

The fit between ladino racial ambivalence, as documented in Chimaltenango, and the emergent mode of governance in post-conflict Guatemala, is far from seamless. In some dimensions, this relationship is one of dissonance, even conflict. I have noted, for example, that ladinos chimaltecos often expressed resentment over central government initiatives that affirmed Maya cultural rights and prerogatives, thereby displacing the traditional ladino role of intermediary. The analysis in chapter 2 emphasized the historical continuity of this dissonance: during the decade of social democratic reforms (1944–1954) and in the period afterward, provincial ladinos acted to contravene the state's assimilationist impulse, in favor of the "separate and unequal" principle. In contemporary times, many provincial ladinos have clung to hopes for assimilation as a counterweight to the threatening prospect of state-endorsed multiculturalism.

While acknowledging this dissonance, we can also note instructive parallels and connections. Ladino racial ambivalence is not the product of Machiavellian calculation. It is a gradually emerging collective response to multiple forces in a rapidly changing world: from direct Maya contestation, to the eroding hegemonic influence of "ladinoization" (that is, the promise and process of becoming ladino), to the assertion that respect for indigenous culture is an indication of full-fledged modern and civilized status. My ethnographic data come from a time when ladinos chimaltecos clearly were struggling (individually, and in rare occasions collectively) to make sense of and respond to these forces; not surprisingly, these data document a range of positions, and lots of outright perplexity. Yet the aggregate political sensibilities point to an implicit compromise, born of a striking realization. To endorse cultural equality does entail risks and provoke anxiety; it does oblige us to rebuke the classic racism of times past. Yet it does not require us to cede racial privilege, and it yields a powerful inoculation against more expansive demands.[27] The rise of neoliberal multiculturalism both helps to constitute this compromise and represents a parallel response to national-level forces of change.

Neoliberal multiculturalism, I contend, will soon displace its counterpart ideology of the previous era: mestizo or ladino nationalism. The key innovations of this emergent mode of governance include the affirmation of cultural difference, the vigorous critique of classic racism, the explicit encouragement of indigenous political participation (and that of other groups defined as culturally different), and a principled openness to the negotiation of rights associated with this Maya efflorescence. Proponents of state-driven mestizo nationalism offered universal citizenship and viewed cultural difference as residual; their multicultural counterparts favor differentiated citizenship, for which cultural pluralism provides the essential rationale. The rise of a multicultural ethic among Latin American states and political-economic elites has been explained as the outcome of three powerful forces of change: grassroots and national mobilization from below, with ample support from "global" allies; neoliberal economic reforms, which eliminated corporate constraints on indigenous politics while accentuating inequality and economic distress; and, finally, democratization, which widened spaces of protest, and necessitated substantive responses from above. My argument does not dismiss any of these explanatory factors but, rather, adds a fourth, which in turn casts the first three in a different light.

Multiculturalism has also developed as a proactive response, born in a realization, strikingly parallel to that of the ladinos chimaltecos: a carefully designed package of cultural rights that are guaranteed not to threaten the fundamental tenets of the capitalist economy, and could actually strengthen them. Even aggressive neoliberal economic reforms, which favor the interests of capital and sanctify the logic of the market, are more compatible with some facets of indigenous cultural rights than many would like to admit. The leading edge of neoliberalism's cultural project is not radical individualism, but rather the creation of subjects who govern themselves in accordance with the logic of globalized capitalism.[28] The pluralism inherent in this equation—the subjects in question can be individuals, communities, or even entire identity groups—makes for a comfortable fit with the multicultural ethos. Governance takes place not through the distinction between forward-looking ladinos and backward Indians, but rather between authorized and prohibited ways of being Indian.[29]

Neoliberal multiculturalism is poised to remake racial hierarchies in national and global arenas, in ways that should be familiar from the local vantage point of Chimaltenango. The rise of cultural rights creates a series of authorized spaces, both in civil society and the state itself, which spokespeople and representatives of the broader indigenous population come to occupy. They do not necessarily submit or conform to the state's purposes; much to the contrary, they are forced to operate within certain constraints, both material and symbolic, associated with the spaces themselves. These spaces carry with them a basic dichotomy between two ways of being Indian. The authorized Indian has passed the test of modernity, substituted "proposal" for "protest," and has learned to be both authentic and fully conversant with the dominant milieu. Its Other is unruly, vindictive, and prone to conflict. These latter traits linger in minds of elites who have pledged allegiance to cultural equality, seeding fears of the havoc that empowerment of the Other Indians could wreak. In Chimaltenango, for example, such fears are fully embodied and expressed in the image of the insurrectionary Indian, discussed in chapter 5. Governance proceeds by proactively rewarding the authorized Indian, while condemning its Other to the racialized spaces of poverty and social exclusion. Those who occupy the category of the authorized Indian must convincingly prove they have risen above the racialized traits of their brethren by endorsing and reinforcing the authorized/prohibited dichotomy. In Chimaltenango this occurs not through explicit declarations of political allegiance, but rather in more subtle concessions: gratefully accepting the expressions of cultural equality, while swallowing the bile produced by the insult of the persisting racial hierarchy that discourses of cultural equality ignore and are not meant to change.

Between Nihilism and Naïveté

Guatemalan history since the middle of the twentieth century could be read as a series of grand political projects that failed, but in this very failure brought about unintended consequences that set the stage for the subsequent struggle. The revolutionary decade (1944–1954), far from achieving the stated goals of universal citizenship and social equality, ended in a bloody coup that polarized the nation, and for many provided incontrovertible proof that a moderate, democratic course of political change was impossible. Yet with the benefit of hindsight, we can now see how part of that agenda of reforms persisted in the post-1954 counterrevolutionary environment, and how state authorities, rather than turning back the clock completely, sought to meld these reforms into their new strategy of governance. The army's rising commitment to an ideology of assimilation, in contrast to the persisting "separate and unequal" ideology of ladino elites in places like Chimaltenango, is but one case in point. The armed revolutionary movement also failed in its basic goal of seizing power and freeing the country from the stranglehold of a rapacious oligarchy. This failure eventually gave way to a burgeoning civil society, whose protagonists asserted autonomy from both sides in the preceding armed conflict, but were much more directly linked to global purse strings and political sensibilities than the still authoritarian state would otherwise condone. This broader transformation yielded highly improbable consequences: a Maya efflorescence, spawned by the previous experience of mobilization in the period of revolutionary fervor and by massive state violence against its civilian base. To what extent has the Maya movement—the most important and promising political project currently on the horizon in Guatemala—ended up following this well-established pattern?

My research, focused on ladinos, can provide only an indirect answer to this question. I did not systematically examine the political aspirations of the organizations that comprise the Maya movement, nor do I scrutinize the political sensibilities of the much wider range of Maya actors who constitute the aggregate effects of the Maya efflorescence. My analysis has been directed, instead, toward the adversaries of these cultural-political initiatives, guided by the hypothesis that these adversaries have changed much more than most Maya activists have been inclined to acknowledge. These new conditions—produced locally by ladino racial ambivalence and globally by neoliberal multiculturalism—have the potential to reshape Maya people's contestation in the image of their adversaries, opening certain spaces while summarily closing others. Stated in theoretical terms, these conditions have a great potential for subject-making, for the interpellation of indigenous people as subjects of the neoliberal multicultural state. One important objective of this work is achieved simply by emphasizing this menace, in hopes that it will motivate further analysis of and reflection on the question that follows. To what extent, and in what ways, have Maya actors been able to occupy these newly opened spaces, putting them to the service of alternative political ends?

While focusing on the menace of neoliberal multiculturalism, my study also brings ladinos solidarios to the fore, asking hard questions about their sensibilities and practice, and the consequences that follow. My analysis of these ladinos solidarios offers a glimpse of transformative possibilities. From a position of dominance in the local racial hierarchy, these ladinos (and mestizos) are reaching out to build bridges of solidarity with Mayas, going clearly beyond the standard responses that racial ambivalence entails. They critique the sanctimony of the cultural equality discourse, drawing attention to its preinscribed limits; they distance themselves from the trappings of ladino hegemony, acknowledging how the ladino identity category itself has been predicated on the premise of indigenous inferiority; some have taken the logical next step of ladino-to-mestizo identity change; in a few cases, they renounce an additional measure of racial privilege, opting to work, for example, in a Maya-run organization.

While documenting these initiatives, the preceding analysis also emphasized their internally generated limits. In the first place, and most seriously in my view, I found a striking dearth of organized interracial political settings in Chimaltenango where these issues were being explicitly addressed. This leaves ladinos solidarios to ponder their predicament alone, perhaps with family members and friends, in fortunate cases (rare, according to my observations) with a trusted Maya friend. The one major inter-racial social movement that occurred in Chimaltenango during the course of my field-work, described in chapter 6, did not explicitly address racial questions, and indeed perpetuated racist precepts in confounding ways. Second, as argued at length in chap-ter 6, the attempts of ladinos solidarios to reach out to Mayas have foundered in part because they incorporate key precepts of the racial hierarchy that they set out to chal-lenge. Militant mestizos, even while affirming Maya cultural difference, tread a very fine line, always at risk of appropriating Indianness while remaining relatively free from the racialization that Indians continue to experience. Ladino dissidents avoid that problem by keeping sharp lines of cultural difference intact, but have a hard time con-vincing Mayas of their egalitarian intent when speaking from a ladino subject posi-tion. It is doubtful that Valentín would be able to hear the words "vos Valentín" come from the mouth of a ladino, any ladino, in any context, without having Guillermo's meaning of the phrase come to mind. It will take a generation or two, at least, for this prior meaning to lose its potency. Finally, my analysis of the ladino political imaginary raises questions about the efficacy of the ladinos solidarios by focusing on what one informant called their "atavistic fears." To fully shake free from the effects of racial ambivalence, ladinos would have to come to terms with the haunting image of the insurrectionary Indian and its more linear counterpart, the indigenous demand for political autonomy. It is not even clear to me where such a process would best start, beyond my vehement, though admittedly weakly supported, assertion that it is better to "out" these fears than to keep them pent up inside.

In contrast to the militant mestizos and ladino dissidents, the new mestizos offer a refreshingly oblique challenge to the racial hierarchy, less apt to go awry because the challenge has no overt political intentions to begin with. New mestizos confound racial boundaries, mixing and mingling in a wide social space where everyone is of indigenous ancestry and no one really identifies as Indian. The new mestizo ethic is perhaps most subversive as it expands to unsettle the boundaries of the established racial identities: nudging ladinos to doubt their presumed superiority over Indians, and encouraging self-identified Indians to adopt a more fluid and flexible identity pol-itics that, in some ways, could be liberating. Yet however compelling and theoretically resonant this subversive stance, it would be hasty to pin immediate hopes for transfor-mative politics on new mestizo sensibilities. They live in racialized spaces, but are not inclined to mount a direct challenge to that racialization; they stand in tension with the Maya movement, with little evidence of bridges being built; they provide much of the wage labor for the neoliberal economy, but have no direct claim to a category of rights that neoliberal multiculturalism has opened. They have great potential to contribute to the subversive reinvention of politics, along the lines that political theorist Cathy Cohen describes, but thus far, at least in my ethnographic rendering, they have demonstrated mainly the individually creative but politically conformist mestizo sensibilities that Chicano writer Richard Rodriguez champions.[30]

In any case, the political affinities that I developed in the course of this study are invoked in chapter 3: a partly imagined, partly historical moment of struggle for progressive social change, including both ladinos and indigenous people, with the interests of the Maya majority as the guiding force. There are many Maya and a few ladinos who embody these sensibilities today, and a few organizations, working under great constraints, that promote them in a more public, systematic, political fashion. One of the most immediate constraints, apart from the omnipresent threat of political violence, is the commonsense understanding of the emergent mode of governance. The argument set forth in these pages is intended to challenge that common sense. My analysis demonstrates how racial hierarchy can persist even when classic racism is no longer a driving force; it shows how the indigenous majority can remain marginalized, even though the state selectively recognizes Maya cultural rights; and it insists that a growing ethos of cultural equality and multicultural citizenship among dominant actors does not necessarily signal the elimination of racism. My principal critique of this new mode of governance is not that the political spaces it allows are too limited (although this certainly is a problem) but, rather, that it discourages expansive thinking about political alternatives. This analysis endorses the need to work within the spaces of neoliberal multiculturalism, while refusing their built-in limits. Refusal, in turn, rests on two basic assertions: that racism is at work as long as racial hierarchy persists and that antiracist politics must confront the root conditions of persisting racial hierarchy, which may not include explicit, public ideologies of racial inferiority.

The strategy that follows from this analysis might be called a politics of "rearticulation," which joins the Maya majority and ladinos solidarios in common struggle. One key focus of rearticulation is relations among indigenous peoples of disparate social locations, bridging differences between rural and urban, between peasants and petty merchants, artisans, maquila workers, and even transnational migrants. By necessity, this would also defy the dichotomy between authorized Indians and their unruly, conflict-prone Others, a dichotomy that has become crucial to the rise of neoliberal multiculturalism. A second focus is the alliance between indigenous peoples and their ladino counterparts, who live in similar material conditions, and have little to lose from substantial Maya empowerment. These ideas are unabashedly utopian. Given the genocidal brutality of Guatemala's ruling elite, amply demonstrated in recent history, state responses to even very modest efforts along these lines are apt to turn ugly. It would be fatalistic to abandon hope in anticipation of this ugliness, but irresponsible to advocate such a strategy without imagining some means to ease the transition, assuage the fears, lessen the polarization.

Here, perhaps, is where the ladino dissidents have an additional role to play. Their sensibilities and social position may be contradictory, but they do offer a bridge to the majority of ladinos, who view Maya efflorescence with deep anxiety and incomprehension. Ladino dissidents have engaged in a process of dialogue and reflection, perhaps even having forged ties of friendship and understanding with Mayas, perhaps even having begun to exorcise the insurrectionary Indian from their own political imaginaries. They still embody the predicament that Francisco Goldman so clearly evokes in the epigraph to chapter 1: as a strong supporter of Maya demands for economic and cultural rights, Moya finds himself having helped to forge a new society that he then feels compelled to flee, "to Paris, with a clean conscience at last, vos!" But the ladino dissidents portrayed here, unlike Moya, have begun to confront and move beyond this racial ambivalence. Yolanda and her family express strong support for Maya rights, but with little inclination to flee to Paris or New York, and with a growing commitment to antiracist practice in the ladino settings where they live and work. Their chosen path of struggle from within is not easy, and it has no guarantees. But at least we can be sure that they will always have a generous endowment of humor chapín to keep spirits up and to ease the pain.

Epilogue

Que no sea solo del diente al labio.

(Do not let this stay only between the teeth and the lips.)

—*Ladino saying*

My first thought was to have Yolanda and Genaro write their reactions to this book and its analysis, letting them have the final word. They seemed to appreciate the invitation, thought about it for a while, and said no. They were probably right: this work is not theirs to conclude. As an alternative, we agreed that I would conduct an interview with each of them, and draw from these reflections to write a brief epilogue. I interviewed Yolanda in December 2004, at the end of an intense weeklong work session, during which she gave me feedback on the entire Spanish translation of the manuscript. The interview with Genaro took place in March 2005, in a quiet corner of the back porch of their house. Both turned out to be wide-ranging conversations about their lives, and their thoughts on identity, racism, relations between Mayas and ladinos, and the courses of political action that might be taken. Unfortunately, the most I can do here is to offer a few selections, giving priority to their reactions to the principal topics of this volume. This is especially unfortunate in the case of Genaro, since that was the first time I had heard his fascinating and inspiring life story, recounted systematically from his youth to the present. Perhaps it is inevitable that projects like this one end having uncovered new stories that need to be told, new books that need to be written.

Yolanda had two principal criticisms of the draft she read in the fall of 2004. First, research for the book spanned a decade of intense change in her life and in her own political sensibilities, yet very little of that evolution was reflected in what I wrote. She is not the same person today as the one depicted in some of those anecdotes. The second criticism, which she and Genaro shared and raised repeatedly over the last year, began with the simple question: *¿y qué?* (And now what? But also, so what?). What political strategy emerges from all this analysis? Where is the plan of action, the "what is to be done?" Both reactions, in my view, are on the mark. Moreover, they focus succinctly on two weak flanks of anthropology—including anthropology that fancies itself to be politically engaged.

Yolanda's reflections on the changes in her own attitudes toward issues of race, racism, and Maya-ladino relations came out in various ways, provoked initially as she remembered what she was doing and thinking in 1993 when we first met. The Maya efflorescence was still building to a crescendo at that time, and ladinos such as Yolanda were being obliged, for the first time ever, to understand and respond to the challenge of sharing Guatemalan society, on equal terms, with Mayas. How many newspaper articles had she read, workshops attended, awkward public exchanges with Maya intellectuals endured, kitchen table discussions of identity politics held in the decade since then? The most striking evidence for change in Yolanda's consciousness came inadvertently, in her response to my query, "Were there passages in the book that you would like me to remove?" At first, she replied, the answer had been yes. For example, she wasn't comfortable with the anecdote (in chapter 1) that depicted her as harboring residual biological notions of race:

> At first I said: why should I appear in the book saying things like that, if I am
> presenting myself as someone who works in solidarity with the Mayas? But
> seven years have passed since that incident, and that is a long time. I do not
> think I would express myself in the same way now; I think I have grown. I
> have begun to be very careful in recent times, to develop an awareness of how I
> speak, and this involves a commitment to eliminate ways of speaking that con-
> tain a certain amount, no a lot, of discrimination.

She was ultimately comfortable with the passage, not because it accurately depicted her present sensibilities, but precisely because it did not. It dramatized how much she had changed. A good argument, I later mused, for such delay in finishing the manuscript.

This evolution had many facets. Yolanda abruptly quit local electoral politics in the late 1990s, putting an end to her incipient ascent in that ladino-dominated world. When Alfonso Portillo won the presidency in 2000, his Chimaltenango deputies maneuvered to have Yolanda replaced as director of DIGEA, with the argument that the director must be Maya. In a previous moment Yolanda might have cried foul, as some of her friends urged her to do; instead she stayed quiet. In her remaining job as university professor, Yolanda worked more and more with Maya students, to the point where some of her colleagues began to make disparaging remarks, "*Como que sólo querés trabajar con indios*" (It looks like you only want to work with Indians). With the heightened awareness of racial issues came also a sharpened gender critique, deployed regularly when male family members, and their anthropologist friend, seemed to be dwelling too single-mindedly on matters of racial hierarchy. In sum, I readily concede the critique: Yolanda has changed profoundly in the period since 1993. Although acutely aware of the fallacy of the "anthropological present," I had fallen, at least partly, into the trap.

This problem is more complicated still because my research, in some small but significant way, contributed to the process of change that I was being asked to depict. These effects culminated when the Spanish language draft of the book arrived for the Valencia family's review. Yolanda described some of the heated discussions that took place over the next few months. Her son Wilfredo berated her for the identity vacillation, described in chapter 6: "You don't really want to appear in the book as ladina, do you?" Yolanda held her ground and the debate raged. In studied reflection in front of a microphone, both Yolanda and Genaro insisted that the identity label mattered much less than one's actual daily practice. But in the raucous exchanges around the kitchen table, the ladino-versus-mestizo debate became a catalyst for larger discussions of what is to be done. Earlier versions of this debate, and innumerable collective conversations where we analyzed my interviews and ethnographic encounters of the preceding day, formed part of the broader process of change on which the family, and Yolanda in particular, had embarked. This no doubt helps to explain why they tolerated, at times even encouraged, my presence as an ethnographer. I asked Yolanda if, in the course of the research, she ever felt used or manipulated. Her answer surprised me:

> No, because I knew what you were doing. Now I do not feel misled or used.
> But there is something I need to tell you. There was a moment when I did feel
> used. There was a time when our communication on these topics broke down.
> It seemed that you had abandoned the book, or perhaps you had too many
> other things to do . . . do you remember? You would come to Guatemala and
> we did not even talk about the book, but about other things. I said to myself,
> "What happened?" Charlie did all this work, and I have no idea what resulted.
> In that moment, I felt used.

The gravest insult to the legions of anthropological subjects over the years, Yolanda seemed to be saying, is not in the act of representation—whether power sensitive and reflexive or otherwise—but rather, in the subjects' lack of opportunity to engage, learn from, affirm, or challenge the product that results.

The interview with Genaro took most of a day. Yolanda previously had explained one reason for his reticence: before having read the manuscript, he had assumed that the book would serve to shore up ladinos' identity, rather than subjecting them to critical scrutiny. In the course of our conversation, Genaro added a second reason:

> I have an allergic reaction to intellectuals, who talk and talk and leave it to
> others to assume serious political commitments. It is like the protest music
> singers: they sing those inspiring songs, about the people united, calling

everyone to the struggle; young people listen, get excited and take to the streets, while the singer packs up his guitar and goes home. The same with intellectuals. I doubted that the book would generate serious political commitments. In the midst of so much intellectual discussion, the problems remain unaddressed. It is as if we were in the Escuintla hospital, and two doctors kept on discussing an especially complex illness, while the patient died.

Voiced by some, this critique could sound like unreflective activism; but that description doesn't fit Genaro in the least. He is one of the most pensive, intensely analytical individuals I have ever met. I take his critique of the intellectual's conceit not as a condemnation of the book's attempt at analysis but, rather, as a reaction born out of his own deep impatience and frustration, at times bordering on visceral disgust, with the state of Guatemalan society. Genaro gave the best years of his life to a political project that would transform these social conditions, only to return to Chimaltenango twenty-five years later to the shock of how little had changed. The human cost was so high, he observed grimly, for the meager concessions that the comandantes were able to negotiate. Genaro's impatience is epochal—so powerful that occasionally it immobilizes him. The rest of the time his gentle humanism, biting humor, and abundant political energy shine through.

Genaro's life story recapitulates the central question this book should have been able to answer, and it partly confirms, but partly confounds, the analysis I have put forth in response. Under what conditions might ladinos play a role, together with Mayas, in dismantling the racial hierarchy that pervades and cripples Guatemalan society? The confirmation is relatively easy to narrate. As a guerrilla doctor Genaro worked for years in settings where he sustained relations of equality with Mayas, as a member of a political collective with the express intent of casting off the dominant ideology, and forging a new society based on an ethos of radical equality.

> We were able to have meaningful and enriching experiences of collective politics. At first I worried that I was romanticizing these experiences. To clear up these doubts, I talked about my memories with various others who had been there with me, and they all expressed the same thing. We had achieved, even if in miniature—absurdly miniature some would say—we engaged in a very interesting effort to put the theories [of political change] into practice; we showed it was possible to live and work together in accordance with basic principles of social justice.

Even if that "new society" was a small group of foot soldiers and civilian supporters, hunkered down in the jungle, frightfully vulnerable, moving constantly from place to place to elude the army, the experience exerted an enormous influence on Genaro's thinking about how society could be organized differently. So much influence that it made Genaro, by his own account, into a "bad" revolutionary: increasingly irreverent toward the leadership, who seemed incapable of acting in accordance with the very principles that supposedly enshrined the struggle they led. A decade later, when that experience had become a distant memory, it still provided the compass for his reactions to the everyday racism that he encountered in Chimaltenango: "I started to reflect on everyday interactions, in the market, in buses, conversations, social relations in general, and I become increasingly aware of how all these relations are deeply infused with discrimination and racism." More disturbing still was his reencounter with Maya guerrilla comrades, people he had joined in struggle a decade earlier:

> They had reentered Guatemalan society. I was especially struck when I visited them: they would use the formal "Usted" with me, creating a social distance. It was as if they had resumed their traditional role. I brought this change to their attention, they laughed, but carried on the pattern. I did not force the issue. I think it was in response to these experiences that I began to take questions of identity more seriously. Something very positive that those years in the jungle left me is that I am very sensitive to these social interactions, and I have a clear perspective on them. I do not want to say that I have eliminated all of my own discriminatory attitudes, but I did develop a heightened awareness of the problem.

As part of this reflection, upon his return to Chimaltenango, Genaro also parted ways with the tired mantra of the revolutionary left that posited,

> Our primary contradiction was between rich and poor, and the central objective was to take power. The struggles between man and woman, and racial discrimination were considered secondary contradictions. Once the primary contradiction is addressed, and once the revolutionary forces take power, these secondary contradictions will quickly fade away, because their structural underpinnings will have been eliminated (*iban a caer por su propio peso*).

Consistent with this critical reevaluation, Genaro adopted the identity of what I called "militant mestizaje," with an accent on the modifier "militant." By the time I got to know him well in the last few years, antiracism had become a prominent and vehemently primary elment in his political thought and practice.

Even while providing a vivid illustration of the race-conscious progressive politics that I argue Guatemala sorely needs, Genaro's story also subtly confounds my analysis. Even taking into account his searing critique of revolutionary hubris and hypocrisy, Genaro remains committed to what might be called universalist humanism; a little more committed than a loyal disciple of critical race theory would comfortably allow. The reasons for the theorists' discomfort are well-known, and I have rehearsed them in this book: that universalism has often served as a guise for the dominance of one particular perspective; that this form of humanism thrives with the assertion of homogeneity, rather than the affirmation of difference. Yet if Genaro's story provides any basis for generalization, to dismiss universalist humanism would be to undermine the very process by which he came to a critical race consciousness, and to shake the foundations of his current commitments. At each step along the way, the most inspiring moments in Genaro's political journey—from middle-class ladino youth, to medical student, to guerrilla doctor, to militant mestizo—emerge from a principled, radical application of universalist humanism. Two illustrative episodes will suffice.

In 1980, while working in the Escuintla hospital, in full support of the increasingly militant worker and peasant politics of that time, Genaro's name appeared on a list of ten subversives to be eliminated. Within a few days, after six of the ten had been killed, he was spirited outside the country. That experience converted Genaro, virtually overnight, from an activist doctor committed to social justice, into a revolutionary. Yet to my surprise, his first assignment was to work as a surgeon in a remote rural hospital in Nicaragua; the Guatemalan organization apparently was not ready to incorporate him. "Weren't you disappointed to be separated from Guatemala, in the heat of the struggle?" I queried.

> I was never, for one moment, separated from the struggle.... I was genuinely anxious to go to El Salvador or to Nicaragua. I really did not care which of these struggles I was aligned with. I deeply believed in the principles of that time, what they called proletarian militancy or something like that—I do not remember the exact term. The idea was that you could join the struggle in any part of the world—a kind of proletarian internationalism—I deeply believed in this idea, and I decided to live my life accordingly.

When he returned to Guatemala two years later, the same reasoning applied. That front of a much broader struggle needed him most.

After Nicaragua, Genaro was sent to head up *servicios médicos* (medical services) in one of the guerrilla encampments of the Ixcán region of the Quiché department. The foot soldiers and mid-level commanders—the only ones with whom he had daily contact—were almost entirely indigenous. Racial hierarchy only became evident at the upper levels of command, which was almost entirely ladino. I asked Genaro whether that experience, of living and working as equals among indigenous people, led him to question his own identity and formation as a ladino. His answer was no:

> The discussion took place in a different register. At least among the people I lived with there was no talk, no real concern [with identity questions]. You would need to ask the Mayas; I have talked with some of them about this, and they confirmed my impression. We felt that we could move beyond many of these problems by treating each other as comrades, working together toward the central objective of taking power. I learned a whole lot from these Maya comrades. I attended their medical needs, we bonded, and from that moment I knew that they would risk their lives for me. They wouldn't go around talking about how they felt. It was a simple, unstated commitment: comrades to the death. They had a way of communicating that is very alien to us [ladinos]; we are accustomed to talking endlessly about these matters. They are discreet and spare with their words, but in practice, their solidarity runs deep.

Perhaps if Genaro already had developed an acutely self-critical mestizo consciousness, this experience of solidarity with his Maya comrades would have been deeper still. Or perhaps not. In any case, it did not happen that way. A radicalized universalist humanism provided the basis for his experience of social transformation, which continues to be the touchstone for Genaro's political commitments to this day.

Rather than drawing firm conclusions from this account, I am inclined to leave it posed as a question. Could it be that theory-driven reasoning has led us to overstate the dichotomy between these two cultural-political logics—universalist humanism on the one hand, and affirmation of cultural-racial difference on the other? One could easily develop a reading of Genaro's story that would wish this question away, and keep the dichotomy firmly in place. Since indigenous combatants had not developed a sharply defined identity as Maya, they were not apt to challenge Genaro's position as ladino, nor to probe the limits of a transformative politics born in universalist humanism. In Chimaltenango a decade later, amid the Maya efflorescence, this same universalist solidarity would ring hollow. Such a reading works, but only to a point. Upon his return to Chimaltenango, Genaro quickly affirmed the politics of Maya cultural difference. He developed a sharp critique of ladino racism, made the case for militant mestizaje, and vehemently defended the basic demands of the Maya movement. Yet throughout this coming of consciousness, and he *does* view it as such, Genaro never stopped turning to those years in the jungle for inspiration, clarity, and guidance.

This firm inclination to keep the experience of revolutionary struggle as his touchstone became clear to me when our conversation turned to what I consider the thorniest analytical problem of the book. With reference to the material in chapter 5, and fully admitting my own perplexity, I asked Genaro about ladino political imaginaries: how could this deepest level of socialization, and the distance it creates between Maya and ladino, be expected to change?

> In order to effect change at the level of the political imaginary, there must be conditions that lead us to consider people as people. When we were in the jungle, I depended on Maya comrades on a daily basis; there were many occasions when they kept me going. Through these experiences, I came to the understanding that they were people just as important and valuable as I. It is not that I spent a lot of time analyzing this while it was happening; these were implicit understandings that emerged from collective experience. In my case, that is how my political imaginary changed.

I am not sure what role this universalist humanism should have in the broader strategy to dismantle racial hierarchy in Guatemala, but it would seem profoundly mistaken simply to dismiss it as superceded and flawed.

This brings us back to Yolanda's second critique, the ¿y qué? question. Both Yolanda and Genaro had been thinking about this a lot in recent months, and their prescriptions, at least in general terms, were the same. Education and critical self-awareness are crucial. Whether as ladina dissident or militant mestizo, they have been reading extensively, attending forums and workshops, engaging in debate with family and friends, educating themselves. Second, they are both acutely aware of the limits of their own initiatives, the danger of speaking for Mayas, rather than being in dialogue with them. As Genaro puts it graphically,

> I can come as mestizo or ladino with the best intentions in the world, saying that we are going to take this or that action with regard to the Mayas. But if I ask them: "What are the conditions that you find most oppressive, that you most want to change?" a whole series of things that I had not even imagined are sure to emerge. The person who is under the boot knows exactly what it feels like to be stepped on, where it hurts most; for anyone else, it is mere speculation. So the most important thing is to listen: I have no doubt that their responses to this question will require me to divest a considerable amount of the privilege (*cuota de poder*) that I have as mestizo or ladino.

Third, they are planning to take action, through the founding of an organization of antiracist ladinos (and mestizos) in Chimaltenango. As this book goes to press, they are still debating what their first activities will be.

In talking over possible plans of action, and the likely responses of ladinos chimaltecos, the basic analysis of this book did seem to have a role to play. Both readily affirmed that their natural allies in Chimaltenango would be few, in part because racism had taken on a new, perhaps more resilient form. Genaro explained,

> With all that has happened in Guatemala recently, the sanctity of superficial appearances (*culto a la apariencia*) has become our greatest concern. One of the dangers that follows is that people come to believe that they can eliminate racism by simple decree. This diverts attention away from the need for structural changes, away from the economic underpinnings [of racism]. To eliminate the discourse of biological inferiority is no guarantee that true equality will result.

Yolanda characterized the problem more succinctly, in good chapín: that the respect for the Maya would be only "*del diente al labio.*" Or, in the terms introduced in this book, they will need to confront not only the classic racism of times past, but also the racial ambivalence that has begun to take hold.

But Yolanda is patient, inclined to seek incremental change, and to tolerate mild hypocrisies. She understands the predicament of racial ambivalence, and to some extent accepts it as an apt self-description. For this reason, Yolanda is more concerned than Genaro about how the ladino community, with whom she still (ambivalently) identifies, will respond to their political initiatives. She is also more concerned about what they will think about her when the book is published. Now, they tend to dismiss her sympathies with lo Maya with a humor-laden reproach: "*Ah, ya viene la Menchú*" (uh oh, here comes that Menchú again), or saying that to be spending so much energy on these things, she must be either a little stupid, or a little crazy. After they read the book, however, their reactions may well be stronger; they might consider her a traitor. In any case, Yolanda and Genaro are both sober and circumspect about the challenge they have taken on: Genaro, with an impatient critique from the outside; Yolanda, with a bemused smile, having just returned from her weekly coffee date with lady friends at Pollo Campero. Both want to focus their efforts on youth, with the assumption that the younger generations are more open to new forms of thought and practice. As an example, Yolanda cites the remarkable evolution, from her father Don Luis, to herself, to her eldest son Wilfredo.

Genaro and I ended our conversation reflecting on an incident involving Wilfredo, which had happened a few months earlier. Wilfredo works for an organization devoted to community-based exhumations of the hundreds of mass graves that are the legacy of the horrendous state violence of the preceding era. Working in a hamlet of San Martín Jilotepeque, Wilfredo's forensic team heard from community members about a much loved community member who, after receiving a serious bullet wound, had been taken to be treated in a jungle hospital, never to be seen again. They wanted to give the man a proper burial, along with the others whose remains had been exhumed. There was little hope of finding him, the forensic team regretfully replied. By chance, Wilfredo mentioned the exchange to Genaro, who immediately remembered the man, how they had tried to save him to no avail, when and how he had been buried. Soon thereafter, the forensic team was able to grant the community members their modest, but deeply important wish.

The image stayed with me. In the Valencia family, the story lent itself to a round of slightly morbid humorous commentary: What hope for a society where one generation buries the dead, while the next generation exhumes them? What futility! *Guatemala no se compone* (Guatemala will never fix itself). But as usual, amid the chingadera, there were glimmers of truth. The conversation changed tone for a moment, as we pondered these more serious interpretations. A bond of mutual respect between generations of politically committed Guatemalan mestizos? A bridge between political visions past and future? But had I tried to push the matter further, as the earnest analyst in me is apt to do, they almost surely would have responded with another round of humor chapín.

Notes

Preface

1. Brosnahan (1995:125).

2. Mack was an anthropologist who researched a series of politically sensitive topics in Guatemala, including the status of the "internally displaced" (people forced to leave their homes by government-instigated violence who remained within the country). She was brutally murdered on 11 September 1990. Through more than a decade of arduous legal and political struggle, human rights activists forced the government to acknowledge responsibility for her murder.

3. Throughout this book I use the Spanish language honorifics "Don" and "Doña" before some, but not all, given names of my informants. My decision of when to use them follows patterns of common usage in Chimaltenango: elderly people of a certain stature are uniformly referred to as Don or Doña so and so. These common usage guidelines are of course thoroughly entangled both with longstanding patterns of racial hierarchy, and more recent changes in these patterns. Ladinos of the elder generation, raised in a milieu of classic racism, were not apt to use these honorifics for any indigenous person, in any circumstance. In contrast, ladinos influenced by the rising ethic of interracial equality were much more inclined to use the honorifics for elderly Indians as well. My usage reflects these latter changes. However, as the analysis of the book should make clear, these changes are substantial, but incomplete and contradictory. I have made no attempt to modify my usage to address the contradictions.

Chapter 1

1. "Maya movement" would be a more conventional phrase, with a widely established meaning. For this very reason, I avoid using it when evoking the multifaceted processes that have brought Mayas into the public sphere as collective actors. While some of these processes have been engendered by actions that fit neatly within the category "social movement," others have a different character. In part, Maya

empowerment has come about as the cumulative effect of many diverse, highly dis-aggregated actions at the family or individual level, from the struggle to provide children an education, to economic advancement, to the remaking of day-to-day relations with the dominant society. While there certainly is mutual influence between collective assertion and these disaggregated actions, to place them all under the rubric of a "movement" seems misleading. The term "efflorescence," that is, "flowering" and the "culmination or fulfillment of something," is meant to evoke this broader array of processes. I keep the phrase "Maya movement" in the chapter title, because it is more readily comprehensible, and because, in the last analysis, it probably is these "movement" activities that members of the dominant society find most threatening.

2. When COCADI reissued the book in 1992, the name of Raxche' Demetrio Rodriguez Guaján appeared as the *compilador*. COCADI later changed its name to COKADI, to reflect the new spelling, Kaqchikel.

3. Indeed caution prevailed with regard to the seminar organizers' proposal, and the Maya participants rejected it outright: "too soon, too fast, too dangerous," concluded the group's informal spokesperson.

4. These concepts come directly from Gramsci (1971) and are explained amply by Adamson (1980).

5. See Cojtí (1989: footnote 3, 126–127). The precise wording of the footnote is that "[Ríos Montt] tried to address 'the indigenous problem' correctly, although he lacked clarity in his analysis and in his solutions."

6. What was most significant about this outlandish assertion is the assumption that there had to be some nonindigenous instigator behind an indigenous political initiative of this magnitude.

7. The literature is immense and has distinct phases that correspond to successive historical moments. An initial phase of literature, epitomized by the edited volume *Harvest of Violence* (Carmack 1988) focuses on the horrors of the political violence and its aftermath; a second phase of literature, epitomized by Warren (1998), Fischer (2001), Nelson (1999), Smith (1990b), and Camus and Bastos (1992), is situated squarely within the Maya efflorescence; a third emergent phase will be characterized by critical engagement with what has become known as the "Maya movement." There is also a distinct genre, situated within the second and third phases, in which Maya intellectuals analyze different facets of their own reality. Prominent actors in this rapidly growing field include: Cojtí Cuxil (1997, 1999), Sam Colop (1996), Otzoy (2001), Velásquez Nimatuj (2002), and Esquit (2002). Separate from all these are the revisionists, whose principal concern is to question existing portrayals of Mayas during the period of revolutionary upheaval. I address these at length in chapter 3.

8. Among the most important of these are Nelson (1999), and Schirmer (1998).

9. For a fascinating and cogent study of the deployment of this interculturali-dad discourse, with conclusions that parallel closely my argument here, see Cumes

(2004). Some analysts posit a sharp distinction between the terms *interculturalidad* and *multiculturalidad*, associating the former with egalitarian interchange and the latter with top-down initiatives. Although such a distinction holds in some cases, my sense is that in Guatemala the terms are fluid and contested, bearing a range of meanings depending on the context.

10. The "against race" and "beyond identity" arguments of Paul Gilroy (2000) and Judith Butler (1993) are indicative.

11. This is, in my view, the principal limitation of the "racial formation" approach, which I otherwise heartily endorse (e.g., Omi and Winant [1987], Winant [2001]). This same limitation applies to much of the Guatemalan literature on ladino-Maya relations, whose authors generally take a dim view of ethnography.

12. See, for example, the demands for territory and autonomy put forth in Cojtí Cuxil (1994a and 1994b). This proposal was met with widespread ladino skepticism, but generated little or no further public discussion since it was published.

13. For a thorough analysis of this process, see Warren (2002).

14. I outline this crisis in an unpublished report to the Ford Foundation (Mexico office). See Hale (n.d.).

15. The prime example here is the Coordinadora Nacional Indígena y Campesina (CONIC). With origins in the *popular* wing of the indigenous movement, and a primary focus on agrarian struggle, CONIC has never figured prominently in analyses of the "Maya movement." I leave it to others to sort out the evolving complexities of the relations between "mayanista" and "popular" forms of indigenous organization. See Bastos and Camus (2003) and the 2005 doctoral dissertation of Irma Alicia Velásquez Nimatuj.

16. For an instructive parallel to this notion of "racial ambivalence," see Howard Winant's (1997) analysis of the "duality" of white identity in the United States since the Civil Rights Movement. My notion of ladino "investment" in racial privilege has been influenced by the writings of Lipsitz, especially (1998).

17. The telling example here is the widespread premise that Indians can become educated and "cultured," and yet never completely shake free from the burden of their racial origins, because culture runs in the veins, because "*no se quita la costumbre*" (custom just doesn't go away).

18. Guatemala is far from having made this transition, and perhaps never will. There is movement in this direction, however, and it is crucial to theorize. Otherwise, there is a constant tendency to think of racism solely in terms of perpetrators, and of individual or collective assertions of racial inferiority, all of which are evidently on the decline. In the emergent mode, racism will have to be understood primarily through its consequences—structured inequities that afflict certain racial groups disproportionately—accompanied by varied and flexible ideological justifications, but *without* recourse to an ideology that casts the disadvantaged racial group as universally inferior. For a cogent argument along these lines, in global terms, see Winant (2001).

19. Since Nader's essay (1969) there have been many such anthropological studies. My own idiosyncratic list includes: Ferguson (1990), Herzfeld (1992), Gusterson (1996), and Gill (2004). There is also a broader gauged project of turning the lens back on the very underpinnings of western epistemologies, best exemplified by the work of Michael Taussig. The principal unfinished agenda, in my view, is an adequate response to the political edge of Nader's call: how to balance the empathy that any good ethnography requires, and the transformative impulse of putting anthropology to the service of certain sharply defined political ends? I grapple with, but do not completely resolve, that tension in this work.

20. The book *Linaje y racismo*, by Marta Elena Casaús Arzú, had begun to circulate, and we had been discussing her shocking discovery that some elite Euro-Guatemalans believe, and were glad to state in interviews, that the best way to resolve the problem of tense relations and inequality between indigenous and ladinos was to exterminate the indigenous population. I contended that no ladino in Chimaltenango would have such views, and Yolanda insisted that I was wrong. Not surprisingly, the interview with Don Frederico produced no such extremism (although, see the epigraph to chapter 7).

21. Gender politics were a major factor in Yolanda's ability to move through these circles in this way, and also, to bring me with her. As a widow, she had an established position in the community; yet as a single woman she had extraordinary freedom of movement and social interaction that would have been nearly inconceivable for a conventionally married middle-class ladina.

22. Throughout this book I use the term "progressive," like its Spanish language counterpart "*progresista*," to mean aligned with the principles of distributive equality, social justice, and democratic empowerment that have been basic tenets of the Left since the nineteenth century. I recognize at least two types of ambiguity in this understanding. First, it has embodied constitutive exclusions or implicit hierarchies, making class or economic inequality matter more than, for example, inequality along the lines of race, gender, or sexuality. Second, among those whose political ideologies clearly fall outside this understanding, there have been objections that their (alternative) tenets are just as deserving of the term "progressive." The first ambiguity is a substantive topic of analysis in this book, and will be addressed extensively in that context. The second keys into a struggle over representations that is part and parcel of politics, and as such, requires analysts to stand their ground.

23. The reference is to Paredes's classic work 1993 [1977].

24. "*Superarse*" is a tricky verb, whose meaning changes with context. If a ladino uses it in reference to another ladino, the more transparent meaning tends to hold. If . the reference is to an Indian, however, the effort to "better oneself" is apt to take on an additional charge. In the traditional ladino mindset, an Indian could not substantively "better himself" without becoming less Indian.

25. See especially, the recent work by Arturo Taracena and his collaborators (2002), by Casaús Arzú (1991), Esquit (2002), and Grandin (2000). Other key

works include McCreery (1994), and Pinto (1986).

26. Grandin's study of the K'iche middle class in Quetzaltenango makes this point in an especially convincing and detailed manner (2000).

27. See, for example, the epigraph to chapter 2, quoted in Palma Murga (1991).

28. The original Spanish language text should be cited in full: "*Desapruebo a toda la indiada que llega los domingos a ensuciar el parque central o Plaza de la Constitución. No sólo es gente que ni se baña…y, por consiguiente, expele olores fétidos, sino que con su presencia espantan a las personas civilizadas. Ya parece zoológico ese lugar, antaño limpio y decente. Allí uno puede ver, los domingos, lo infeliz que estamos en Guatemala: indígenas alienados exhibiendo el más puro subdesarrollo cultural. Tan burros que son esos estropajosos! Yo que el presidente los fumigaba.*" The piece was titled: "Amarren a los Cochambrosos" (Clean out the Scum) *Prensa Libre* 9/2/1995.

29. This turned out to be a long, arduous process, whose results were far from satisfactory to those who originally pushed for the legislation. For more details, see the doctoral dissertation of Irma Alicia Velásquez Nimatuj (2005). Both the fact that the process occurred, and its unsatisfying results, nicely exemplify the larger argument put forth here. In a similar vein, outcry against the crude racism of the "cochambrosos" ("scum," also, "slobs") editorial did not keep its author, Eddy Alfaro Barillas, from continuing to publish inflammatory columns in the *Prensa Libre*.

30. For a cogent review of the strange trajectory of the race concept in the study of Guatemala, see Smith (1999). I delve into this issue at greater length in chapter 4.

31. See Guzmán Böckler and Herbert (1971); they developed a large following among Guatemalans, and reportedly exerted direct influence on those who would later form the Revolutionary Organization of the People in Arms (ORPA). Fragments of the early ORPA statements on racism are reproduced in CEIDEC (1990).

32. Two related factors were at work here as Maya activists imbued these ideas with greater power and urgency. On the one hand, the mere fact that Mayas were now voicing them transformed their political content and impact. On the other hand, some readings of the Guzmán Böckler–Herbert thesis have found a class reductionism underlying the apparent shift to an emphasis on race and culture (See, e.g., Carol Smith [1992]). This latter reading, in turn, would stress a greater substantive distance between the Guzmán Böckler–Herbert thesis and the Maya activists' position.

33. For an intellectual history of Boasian thought with specific relation to race, see Baker (1998). A cogent critique of the Boasian turn to culture, and its reverberations for racial analysis, can be found in Visweswaran (1998).

34. Others such as Goldberg (2002) endorse a variant of this position as well. See also, the edited volume on racism published by AVANCSO (Arenas, Hale, and Palma Murga 1999), and Heckt and Palma Murga (2004), a subsequent volume in the series.

35. See López Larrave (1976). For a description of his killing, see Comisión para

el Esclarecimiento Histórico (1999), *Guatemala Memoria del Silencio,* Tomo VI, Casos Ilustrativos, Anexo 1. His is "illustrative case" #28, pp. 105–110.

36. For an excellent account of both the intense, widespread indigenous revolutionary mobilization and its ultimate subordination to ladino guerrilla authority, see Carlota McAllister's dissertation (2003). In a succinct summary of the central contradiction, she writes: "To remain grounded in the people, the Ejército Guerrillero del Pueblo (People's Guerrilla Army or EGP) had to recognize, even elicit, indigenous demands; to remain the people's army, however, the EGP had to reserve the right to judge which of these demands counted and which did not." (2003:189).

37. A good example is the invective of Carlos Manuel Pellecer, an influential ladino intellectual, on the occasion of the meeting of the anti-quincentenary movement in Quetzaltenango, in 1991. See "¡Cuidado con la Guerra Indianista!" *Prensa Libre* 23 September 1991.

38. Edward Fischer (2001) makes the same observation, with a different analytical conclusion, in his recently published book.

39. For one summary, among many, of this shift, see Demmers, Fernández Jilberto, and Hogenboom (2001).

40. For a good example of this narrative, see Edwards (1995). In contrast, the previous model (known as import substitution industrialization) and its accompanying analytical frame (known as dependency theory) posited a need for heavy state involvement both to combat these perversities and to set the economies on a course of autonomous, egalitarian self-sustaining development.

41. At issue here, also, is whether supporters of these new arrangements actually have taken on "neoliberalism" as an apt self-descriptive term. My impression is that, unlike the case of its close cognate, globalization, neoliberalism has relatively little unconditional support. In part, this could be an indication that critics have won the battle over representation; it could also be that supporters never really waged the battle, on the grounds that the term "neoliberalism" quickly came to signify something very different from what they advocate and do. In any case, this divergence has complicated the analytical terrain, such that the critics can view a whole range of practices as "neoliberal" while the actual protagonists decline (or even actively contest) the appellation.

42. See especially, the recently published study of Deborah Yashar (2005). The work of Van Cott (2000) also follows this line of explanation. See also Yashar (1998).

43. For elaboration on this point, see David Theo Goldberg (2002), Uday Mehta (1999), and Stuart Hall (2000).

44. For a cogent account of this inclination in favor of collectivities, in "advanced liberalism," see Nikolas Rose (1999), and various essays in Burchell, Gordon, and Miller (1991). The phrase "strategies of exclusion" comes from Mehta (1997).

45. For a sophisticated analysis of the trap of neoliberal multiculturalism in another settler society, see Povinelli (2002). Povinelli focuses especially on the way

neoliberal multiculturalism "inspires impossible desires" in the subjects of newfound rights. "Multicultural domination seems to work…," she argues, "by inspiring subaltern and minority subjects to identify with the impossible object of an authentic self-identity" (2002: 6). For Guatemala, I place greater emphasis on the neoliberal prerogative to distinguish between legitimate and "illiberal" demands and comportment.

46. For an analysis of the internal dynamics of World Bank reform, see Fox and Brown (1998) and Thorne (forthcoming).

47. Voter turnout was extremely low, key Maya movement leaders were divided, and campaigns against the reforms whipped up ladino fears of Maya ascendancy. Whatever the precise reasons, the "no" vote was a significant setback for Maya cultural activism.

48. Povenelli (2002) makes this point strongly in chapter 1, "The Cunning of Recognition."

49. See Gillian Hart (2002), especially chapter 1 for a cogent exposition of this critique.

50. For a collection of essays that, considered together, make this point forcefully, see Warren and Jackson (2002).

51. In a previous moment, many of these ladinos would have been sympathetic to, or actively aligned with the revolutionary Left. By the time I began my study, the opposite was true: ladino intellectuals with progressive inclinations had, almost to a person, renounced affinities with the organized Left, which now had become legal and had its own political party.

52. I'm thinking here of Visweswaran's essay, "Feminist Ethnography as Failure" (1994).

53. I presented the work in Guatemala in a number of informal settings, and in at least three public lectures, two to an exclusively Maya audience. I also published a significant portion of this material in essays that first appeared in Spanish, in venues especially accessible to Guatemalans. The greatest impact along these lines, however, will certainly come with the simultaneous Spanish language publication of the book.

54. The concept comes from Gramsci. See for example, Gramsci (1971:333).

55. In an otherwise insightful and instructive book on "racism without race" in the United States, Bonilla-Silva (2003) takes this course, in an attempt to keep the analysis from focusing on individuals. The individuals he interviews, then, become representatives of structural categories or types, rather than actors in their own right.

56. Such a question can be traced most directly to the influence of Foucault's notion of "governmentality" (Foucault 1991). See also, Gordon (1991). While I do not subscribe uncritically to a Foucauldian perspective, in this case I believe the question is on the mark.

57. This phrase comes from William Roseberry (1994:355–366), and his distinctive Gramscian reading of how hegemony is forged.

58. For more on this notion of the "indio permitido" see Hale (2004) and Hale and Millamán (n.d.).

59. I borrow the term from Harlon Dalton, who wrote a book focused on race relations in the United States titled *Racial Healing: Confronting the Fear between Blacks and Whites* (1995). A centerpiece in Dalton's argument is the need to confront, through candid, head on dialogue, the most difficult issues that a history of racial inequality produces.

Chapter 2

1. The twists and turns of the ultimately frustrated attempt to bring the assassins to justice are too complex to summarize here. Thorough reports on the judicial process have been written by Francisco Goldman (1999, 2002). His investigative reportage often reads like magical realist fiction.

2. The phrase draws on the historical work of Taracena and his collaborators (2002, 2004). In the latter work, Taracena uses the term *"tutelar"* (tutelary) to invoke the key premise of separate and inferior status. My use of the phrase inevitably brings the Jim Crow South in the United States to mind. I acknowledge the many differences in ideologies of racial inferiority and in the character of racial hierarchy in the two locales, especially the greater fluidity in boundaries between Indian and ladino. However, my analysis also contests Latin American racial exceptionalism, which moves from these differences to a denial of racism as a central force structuring relations between dominant and subordinate actors in these societies. Until recently, this exceptionalism was a widespread feature of historical and anthropological analysis in Guatemala; Taracena's work has done much to move us beyond this problem.

3. Taracena's recent work (2004), which traces state ideologies toward Indians from the 1944 period to the present, provides the terminology, and an extensive empirical basis, for this assertion.

4. General Otzoy's statement to this effect can be found in an interview, published in Ortego (1994).

5. See Taracena (2002).

6. For a good historical account of this period, see the relevant chapter in James Dunkerley's text (1988).

7. For the most thorough research on these events, see R. N. Adams (1990, 1992). For a fascinating fictional rendition of the events, see Dante Liano's *Misterio de San Andrés* (1996).

8. During the Arbenz years (1950–1954), Don Beto Pájaro was a leader of an active peasant syndicate, which in turn had close ties with the Guatemalan Workers Party (PGT). Pájaro insists that very little land could be redistributed in Chimaltenango, because Decree 900 applied only to "idle" lands. For that reason, his group began a process of obtaining additional lands on the south coast near Escuintla. Regardless, the syndicate's opponents accused them of being Communists, an accusation that still nettled Pájaro fifty years later. He was among about fifty or sixty syndi-

cate activists, all indigenous, who were jailed after the Liberation. The two Chimaltenango leaders of the PGT were Eduardo Simon and Manuel Perez, indigenous and ladino respectively. (Interview with Pájaro, 2 July 2001)

9. This assertion is backed by the historical research of Handy (1989), and more implicitly by his later study (Handy 1994). Cindy Forster (1998), in a study of peasant politics in San Marcos, also makes a strong argument for the rise of race consciousness (fused with worker demands), especially in the last years of the revolutionary decade. Greg Grandin (2004), in a historical account of successive generations of K'ech'i political organization prior to the Panzós massacre of 1978, further substantiates this general picture of local indigenous activists, working under the umbrella of universalist reforms to pursue their own objectives.

10. Evidence for this assertion comes from interviews with the Valencia family, especially Genaro and Yolanda. It is possible, of course, that more egalitarian spaces might have existed in relations between lower-class ladinos and indigenous. But the general pattern seems to have been otherwise: membership in the ladino identity category, even (or especially!) if one was poor, was predicated on sharp enforcement of the racial divide.

11. Quoted in Barrett (1970). Barrett's account of López's accomplishments and outlook provides a fascinating window on the initial phase of indigenous organizing in the late 1950s and 1960s.

12. *Estadísticas agrarias 1955–1969, Departamento de colonización y desarrollo agrario.* Publicación No. 1, INTA, Guatemala, 1971. Although according to the Instituto de Transformación Agraria (Institute of Agrarian Transformation, or INTA) records these acts were legally consummated between 1956 and 1958, they respond to demands that almost certainly arose during the period of ferment in the final part of the revolutionary decade.

13. Unfortunately, the census does not provide municipio-level data that specifies size of holding.

14. The López family story in Patzún is again illustrative. The San Bernadino School was founded in 1955. Barrett reports in 1970 that the school (grades 1 through 9) had an enrollment of 450, the majority Indian. All eight of the López Raquec children in school during this time were in various stages of education that would lead them to careers as professionals.

15. This data is based on a year-by-year count of the graduates, using last name as a proxy for identity. While this proxy is far from infallible, I had the help of a long-time (ladino) teacher who knew many of the student graduates. For additional discussion of this data collection exercise, see chapter 6.

16. The best early source on the social and economic effects of these "green revolution" technologies in Guatemala is Falla (1972).

17. Edwin Morquecho, interview 28 November 1994.

18. Catholic Action programs and their effects on indigenous communities have been the subject of extensive ethnographic description and analysis. See for example,

Warren (1989), Falla (2001), Brintall (1979), Adams (1970), and Manz (2004).

19. A native of the neighboring municipio of San Martín Jilotepeque, Morales grew up steeped in an ideology of ladino dominance and still evinced many of these premises in November and December 1994 when I interviewed him at length.

20. Barrett (1970) describes this struggle in his summary of López's life. The evaluation of the *alcaldes indígenas* would change radically in the subsequent period, when the principles of indigenous autonomy started to be viewed in a more positive light. For a study of the acaldes indígenas produced in the context of this reevaluation, see Barrios (1998).

21. See chapter 3 for an extended analysis of this "narrative frame" problem: events of this period have generally been retold through narrative frames that are, themselves, products of the violent polarization that followed.

22. The coordinates of the earthquake epicenter were: 15.4 N, 88.7 W.

23. According to Adams (1978), San Martín Jilotepeque had an indigenous mayor during the revolutionary decade.

24. The four municipios that elected ladino mayors that year were: Zaragoza, Acatenango, Parramos, and Tecpán. The first three can be explained by the especially powerful ladino sectors, which placed limits on the possibilities for indigenous electoral mobilization. The election of Catarindo Galindo as mayor of Tecpán that year is an anomaly. Galindo had close family ties with powerful national-level political actors, which he used to his advantage. He was killed in November 1981 when guerrilla forces briefly occupied the town center.

25. José Lino Xoyón (Chimaltenango) became the secretary general; Joaquín Quiná (Santa Cruz Balanyá), the official spokesperson; others whose names appeared frequently in news reports on the FIN include Nehemías Cumes and Miguel Angel Curruchiche (Comalapa), Jesús Chacach (San José Poaquíl), Roso Juracán (Tecpán), and Francisco Sisimit (Santa Apolonia).

26. *Gráfico*, 18 September 1978. Opposition spanned the entire political spectrum, with arguments that varied according to political ideology of the exponent, but also shared to a striking degree the assertion that indigenous electoral mobilization could only deepen racial tensions and threaten to dismember the nation. For example, Jorge Carpio Nicolle, a center-left politician who played an important role in national politics until he was assassinated in 1993, argued that the FIN formed part of an indigenous political current "based on profound but hidden neocolonial resentment, which will tear the country apart" (*Gráfico*, 15 December 1976).

27. *Impacto*, 6 March 1977.

28. Meloto was replaced in the early 1980s by Monseñor Julio Fuentes, also one of the more conservative bishops. Fuentes continued to exert substantial influence on the course of political events in Chimaltenango, marking a great contrast with the more progressive bishops in Quiché and San Marcos.

29. Additional information on the Zone 5 house, with a highly critical slant, can be found in Le Bot (1995). Confirmation of the distinction between PROMICA and

the Zone 5 Jesuits comes from a series of interviews with Enrique Corral in June and July 1998.

30. For accounts that portray indigenous social mobilization as largely a product of guerrilla instigation, see Stoll (1993)—who writes specifically on the Ixil triangle—and Le Bot (1995). For an account from southern Quiché, which follows much more closely the pattern in Chimaltenango, see McAllister (2003) and Manz (2004).

31. For example, Enrique Corral, in a 1998 interview, remembers harboring suspicions toward those who emphasized cultural rather than political-economic demands. More generally, as analyzed in chapter 3, revolutionary intellectuals had only a limited tolerance for a Maya cultural rights perspective. It is quite possible, of course, that leftist organizers advanced a universalist message, which indigenous participants interpreted and reproduced in a Maya-centric frame. This is especially likely given that, as argued in chapter 3, the chasm between left-universalist and Maya-centric politics was much less deep in the 1970s, and to some extent emerged from the armed conflict itself.

32. For example, a well-connected long-time ladina resident of Chimaltenango told me one day that she knew the true story behind the assassination of José Lino Xoyón, the popular indigenous mayor of Chimaltenango (1978–1980). She knew, reportedly, because the assassin, the father of prominent ladino merchants in town, had boasted about his role in the feat in a private conversation with her. The point, of course, is not the veracity of this account, but the fact that it, and hundreds others like it, circulate constantly, keeping memories of the violence alive.

33. *La Hora*, 4 December 1981; *Imparcial,* 20 November 1981.

34. The four were: (1) the Q'anjob'al and Chuj Maya of Huehuetenango; (2) the Ixil Maya of Quiché; (3) the K'iche' Maya of Quiché; and (4) the Achi Maya of Baja Vera Paz. The methodology and juridical basis for the findings are detailed in the report of the Comisión para el Esclarecimiento Histórico (1999).

35. This memorable phrase comes from an early report by Carol A. Smith (1990c). The most forceful intervention along these lines in the English language anthropological literature comes from Sanford (2003), who argues that the commission seriously understated the extent of the genocide by applying the term to specific regions, rather than to the entire Guatemalan highlands.

36. Casaus Arzú (1991) presents evidence for deep support among Guatemalan elites for the policy alternative of "exterminating" Indians who cause social and political problems.

37. Support for this assertion comes from Schirmer's account of the "military project" (1998), and from the analysis of Stepputat (2001) from Huehuetenango.

38. Personal communication with the Chimaltenango research team of the Commission for Historical Clarification.

39. This pattern continued even after the return to democracy in 1985. For example, while the governmental decentralization policies (known as the Constitucional 8%), implemented soon after Vinicio Cerezo came to power in 1986,

did bolster municipio autonomy, it also opened the municipio to influence of the state in powerful ways. Political parties acquired new incentives to become much more intimately involved in local power relations; municipal authorities now needed to partner with the state to execute public works projects; although the municipios began to receive their own funds, they now submitted to a rigorous process of state-directed *fiscalización* (fiscal accountability).

40. Army analysts reportedly considered and rejected the option of rapid, forced assimilation, and they viscerally opposed any hint of Maya collective rights. The middle ground stance they embraced was meant to win at least passive indigenous support while placing them on the long-term course toward integration, as described by my informant, Cifuentes. Schirmer lays out these three options, and the army rational for choosing the third (1998:104–107). While the Ixiles are the specific object of analysis in this passage, one assumes that similar rationale applied across the board.

41. For detailed background information on the comisionados and their prior role, see Adams (1970).

42. One especially sweeping claim along these lines can be found in Fischer (2001).

43. I find especially strong support for this assertion in the provocative essay by Finn Stepputat (2001). Additional support, focused specifically on Chimaltenango, comes from Little (2004).

44. For documentation of these early efforts to recuperate Tecún Uman as an army hero, see *Ejército de Guatemala* (1963) and Otzoy (2001).

45. Reportedly, among the most active members of this organization of San Martinecos in the United States are the members of an indigenous family, who were active in the revolutionary movement but left just before the debacle and have grown wealthy from a food concession business that caters to Central Americans. In general, while Indian-ladino divisions in such organizations are not unknown, the lines tend to blur and fade, yielding to the commonalities under the rubric "latino immigrant" in the US context.

46. It makes sense that the first inklings of this shift would come from the Ministry of Education where multiculturalism has less threatening implications, and also where Alfredo Tay Coyoy was the first Maya to hold a cabinet-level post. In 1991 the government promulgated a new National Education Law, which affirmed for the first time the multiethnic and pluricultural character of Guatemalan society. By the signing of the definitive Peace Accords in December 1996, these principles had been established beyond question at the level of political discourse. Implementation of the principles is another issue entirely. For a critical analysis of educational reforms and their effects, see AVANCSO (1998).

47. The Academia received full legal recognition on 15 November 1990. For a detailed description of the process see Nelson (1999:152–155), and for a critical assessment of its initial years, see England (1998).

48. The whole notion of "civil society" as a fully constituted political actor was just emerging at this time; one of the primary elements of this definition was the sharp differentiation from the revolutionary movement. This differentiation was still incipient in the early 1990s: the guerrilla movement still had organizations that operated as their "civil society" appendages, which blurred any clear distinction between the two.

49. A full account of this heyday of Maya civil society and the subsequent period of crisis can be found in my unpublished report to the Ford Foundation (Hale n.d.); another account, following roughly similar lines, can be found in Bastos and Camus (2003).

50. One prominent example of this shift is the health rights activist organization, called ASECSA (Association for Community Services).

51. Some of these interviews were carried out by Silvia Barreno, my research assistant.

52. For example, in response to pressure from multiculturalist constituencies, both Guatemalan and international, the national census started for the first time ever to ask the question: "*¿Es usted indígena?*" Interestingly enough, they still do not ask the counterpart question, "*¿Es usted ladino?*" Questioned on this apparent inconsistency, a national census official told me that "ladino is an insult. You look it up in an encyclopedia and you see a bunch of bad words. ""What would you say if I asked you, 'What is your identity?'" She responded, "I would say no-indígena." But what identity, I pressed on. She answered, "*Saber* [who knows].... There is no category. We would be objects of ridicule if we arrived at an international conference saying that we have this or that number of ladinos. The only ones who count are indigenous. No one cares about the rest."

53. This image of diffuse and multiple forms of governance coincides with Trouillot's (2001) notion of "state effects." Trouillot makes a broad programmatic call to study the workings of governance as diverse, decentralized spaces that operate with a certain autonomy from state institutions.

54. The most prominent of these in the late 1990s were the mayors of Patzún, San Martín Jilotepeque, and San José Poaquíl.

Chapter 3

1. The term "memory work" refers to the diverse, loosely related series of activities initiated in the early 1990s, which would allow people to come to terms with their traumatic experiences of political violence. These included two major initiatives to document the violence, organized exhumations of mass graves, and numerous collective efforts to process memories and console the survivors. I would also include, under the umbrella term "memory work," historical and analytical engagement with that period, such as this chapter. For an earlier essay that uses this term, see Hale (1997).

2. Interview with Genaro Xoyón, the deceased mayor's brother, on 20

November 1995. Both Don Genaro and Don José Lino's wife left the country shortly thereafter in response to further threats.

3. The EGP's slogan that year was triumphalist in the extreme: "overthrow Lucas, take state power, establish a popular revolutionary government." However, what indigenous chimaltecos saw all around them—an outpouring of political energy from below, with little countervailing institutional presence of the state—must have been much more influential than any political slogan.

4. This deployment reportedly not only emptied the barracks but depleted security forces in the principal capital city prison, setting the stage for the spectacular escape of Emeterio Toj, campesino activist, later to become an EGP stalwart. He would be one of a handful who survived imprisonment during this phase of the armed conflict. See "A Guerrilla is Captured, Confesses, Then Escapes" in Fried et al. (1983).

5. This data comes from *Guatemala Memoria del Silencio*, Tomo VIII, pp. 198–211. Comisión para el Esclarecimiento Histórico (1999). This same counterinsurgency campaign continued northward to the Ixcán region of the Quiché department, with results documented in detail by Ricardo Falla (1994). The Truth Commission documented a handful of massacres perpetrated by the guerrilla in this period. Government forces and aligned groups certainly committed ample acts of violence before the major counterinsurgency campaign of November 1981. The Truth Commission report records seventeen massacres and large numbers of extra-judicial killings before that date. But the number and magnitude of the massacres clearly increases from November on, that is, after guerrilla forces have essentially been forced from the area.

6. Warren's (1998) analysis of the violence in San Andrés Semetabaj, for example, emphasizes anxieties, ambiguities, and inherently blurred boundaries between what is known, unknown, and unknowable. See especially her fourth chapter, "Civil War. Enemies without and within."

7. Rigoberta Menchú (1984).

8. Héctor's father also apparently had doubts about the basic story line. While in the midst of a prolonged process of petition with the government, he thought he sighted his wife in a busy street of Zona 1 in Guatemala's capital city. For a number of years after, when the family visited the capital, Héctor's father would walk with the children the city blocks around where the sighting had taken place, in hopes of seeing her again, using the children's presence to convince her to come back home. Héctor only recently came to understand the reason for this mysterious block walking of his youth, twenty years earlier.

9. Two prominent examples are Julio César Macías (1997) and Yolanda Colóm (1998).

10. Marcie had worked in the department in the late 1970s and later coordinated research in Chimaltenango for the Comisión de Esclarecimiento Histórico, the U.N.-supervised "Truth Commission" mandated by the peace accords. Marcie and I

worked together intensively on the analysis in this chapter. Since conditions did not permit us to collaborate in the writing phase, I assume authorship and use the singular pronoun in reference to the conclusions reached. When I use the first person plural pronoun, it is to signal positions that were discussed sufficiently to merit them being presented as collective. I am deeply grateful to Marcie for this collaboration, including many late night sessions of analysis and reflection, from which I learned an immense amount. Her acute comments on earlier drafts of this chapter also improved it greatly.

11. Ricardo Ramírez (Rolando Morán) (1969).

12. This vanguardism did not apply only to Indians, of course. For a thorough analysis of the parallel phenomenon, as it affected urban ladino workers, see Levenson (1994). The point is, rather, that given the history of racism and racial hierarchy in Guatemala, vanguardism had different and especially noxious effects when the enlightened leaders in question were ladinos, and the foot soldiers Indians.

13. Enrique Corral, an EGP leader introduced more fully below, had this to say about "ethnic" demands: "For us, the ethnic question was cultural…to revalue culture, but not to give this position a political character.... We were worried that the ethnic groups would undermine the national focus of the struggle, and so we did not advance any specifically ethnic-cultural demands." This interview took place in June 1998.

14. Tezagüic was originally from an aldea of Santa Cruz Balanyá, Chimaltenango, called Chimazat. He became a teacher, lived most of his adult life in Guatemala City, and when elected to Congress he had recently moved to Sololá to take up a teaching job. If there were earlier cases, during the October Revolution (1944–1954), they were few and far between.

15. The second indigenous deputy to enter the Congress in this election was Pedro Verona Cumes, from Comalapa, a long-time affiliate of the DC. Cumes consistently opposed the FIN, portraying it as an opportunistic maneuver of the PR, designed to steal votes from the DC and to divide the indigenous movement. The details of this fascinating account of the DC, and its closely entwined relationship to the incipient indigenous movement, will have to await a separate essay.

16. Interview with Marcial Maxia, June 1998.

17. *La Nación*, 24 April 1977. Ricardo Falla (1978), in contrast, claims that Tezagüic promised numerous times to resign from the PR but never consummated the act. Tezagüic himself, in a June 2000 interview, claims that he did resign. The matter has a crucial bearing on one's interpretation of the fateful events that followed.

18. *Impacto*, 6 March 1977. Whether or not the FIN ever had the potential for massive electoral strength remains an open question, but there is no doubt that ladino observers believed in and deeply feared this possibility. When the government finally emitted a formal decision to deny the FIN's request for legalization, the reported logic went as follows: "it will not be authorized because it is feared that if

it were permitted, the other political parties would cease to function, given that many of the other parties have majority indigenous members who would abandon ranks, leading these other parties to disappear." *Gráfico*, 18 September 1978.

19. For example, Jorge Palmieri, a columnist for *La Hora*, wrote on 4 August 1977: "Indigenous people are not qualified to occupy legislative seats, in addition to the fact that they have no experience." They would need to be educated first, Palmieri continued, otherwise "it would be like voting children into the legislature."

20. The election took place in an atmosphere of intense political crisis, leading to the lowest voter turnout in Guatemalan history (64 percent abstention). Comisión para el Esclarecimiento Histórico (1999). In general, the elections between the 1954 coup and the 1986 election of Cerezo, were viewed at the time, and subsequently have been portrayed as having very little legitimacy.

21. Interview with Maxia, June 1998.

22. The analytical strategy followed in this chapter—a close reading of an epitomizing text, as a means to elucidate a given narrative frame—runs into certain difficulties, which are best addressed from the outset. Ricardo Falla is a prolific and widely respected analyst of diverse topics in Guatemalan and Central American cultural politics over some thirty-five years. I make no attempt in my analysis to capture the full scope and diversity of his oeuvre, nor do I assert that the 1978 essay is representative of his larger work. To the contrary, many of his writings before and after this essay take different positions on key issues. My analytical strategy is to choose the most persuasive textual example of the narrative frame in question in order to put my argument most fully to the test. Since I did not interview Falla (nor Le Bot or Cojtí) on the issues raised in this essay, it is crucial to think of the analysis as focused on the narrative frame in general, not on the author of the text in particular.

23. Signaling the potential for massive slippage between social process and abstract terminology with vague and variable meanings, Falla notes at the outset, with dismay, that both the EGP and the vice president elect under Lucas, Francisco Villagrán Kramer, recently had used the term "nationalities" in reference to Guatemalan indigenous peoples. Given these disparities, and the fluid character of theoretical debate, Falla's theoretical clarifications are less relevant to the argument here than his political analysis.

24. This assertion must contain a measure of revisionism, since the CUC took shape in 1978, after the FIN's day already had passed. It seems more plausible that among founding members of the CUC were some who had been active in the FIN over the prior two years. More generally, it is striking that Maxia registers no political-ideological antagonism between the two organizations.

25. The term is my own. Falla avoids epithets altogether. In his analysis, FIN's errors are twofold: to organize separately as Indians "against the nation" and to opt for struggle within rather than align with the Left against the dominant bloc. I use the term "indianista" to evoke those two criticisms.

26. José Lino Xoyón, according to his brother Genaro who also was active politically at the time, won by appealing to the poor and downtrodden of the municipio, and governed actively on their behalf. Some have attributed his assassination in 1980 to later involvement in the CUC or another "subversive organization"; others vehemently deny this. In any case, running a highly participatory and progressive municipal government that challenged the traditional ladino power structure was more than enough to merit a death warrant.

27. According to Don Genaro, José Lino also reflected publicly on his own family: "He would say, 'it's not only me, but also so and so who has a ladina wife, and now what are we going to do? For us, it is not a problem, my wife and I can get a divorce...I would have to choose the indigenous movement, because I deeply identify as Indian; but what about our children? What will we do with them?' This is how he made people think."

28. See, for example, the petition for legalization, which promises to "promote true national culture," and Xoyón's statements to the press at the time, which commit the FIN to "work for the creation of an authentic nationality...to stimulate human values and work for the realization of a Constitutional mandate to prohibit all forms of discrimination" (*Impacto*, 20 April 1977). While these exhortations always refer to a reconstituted nationalism with indigenous culture as its centerpiece, they also include ladinos and seem framed around a notion of Guatemalan, not indigenous, national identity.

29. *La Tarde*, 23 November 1976.

30. He interpreted the change from indígena to integración, for example, as evidence of ideological "incoherence" and vacillation.

31. Interview with Fernando Tesagüic, June 2000.

32. This affirmation comes from a follow-up interview with Maxia, conducted by Silvia Barreno in 1999.

33. See, for example, various government statements collected in Fried et al. (1983).

34. In his concluding reflections, Le Bot goes further to note a structural-symbolic parallel between the modernizantes and the revolucionarios: "The Latin American revolutionaries are, at the same time, children of las Luces, as if they were characters out of an Alejo Carpentier novel, and 'children of rigid ecclesiastical societies,' as Carlos Fuentes claims. They conceive of change in the mode of a religious conversion: rapid, complete, necessary.... The modernizing Indians, as they tried to incorporate themselves into the tradition of las Luces, also remain...children of rigid ecclesiastical societies. It is no surprise that the message and the gesture of these Christian revolutionaries found a welcome home with them" (1992:301–302).

35. However, Jennifer Schirmer's (1998) detailed account of the Cerezo government, drawing on hours of interviews with General Héctor Gramajo, Cerezo's minister of Defense, calls the civilian version of the dos demonios political discourse fundamentally into question. Schirmer shows that the Armed Forces controlled and

orchestrated the democratic transition, while passing a major quota of public responsibility on to civilian politicians. Every criticism of the army was in essence approved (if not conceived) in advance by Gramajo himself. In this sense, it is most accurate to say that the dos demonios narrative originated with the military itself, as intellectuals such as Gramajo sought to disassociate themselves from the atrocities they had just finished committing. Gramajo can be credited with the demented brilliance of seeing how this move could best be achieved through "ventriloquism": if Cerezo, the head of state, voiced the critique, then no explicit military disavowal would be necessary.

36. Demetrio Cojtí (1997), among others, makes this three-part historical allusion. The first two holocausts are the Conquest and the liberal revolution of 1871.

37. To my knowledge, this manifesto has never been published. It has circulated widely in mimeo form, with varying dates and titles. Mine ends with the following: "Movimiento Indio Tojil" Guatemala, enero de 1985. I am reasonably sure that other versions have earlier dates.

38. This interpretive quandary runs parallel to one of the founding debates in South Asian "subaltern studies" literature, around the narrative frames one uses to interpret peasant rebellions. Cojtí may well be taking a position similar to that of Ranajit Guha (1988) in his classic essay "The Prose of Counter-Insurgency." But Cojtí doesn't tell us quite enough to draw an informed conclusion.

39. This interview took place in February 1998.

40. It would be interesting and instructive to capture the political positions of foreign scholars in 1980 and 1981, when Maya participation in the revolutionary movement was at a height, before the disastrous consequences of the army's counterinsurgency campaign were well known. My guess is that a general expression of militancy and support could probably be found, although quickly disavowed as conditions changed.

41. This problem is brought to the fore dramatically, if in part inadvertently, in the recently published book by Victoria Sanford (2003).

42. The unpublished work of Bastos and Hernández Ixcoy (2004) contains the first continuous narrative of the Maya movement, from the 1970s through the 1990s, that I have read. As such, it represents a major step toward overcoming the problem noted here. Still, in that narrative, the relationship to the guerrilla is underanalyzed and many complexities left unaddressed.

43. Don Orlando does portray indigenous chimaltecos as protagonists, out to settle racial accounts. But it is also common for ladinos of his ilk to add, at this point in their narrative, a note on ladino guerrilla manipulation. Such a note would make Don Orlando's account merge neatly with the dos demonios narrative frame. Interviewed in August 1994.

44. This is true even of the first Truth Commission report, that of REMHI. See for example, the section titled "Las víctimas" (pp. 125–126) of the second volume of that report, *El entorno histórico*. Gerardi's assassination proves, however, that the sym-

bolic and material importance of REMHI's work reached well beyond the analytical message contained in the written text of the findings.

Chapter 4

1. There is no translation for the term "pixuco." It is one of the wide array of deprecating racial epithets that ladinos have for Indians.

2. This is another slang word for "Indian," a reference to the indigenous skirt, which the woman wraps around her torso. Since it is inconceivable that ladinas would wear indigenous clothing, to be "envuelta" is to be Indian.

3. The proposed constitutional reforms, growing out of the Peace Accords, had just been introduced into the arena of public debate, and therefore were on everyone's minds. They would not be voted on until May 1999. For details on the reforms and the vote, see Warren (2002).

4. The work of Ruth Frankenburg (1994) has been especially important in making this point. See also Goldberg (2002) and Roediger (2002). Alberto Memmi (1965) addresses similar concerns in a much earlier, strikingly prescient study.

5. The first North American to systematically challenge this orthodoxy in a mainstream anthropological publication was Douglas Brintall (1979).

6. Critics included Carlos Guzmán Böckler and Herbert (1971) and Severo Martínez Peláez (1971) on whom I comment further below. Social scientists who supported this viewpoint included most of those associated with the Instituto Indigenista de Guatemala and the publications of the Seminario Guatemalteco de Integración Social. For a thorough summary of the contribution of the Seminario to broader political thought and practice toward Indians, see Taracena Arriola (2004).

7. For another useful overview of this elite discourse, see González Ponciano (1993).

8. This could be part of the explanation for the puzzle: perhaps because highland ladinos and ladinos/whites of the oligarchy lived in such different worlds, descriptions of their attitudes toward Indians could have been so sharply divergent. Yet this would only be convincing to a point, since I found altiplano ladinos also regularly biologize race and they must have to a greater extent in Tax's time. Moreover, it would not explain the social spaces, most notably the fincas, where these two worlds overlapped. See, for example, Pansini (1977).

9. The full text of the thesis has been reprinted. See Asturias (1923).

10. This exchange was initiated with a column by Estuardo Zapeta in the *Siglo XXI*, titled "Del racismo radical al realismo trágico" (18 July 1995). An example of the many responses, which defends Asturias while establishing a safe distance from the obvious racism of Asturias's thesis, is that of Luz Méndez de la Vega (*Siglo XXI*, 29 July 1995).

11. Although it does, in a later passage (IIA1), make reference to "the reality of racial discrimination." The Peace Accords have been published in a number of forms.

This is cited from a pamphlet published by MINUGUA in August 1995.

12. The early work of Richard Adams (1956) and that of Guzmán Böckler and Herbert (1971) constitute noteworthy exceptions to this reductionism, even if the analytical contents are diametrically opposed. Other exceptions include Méndez Domínguez (1967) and Moore (1973). Examples of recent work that has begun to fill this gap include Jafek (1992), Rodas (2004), Nelson (1999), and especially Casaús Arzú (1991).

13. This interview was conducted in four sessions in November 1995.

14. The muncipio of Zaragoza, inhabited almost completely by ladinos, is the exception.

15. Seven major Maya NGOs have their headquarters in the city of Chimaltenango: Saqb'e, COCADI, Pop Wuj, Comunidad Kaqchikel de la Academia de Lenguas Mayas, COMG, ULEU, and Pueblos Mayas. The list would grow by dozens more if smaller and municipio-based organizations were included.

16. I am reasonably sure that ladino identity and consciousness in Chimaltenango does not diverge radically from that of ladinos in other highland departments. The case of middle-sector and elite ladinos from the capital city is a much more open question. On the one hand, it would seem likely that because capital city ladinos do not face the daily challenge of indigenous ascendancy they can afford to be more liberal and tolerant. On the other hand, those who hold the most extremist views, of the type documented by Casaús Arzú (1991), are almost exclusively concentrated in the capital city.

17. I also read the passage of Don Antonio's words to Yolanda, who assured me that these sentiments would be shared by many people she knows.

18. In a ceremonial lunch in Zaragoza, attended by then-president de Leon Carpio, the departmental governor of Chimaltenango is reported to have eulogized Zaragozans for having responded so readily to the Patzicía ladinos' call for help in squelching the Indian rebellion. "You sharpened your machetes, mounted your horses, and galloped off without a second thought," he recalled poetically. Adams (1992) reports that ladinos from Patzicía were more reticent in talking about these events, which would make sense since the history forms part of their direct experience. I have not extensively interviewed ladinos from Patzicía.

19. Interviewed in June 1995. In one variation, the plan is said to have encompassed the entire department. Patzicía was to be the catalyst for this broader uprising. For reference to the neighboring municipio of San Andrés Itzapa, see chapter 5.

20. Adams (1990, 1992) has done the most exhaustive research reconstructing the details of the conflict.

21. The exceptions to this rule are those few ladinos who, for various reasons, have developed a relationship of unusual solidarity with indigenous chimaltecos. In the case of one such man, the thrust of his recollection is almost exactly the inverse: "they killed many Indians." See chapter 6.

22. Interviewed in December 1994 and late 1997. I take this reference as further

confirmation of the prominence of the Patzicía conflict in ladino collective memories. Though it is of course possible that an insurgent attack was planned to commemorate the events of Patzicía, this seems unlikely. If the guerrilla assigned a special importance to October 19, it is much more likely it had to do with the national significance of that date (inception of the 1944 revolution), rather than the local history.

23. The story continues as a family member reportedly assures the mayor that his power isn't eternal either, and "fijese Ud. soon thereafter the earthquake leveled the building to rubble." This version is clearly apocryphal because the mayor in question came to power after the earthquake of 1976. In less guarded circumstances, the coda might well have taken a slightly different course: "Fijese Ud., soon thereafter the mayor was assassinated." The mayor was killed on the street in October of 1980.

24. The term "raza ladina" (ladino race) is frequently used by ladinos chimaltecos but, upon further questioning, rarely defended in strictly biological terms. Unlike the oligarchy studied by Casaús Arzú, these ladinos generally admit to some distant ancestral admixture of "Indian blood" in their family lines, or at least answer the question equivocally.

25. Don Rolando's bitterness also has a much more personal source. When the guerrilla occupied Comalapa in 1981, they killed his brother. I lack clear information about why Rolando's brother was targeted.

26. Interview in late 1995, date unknown.

27. "Overlap" often implies direct competition, most evident in the case of development-oriented NGOs, which in turn certainly plays a part in the tensions. Competition does not only occur between ladino-controlled and Maya NGOs. It is well known in Chimaltenango that certain of the major Maya NGOs sustain fierce rivalries among themselves. It is significant how easily these tensions become racialized.

28. Interview in October 1995.

29. This includes many ladinos whose contact with Maya organization is minimum to nil. They are much more apt to comment, for example, on Rigoberta Menchú's prominence in the news media ("she has passed us by"), on frustrations with an Indian boss in their workplace, or difficulties in getting young Indian girls to work as domestics, than on Maya activism in language policy, educational reform, or other areas.

30. Those who seem disinclined to use the discourse are, first, strongly Maya-identified ladinos, who do not perceive Maya activism as offensive or exclusionary; second, ladinos who espouse such an extreme racism that they have trouble even imagining Indians with enough initiative to generate an ideology of reverse racism; and third, those who identify as neither indígena nor ladino, or perhaps as both. The first two groups are not large enough to invalidate the claim; the third raises more complex issues, addressed in chapter 6.

31. Although personal and professional rivalries should not be ruled out of

consideration, the divergent contents of the two books' theses, and the highly charged character of the issues involved, go a long ways toward explaining the sharp disagreement and mutual critique that resulted.

32. This made ladinos oppressors, not as initiators but as servile intermediaries, utterly dependent—culturally, economically, politically—on the European metropole. As noted in chapter 1, Guzmán Böckler dubbed the ladino a ser ficticio, defined by the negation of everything Indian, and inclined toward *vasallaje intelectual* (intellectual subordination) in the face of everything European. Guzmán Böckler and Herbert denounced ladino racism with a vigor without precedent in Guatemalan social science. For a more fully elaborated analysis of ladino identity, see also Guzmán Böckler (1975).

33. This sentence does not begin to do justice to Martínez's historical narrative; indeed, it is taken more directly from his later (1973) essay, written as a polemic against the Guzmán Böckler–Herbert thesis. Nonetheless, the premises of this later essay are all present, woven into the historical narrative of *La patria del criollo*, and more explicitly stated in that book's final chapter.

34. Martínez Peláez (1973:37). His concerns about the growing popularity of Guzmán Böckler's thesis are revealed later on in the essay, in a reference to "many young intellectuals…that passionately embrace the thesis of racial struggle in Guatemala…acknowledge in themselves some autochthonous racial features, and…make the mistake of believing that these features are the motive for the bourgeoisie to scorn them" (1973:42).

35. Interview with Dr. Carlos Guzmán Böckler, September 1995.

36. For more on the FIN, see chapters 2 and 3.

37. My evidence on this point is anecdotal. I suspect that contemporary Maya intellectuals tend to downplay the influence of this text to avoid giving the impression that their own intellectual bearings were unduly influenced by the writings of a ladino.

38. These assertions are based largely on Guzmán Böckler's own recollections and analysis; they are corroborated by Yolanda, who attended his lectures during precisely this period.

39. I have been surprised to hear, more than once, ladinos use the charged reflexive verb *"civilizarse"* to describe changes in their own consciousness and practice toward indígenas. This is another indication, in my view, that ladino racial consciousness is deeply marked by a general awareness of the history of their relations of racial oppression with Indians.

40. Public Education is perhaps the most prominent place where this new set of conditions prevails. See chapter 2 for data on teachers and educational administrators in Chimaltenango.

41. I use the term "hegemony" in the Gramscian sense (Gramsci 1971), to refer to the active mobilization of consent by partial concessions to subordinate peoples' demands, and articulation of their consciousness to the logic of the dominant bloc.

Ladinos make an active critique of classic racism, which in turn allows them to use the mantle of antiracist principle to strengthen their position. The reference, then, is to a process of cultural-political struggle, not simply to the coercive political domination. Secondary sources that have guided my understanding of the term include Hall (1986), Adamson (1980), and Mouffe (1979).

42. Ladino politicians and public figures now are beginning to monitor their speech to avoid racial insensitivities, lest attention be called to them by colleagues or by the media. For example, in a recent speech a ladino candidate for mayor in Chimaltenango used the phrase "raza indígena," which afterward was the subject of critique by others connected with the campaign who knew better.

43. Such scrutiny would need to be focused on commonsense premises associated with the inequities to which indígenas are subject. Examples would include the assumption that indígenas are rural, poor, and uneducated; the association of negative "cultural" attributes to indigenous people (e.g., impulsive, tradition bound, authoritarian); and so on. Those who perpetrate these assumptions might well subscribe to the critique of biological precepts as well.

44. This definition does have its share of ambiguities. How much structural-institutional power does one group need in order to be "racist" toward another? By this definition, is it not conceivable that two groups each have sufficient power to be "racist" toward the other? These questions have no simple answer. They do demonstrate the principal advantage of this definition: to focus the analyst's attention on institutionalized power relations rather than individual discourse and practice. For a sustained analysis of racial processes that puts this definition to productive use, see Winant (2001).

45. For an example of Morales's notion of Maya racism toward ladinos, see his "Otra vuelta de la misma tortilla tostada," Parts 1, 2, and 3, dated 28 August, 30 August, and 2 September 1995, respectively, all published in *Siglo XXI*.

46. See the exchange between Juan Zevallos Aguilar (*La Hora*, 18 March 1995) and Mario Roberto Morales (*Siglo XXI*, 28 August, 30 August, and 2 September). The assertion regarding Maya "strategic essentialism" is made by Zevallos.

47. Theorists of the new racism include: Gilroy (1987), Balibar (1991), Goldberg (1993, 2002), Michaels (1992), and Taguieff (2001).

48. In the European context, the immediate object of this line of reasoning is the culturally different immigrant (African, Afro-Caribbean, Indian, Muslim, Turkish, etc.), and the policy mandate to separate off those who have arrived and to prevent more from coming. In the United States, especially California, the logic is slightly different, since so much hinges on the (more blatantly cynical) alleged unfairness of illegal immigrants who are burdening the state, "getting something for nothing."

49. As feminist theorists have amply demonstrated, the effort to situate oneself as the producer of knowledge is fundamental to the formal content of the knowledge itself. By extension, the standpoint of the critic forms part of the content of the

criticism itself. See, among many others, Collins (2000), Haraway (1988), and Harding (1993).

50. This interview with General Otzoy was done by the Spanish journalist Enrique Ortego (1994).

51. It would make little sense to expend this effort if ladinos were completely intransigent, unalterably committed (materially or ideologically) to the emergent struggle for hegemony. But I contend that, at least in Chimaltenango, most do not clearly fit this description. Their stance is much more ambivalent.

Chapter 5

1. The image appears in Taussig's (1993) book, *Mimesis and Alterity*.

2. Key works, encompassing various perspectives, include Schirmer (1998), Green (1994), Le Bot (1995), Stoll (1993), Falla (1994), Figueroa (1991), and Carlsen (1997).

3. This interview took place in November 1995.

4. These were Eduardo Stein, minister of Foreign Relations, and Gustavo Porras, secretary of the President.

5. A number of the essays in the collection titled *¿Racismo en Guatemala? Abriendo debate sobre un tema tabú* (Arenas, Hale, and Palma 1999), engage with and advance this notion of "new racism." See especially, Casaús Arzú (1999) and Cojtí (1999).

6. Myself included. The review of current thinking on ethnicity in my book on Nicaragua is largely dismissive of the theoretical notion of primordialism (Hale 1994b).

7. For a full rendition of this argument, see Maybury-Lewis (1994).

8. This is one of the principal methodological tenets of the "ethnography of speaking" approach in linguistic anthropology, pioneered by Joel Sherzer (1983) and others.

9. This interview took place in November 1995.

10. He probably means the Rabina Ajau in Cobán.

11. See Omi and Winant (1987). An updated volume was published in 1994.

12. This phrase comes from Aretxaga's posthumously published review essay, "Maddening States" (2003).

13. Examples of the former would be Castoriadis (1987) and Žižek (1997). Gaonkar (2002) makes the cogent point that this approach inevitably ends up substituting a new master narrative for the one that is displaced.

14. The closest he gets is to suggest that, in the study of identity politics, the "suture" between interpellation and self-making can ultimately be understood with recourse to the analysis of psychic processes. See, for example, Hall (1996b). While this acknowledgement is a major step toward Lacan, it remains a long way from a useful synthesis of the two analytic frames.

15. See, for example, McCreery (1994), Smith (1990d), Taracena (1997), Rodas (1999), Pinto (1986), and especially the recently published CIRMA study on interethnic relations coordinated by Arturo Taracena Arriola (2002). Another recently published study by Isabel Rodas Nuñez (2004) places the key transformation somewhat earlier, in the final phase of colonial rule.

16. A major point of disputed historical interpretation concerns the relationship between these two groups within the historic bloc. C. A. Smith tends to portray "the white Creole elite" as the "real owners and rulers of Guatemala" and ladinos as their "agents" (1990d:89). Taracena, in contrast, argues that after 1871 ladinos took power in political and economic terms, relegating Euro-Guatemalans to the role of powerful allies in a ladino-controlled project of nation-state building (personal communication and Taracena [1997]). Important implications for the development of the ladino and white identity categories follow. These issues, though crucial, cannot be pursued here.

17. The term comes from Brackette Williams (1989), who also provides a useful framework for understanding nation-state building in multicultural societies.

18. There is a certain similarity here to the way Richard Flores writes of the Alamo as "master symbol." The Alamo, he explains, is "constitutive, not merely reflective, of the material and social changes...of Texas modern" (Flores 2002:10). There is a key difference, though, in the sense that the insurrectionary Indian, as epitomizing symbol, plays a shadowy and intermittent role in public discourse, rather than a central and explicit one. This primary location in the social imaginary gives my use of "epitomizing symbol" a different valence. It would be interesting, by extension, to identify the more direct analogue of the "insurrectionary Indian" in the story that Flores tells of the emergence of "Texas modern."

19. This is not to say that ladinos never came up with specific evidence to substantiate their fears. My taxista once reflected on his childhood relations with Indians in this way: "We grew up playing together and all that. We were *cuates* [friends and peers]. But there came a moment when they started acting really strangely. What I remember most is when they said 'We're going to take your women.' Or, 'I'm going to take your sister.' I didn't understand why they were saying this."

20. I have Yolanda to thank for orchestrating this conversation. She knew Samuel, and probably assumed that a rum drinking session among the three of us at *Los Aposentos* would bring out some good material for my study. At one point early on in his discourse on indigenous sexuality, he turned to Yolanda and indicated that perhaps he should stop out of respect for her. She protested vigorously, urging him to continue in the interest of "anthropological knowledge." Samuel concluded his monologue with a smug grin, asserting that the ladino man has a much greater ability to satisfy the indigenous woman because the Indian man copulates simply "out of physical necessity, animal needs of reproduction. That's why so many indigenous women prefer ladinos." This conversation, like so many in the genre, had a

tongue-in-cheek quality, alternating between straightfaced assertions and "humor chapín." Although the context does demand that we take all that was said with a grain of salt, Samuel's tone indicated that a good part of what he said was serious, and that this was something he had repeated to others many times before.

21. "La hija de nadie" from *15 Exitos de Yolanda del Río* (RCA 1983).

22. In one case, a prominent ladino writer and social scientist named Mario Monteforte Toledo reportedly engaged in a biological experiment: having a child with an indigenous woman, and raising the child in a ladino milieu, to see what the effects of mestizaje might be. This experiment, well known in ladino intellectual circles, was too explicit and brazen to fit within the general pattern of normalized transgression. More details of the case are provided by Nelson (1999:227–228), without naming the individual.

23. I enlisted a ladino psychologist, Renato Gellner, to help me think through this topic, using his own upbringing in the capital city as point of departure. At a certain point in the interview, the discussion brought up his own memory of having been with a group of young adult men who encountered an Indian woman at night alone. Some of the boys raped her, while Gellner watched in horror. After telling the story he reflected on the underlying mentality: "The indigenous woman is seen as an object to be hunted, trapped, and used sexually. That's the way I interpreted that incident and *me shockió tremendamente* (it shocked me deeply) because it was the first time I had been exposed to such behavior."

24. As Borneman (1998) convincingly notes in his analysis of sexual violence in the Bosnian conflict, although the general practice is widespread, explanations need to be tied carefully to the specifics of each case. Better answers to this "why" question in the context of the state violence of the 1980s would no doubt shed light on the specific explanatory problem at hand here: ladino fears of Maya ascendancy that include sexual violence against them. Yet, given this admonition, Borneman's own explanation—a general assertion that "state sovereignty" and "reproductive hetero-sexuality" are deeply intertwined—seems too sweeping. It calls crucial attention to a general relationship, but does little to specify a process that could then be examined in other contexts.

25. After reading this chapter, Yolanda agreed with the basic analysis, but argued that my ethnographic evidence in the psychosexual realm came almost exclusively from men. Ladina women, she claimed, rarely express such anxieties in the same terms, which so clearly construct women as an extension of male property, seized and violated by the "insurrectionary Indian" in much the same way as they would land or other goods. Ladina women, Yolanda claimed, are much more concerned about their own social position. Their anxieties, then, tend to revolve around competition from Indian women and, by extension, from any social interaction that might minimize the social distance between themselves and Indians. In Yolanda's view, ironically enough, ladino men fear being displaced by Maya men, while ladina women fear being mistaken for Maya. Since Yolanda is completely right that my

evidence on this point comes almost wholly from males, I will let her correction stand without further commentary.

26. For further analysis along these lines, see Hale (1999).

27. Marco Antonio Flores (1996:3).

28. For a thorough analysis of this political process surrounding the Consulta Popular, see: Warren (2002). Demetrio Cojtí, vice-minister of Education under Portillo, explained in a public lecture how hearing the epithet "xumos" assigned to the FRG convinced him to join the party. The epithet is one of a host of derogatory terms for lower-class Indian.

Chapter 6

1. The classic reference is Althusser (1971). For a good recent anthropological analysis of subject formation (or what she calls "subject making" in especially nuanced terms, see Ong (1996). Stuart Hall (1996b) has laid out the subject formation/self-making relationship with characteristic clarity.

2. The concept of everyday resistance comes originally from Scott (1990); for an anthropological critique of resistance with a similar message see Abu-Lughod (1990). My assertion is not meant to dismiss everyday resistance, but rather to insist on asking questions about its articulation to broader political processes, in the Gramscian sense.

3. See, for example, figure 6.1 and the epigraph for chapter 7.

4. On the one hand, ladinos have at times lashed out against the Euro-Guatemalan elite—a political initiative generally explained in antioligarchical class terms, with only faint racial undertones; on the other hand, Guatemalan political history since the nineteenth century shows evidence of fusion, whereby Euro-Guatemalans assume a place within the omnibus ladino identity category, at least in the context of public political machinations. Key contributions to this debate come from Taracena (1997), Casaús Arzú (1991), Rodas Núñez (2004), and Smith (1990d).

5. For a thorough examination of this mestizaje ideology, see Gould (1998), Stutzman (1981), and Wade (1997).

6. For evidence of widespread sexual transgression, see chapter 5.

7. Ironically, this policing amounted to a parochial version of the same practice in which elite Euro-Guatemalans engaged, except that the targets in these cases were ladinos themselves (and Indians too, of course, but this threat was much more remote). Marta Elena Casaús Arzú, author of the 1991 path-breaking study of "racism and lineage" among Guatemala's elite, recounted to me how, on the eve of the book's Guatemalan publication, she received an urgent phone call from the patriarch of the Díaz Durán family, who pleaded with her to excise evidence that represented his family as mixed with ladinos. Díaz Durán and her other interview subjects apparently were much more concerned about her representation of

impurities in their bloodline than of the shockingly racist sensibilities that this very concern, and much of Casaús Arzú's interview material, substantiates.

8. Indian challenges, both resistance and more subtle forms, have been much studied by others and are beyond the scope of this work. See Handy (1989), Grandin (2000), Martínez Peláez (1991), and Smith (1990a) among many others.

9. Depending on one's interpretation, the search for prior challenges could begin much further back, to the early colonial church-crown disputes over the status of Indian souls. I have delimited the topic considerably (and somewhat arbitrarily) to begin with the decade of the October Revolution on the grounds that this is the earliest period that exerted direct influence on ladinos I interviewed in the present.

10. See, for example, Handy (1989) and Forster (1998). On racial formation in general during the decade of social reform, see Palma (1991), Wasserstrom (1975), and Adams (1970, 1990).

11. Of my roughly twenty-five interviews with ladinos solidarios, at least three others espoused views very close to those of Morquecho. All three had work trajectories roughly similar to his.

12. As Arturo Taracena and his CIRMA colleagues have argued (2002), in an exhaustive historical review of state policies and practices toward Indians since the late nineteenth century, ladino statecraft proceeded according to an insistent principle of separate and unequal, veiled in a thin veneer of liberal universalism.

13. Two of the four, the Xinca and the Garífuna, are tiny numerically, but important for their role in cementing the model of various peoples coming together under a single state.

14. The initiative had great progressive potential, not for the substance of the tax itself (which, in fact, was already on the books but abysmally enforced), but rather for the stipulation that it be collected and used by local governments.

15. The most intense disturbances around the announcement of the IUSI took place in the department of Totonicapan. The government accused the protestors of being manipulated by opposing political forces, and the protestors countered demanding respect for their dissent. See, for example, "Piden respeto del Presidente" (*Prensa Libre*, 12 March 1998).

16. I do not have a good explanation for this racial epithet. The term "negro" is occasionally used as a deprecatory reference to Indians, but in my experience in Chimaltenango this is uncommon. A more likely explanation, in my view, is that the author of the graffiti sought the most powerfully denigrating epithet in the transnational racial vocabulary, and settled on "negro" as the chosen term. For another example along similar lines, see the epigraph to chapter 7.

17. See Rodriguez (2002). This is one of a rapidly growing genre of academic, high-brow popular, and mainstream interventions with a similar message.

18. The reader should keep in mind that these figures are specific to 1998 levels and exchange rates.

19. I never had the chance to interview Yuri's younger sister. Judging from

Yuri's description, it would have been fascinating as well: "My sister…is half-crazy in a lot of ways. She does well in school, but she has a lot of crazy ideas. She wants to be in the army, but in her notebooks she has pictures of Comandante Marcos and Ché Guevara. She is super rebellious, but she says that she wants to do something to defend the country. When the high school principal brought a television in for people to see the Soccer World Cup, she protested. She likes to dance and all that: when she sees someone do a mortal she gets all excited."

20. These words translate roughly as "shrewd," "rascal," "lazy," and "foxy."

21. The rough equivalent of whites addressing adult African Americans as "hey boy." The added complexity is the "vos"—a familiar pronoun that would never be used between two strangers of equal status.

22. The use of "usted" in Guatemala is more complicated still because it can be a marker of both hierarchy or distance, and great intimacy. This latter permutation, well beyond the scope of my analysis here, does not affect the basic observation on Berta's dilemma.

23. In the Leonidas high school's anonymous survey of student identities, 45 percent answered indigenous, 38 percent answered mestizo, and 17 percent ladino. In a survey of a class on the USAC Extension campus, a few years earlier, the percentages were 9, 44, and 34, respectively. Mestizo clearly is an identity category that analysts of Guatemalan identity politics must come to terms with.

24. A similar phrase is apparently common in Brazil. See Ramos (1998:69).

25. About one-fourth of my total sample of twenty five ladinos solidarios identified as ladino. The Franja group (see chapter 5) split 50-50 on this basic ladino-mestizo identity question.

26. I am indebted to Arturo Taracena Arriola, who shared with me his unpublished manuscript, a historical study of Guadalupanismo in Guatemala (n.d.).

27. I was unfortunately unable to interview Blanca Gálvez.

28. For references on hybridity theory as they relate to this argument, see my essay (Hale 1999).

29. Mario Roberto Morales (1998) has deployed this ostensibly progressive cultural theory to deconstruct the Maya movement to the dismay of his advisor, leading cultural studies theorist John Beverley. Diane Nelson (1999) avoided this problem by deploying this theory mainly to deconstruct dominant actors and the state. Even her "Maya hacker" gains substance mainly in his/her critique of the dominant; if the theory were applied across the board to include the Maya as well, it is hard to see how she would avoid convergence with the position Mario Roberto Morales defends.

30. This is a standard pattern in Latin America. See Smith (1995), Stolcke (1991), and Gilliam (1988) for summaries.

31. It is unclear to me why Yolanda remembered the scandal so clearly for Don Rigoberto's sister and not for him. In part, this follows the standard "whitening" pattern, whereby an ambitious and economically ascendant "Indian" gains the right

to "marry up." This path would generally be much more accepted for men than for women, thus the greater reaction when a woman crossed the race line.

32. My evidence on this point is anecdotal, mainly from discussions with friends who work in the Landivar University in the capital city, who described the sensibilities of their students from mainly elite backgrounds. This identity issue became more charged with the entrance of a large number of indigenous fellowship students into the university in the late 1990s. The fellowships were financed by USAID.

33. João Vargas's (2004) essay on the hyperconsciousness of race in Brazil influenced my thinking on this point.

34. Don Luis, Yolanda's father, epitomizes this point of view. It is also epitomized by the ladinos of Zaragoza, where Abelardo works as a teacher, and where he made his defiant gesture of resistance to the "identity" form. This is significant because the other teachers from Zaragoza marked "ladino," with full claims to the associated prerogatives. To mark only "Guatemalan" in this context, is—at least rhetorically—to renounce those prerogatives.

35. In his response to the "identity question," he said, "I am of mixed ancestry," a family split between ladino and indigenous branches. Many have the tendency, in this case, to suppress the indigenous in favor of the ladino hegemony. Zavala advocates a different solution: "neither indigenous nor ladino, but Christian."

36. The most extended work of Morales on this topic is his book, *La articulación de las diferencias* (1998)

Chapter 7

1. See for example, "Brown v. Board, 50 Years Later," a four-part series in the *Detroit News*, available at http://www.detnews.com/specialreports/2004/brown-vboard/; "*Brown* At 50: King's Dream or Plessy's Nightmare?" (17 January 2004) available at http://www.civilrightsproject.harvard.edu/research/reseg04/resegregation 04.php.

2. This is not as radical a departure from recent work on Guatemala as it might seem. Diane Nelson (1999), for example, emphasizes convergent premises in deployments of racial and ethnic terminologies, and avoids both as theoretical frames; Kay Warren (1997) details the fallacies associated with the deployment of ethnicity in Maya studies, and in general seems to rely very little on ethnicity theory to frame her analysis. Carol Smith (1999), in a comprehensive overview of Maya studies, calls for greater attention to racial processes.

3. For an example of this comparative approach, see chapter 4 of E. T. Gordon's *Disparate Diasporas* (1998); one of the only general contemporary treatments is Wade (1997).

4. In a lengthy polemic against the sloppy overuse of the related concept "identity," Brubaker and Cooper (2000) draw a basic distinction between "categories of practice" deployed by "ordinary social actors" for political purposes *versus* the "cate-

gories of analysis" used for strictly academic ends. This firewall between political and analytical terminologies, in turn, purportedly offers a ready rationale for "our" continued use of terms such as "ethnic" despite dissent on the part of indigenous intellectual-activists. I find this absolute distinction impossible to defend on either ethical or analytical grounds. Granted, analysts and actors do develop specialized and shorthand ways of thinking about what they do and communicating this to others. But actors also analyze, and the work of analysts can have great political impact. To erect the firewall is to suppress these complexities, rather than subject them to critical scrutiny as well.

5. See, for example, Appelbaum, Macpherson, and Rosenblatt (2003), de la Cadena (2000), Poole (1997), Smith (1995), and Weismantel (1997, 2001). Among Guatemalan scholars, prominent examples include the collection of essays in Hecht and Palma (2004) and the work of Casaús Arzú (1991, 1999). That the AVANCSO series on racism will include the present volume is another example.

6. The fact that this same trend did not occur in scholarship on black Latin Americans is what gave rise to the uncomfortable analytical divergence mentioned earlier. To my knowledge, the intellectual genealogy of this divergence has yet to be explored, although Wade (1997) has laid some important groundwork.

7. Scholarship on whiteness has burgeoned in recent years and I have no intention of providing either an exhaustive review of or a systematic analytical engagement with its many currents. I have drawn principally on the classic originating works, beginning with W. E. B. Du Bois and through the more contemporary contributions of Frankenberg (1994), Roediger (1991), Morrison (1992), and Lipsitz (1995). The edited collections I have reviewed and found useful include those edited by Frankenberg (1997), Fine et al. (1997), and Levine-Rasky (2002). Robyn Wiegman's recent review essay exerted an orienting influence on my analysis (1999), and I am especially grateful to John Hartigan, for allowing me to read two chapters of his forthcoming book *Odd Tribes* (2005), which provides an extensive review of and critical engagement with the whiteness literature.

8. I have never forgotten a time, early on in my dissertation research in Nicaragua, when a black (Creole) Nicaraguan introduced me in a community meeting of Creoles and Miskitu Indians: "This is Charlie; he's an anthropologist; anthropologists study" he paused, unsure how to finish his own sentence, and then finally found his voice, "anthropologists study people like us."

9. Since the debate on racial formation in Guatemala is recent and incipient, the back and forth cannot be referenced in the published scholarly literature. I have gleaned these three objections from dialogue with colleagues, both Guatemalan and foreign, in a diversity of settings.

10. The racial formation approach was originally named by Omi and Winant (1987), following on a long tradition of race-centered analysis. Winant's more recent book (2001) extends this analysis in important ways. Even to call it an "approach" may exaggerate the extent to which it is bounded and unitary. See also: Goldberg

(2002) and Harrison (1995). In developing these ideas, I have been especially influenced by the writing of, and ongoing dialogue with, Edmund T. Gordon.

11. This debate is most well developed in relation to race in Brazil, especially since Pierre Bourdieu and Lois Wacquant (1999) launched their critique of Michael Hanchard's monograph, *Orpheus and Power* (1994). Voluminous commentary around that exchange followed, including Hanchard's (2003) response.

12. Most of the extensive writing in the tradition of the Latin American nationalist and revolutionary Left strikes these themes. A classic work along these lines is Eduardo Galeano's, *Open Veins of Latin America* (1971). For a historical work that advances an especially trenchant version of this argument, see Burns (1980).

13. On blanqueamiento, see Gilliam (1988); specifically in relation to Guatemala, see Guzmán Böckler and Herbert (1971).

14. For an excellent summary of the Du Boisian legacy in anthropology, with implications for this broader realm of analysis, see Harrison (1992).

15. Key works in racial formation theory can be found in note 10 of this chapter.

16. See, for example, the recently published work of Ana Cumes (2004), and various works in the edited volume *Racismo en Guatemala* (Arenas, Hale, and Palma 1999). Diane Nelson (1999) also makes this point.

17. George Lipsitz (1998) has written extensively on this concept; see also Frankenberg (1997), McIntosh (1995), and Dalton (1995).

18. *Against Race* is the title of Paul Gilroy's recent text (2000). The thrust of much of Judith Butler's work urges us to move "beyond identity." See Butler (1990, 1993).

19. This is the principal critique of the "beyond identity" genre put forth by the authors of the edited volume *Reclaiming Identity* (Moya and Hames-Garcia 2000).

20. The critique of identity-based racial politics is best exemplified by the recent work of Paul Gilroy (2000, 2003). The questioning of antiracist politics grounded centrally in an analysis of racial dominance is a recurrent theme in John Hartigan's forthcoming book *Odd Tribes* (2005). Skepticism of racial formation as a generalized analytical approach is the principal issue at play in Bourdieu and Wacquant's (1999) critique of Michael Hanchard.

21. An example here would be Aiwa Ong's (1996) analysis of racial processes among Asian Americans in the United States. While promising to provide a balanced view of subject formation and self-making, her emphasis is almost completely on the former. To be fair, this imbalance may be attributed in part to her effort to contest work on cultural citizenship in which she sees the pendulum as having swung too far in the opposite direction.

22. This is my criticism of the otherwise insightful and valuable work of Eduardo Bonilla-Silva on "racism without racists" (2003).

23. This is my impression, for example, of many of the works in the collection, *Critical Race Theory* (Delgado 1995).

24. When Stuart Hall, the master synthesizer of complex theoretical ideas, argued a few years ago that the critical problem in theories of identity is the "suture" between processes of subject formation on the one hand, and self-making on the other, it was hard not to hear echoes of that previous formulation (1996b). His essay continues to serve as a key theoretical reference for the ideas presented in this paragraph.

25. Black feminists have been central in developing the notion of intersectionality. Key works that I consulted include Carby (1982), Collins (2000), Combahee River Collective (1983), hooks (1984), and Sudbury (1998).

26. This does not fully render the charged racial meanings of the use of the "vos" form between ladinos and Indians. For more explanation of this point, see chapter 6.

27. There is an interesting historic parallel here in the debates over the elimination of forced labor during the final period of the decade of social democratic reforms (1944–1954). Those who opposed the measure feared that they would deprive coffee plantations of essential labor to harvest the crop. Once promulgated, however, these reforms provided an even more effective guarantee: "voluntary" participation in the labor market based on economic need.

28. This approach to understanding neoliberalism draws on critiques of liberalism (e.g., Mehta [1997]), and on theories of governmentality inspired by Foucault (e.g., Gordon [1991], Rose [1999]) as well as more epochal analyses, such as that provided by Hardt and Negri (2000). I differ from these theorists, however, in my preference to interpret the transformations through a Gramscian lens. See, for example, Hale (2002).

29. I develop this argument further in Hale (2004).

30. See Cohen (2004) and Rodriguez (2002).

Glossary

abolengo, high race-class lineage

alcadías indígenas, indigenous mayoralties

blanqueamiento, whitening

caballería (unit of land area), equivalent to 47 hectares and 114 acres

cabecera municipal, county seat

camaradas, comrades

cangrejos, literally, crabs; figuratively, backward-looking reactionaries

chapín, Guatemalan

chavo, neighborhood peer

chingadera, banter laden with humor, irony, and mutual ribbing

choleros, bearers of Indian blood

cofradías, religious brotherhoods

comandante, political-military commander

comisionado militar, military commissioner

costumbristas, those loyal to longstanding indigenous customs

de corte, indigenous

dos demonios, two devils

emancipación india, Indian emancipation

feria, festival

guerra étnica, ethnic war

guerrillero, guerrilla combatant

humor chapín, Guatemalan sense of humor

indianista, Indianist

indio permitido, authorized Indian

inidios bochincheros, unruly redskins

injerto, graft

interculturalidad, tolerance and mutual respect

ladinos solidarios, ladinos who practice solidarity toward Indians

lo cristiano, the notion of things Christian

lo guatemalteco, the notion of things Guatemalan

lo maya, the notion of things Maya

lucha racial, racial struggle

mara, youth gang

mancha mongólica, patch of dark skin on the lower back of a newborn

manzana (unit of land area), .7 hectares

mestizaje, assimilationist ideology of racial mixture

miedos atávicos, atavistic fears

modernizantes, modernizers

municipio, township, municipality

patojo/a, young man/woman

patrón, boss

petate, woven mat

pueblo, nation, masses

racismo al revés, reverse racism

raza, race

raza indígena, the indigeous race

ropa tumbada, baggy clothing

salón, hall

señoríos, nobility

ser ficticio, ficticious being

sí pero, yes, but

superación, betterment

técnicos, staff teachers

tío, uncle

traje típico, Indian clothing

traje, clothing

trato de iguales, treatment as equals

vos, term of familiar address

¿verdad?, You know what I mean?

¿y qué?, And now what? But also, so what?

References

Abu-Lughod, Lila
1990 The Romance of Resistance: Tracing Transformations of Power through Bedouin Women. *American Ethnologist* 17(1):41–55.

Adams, Richard N.
1956 Encuesta sobre la cultura de los ladinos en Guatemala. Guatemala: Seminario de Integración Social Guatemalteca.
1970 *Crucifixion by Power.* Austin: University of Texas Press.
1990 Ethnic Images and Strategies in 1944. In *Guatemalan Indians and the State, 1540–1988.* C. A. Smith, ed. Pp. 141–162. Austin: University of Texas Press.
1992 Las masacres de Patzicía en 1944: Una reflexion. *Winak* 7(1–4):3–20.

Adams, Tani Marielena
1978 "San Martín Jilotepeque: Aspects of Political and Socioeconomic Structure of a Guatemalan Peasant Community." BA Thesis, University of Texas.

Adamson, Walter L.
1980 *Hegemony and Revolution: A Study of Antonio Gramsci's Political and Cultural Theory.* Berkeley: University of California Press.

Althusser, L.
1971 *Lenin and Philosophy.* New York: Monthly Review Press.

Appelbaum, Nancy P., Anne S. Macpherson, and Karin Alejandra Rosenblatt
2003 *Race and Nation in Modern Latin America.* Chapel Hill: University of North Carolina Press.

Arenas, Clara, Charles R. Hale, and Gustavo Palma Murga
1999 *Racismo en Guatemala? Abriendo debate sobre un tema tabu.* Guatemala: AVANCSO.

Aretxaga, Begoña
2003 Maddening States. *Annual Review of Anthropology* 32:393–410.

Asturias, Miguel Ángel
1923 *Sociologia Guatemalteca.* M. Ahern, trans. Tempe: Arizona State University Center for Latin American Studies.

AVANCSO

1998   *Imágenes homogéneas en un país de rostros diversos: El sistema educativo formal y la conforma-ción de referentes de identidad nacional entre jóvenes Guatemaltecos.* Guatemala: AVANCSO.

Baker, Lee

1998   *From Savage to Negro. Anthropology and the Construction of Race, 1896–1954.* Berkeley: University of California Press.

Balibar, Etienne

1991   Is there a "Neo-Racism"? In *Race, Nation, Class: Ambiguous Identities.* E. Balibar and I. Wallerstein, eds. Pp. 17–29. London: Verso.

Barrett, Dennis

1970   Gente: Esteban Lopez. *Fijese* 1:22–37.

Barrios, Lina E.

1998   *La alcaldía indígena en Guatemala: De 1944 al presente.* Guatemala: Universidad Rafael Landivar, Instituto de Investigaciones Económicas y Sociales.

Bastos, Santiago, and Manuela Camus

2003   *Entre el mecapal y el cielo.* Guatemala: FLACSO.

Bastos, Santiago, and Domingo Hernández Ixcoy

2004   Violencia, memoria y diferencia: Resarcimiento y Pueblo Maya en Guatemala. P. 35. Unpublished report in author's possession.

Bhabha, Homi

1990   The Third Space. Interview with Homi Bhabha by J. Rutherford. In *Identity*, edited by J. Rutherford. London: Lawrence and Wishant.

Bonfíl Batalla, Guillermo

1987   *Mexico profundo: Una civilizacion negada.* Mexico: Secretaria de Educación Pública, CIESAS.

Bonilla-Silva, Eduardo

2003   *Racism without Racists: Color-Blind Racism and the Persistence of Racial Inequality in the United States.* Oxford: Rowman and Littlefield.

Borneman, John

1998   *Subversions of International Order: Studies in the Political Anthropology of Culture.* Albany: SUNY Press.

Bourdieu, Pierre, and Loïc Wacquant

1999   On the Cunning of Imperialist Reason. *Theory, Culture, and Society* 16(1):41–58.

Brintall, Douglas

1979   *Revolt against the Dead: The Modernization of a Mayan Community in the Highlands.* New York: Gordon and Breach.

Brosnahan, Tom

1995   *Guatemala, Belize, and Yucatan. La Ruta Maya*. Hawthorn, Australia: Lonely Planet Press.

Brubaker, Rogers, and Frederick Cooper

2000   Beyond Identity. *Theory and Society* 29:1–47.

Burchell, Graham, Colin Gordon, and Peter Miller

1991   *The Foucault Effect: Studies in Governmentality*. Chicago: University of Chicago Press.

Burns, E. Bradford

1980   *The Poverty of Progress: Latin America in the Nineteenth Century*. Berkeley: University of California Press.

Butler, Judith

1990   Gender Trouble, Feminist Theory, and Psychoanalytic Discourse. In *Feminism/Postmodernism*. L. Nicholson, ed. Pp. 324–340. New York: Routledge.

1993   *Bodies that Matter: On the Discursive Limits of "Sex."* New York: Routledge.

Camus, Manuela, and Santiago Bastos

1992   *Quebrando el silencio.* Guatemala: FLACSO.

Carby, Hazel

1982   White Woman Listen! Black Feminism and the Boundaries of Sisterhood. In *The Empire Strikes Back: Race and Racism in {19}70s Britain*. Center for Contemporary Cultural Studies, ed. Pp. 214–233. London: Hutchinson.

Cardoza y Aragón, Luis

1976   ¿Que es ser Guatemalteco? Alero 20: Tercera Epoca.

Carlsen, Robert S.

1997   *The War for the Heart and Soul of a Highland Maya Town*. Austin: University of Texas Press.

Carmack, Robert

1988   *Harvest of Violence: The Maya Indians and the Guatemalan Crisis*. Norman: Oklahoma University Press.

Casaús Arzú, Marta Elena

1991   *Linaje y racismo*. San José: FLACSO.

1999   La metamorfosis del racismo en la elite de poder en Guatemala. In *¿Racismo en Guatemala? Abriendo debate sobre un tema tabú*. C. Arenas, C.R. Hale, and G. Palma, eds. Pp. 47–92. Guatemala: Ediciones Don Quijote.

Castoriadis, Cornelius

1987   *The Imaginary Institution of Society*. Cambridge: MIT Press.

CEIDEC

1990   *Seminario sobre la realidad étnica en Guatemala*. Guatemala: Editorial Praxis.

COCADI

1989   *Cultura Maya y políticas de desarrollo*. B'okob', Guatemala: COCADI.

Cohen, Cathy J.

2004   Deviance as Resistance? A New Research Agenda for the Study of Black Politics. *Du Bois Review: Social Science Research on Race* 1(1):27–45.

Coj Ajbalam, Pedro

1978   Algo sobre la naturaleza del Ixim. *IXIM* 13.

Cojtí Cuxil, Demetrio

1989   Problemas de la "identidad nacional" Guatemalteca. In *Cultura Maya y políticas de desarrollo*. COCADI, ed. Pp. 139–162. Chimaltenango: Ediciones COCADI.

1994a   *Políticas para la reinvindicación de los Mayas de hoy*. Guatemala: Cholsamaj.

1994b   "Unidad del estado mestizo y regiones autónomas mayas." *Siglo Veintiuno*, 28 agosto 1994.

1997   *Ri Maya' Moloj pa Iximulew. El movimiento Maya*. Guatemala City: Editorial Cholsamaj.

1999   Heterofobia y racismo Guatemalteco. In *¿Racismo en Guatemala? Abriendo debate sobre un tema tabú*. C. Arenas, C.R. Hale, and G. Palma, eds. Pp. 193–216. Guatemala: Ediciones Don Quijote.

Collins, Patricia Hill

2000   *Black Feminist Thought: Knowledge, Consciousness, and the Politics of Empowerment*. Boston and London: Unwin Hyman.

Colom, Yolanda

1998   *Mujeres en la alborada*. Guatemala: Artemis y Edinter.

Combahee River Collective

1983   The Combahee River Collective Statement. In *Home Girls: A Black Feminist Anthology*. B. Smith, ed. Pp. 264–274. New York: Kitchen Table Press.

Comisión para el Esclarecimiento Histórico

1999   *Guatemala Memoria del Silencio*. 12 vols. Guatemala: UNOPS.

Cumes, Ana

2004   "Aquí no hay racismo, aquí hay interculturalidad...." Experiencias de trabajo en la Escuela Normal Pedro Molina en Chimaltenango, Guatemala. In *Racismo en Guatemala: De lo políticamente correcto a la lucha antirracista*. M. Heckt and G. Palma Murga, eds. Pp. 41–76. Guatemala: AVANCSO.

Dalton, Harlon

1995   *Racial Healing: Confronting the Fear between Blacks and Whites*. New York: Anchor.

de la Cadena, Marisol

2000   *Indigenous Mestizos: The Politics of Race and Culture in Cuzco, Peru, 1919–1991*. Durham: Duke University Press.

Delgado, Richard
1995   *Critical Race Theory.* Philadelphia: Temple University Press.

Demmers, Jolle, Alex E. Fernández Jilberto, and Barbara Hogenboom
2001   The Transformation of Latin American Populism: Regional and Global Dimensions. In *Miraculous Metamorphoses: The Neoliberalization of Latin American Populism.* J. Demmers, A.E. Fernández Jilberto, and B. Hogenboom, eds. Pp. 1–21. London: Zed.

Dirlik, Arif
1996   The Global in the Local. In *Global/Local: Cultural Production and the Transnational Imaginary.* R. Wilson and W. Dissanayake, eds. Pp. 21–46. Durham: Duke University Press.

Dunkerley, James
1988   *Power in the Isthmus.* London: Verso.

Edwards, Sebastian
1995   *Crisis and Reform in Latin America: From Despair to Hope.* Oxford: Oxford University Press.

Ejército de Guatemala
1963   La muerte de Tecún Umán: Estudio critico de la conquista del altiplano occidental de Guatemala. Guatemala: Editorial del Ejército.

England, Nora
1998   Mayan Efforts toward Language Preservation. In *Endangered Languages, Current Issues and Future Prospects.* L.A. Grenoble and L.J. Whaley, eds. Pp. 99–116. Cambridge: Cambridge University Press.

Esquit, Édgar
2002   *Otros poderes, nuevos desafíos. Relaciones interétnicas en Tecpán y su entorno departamental (1871–1935).* Guatemala: Instituto de Estudios Interétnicos.

Falla, Ricardo
1972   Hacia la revolución verde: Adopción y dependencia del fertilizante químico del Quiche, Guatemala. *Estudios Sociales* 6(6):16–51.
1978   El movimiento indígena. *Estudios Centroamericanos* 356/357(junio–julio):437–461.
1994   *Massacres in the Jungle.* Boulder: Westview.
2001   *Quiche Rebelde: Religious Conversion, Politics, and Ethnic Identity in Guatemala.* Austin: University of Texas Press.

Ferguson, James
1990   *The Anti-Politics Machine: "Development," Depoliticization, and Bureaucratic Power in Lesotho.* New York: Cambridge University Press.

Figueroa Ibarra, Carlos
1991   El recurso del miedo: Ensayo sobre el estado y el terror en Guatemala. San José, Costa Rica: Editorial Universitaria Centroamericana.

Fine, Michelle, Lois Weis, Linda C. Powell, and L. Mun Wong
1997   *Off White: Readings on Race, Power, and Society*. New York: Routledge.

Fischer, Edward F.
2001   *Cultural Logics and Global Economics: Maya Identity in Thought and Practice*. Austin: University of Texas Press.

Fish, Stanley
1993   Reverse Racism, or How the Pot Got to Call the Kettle Black. *Atlantic Monthly*, November 1993.

Flores, Marco Antonio
1996   Todos somos mestizos. *La Ermita*:2–4.

Flores, Richard
2002   *Remembering the Alamo: Memory, Modernity, and the Master Symbol*. Austin: University of Texas Press.

Forster, Cindy
1998   Reforging National Revolution: Campesino Labor Struggles in Guatemala, 1944–1954. In *Identity and Struggle at the Margins of the Nation-State: The Laboring Peoples of Central America and the Hispanic Caribbean*. A. Chomsky and A. Lauria-Santiago, eds. Pp. 196–226. Durham: Duke University Press.

Foucault, Michel
1991   Governmentality. In *The Foucault Effect*. E.A.G. Burchell, ed. Chicago: University of Chicago Press.

Fox, Jonathan A., and L. David Brown
1998   *The Struggle for Accountability: The World Bank, NGOs, and Grassroots Movements*. Cambridge: MIT Press.

Frankenberg, Ruth
1994   *White Women, Race Matters: The Social Construction of Whiteness*. Minneapolis: University of Minnesota Press.
1997   *Displacing Whiteness: Essays in Social and Cultural Criticism*. Durham: Duke University Press.

Fredrickson, George M.
2002   *Racism: A Short History*. Princeton: Princeton University Press.

Fried, Jonathan L., Marvin E. Gettleman, Deborah T. Levenson, and Nancy Peckenham
1983   *Guatemala in Rebellion*. New York: Grove Press.

Gaonkar, Dilip Parameshwar
2002   Toward New Imaginaries: An Introduction. *Public Culture* 14(1):1–19.

Galeano, Eduardo
1971   *Las venas abiertas de América Latina*. Montevideo: Universidad de la República, Departamento de Publicaciones.

García Canclini, Nestor

1989   *Culturas híbridas: Estrategia para entrar y salir de la modernidad.* Mexico: Grijalbo.

Gill, Lesley

2004   *The School of the Americas: Military Training and Political Violence in the Americas.* Durham: Duke University Press.

Gilliam, Angela

1988   Telltale Language: Race, Class and Inequality in Two Latin American Towns. In *Anthropology for the Nineties.* J. Cole, ed. Pp. 522–531. New York: Free Press.

Gilroy, Paul

1987   *"There Ain't No Black in the Union Jack": The Cultural Politics of Race and Nation.* London: Hutchinson.

2000   *Against Race: Imagining Political Culture beyond the Color Line.* Cambridge: Harvard.

2003   After the Great White Error…The Great Black Mirage. In *Race, Nature and the Politics of Difference.* D.S. Moore, A. Pandian, and J. Kosek, eds. Pp. 73–98. Durham: Duke University Press.

Goldberg, David Theo

1993   *Racist Culture: Philosophy and the Politics of Meaning.* London: Blackwell.

2002   *The Racial State.* Malden, MA: Blackwell.

Goldman, Francisco

1999   "Murder Comes for the Bishop." *New Yorker:* 61–77.

2002   Victory in Guatemala. *New York Review of Books* 49(9).

González Ponciano, Jorge Ramón

1993   Guatemala, la civilización y el progreso: Notas sobre indigenismo, racismo e identidad nacional, 1821–1954. Estudios 3a. *Epoca:*33–120.

1999   "Estas sangres no estan limpias": Modernidad y pensamiento civilizatorio en Guatemala (1954–1977). In *Racismo en Guatemala? Abriendo el debate sobre un tema tabú.* C. Arenas, C.R. Hale, and G. Palma, eds. Pp. 15–46. Guatemala: AVANCSO.

Gordon, Colin

1991   Governmental Rationality: An Introduction. In *The Foucault Effect.* G. Burchell, C. Gordon, and P. Miller, eds. Pp. 1–52. Chicago: University of Chicago Press.

Gordon, Edmund T.

1998   *Disparate Diasporas: Identity and Politics in an African-Nicaraguan Community.* Austin: University of Texas Press.

Gould, Jeffrey

1998   *To Die in This Way: Nicaraguan Indians and the Myth of Mestizaje, 1880–1965.* Durham: Duke University Press.

Gramsci, Antonio

1971   *Selections from the Prison Notebooks of Antonio Gramsci.* London: Lawrence & Wishart.

Grandin, Gregory

2000   *Blood of Guatemalans: A History of Race and Nation.* Durham: Duke University Press.

2004   *The Last Colonial Massacre: Latin America in the Cold War.* Chicago: University of Chicago Press.

Green, Linda

1994   Fear as a Way of Life. *Cultural Anthropology* 9(2):227–256.

Guha, Ranajit

1988   The Prose of Counter-Insurgency. In *Selected Subaltern Studies.* R. Guha and G. Spivak, eds. Pp. 45–88. New York and Oxford: Oxford University Press.

Gusterson, Hugh

1996   *Nuclear Rites: A Weapons Laboratory at the End of the Cold War.* Berkeley: University of California Press.

Guzmán Böckler, Carlos

1975   *Guatemala: Colonialismo y revolución.* Mexico: Siglo XXI.

Guzmán Böckler, Carlos, and Jean-Loup Herbert

1971   *Guatemala: Una interpretación histórica social.* Mexico: Siglo XXI.

Hale, Charles R.

1994a   Between Che Guevara and the Pachamama: Mestizos, Indians and Identity Politics in the Anti-Quincentenary Campaign. *Critique of Anthropology* 14(1):9–39.

1994b   *Resistance and Contradiction: Miskitu Indians and the Nicaraguan State, 1894–1987.* Stanford: Stanford University Press.

1997   Consciousness, Violence, and the Politics of Memory in Guatemala. *Current Anthropology* 38(5):817–838.

1999   Travel Warning: Elite Appropriations of Hybridity and Other Progressive Sounding Discourses in Highland Guatemala. *Journal of American Folklore* 112(445):297–315.

2002   Does Multiculturalism Menace? Governance, Cultural Rights and the Politics of Identity in Guatemala. *Journal of Latin American Studies* 34:485–524.

2004   Rethinking Indigenous Politics in the Era of the "Indio Permitido." *NACLA* 38(1):16–20.

n.d.   Indigenous Organization in Guatemala: The National Context. P. 40. Unpublished report. Austin, Texas: Caribbean Central American Research Council.

Hale, Charles R., and Rosamel Millamán

n.d.   Cultural Agency and Political Struggle in the Era of the "Indio Permitido." In *Cultural Agency in the Americas.* D. Sommer, ed. Forthcoming. Durham: Duke University Press.

Hall, Stuart

1986   The Problem of Ideology: Marxism without Guarantees. *Journal of Communications Inquiry* Summer:29–43.

1995   Fantasy, Identity, Politics. In *Cultural Remix: Theories of Politics and the Popular.* E. Carter, J. Donald, and J. Squires, eds. Pp. 63–69. London: Lawrence and Winehart.

1996a Gramsci's Relevance for the Study of Race and Ethnicity. In *Critical Dialogues in Cultural Studies*. D. Morley and K-H Chen, eds. Pp. 413–440. New York: Routledge.

1996b Introduction: Who Needs Identity? In *Questions of Identity*. S. Hall and P.D. Gay, eds. Pp. 1–16. London: Sage.

2000 Conclusion: The Multi-Cultural Question. In *Un/Settled Multiculturalisms: Diasporas, Entanglements, "Transruptions."* B. Hesse, ed. Pp. 209–241. London: Zed.

Hanchard, Michael George

1994 *Orpheus and Power: The Movimiento Negro of Rio de Janeiro and Sao Paulo, Brazil, 1945–1988*. Princeton: Princeton University Press.

2003 Acts of Misrecognition: Transnational Black Politics, Anti-Imperialism, and the Ethnocentrism of Pierre Bourdieu and Loïc Wacquant. *Theory, Culture, and Society* 20(5–29).

Handy, Jim

1989 "A Sea of Indians: Ethnic Conflict and the Guatemalan Revolution, 1944–1952." *The Americas* 46 (October): 189–204.

1994 *Revolution in the Countryside: Rural Conflict and Agrarian Reform in Guatemala, 1944–1954*. Chapel Hill: University of North Carolina Press.

Haraway, Donna

1988 Situated Knowledges: The Science Question in Feminism and the Privilege of Partial Perspective. *Feminist Studies* 14(3):575–599.

Harding, Sandra

1993 Rethinking Standpoint Epistemology: What is "Strong Epistemology"? In *Feminist Epistemologies*. L. Alcoff and E. Potter, eds. Pp. 49–82. London and New York: Routledge.

Hardt, Michael, and Antonio Negri

2000 *Empire*. Cambridge: Harvard University Press.

Harrison, Faye V.

1992 The DuBoisian Legacy in Anthropology. *Critique of Anthropology* 12(3):239–260.

1995 The Persistent Power of "Race" in the Cultural and Political Economy of Racism. *Annual Review of Anthropology* 24:47–74.

Hart, Gillian

2002 *Disabling Globalization: Places of Power in Post-Apartheid South Africa*. Berkeley: University of California Press.

Hartigan, John

2005 *Odd Tribes: Toward a Cultural Analysis of White People*. Durham: Duke University Press.

Heckt, Meike, and Gustavo Palma Murga

2004 *Racismo en Guatemala: De lo políticamente correcto a la lucha antirracista*. Guatemala: AVANCSO.

Herzfeld, Michael

1992   *The Social Production of Indifference: Exploring the Symbolic Roots of Western Bureaucracy.* New York: Berg.

hooks, bell

1984   *Feminist Theory: From Margin to Center.* Boston: South End Press.

Jafek, Timothy B.

1992   "Looking at and Speaking about: Non-Indian Discourses on Indians in Guatemala, 1940s–1990s." BA Thesis, Swarthmore College.

Le Bot, Yvon

1995   *La guerra en las tierras Mayas: Comunidad, violencia y modernidad en Guatemala, 1970–1992.* Mexico: Fondo de Cultura Economica.

Levenson, Deborah T.

1994   *Trade Unionists against Terror. Guatemala City 1954–1985.* Chapel Hill: University of North Carolina Press.

Levine-Rasky, Cynthia

2002   *Working through Whiteness.* New York: SUNY Press.

Liano, Dante

1996   El misterio de San Andrés. Mexico: Editorial Praxis.

Lipsitz, George

1995   The Possessive Investment in Whiteness: Racialized Social Democracy and the "White" Problem in American Studies. *American Quarterly* 47(3):369–387.

1998   *The Possessive Investment in Whiteness.* Philadelphia: Temple University Press.

Little, Walter

2004   Outside of Social Movements: Dilemmas of Indigenous Handicrafts Vendors in Guatemala. *American Ethnologist* 31(1):43–59.

López Larrave, Mario

1976   *Breve historia del movimiento sindical guatemalteco.* Guatemala: Editorial Universitaria.

Macías, Julio César

1997   *La Guerrilla fue mi camino.* Guatemala: Editorial Piedra Santa.

Manz, Beatriz

2004   *Paradise in Ashes: A Guatemalan Journey of Courage, Terror, and Hope.* Berkeley: University of California Press.

Martínez Peláez, Severo

1971   *La patria del criollo.* Guatemala: EDUCA.

1973   ¿Que es un indio? *Alero*, Número 1, Tercera Epoca (julio-agosto), pp. 36–46.

1991   *Motines de indios.* Guatemala: Ediciones en marcha.

Maybury-Lewis, D.

1994 Ethnic Conflict: The New World Order? Special Issue. *Cultural Survival Quarterly* 18(2/3).

McAllister, Carlota

2003 "Good People: Revolution, Community, and Conciencia in a Maya-K'iche Village in Guatemala." PhD dissertation, Department of Anthropology, Johns Hopkins University.

McCreery, David

1994 *Rural Guatemala, 1760–1940.* Stanford: Stanford University Press.

McIntosh, Peggy

1995 White Privilege and Male Privilege: A Personal Account of Coming to See Correspondences through Work in Women's Studies. In *Race, Class, and Gender: An Anthology.* M.L. Andersen and P.H. Collins, eds. Pp. 291–299. Belmont, CA: Wadsworth Press.

Mehta, Uday Singh

1997 Liberal Strategies of Exclusion. In *Tensions of Empire: Colonial Cultures in a Bourgeois World.* F. Cooper and A.L. Stoler, eds. Pp. 427–454. Berkeley: University of California Press.

1999 *Liberalism and Empire: A Study in Nineteenth-Century British Liberal Thought.* Chicago: University of Chicago Press.

Memmi, Alberto

1965 *Colonizer and the Colonized.* New York: Orion Press.

Menchú, Rigoberta

1984 *I, Rigoberta Menchú: An Indian Woman in Guatemala.* London: Verso

Méndez Domínguez, Alfredo

1967 *Zaragoza: La estratificación social de una comunidad ladina Guatemalteca.* Guatemala: Seminario de Integración Social Guatemalteca.

Michaels, W. B.

1992 Race into Culture. *Critical Inquiry* 18:655–685.

Moore, Alexander

1973 *Life Cycles in Atchalan: The Diverse Careers of Certain Guatemalans.* New York: Teachers' College Press.

Morales, Mario Roberto

1998 *La articulación de las diferencias, o, El sindrome de Maximon: Los discursos literarios y políticos del debate interétnico en Guatemala.* Guatemala: FLACSO.

Morrison, Toni

1992 *Playing in the Dark: Whiteness and the Literary Imagination.* Cambridge: Harvard.

Mouffe, Chantal

1979 Hegemony and Ideology in Gramsci. In *Gramsci and Marxist Theory.* C. Mouffe, ed. Pp. 168–204. London: Routledge and Kegan Paul.

Moya, Paula, and Michael R. Hames-Garcia

2000   *Reclaiming Identity: Realist Theory and the Predicament of Postmodernism.* Berkeley: University of California Press.

Nader, Laura

1969   Up the Anthropologist—Perspectives Gained from Studying Up. In *Reinventing Anthropology.* D. Hymes, ed. Pp. 284–311. New York: Vintage.

Nelson, Diane

1999   *A Finger in the Wound: Body Politics in Quincentennial Guatemala.* Berkeley: University of California Press.

Omi, Michael, and Howard Winant

1987   *Racial Formation in the United States.* New York: Routledge.

Ong, Aihwa

1996   Cultural Citizenship as Subject-Making. *Current Anthropology* 37(5):737–762.

Ortego, Enrique

1994   Entrevista con General Otzoy. *Tendencias* 32(July/August): 10–14.

Otzoy, Irma

2001   "Tekum Umam: From Nationalism to Maya Resistance." PhD dissertation, University of California, Davis.

Palma Murga, Gustavo

1991   *El estado y los campesinos en Guatemala durante el periodo 1944–1951.* Guatemala: Universidad San Carlos.

Paredes, Américo

1993   On Ethnographic Work among Minorities. In *Folklore and Culture on the Texas-Mexican Border.* R. Bauman, ed. Pp. 73–112. Austin: University of Texas Press.

Pasini, Joseph J.

1977   "'El Pilar,' A Plantation Microcosm of Guatemalan Ethnicity." PhD dissertation, University of Rochester.

Pinto, Julio

1986   *Centroamerica, de la colonia al estado nacional (1800–1940).* Guatemala: Editorial Universitaria.

Poole, Deborah

1997   *Vision, Race, and Modernity: A Visual Economy of the Andean Image World.* Princeton: Princeton University Press.

Povinelli, Elizabeth A.

2002   *The Cunning of Recognition: Indigenous Alterities and the Making of Australian Multiculturalism.* Durham: Duke University Press.

Ramírez, Ricardo (Rolando Morán)

1969   *Turcios Lima.* La Habana: Instituto del Libro

Ramos, Alcida Rita

1998   *Indigenism: Ethnic Politics in Brazil.* Madison: University of Wisconsin Press.

Rodas Núñez, Isabel

1999   Identidad, asentamiento y relaciones de parentesco de los Espanoles de Patzicía (Siglos XVI–XVIII). In *Entre comunidad y nación.* J. Piel and T. Little-Siebold, eds. Pp. 19–36. Antigua, Guatemala: CIRMA.

2004   De españoles a ladinos. Cambio social y relaciones de parentesco en el Altiplano central colonial guatemalteco. Guatemala: Ediciones ICAPI.

Rodriguez, Richard

2002   *Brown: The Last Discovery of America.* New York: Viking.

Roediger, David R.

1991   *The Wages of Whiteness: Race and the Making of the American Working Class.* London: Verso.

2002   *Colored White: Transcending the Racial Past.* Berkeley: University of California Press.

Rose, Nikolas

1999   *Powers of Freedom: Reframing Political Thought.* Cambridge: Cambridge University Press.

Roseberry, William

1994   Hegemony and the Language of Contention. In *Everyday Forms of State Formation.* G. M. Joseph and D. Nugent, eds. Pp. 355–366. Durham: Duke University Press

Sam Colop, Enrique

1996   The Discourse of Concealment and 1992. In *Maya Cultural Activism in Guatemala.* E. F. Fischer and R. M. Brown, eds. Pp. 107–113. Austin: University of Texas Press.

Sanford, Victoria

2003   *Buried Secrets.* New York: Palgrave.

Schirmer, Jennifer

1998   *The Guatemalan Military Project: A Violence called Democracy.* Philadelphia: University of Pennsylvania Press.

Scott, James C.

1990   *Domination and the Arts of Resistance: Hidden Transcripts.* New Haven: Yale.

Shapiro, Michael J.

1994   Moral Geographies and the Ethics of Post-Sovereignty. *Public Culture* 6:479–502.

Sherzer, Joel

1983   *Kuna Ways of Speaking: An Ethnographic Perspective.* Austin: University of Texas Press.

Smith, Carol A.

1990a   Conclusion: History and Revolution in Guatemala. In *Guatemalan Indians and the State, 1540–1988.* C.A. Smith, ed. Austin: University of Texas Press.

1990b   *Guatemalan Indians and the State, 1540–1988.* Austin: University of Texas Press.

1990c   Militarization of Civil Society in Guatemala: Economic Reorganization as a
         Continuation of War. *Latin American Perspectives* 17:8–41.
1990d   Origins of the National Question in Guatemala: A Hypothesis. In *Guatemalan
         Indians and the State, 1540–1988*. C.A. Smith, ed. Pp. 72–96. Austin: University of
         Texas Press.
1992   Marxists on Class and Culture in Guatemala. In *1492–1992: Five Centuries of
         Imperialism and Resistance*. L. Brown et al., eds. Pp. 189–212. Halifax, Nova Scotia:
         Fernwood Press.
1995   Race-Class-Gender Ideology in Guatemala: Modern and Anti-Modern Forms.
         Comparative Study of Society and History 37(4):723–749.
1999   Interpretaciones Norteamericanas sobre la raza y el racismo en Guatemala. In
         ¿Racismo en Guatemala? Abriendo debate sobre un tema tabú. C. Arenas, C. R. Hale, and
         G. Palma, eds. Guatemala: AVANCSO.

Stepputat, Finn
2001   Urbanizing the Countryside: Armed Conflict, State Formation, and the Politics of
         Place in Contemporary Guatemala. In *States of Imagination: Ethnographic Explorations
         of the Postcolonial State*. T. B. Hansen and F. Stepputat, eds. Pp. 284–312. Durham,
         NC: Duke University Press.

Stocking, George
1993   The Turn of the Century Concept of Race. *Modernism/Modernity* 1(1):4–16.

Stolcke, Verena
1991   Conquered Women. *NACLA* XXIV(5):23–28.

Stoll, David
1993   *Between Two Armies in the Ixil Towns of Guatemala*. New York: Columbia University
         Press.
1999   *Rigoberta Menchú and the Story of all Poor Guatemalans*. Boulder: Westview.

Stutzman, Ronald
1981   El Mestizaje: An All-Inclusive Ideology of Exclusion. In *Cultural Transformations and
         Ethnicity in Modern Ecuador*. N. Whitten, ed. Pp. 45–93. Urbana: University of
         Illinois Press.

Sudbury, Julia
1998   *"other kinds of dreams": Black Women's Organizations and the Politics of Transformation*.
         London: Routledge.

Taguieff, Pierre-André
2001   El racismo. *debate feminista* 24(Octubre): 3–14.

Taracena Arriola, Arturo
1997   *Invención criolla, sueño ladino, pesadilla indígena. Los altos de Guatemala: de región a
         estado, 1740–1850*. San José, Costa Rica: Editorial Porvenir.
2002   *Etnicidad, estado y nación en Guatemala, 1808–1944*. Guatemala: Nawal Wuj.
2004   *Etnicidad, estado y nación en Guatemala, 1944–1985*. Guatemala: CIRMA.

n.d. El Guadalupanismo en Guatemala: Reflexiones históricas sobre la tradición de un transvestismo penitente. Unpublished manuscript.

Taussig, Michael
1993 *Mimesis and Alterity: A Particular History of the Senses.* New York: Routledge.

Tax, Sol
1942 Ethnic relations in Guatemala. *America Indigena* 2:43–47.

Thorne, Eva
n.d. *Protest and Accountability: The World Bank and the Politics of Safeguard Policy Compliance.* Manuscript in the author's possession.

Trouillot, Michel-Rolph
1995 *Silencing the Past: Power and the Production of History.* Boston: Beacon.
2001 The Anthropology of the State in the Age of Globalization. *Current Anthropology* 42(1):125–138.

Van Cott, Donna Lee
2000 *The Friendly Liquidation of the Past: The Politics of Diversity in Latin America.* Pittsburgh: University of Pittsburgh Press.

Vargas, Joao
2004 Hyperconsciousness of Race and its Negation: The Dialectic of White Supremacy in Brazil. *Identities* 11:443–470.

Velásquez Nimatuj, Irma Alicia
2002 *La pequeña burguesía indígena comercial de Guatemala.* Guatemala: Cholsamaj.
2005 Indigenous Peoples, the State, and Struggles for Land in Guatemala: Strategies for Survival and Negotiation in the Face of Globalized Inequality. Ph.D. dissertation. University of Texas, Austin.

Visweswaran, Kamala
1994 *Fictions of Feminist Ethnograpy.* Minneapolis: University of Minnesota Press.
1998 Race and the Culture of Anthropology. *American Anthropologist* 100(1):70–83.

Wade, Peter
1997 *Race and Ethnicity in Latin America.* London: Pluto.

Warren, Kay B.
1989 *The Symbolism of Subordination: Indian Identity in a Guatemalan Town.* Austin: University of Texas Press.
1997 Identidad indígena en Guatemala: Una crítica de modelos norteamericanos. *Mesoamerica* 18(33):73–91.
1998 *Indigenous Movements and their Critics: Pan-Mayan Activism in Guatemala.* Princeton: Princeton University Press.
2002 Voting against Indigenous Rights in Guatemala: Lessons from the 1999 Referendum. In *Indigenous Movements, Self-Representation, and the State in Latin America.* K.B. Warren and J.E. Jackson, eds. Pp. 149–180. Austin: University of Texas Press.

Warren, Kay B., and Jean E. Jackson

2002   *Indigenous Movements, Self-Representation, and the State in Latin America.* Austin: University of Texas Press.

Wasserstrom, Robert

1975   Revolution in Guatemala: Peasants and Politics under the Arbenz Government. *Comparative Studies in Society and History* 17:443–478.

Weismantel, Mary J.

1997   White Cannibals: Fantasies of Racial Violence in the Andes. *Identities* 4(1):9–44.

2001   *Cholas and Pishtacos: Stories of Race and Sex in the Andes.* Chicago: University of Chicago Press.

Wiegman, Robyn

1999   Whiteness Studies and the Paradox of Particularity. *boundary* 2 26(3):115–150.

Williams, Brackette

1989   A Class Act: Anthropology and the Race to Nation across Ethnic Terrain. *Annual Review of Anthropology* 18:401–444.

Williams, Raymond

1977   *Marxism and Literature.* New York and Oxford: Oxford University Press.

Winant, Howard

1997   Behind Blue Eyes: Whiteness and Contemporary U.S. Racial Politics. In *Off White: Readings on Race, Power and Society.* M. Fine, L.C. Powell, L. Weis, and L.M. Wong, eds. Pp. 40–56. New York: Routledge.

2001   *The World is a Ghetto: Race and Democracy Since World War II.* New York: Basic Books.

Yashar, Deborah

1998   Contesting Citizenship: Indigenous Movements and Democracy in Latin America. *Comparative Politics* 31(1):23–42.

2005   *Contesting Citizenship in Latin America: The Rise of Indigenous Movements and the Postliberal Challenge.* Cambridge: Cambridge University Press.

Žižek, Slavoj

1993   *Tarrying with the Negative.* Durham: Duke University Press.

1997   Multiculturalism, or, the Cultural Logic of Multinational Capitalism. *New Left Review* (225):28–51.

Index

Note: Numbers in *italics* indicate figures

Gerardi, Monseñor Juan José, 47–48, 50, 71, 86
Gerardo, 86, 188
globalization, 162
Goldman, Francisco, 224
Gramajo, Héctor, 251–52n.35
Gramscian analysis, 14, 155, 208, 256n.41, 241nn.54, 57
Guadalupanismo, 188–90
Guatemala: De la republica burguesa centralista a la república popular federal, 102
Guatemala: Una interpretación histórico-social (Guzmán and Herbert), 126
Guatemalan army, and assimilation and multiculturalism, 49; and counterinsurgency in Chimaltenango, 84; and disciplinary assimilation, 68, 70; and *dos demonios* narrative, 94; massacres, 248n.5; and Maya ascendancy, 135; and racism, literature on, 140, 258n.2
Guatemalan Left, 32, 33, 34, 170
Guatemalan national identity, 158, 195
Guatemalan National Revolutionary Unity. *See* Unidad Revolucionaria Nacional Guatemalteca (URNG); *see also* guerrilla movement
Guatemalan Republican Front. *See* Frente Republicano Guatemalteco (FRG)
Guerra en tierras mayas, La (Le Bot), 95–96
Guerrilla Army of the Poor. *See* Ejército Guerrillero de los Pobres (EGP)
guerrilla movement: in Chimaltenango Department, 66, 84–85, 100; and FIN, 92; and indigenous organization (1976–1984), 64; reintegration of combatants, 86
Guillermo, 150–55, 158, 160, 217
Guzmán Böckler, Carlos, 17, 126, 127, 239n.31

Hall, Stuart, 30, 156–57
Héctor, 6–7, 83, 84, 85, 114, 126, 134–35
Herbert, Jean-Loup, 17, 126, 127, 239n.31
Heredia, Dr. Américo, 184–85
Hermelindo, Don, 149
humor chapín (Guatemalan sense of humor), 8, 24, 176, 200, 224, 233

hybridity theory, 162, 191, 192

I, Rigoberta Menchú (Menchú), 85
identity politics, 37
Igor, 141–43, 144, 145, 159, 162
Impuesto Único Sobre Inmuebles (IUSI), 175–76
indigenous autonomy, 18, 37, 102, 237n.12
indigenous mayors, 59, 61–62, 62, 64, 80, 244n.24
indigenous mobilization, 59–63, 100–104
Indigenous National Front/National Front for Integration. *See* Frente Indígena Nacional/Frente de Integración Nacional (FIN)
indigenous organization, 57, 61–63, 62, 162, 240n.36
Indigenous Revolutionary Front. *See* Frente Indígena Revolucionaria
indio permitido (authorized Indian), 45, 241n.58
Instituto de Estudios Étnicos, 192
insurrectionary Indian, 158–61; 163; 165; 217; 259n. 18. *See also* atavistic fears
Interamerican Development Bank (IDB), 35
interculturalidad (tolerance and mutual respect), 17, 110, 140, 143, 146, 165
Irene, 105
Itzapa (municipality), 61, 63, 64, 70
IUSI (Unified Property Tax), 175–76
Ixim (newspaper), 63, 98

Jesuit organizers, 63, 90
Juana, 182

Kaqchikel (also Cakchikel) Maya, 1, 63, 68
kissing, among Indians, 159–60
kite festival, 194

ladino anxiety, 14, 19, 82, 114
ladino dissidents, 169, 196–97, 188–92, 193, 200, 223–24
ladino identity: 16–18, *16*; formation of, 157; literature on, 259n.15; and neoliberal multiculturalism, 37–38; and racial privilege, 237n.16; and whitening, 205–206. *See also* Guatemalan national

identity

ladino nationalism, 219, 207

ladino racial dominance, 48–49, 204–205, 214–15

ladino racism, 126, 163, 254n.12, 256n.32

ladinos chimaltecos (ladinos from Chimaltenango), 18–19, 81–82

ladinos solidarios (ladinos who practice solidarity toward Indians), 40, 42,138, 169, 198, 221–22

Lalo, Don, 52–53

Lampo, Don. *See* Caralampio, Don

Le Bot, Yvon, 95–96, 97–99, 108

León Carpio, Ramiro de, 74

Leti, Doña, 172

liberalism, 240n.43

Liberation. *See* October Revolution

Liliana, 124

Lino, José. *See* Xoyón, José Lino

López, Esteban, 54, 59

Lipsitz, George, 237n.16

López Lavarre, Mario, 32, 33

Lucas García, General Romeo, 84, 90, 93, 111

Luis, Don. *See* Valencia, Don Luis

Mack, Myrna, 5, 235n.2

Maribel, Doña. *See* Valencia, Doña Maribel

Marielena, 113, 114

Martín, Tío, 112

Martínez Peláez, Severo, 126–27, 256nn.33, 34

Maxia, Marcial, 90, 92, 93

Maya cultural rights activism: appropriation of, 31; in Chimaltenango, 63, 121; collective rights, 74; and discourse of reverse racism, 133; and neoliberal multiculturalism, 34, 35

Maya efflorescence: 80, 13–14,143–44, 235n.1 (ch. 1); and Guatemalan national identity, 158; ladino responses to, 20, 155; literature on, 236n.7; and Maya political impasse, 18; and primary education, 55–56, 59; and reverse racism, 129. *See also* Maya movement

Maya intellectuals, 39, 236n.7. *See also* Cojtí Cuxil, Demetrio; Rodríguez Guaján,

Raxché Demetrio

Maya movement, 14, 31, 59, 252n.42, 235n.1 (ch. 1). *See also* Maya efflorescence, Maya political impasse

mayanista politics, 64, 92, 104

mayanista vindication narrative frame, 87, 102–104

mayanization, 78, 144

Maya political impasse, 18, 31, 37, 45, 197, 202. *See also* Maya movement

MAYAS (Movement for Solidary Aid and Action), 102–103

mayors, indigenous, 61–62, 64

memory work, 84, 247n.1

Menchú, Rigoberta, 5–6, 18, 19, 85, 107, 112

Mersky, Marcie, 41, 87, 88, 248n.10

mestizaje: and assimilationism, 51; from below 183, 197; literature on, 261n.5; and racial ambivalence, 20; and youth gangs, 180. *See also mestizo/a*

mestizo/a: 168, 185–88, 212, 214–15; militants, 170, 184–88, 199, 218, 222; nationalism, 219; new mestizos, 169, 206, 222–23; universalists, 173–74. *See also mestizaje*

Miguel, Don, 150–52, 155, 158, 159

MINUGUA (United Nations Verification Mission in Guatemala), 76

Miriam, 25, 26, 29

Misión de Verificación de las Naciones Unidas en Guatemala (MINUGUA), 76

mistado ideology, 171–73, 183, 187, 206, 262n.8

modernizantes, 58, 95, 251n.34

Monjardín, Berta, 186

Monteforte Toledo, Mario, 260n.21

Montes, César, 92

Morales, Father Antonio, 58, 63, 118–20, 122, 124, 128, 129, 131, 136

Morales, Mario Roberto, 132, 199, 257nn.45, 46

Morán, Rolando, 88

Morquecho, Edwin, 173–74, 188

Movement for Solidary Aid and Action. *See* Movimiento de Ayuda y Acción Solidaria (MAYAS)

Movimiento de Ayuda y Acción Solidaria (MAYAS), 102–103

Movimiento indígena, El (Falla), 90

Movimiento Indio Tojil (Tojil Indian Movement), 101, 252n.37

Movimiento Maya, El (Cojtí Cuxil), 102

multiculturalism. *See* neoliberal multiculturalism

multilateral organizations, 74, 81, 163. *See also* World Bank, Interamerican Development Bank

neoliberal multiculturalism: 1992 to present, 74–76, 81; and classic racism, 210; in global context, 218–20; and Maya political impasse, 18, 31–38, 197; and memories of cultural politics, 87

neoliberalism: 240n.41; and governance, 34–35; literature on, 240nn.39, 42, 44–45, 267n.27; and racial ambivalence, 20, 36. *See also* neoliberal multiculturalism

new racism, 133–34, 257nn.47–48, 258n.5

North American identity, 207

October Revolution, 27, 32, 52–54, 150, 169–70, 173, 220, 262n.10

OKMA (Oxlajuuj Keej Maya' Ajtz'iib' [Maya linguistics collective]), 21

Omi, Michael, 155. *See also* racial formation

Organización Revolucionaria del Pueblo en Armas (ORPA), 127, 239

ORPA (Revolutionary Organization of the People in Arms), 127, 239

Otzoy, General, 51, 258n.50

Otzoy, Irma, 27

PAC (Civilian Auto-Defense Patrols), 67, 84

Padre Antonio. *See* Morales, Father Antonio

Palma, Eustaquio, 73

PAN (Party of National Advancement), 80, 176

Paredes, Américo, 24

Parramos (municipality), *57*, 77

Partido de Avanzada Nacional (PAN), 80, 176

Partido Cristiano Demócrata (DC), 61, 62,

89, 90, 99

Partido Revolucionario (PR), 62, 89

Party of National Advancement. *See* Partido de Avanzada Nacional (PAN)

Patinamit (organization), 89

Patria del criollo, La (Martínez Peláez), 126

Patrullas de Auto-Defensa Civil (PAC), 67, 84

Patzicía conflict, 52–53, 122–23, 129, 142, 245nn.18–20

Patzicía (municipality), 57, 77

Patzún (municipality), *57*, 77

Peace Accords (1996), 74, 76, 113, 143, 246n.46

Pellecer, Carlos Manuel, 240n.37

Pérez, Ignacio, 185

Pérez, Luis Enrique, *116*, 117

Pinzón, José, 93

Poaquíl. *See* San José Poaquíl

Pochuta (municipality), *57*, 77

political imaginary, 139, 146, 147, 156, 162, 231

Ponce Vaides, General Federico, 52

Portillo, Alfonso, 226

PR (Revolutionary Party), 62, 89

Prensa Libre (newspaper), 27

Producto 2 (second product), 40

Programa Misionero Cakchiquel (PROMICA), 63

PROMICA (Cakchiquel Missionary Program), 63

Quemé, Rigoberto, *164*, 165

Quetzaltenango (municipality), *164*, 165

race: and biology, 24; critiques, 212; and culture, 28–29, 239nn.33, 34; vs. ethnicity 29, 203, 210–11, 264nn.2, 3, 4; in Guatemala, 115, 239n.30; studies in Latin America, 265n.5

racial ambivalence: 18–20; characteristics of, 28; and cultural racism, 144; and *dos demonios* narrative, 108; emergence of, 237n.18; and Guatemalan left, 15; and ladino dominance, 31; and politics of racial difference, 44; and racial dominance, 217–18, 219; and racial privilege, 211; and reverse racism, 132–34; and World Bank, 37. *See also* reverse racism

racial categories, 214

racial dominance. *See* ladino racial dominance

racial formation, framework, 204–205, 208, 235n.11; and ethnography, 208, 211–14; and ladino identity, 17; literature on, 208–209, 265–66n.10; and political imaginaries, 155; and racial hierarchy in Guatemala, 29, 209–10; and racial privilege in Guatemala, 211, 266n.17

Racial Formation in the United States (Omi and Winant), 155

racial healing, 10, 45, 197

racial violence. *See* atavistic fears

racism. *See* ladino racial dominance; race; racial ambivalence; racial formation

Ramírez, Ricardo, 88

Ramón, 179, 181–82, 188

rape, 160–61

Rayo Ovalle, Don Miguel Ángel, 6, 54

raza (race), 78–79

raza indígena (indigenous race), 123, 126, 136, 257n.43

Rebel Armed Forces. *See* Fuerzas Armadas Rebeldes (FAR)

reformist decade. *See* October Revolution

Regional Center for Research on Mesoamerica. *See* Centro de Investigaciones Regionales de Mesoamérica (CIRMA)

REMHI (Project for the Recuperation of Historical Memory), 47, 252–53n.44

Reparations Commission, 106

Reparto de Tierras, El (Rivera), 33

reverse racism, 117–18, 125–26, 127, 255nn.29, 30; and ladino hegemony, 134–36; political consequences of, 129–32

revolutionary decade. *See* October Revolution

Revolutionary Organization of the People in Arms. *See* Organización Revolucionaria del Pueblo en Armas (ORPA)

Revolutionary Party. *See* Partido Revolucionario (PR)

revolutionary triumphalism narrative frame, 87, 88–94

Rigoberto, Don, 10, 11, 149, 193

Ríos Montt, General Efraín, 15, 67, 68, 111

Roberto, Father, 70, 71, 73

Rodríguez Guaján, Raxché Demetrio, 236n.2

Rodriguez, Richard, 178, 223

Rolando, Don. *See* Fernández, Rolando

Rosario, 83, 85, 88, 112, 134

Rose, Jacqueline, 156

Rufino Barrios, Justo, 52

Sacatepéquez. *See* San Pedro Sacatepéquez

San Andrés Itzapa (municipality), 57, 77, 148

San Carlos University (USAC), 127

Sánchez, Gregorio, 125–26

San José Poaquíl (municipality), 57, 77

San Martín Jilotepeque (municipality), 57, 77

San Pedro Sacatepéquez (municipality), 52, 120

Santa Apolonia (municipality), 57, 77

Santa Cruz Balanyá (municipality), 57, 77

separate and unequal principle, 54, 79, 81, 219

sexual violence, 158–62, 217

Shapiro, Michael, 162

Smith, Carol, 14

SNJ (Solidarity with Children and Youth), 41, 175, 179

Solares, Jorge, 192

Solidaridad con la Niñez y la Juventud (SNJ), 41, 175, 179

Solidarity with Children and Youth. *See* Solidaridad con la Niñez y la Juventud (SNJ)

Space for Intercultural Dialogue. *See* Franja para el Diálogo Intercultural

state violence, 70, 84–85, 95, 108, 140, 236n.7, 248n.6. *See also* Guatemalan army

Stocking, George, 29

Stoll, David, 95, 107

subject formation, 20, 35, 261n.1